D0770966

RESURGENT

How Constitutional Conservatism
Can Save America

KEN BLACKWELL

AND KEN KLUKOWSKI

THRESHOLD EDITIONS

NEW YORK   LONDON   SYDNEY   TORONTO

Threshold Editions
A Division of Simon & Schuster, Inc.
1230 Avenue of the Americas
New York, NY 10020

First Threshold Editions hardcover edition May 2011

THRESHOLD EDITIONS and colophon are trademarks of Simon & Schuster, Inc.

For information about special discounts for bulk purchases,
please contact Simon & Schuster Special Sales at 1-866-506-1949
or business@simonandschuster.com.

The Simon & Schuster Speakers Bureau can bring authors to your live event.
For more information or to book an event contact the
Simon & Schuster Speakers Bureau at 1-866-248-3049
or visit our website at www.simonspeakers.com.

Designed by Ruth Lee-Mui

Manufactured in the United States of America

1   3   5   7   9   10   8   6   4   2

Library of Congress Cataloging-in-Publication Data
Blackwell, J. Kenneth, 1948–
Resurgent : how constitutional conservatism can save America /
Ken Blackwell and Ken Klukowski.
p.   cm.
1. Conservatism—United States.   2. United States—Politics and
government—2009–   3. Constitutional history—United States.
4. Obama, Barack.   I. Klukowski, Ken.   II. Title.
JC573.2.U6B55 2011
320.520973—dc22   2011001439

ISBN 978-1-4516-2926-2
ISBN 978-1-4516-2928-6 (ebook)

CONTENTS

INTRODUCTION

THE PRODIGAL NATION

"You and I have a rendezvous with destiny. We will preserve for our children this, the last best hope of man on Earth, or we will sentence them to take the last step into a thousand years of darkness."

—Ronald Reagan, "A Time for Choosing," October 27, 1964

Re • sur • gent (ri-'sər-jənt): *adj.* 1. Exhibiting renewal or revival; 2. Surging back again.

The democratic republic created by the Framers of our Constitution—and designed with the hope of enduring forever—is hanging by a thread. Are you willing to do your part to save it?

The United States faces a crisis unlike anything we've ever confronted in our 235 years. We are facing economic threats like no other, social threats like no other, and national security threats like no other, all at the same time. Our country teeters on the brink—the very edge of a precipice—and only determined, courageous, and principled leadership will pull us back from what will otherwise be a series of catastrophes that could literally end the United States as we know it.

The Constitution of the United States was designed to save America in exactly such a situation as this. *Constitutional conservatism*—the

1

principles arising from the Constitution that form a vision and system of limited government—forms the foundation of the economic, social, and national security policies that we need—right now—to not only pull back from the edge of the abyss, but to then move forward and prosper in enjoying our God-given rights to life, liberty, and the pursuit of happiness.

It took decades to get into our current predicament. Both parties are to blame, and we the voters are also to blame for letting politicians do what they've been doing to drive our beloved country into a ditch. Principled leadership is rare, but it would be more common if voters would consistently fire those politicians who fail to live up to their oath of office to support and defend the Constitution of the United States.

The Ship of State Is Sinking—All Hands on Deck

Two friends of ours provided a vivid image that explains just how dire this situation is for every person living in America today. We've been given this image separately by two retired military officers. Both served the United States during wartime, and both were commanding officers.

A capital ship in the U.S. Navy is one of the big ships, such as an aircraft carrier or a battleship. When you're commanding a naval ship during a war, there are always competing concerns and priorities about how you allocate resources. An aircraft carrier has several thousand personnel on board, carrying a vast array of military aircraft and assets, and must maintain the ship in such condition that it's able to perform all of its functions. A carrier is always abuzz with activity, with thousands of people moving about on its many decks, performing their duties.

Such is the scene on a carrier on any given day. But then imagine what happens if a missile launched by a hidden enemy suddenly strikes the ship without warning.

Immediately the ship goes to general quarters. All hands to battle stations. Whatever you're doing, you drop it and rush to your assigned station.

The entire aircraft carrier has only two concerns at that moment. The first is to put the ship into a combat posture to defend itself. The threat must be identified and steps taken to prevent a second attack, or to launch a counterattack.

The second is damage control. Watertight hatches are sealed throughout the ship. Water containment and pumping teams go into action, and firefighters prevent fires from spreading. If not immediately countered, either the fire or the water can destroy the ship.

Both of those concerns serve a single mission: Save the ship. The ship has been hit. Every effort is focused on containing and repairing that damage, while heading off any new damage. Whatever you were working on five minutes ago no longer matters. If the ship goes down, we all go down. Although some might escape aboard lifeboats, the loss of the ship will be devastating on a scale that nothing else compares to.

That is the crisis state the United States is currently experiencing. The USS *America* has been hit by a missile—an economic and governmental missile. Unless all citizens muster to general quarters, our ship of state will go down.

You need a captain (president) who is able to keep the ship afloat in the midst of this emergency, while directing the forces to repair the damage and restore the ship to its full operational capacity. But no captain can do it by himself; every crew member must do his or her part to save the ship.

The missile that has struck the ship of state is one of government policy on three fronts: economic mismanagement, trillions of dollars of deficit spending, and massive entitlements that cannot possibly pay what they've promised. The 111th Congress (2009 and 2010) amassed more debt—$3.22 *trillion*—in just two years than the first one hundred Congresses *combined* over a period of two hundred years. That's $10,429 per person—including each child—in the United States, just in the past two years.[1] And that number doesn't even touch our other $11 trillion in debt, or $88 trillion in unfunded entitlements.

This book talks about going to general quarters to contain that damage and prevent the ship from going down. It also talks about the other functions of our ship of state—our culture, our security, and for that matter our overarching vision of the nature of our society and the proper role of government in our free society—that must be addressed to repair it and bring us to our full capacity, and get us back on course.

One of the naval officers who described this scenario used to be at the helm of an aircraft carrier, directing the movement of the colossal ship. He explained that it can take a ten-mile radius to turn a carrier.

Our ship of state is bigger than any aircraft carrier. Instead of thousands of personnel, we have over 300 million people. Instead of a size that can be measured in terms of a number of football fields, we cover half a continent. And instead of billions of dollars of military assets, we have a $14 trillion economy. It will take an enormous turn to bring the USS *America* around and set her back on her constitutional course.

Some of these problems have taken many years to develop. One leading problem has been building for seventy-five years. But the past decade has set these problems on a collision course, and the past two years have exacerbated these problems to catastrophic proportions. They have become the missile that is now striking us, and we must take drastic, immediate action to save the ship of state and come about on a new course.

THE AMERICAN BODY WITH
A LIFE-THREATENING DISEASE

Another way to understand how to successfully grapple with our current emergency is to consider a person facing a life-threatening situation.

The body of every human being is always beset by countless dangers. We are constantly surrounded by bacteria and viruses that will take us down in short order if they can make it past our bodies' protective layers. That's why an open wound can prove fatal.

Uncle Sam has some serious medical conditions that are endangering his health. These social issues, of families breaking down, the loss of the concepts of moral absolutes and transcendent truths, the sense of being accountable to a being greater than yourself, these principles that drive you to sacrifice your own comfort so that your children can have a better life, and the decline of the firm conviction that there are things worth dying for, are a cancer in our national body. If we fail on issues such as the sanctity of life and marriage, or the honored place of faith in our nation's life, we will slide from decadence, to apathy, to craven-ness, and collapse under attacks both from without and within.

The economic issues confronting us, however, are like a sudden heart attack. We are faced with a situation unlike anything in our national existence. The American people are burdened with personal debt on a level undreamed of by any who came before us. Our govern-ment, during brief times of unparalleled liberalism, established entitle-ment programs that have created *trillions* of dollars in obligations that there is simply no way to ever pay. Taken with the other factors we'll look at in this book, our economy teeters on the edge of a cliff.

Economically, in our metaphor we have sky-high cholesterol and triglycerides. We're morbidly obese. Every day we're eating a mountain of greasy fried food, smothered in cheese. We refuse to exercise, cut our portions, or eat salads and vegetables. If something radical doesn't change right now, we're going to have a catastrophic heart attack. As a nation we're going to be crippled and disabled—*at best*. At worst, we'll be dead.

We face a war on two fronts. America is going bankrupt eco-nomically and morally. Without fundamental change, we're going to be struck dead from our fiscal heart attack or we're going to slowly waste away until dead from our moral cancer.

We must act now to save the Republic.

THIS IS ABOUT MORE THAN MONEY, IT'S ABOUT SAVING WESTERN CIVILIZATION

There are many trying to define the current political crisis as entirely about cost of government and size of government. They're dead wrong, shortsighted, and failing to understand the big picture of the inter-dependent nature of the American body politic and the precepts that are absolutely essential to sustaining limited government over a multi-generational time span. America cannot recover unless we overcome this profoundly wrongheaded idea, which is based on a modern liberal delusion regarding human nature, as explained in Chapter 5.

The other issues on the table—whether we compare them to turn-ing an aircraft carrier or battling cancer—are every bit as critical to the survival of our way of life. If we don't overcome the threats to our culture and national security, they will destroy American civilization as it has existed since the Founding. If we rein in spending, overhaul our entitlement systems, and get government out of the areas of the economy where interference stifles growth and productivity, but do not address these cultural and security issues, then the America we know will cease to exist, just as surely as it would from an economic collapse.

Not only that, but—and we want to emphasize this point as absolutely critical—if we succeed on the economic issues, but fail either on security or on social issues, the *economic* issues will end up falling apart *again* anyway in later years. Should that happen, then after perhaps a decade of paying the price to turn around the economy, a price that will be a real hardship for us, then within thirty years we'll be back in exactly the same place. Principled leadership is about *permanently* solving these problems, not kicking them down the road for a quarter century, condemning our children to confront them.

We explain all this in Chapter 3. Failure to grasp that we cannot solve our economic problems without solving our cultural problems stems from failing to consider the Founders' concept of what elements are essential for enlightened self-government. The reality is that when families break down, government steps in with bigger programs and bigger spending. Government grows when families fail.

True leadership is about more than ten years. It's about looking thirty, fifty, and a hundred years down the road and laying a foundation for long-term prosperity and happiness. If we fail to recapture constitutional conservatism in any of its three aspects—economic, social, or national security—then we will lose *all three* in the long term.

Government Grows When Families Fail

Too many political leaders—within the leadership of the Republican Party and even those who call themselves "conservative leaders" but who don't support the social issues of faith, life, and marriage—fail to comprehend the self-defeating agenda they are pursuing. In doing so, they also reject the Framers' concept of limited government.

People require government. They either govern themselves, or someone else will govern them. The family unit is the basic human unit of government. Stable traditional families constrain personal behavior and focus economic energies to generate productive outcomes. As explored in the coming chapters, there is one inescapable truth: Wherever family fails, growth of government to fill the void is unstoppable.

The Republican Party—and with it the American Republic—cannot be resurgent without understanding this point. Conservatism is built upon this truth, because the Constitution and the Declaration of Independence accept it as a foundational premise. As the Founders of this country understood all too well, self-government endures only when people govern themselves in an honorable and moral fashion, with strong families to raise the next generation with all the values necessary to perpetuate self-government.

You cannot stop a decades-long march toward a socialist and authoritarian state if the family breaks down. Those who say we need to maintain a laser focus on government spending miss the forest for the trees, or refuse to accept what the Founders embraced. If we balance the budget and rein in government but do not rebuild and protect families, then the popular will for government intervention will irresistibly grow over time. Whenever that happens, massive government programs displace families and churches, and funding for these intrusive nanny-state programs inevitably follows.

Transformational Shift

A profound shift in attitudes and priorities is transforming America. Critical issues that languished for years now enjoy majority support, and Americans are ready to vote for serious change in national leadership to bring about a sea change in national policy.

America is polarized at levels unseen since polls started asking about the liberal-conservative divide in 1992. As of the most recent polling, 42% of American adults call themselves conservative, as opposed to 20% liberal and 35% moderate. That's the highest level ever for conservatives (the previous high was 40%, in 2003, 2004, and 2009). It's also relatively high for liberals, who in recent years polled under 20%.[2]

The casualty here is moderates. In 1992, moderates were 43%. The number held steady at 40% for almost a decade. And it had never dropped below 36% since polling began.[3] What this shows is that an increasing number of Americans understand they can't sit on the fence. Whereas 53% of Americans called themselves either liberal or conservative in 1992, that number is now at 62%. Tens of millions of Americans no longer call themselves moderate, either throwing in their lot with big-government collectivism and wealth redistribution, or committing themselves to the Constitution, economic freedom, traditional families and values, and strong national defense.

This represents a crystallizing in American thinking. People are realizing the folly of a "moderate" budget deficit, which will still bankrupt you. They're coming to understand that a "moderate" judge, who follows the Constitution half the time but ignores it half the time, is still toxic to the rule of law. People understand the status quo is unacceptable; we're at a fork in the road, and we're either going toward European-style socialism under an authoritarian government, or returning to a constitutional republic that protects families and empowers them to pursue the American dream in a free-market system.

But polls are showing another shift that is utterly unprecedented in this country since records began. Only 11% of Americans have confidence in the federal government. Beyond that, fully 50% have no confidence in it, the worst showing since pollsters started asking in 1973.[4] Similarly, confidence in Congress has now hit an all-time low since polling began, with only 13% of Americans approving.[5] This disapproval resulted in Republicans picking up sixty-three House seats in 2010.

What this means is that there's political will in this country for historic action. The American people are taking sides, and the majority support what constitutional conservatism calls for to restore our republic.

Collision of Worldviews

People are trying to make sense of what's happening in America. There's tremendous disunity among the American people. Although we've always been a people with diverse backgrounds, priorities, and views, there's been some consensus on certain fundamentals.

Not so anymore. America's political life and overall direction are in a state of remarkable change that carries both tremendous opportunities and profound dangers.

Today's division comes from a collision of worldviews. A worldview is a paradigm, an overall philosophy by which we understand our lives and the world around us. We each have certain core beliefs regarding self, family, other people, government, etc., and when we pull all of those basic beliefs together, there's our worldview.

There is a clear fault line in America's current political divide, resulting from the clash of two opposing worldviews. On one hand are people who believe that government is a source for positive good that can effectively solve social ills. They are distrustful of private business, because they think private-sector workers try to get rich. Capitalism and the desire to accumulate wealth are ignoble, so those who focus their careers on achieving such things are somehow morally deficient. Those who work in professions devoted to serving other people and especially those in need—in other words, government bureaucrats—are to be trusted more than private-sector workers.

Given all this, it's not only acceptable that good-natured servants in government should take money and resources from those venal creatures in corporate America, it's preferable. Such a transfer of wealth is ideal. These people also believe that every person is entitled to a great many things, and that no one has a right to accumulate vast sums of wealth, because such amassing is done through greedy materialistic pursuits that consume resources needed more by other people. So it's the role of government to develop programs that provide for those with less, and take from those with "too much" however much is necessary to fund these generous new programs.

On the other hand are those who believe that government is unavoidably inefficient and wasteful. Although many government employees are well-meaning, many are process-obsessed bureaucrats whose sole ambition is to keep doing whatever they're doing, regardless of the results. These people think in terms of "return on investment" and see the government's return on tax dollars as embarrassing. They think that anything government does that the private sector could also do, the private realm will do better, because private-sector workers are driven by the carrot of greater profits and thus bigger bonuses, as well as by the stick—the fear of getting fired for unacceptable job performance (as opposed to government workers, whom it is almost impossible to fire no matter how inept they are).

These people view government as an unfortunate necessity. You need government for things such as protecting the country and building highways, but aside from that, government should be kept as small as possible. People tend to be better stewards of their own property and put that property to more productive uses. Thus government should enact a system of uniform and reliable laws that respect people's rights to life, liberty, and property and secure justice for them when injured, but aside from that it should not try to dictate how people make decisions.

This latter view is essential to the American Dream, which is still alive and well in the hearts of countless Americans. You cannot be free to succeed without also being free to fail. Government cannot provide you a cushy safety net that eliminates the fear of losing without also putting such shackles on you and a low enough ceiling that you can't succeed. Government corrodes the economic forces necessary to achieve massive success, and government interference in families cannot do anything other than undermine parents in a household.

As he so often did as the Great Communicator, President Ronald Reagan summed up the view of this second group of people: "Government is not the solution to our problems. Government *is* the problem."

This divide has been sorting out over four decades, and recent events have finally crystallized it. The concept of a nanny state was first conceived in America in the 1930s, though even its proponents wanted only to create a safety net, not subsidize the lives of millions. But the nature of government is to grow and consume, and so it did. It mushroomed in the 1960s, then oscillated and occasionally retreated a step in the 1980s. But it grew in the 1990s, grew again under a *Republican* president in the early 2000s, and now has exploded over the past two years.

In the 1960s, Democrats embraced social liberalism alongside their entitlement mentality. Then with the rise of Ronald Reagan, Republicans embraced family-centered conservatism alongside pro-business policies. Although some politicians tried to straddle the fence, and many did on certain issues, the parties eventually started to differentiate.

The final stage has occurred in recent years, with the abject failure of moderate policies confirmed to countless millions. Just as you can't be a little bit pregnant, either government has the answers and is the way to go, in which case we need to give it all of the power and resources it says it needs, or government is the problem—not the solution—and we need to get it out of our lives, where it has no business, and take back the money that it needlessly wastes to the impoverishment of us all, reclaiming those resources to provide for ourselves, our families, and our future.

Between Ronald Reagan in the 1980s and Barack Obama right now, America sees the full picture of these two views, setting them in stark contrast with one another. Ronald Reagan was a consistent and devoted conservative. Barack Obama is a committed and unapologetic liberal. If someone arises in the GOP carrying the truly conservative mantle of Ronald Reagan to challenge President Obama in 2012, the American people will have to choose between these two worldviews.

A CLASH OVER HUMAN NATURE

This divide over the role of government comes from a fundamental divide on human nature. Which of the two general visions of the role of government you embrace stems from which of these two views of human nature you accept. One naturally flows from the other.

The classical view of humanity is the one that was dominant from before Christ until the early 1800s, and is foundational to Judeo-Christian philosophy, theology, and sociology.[6] In this view human beings are imperfect and morally flawed creatures. In biblical terms, we're all sinners. We all have unwholesome, counterproductive, and harmful desires and impulses, and need to resist and control these thoughts and urges. People are profoundly egocentric—self-focused and self-centered. Because of these flaws, we need government to protect us from others and occasionally from ourselves. Government is necessary to protect the weak from the strong, for fear of retribution to constrain individuals from acting out of anger, malice, or wanton disregard for others.

In contrast, the romantic view of humanity emerged around 1800 as a reaction to rationalism and the Enlightenment, and arose in spiritualism and philosophies such as transcendentalism and existentialism. The romantic view is that human beings are inherently good and virtuous, perfectible beings with infinite upward potential. Mankind can evolve to a state where government isn't even necessary because everyone could live harmoniously in a man-made paradise. But until that utopia arrives, government is a benevolent force to help plan people's lives and redistribute assets to create a fair and equitable society.

Countless works have been written on these topics, most of them religious. Even after the rise of romanticism, however, many works without theological premises bear out the truth of the classical view of humanity. Scholars of other disciplines arrive at the same classical-view conclusions, as seen for example when economist Thomas Sowell explores this issue in nonreligious terms in *Conflict of Visions*. In it Sowell speaks of those holding the tragic view of humanity—that man is constrained by his imperfections—versus those holding a utopian view of humanity—wherein people are devoid of inherent moral defects. Many great works of philosophy and theology examine this ageless debate.

History proves the classical model correct. In the 1800s, some romantics predicted the twentieth century would be the golden age of humanity. These prognosticators predicted that wars, poverty, and famine would cease. Instead the twentieth century saw the two most devastating wars in human history, and more than 200 million human beings killed by the totalitarian and authoritarian regimes of the Soviet Union, North Korea, China, Germany, and Japan, and in the massacres of Cambodia and Rwanda, among other places.

This is why communism fails, both in predicting how people will act individually and also collectively when working in government. Communism rests upon the romantic premise that man is naturally willing to give up all personal property, that individually he will labor productively with no incentives of personal gain or fear of loss, that he will freely give to his fellow man, and that he will consume only what he needs as opposed to what he wants. Communism also argues that government can be trusted to effectively and benevolently transfer and redistribute economic resources and outputs according to each person's needs. Instead people act according to the classical view, and because they do, communism leads to destitution, starvation, genocide, and tyranny.

It's clear beyond any doubt that the Founders adhered to the classical view of humanity. As James Madison famously said in *The Federalist* No. 51, "If men were angels, no government would be necessary."[7] Because of humanity's flawed nature, however, government also had to be strictly limited: "If angels were to govern men, neither external or internal controls on government would be necessary."[8] In other words, we need government because people are prone to destructive behavior. But we need to always mistrust and constrain government, because government is populated by people every bit as flawed as those they are charged with governing.

In Chapter 5 we explore the tenfold promise of America. We look at the specific promises the Founders gave us in the Declaration of Independence and the Constitution. The governmental design in those documents shows the Founders' abiding lack of faith in government, how they diligently worked to limit federal power, set the federal government against the states, set states against the feds, and within the central government, to break governing power into three branches, and then set each of the branches against the others.

So the collision of worldviews underlying our current divide is between those with faith in government to do what's right and those who understand enough about human nature to never put their trust in any government, which inevitably wields vast and sometimes terrifying power over other people.

The End of Federalism

Part of the genius of the U.S. Constitution is that it sets up a federal system as an aspect of limiting government power. The United States is a federation of sovereign states united around common principles. Current violations of our constitutional framework amount to the abolition of federalism.

We are unlike most countries in that our states are not merely provinces. In most countries, provinces handle various local affairs but aren't sovereign in their own right. Provinces exist at the sufferance of the national government, as political subdivisions of the nation, and must obey the central government. A province in this system is similar to the county in which you live, which is a subservient subdivision of your state.

Not so in America. Each state is a sovereign republic, free to make its own laws and policies in most matters, and conduct its affairs as it sees fit. Only certain narrow policy areas are given to the central government, and the Constitution that creates that government is also the one that specifies over what areas of law and policy the federal government has jurisdiction. Everything else is left to the states to decide.

The genius of this system is that it maximizes every citizen's ability to live under laws reflecting his or her needs, values, and priorities. Citizens vote for a governor as their chief executive, and for state representatives and state senators, who in turn vote on laws to govern the daily lives of those voters.[9] While each member of the U.S. House represents roughly 650,000 Americans, the typical state house member might represent around 60,000. Thus each voter has perhaps ten times the voting power to decide whether that state representative continues to hold office, which in theory makes him roughly ten times as responsive to his constituents. Moreover, being chosen from the local community also means that more people will know him, and he's more likely to represent the true needs and wishes of his constituents.

As we'll see in Chapter 4, the Supreme Court referred to states as the "laboratories of democracy" in our system of government. It allows for a united people with common characteristics to experiment on ways to address social needs. If one state succeeds in a big way, then other states can decide whether to imitate it. If a state fails miserably on an issue, then other states can treat that as a cautionary tale and avoid the same mistake.

People get to vote with their feet in America's federal system. If you don't like how things are run in your state—whether it's taxes, education, or a plague of corruption—then you get to move to a state that better reflects your views and values.

Both parties have been killing our federal system. Republican actions such as centralizing education policy in the No Child Left Be-hind Act undermine local control. Democrats' actions have been worse by an order of magnitude, from healthcare to labor to environmental regulations. Some Democrats go further, advocating that the federal government become a truly national government, creating national standards on everything. As part of this, the government would begin asserting a "police power" (explained later) of making laws for public health, safety, and welfare in every area of life.

As we'll also see in Chapters 4, 5, and 6, however, federalism is also in danger from radical libertarians (not ordinary libertarians). Feder-alism is one of the promises of the U.S. Constitution, a promise that some people who cannot win a single election at the ballot box are trying to break, forcing a bizarre form of judicial activism down Ameri-cans' throats.

Federalism is thus being eroded from multiple directions, assaulted in all three branches of government. It's just the latest proof of Thomas Jefferson's observation: "The natural progress of things is for liberty to yield and government to gain ground." This end of federalism is part of a broader threat to our republic: It means we are in a constitutional crisis.

The Constitution in Crisis

We are at a fork in the road with the Constitution. The issues we con-front this decade will push us past the point of no return if we choose wrongly. For decades various principles of constitutional law have been increasingly ignored, or stretched to a point that would be unrecogniz-able to the Founders of this nation.

For decades, legal commentators have wondered about various limits in the Constitution, theorizing, "What if this would happen?" or "What about that?" But they've been entirely academic conversations. The courts were silent (as they should be), because no government ac-tion forced lawsuits that required the courts to determine the outer edge of what the Constitution allowed on these issues and strike down any laws to the contrary.

Now that's changed.

As you'll read in this book, the Constitution is being violated in unprecedented ways, with cases now moving toward the Supreme Court that would have been unfathomable a generation ago. Our Supreme Law is being challenged as never before, on economic issues such as the scope of government power over private businesses and personal decisions, social issues that could redefine the most basic institutions of human civilization, and national security issues such as how to protect Americans against a wartime enemy.

Our friend Congressman Trent Franks of Arizona is fond of quoting Daniel Webster in speeches. One line from Webster that Congressman Franks often uses bears repeating here: "Hold on, my friends, to the Constitution and to the Republic for which it stands. Miracles do not cluster and what has happened once in 6,000 years, may not happen again. Hold on to the Constitution, for if the American Constitution should fail, there will be anarchy throughout the world."

Daniel Webster's wisdom from 1851 still holds true. Webster was one of the greatest statesmen in American history, serving both as a senator and our most famous Supreme Court lawyer. This American giant—who possessed a deep grasp of history, philosophy, and biblical truth, as well as of the Constitution—took the long view of history and the broad view of the world's cultures, and considered the U.S. Constitution nothing short of a miracle.

The Resurgent Constitution

What do we mean by "Resurgent"? There is a resurgence under way in this country, a rising wave of something that was once dominant, then faded, and now is ascendant again. But a resurgence of *what*? There are three possible answers. And ironically whether one or all of these are true will dictate whether we recover and flourish as a free, prosperous, and honorable nation.

In the immediate, visible sense that you can see on a TV screen, the Republican Party is resurgent. Despite the media's glee at the thought that the GOP had been dealt a mortal blow between the 2006 and 2008 elections (a magazine cover showed an elephant with the label "Endangered Species"), we survived. After 2008, Republicans were leaderless, voiceless, and lacking a plan because we lacked a clear philosophy.

Three people fixed all that. Nancy Pelosi's self-righteous and wide-eyed San Francisco liberalism alienated Middle America. Harry Reid's curmudgeonly demeanor and occasional low blows kept ordinary folks from connecting with this otherwise-ordinary guy. And of course, Barack Obama took the cake, mixing detached and self-satisfied effete elitism with a far-left, out-of-touch agenda, and responded to criticism and opposition with an unbecoming mixture of complaining, inappropriate jokes, and blame-the-previous-guy rhetoric, amounting to a picture of unpresidential conduct. Together with the president's aides, including a loudmouthed communist, a foulmouthed chief of staff, at least one avowed socialist, and a troupe of far-left zealots, this created a shocking tapestry of unmitigated liberalism utterly foreign to the American people, the American spirit, and the American Constitution.[10]

America is a center-right country. The contrast was too stark, and as the American people pulled back, Republicans reacted. Some were backbenchers on account of their conservative ideas on one issue or another, and these principled statesmen suddenly had a seat at the table. Others were full-spectrum conservatives to begin with, like Congressman Mike Pence of Indiana, who, instead of locking horns with GOP leadership, suddenly had a wide-open national stage for GOP leadership. Others are opportunists, who despite a long record of moderate policies suddenly found it advantageous to sound conservative, and jumped on the bandwagon. Who knows? Some of these conversions might even be genuine. Time will tell (if they survive their primaries).

This combination of truly conservative candidates coming to the fore, somewhat conservative politicians moving to the right, and some fakers who could sense the political winds led to a Republican resurgence. Republicans gained sixty-three seats in the House, creating the largest Republican majority in the better part of a century. We also took six Senate seats, six governorships, and numerous statehouses. The 2010 Republican victory is one of the greatest ever.

In another sense, however, *conservatism* is resurgent. Rhetoric about low taxes has always been popular outside the far-left socialist circles where President Obama recruits his "czars." But now instead of just talking about not spending more on government, you could actually get applause for talking about *cutting* government. You could even touch the "third rail" of Social Security and Medicare, flatly declaring that entitlements must be fundamentally reformed. Increasingly, you can speak openly about your faith, even if your faith is the only politically incorrect faith on earth (that is, Christianity). And you could push back against the politically correct tide of appeasement and globalism, in favor of protecting American lives and interests.

Gone were the justifications for George H. W. Bush's tax hike. Gone were Bob Dole's moderate, big-government policies. Gone also was George W. Bush's "compassionate conservatism." Moderate policies put us in a ditch; liberal policies only dug the hole deeper. Faced with the abject failure of government, millions of Americans became interested in truly limited government.

But ultimately, the best way to describe what's going on in America today is that the *Constitution* is resurgent. The Constitution of the United States, which since the rise of big government in the 1930s— and especially since the invasion of full-bore liberalism in the 1960s— has been seen as increasingly irrelevant to our government policies, is suddenly a topic of mainstream political discussion, instead of being an afterthought. Senior public officials now regularly make the case that numerous things—whether Obamacare, White House czars, or censoring conservative political voices on radio and television—violate the U.S. Constitution.

Therein lies our great hope as a people and a nation. Although no government is perfect, as a singular blessing of divine providence the U.S. Constitution is the greatest charter of government ever penned by man. Through its genius, we have the best shot any group of imperfect human beings could ever have to live as a free and happy people. And through its resurgence, we might just have one last chance for our republic to succeed again.

Republicans had a good night on November 2, 2010. But whether they will continue to have good nights—that is, whether the 2010 election was a flash in the pan driven by voter anger, or instead begins an enduring resurgence signaling a turning point for America—depends on whether the Republican Party has at long last become a conservative party. And whether the GOP is truly a conservative party turns on whether the GOP is finally dedicating itself to strict adherence to the U.S. Constitution.

The Prodigal Nation

In the Bible, the Lord Jesus Christ told the Parable of the Prodigal Son. In it, a wealthy man had two sons. One was hardworking and dependable. The other was lazy and selfish. One day the second son went to his father and said, "I don't want to wait around for you to die for me to get my inheritance. It's not right for me to have a reason not to be sad over you dying. How about giving me my half of your estate now?" The father loved his son, and gave him money for half of all the father owned.

Instead of building a house next door so he could be near his loving father, or living in a nearby town, Jesus says that the son then went off to a far country, where he lived large, partying every night. He spent every dime he had on lavish food, alcohol, and prostitutes. Left broke and destitute, the son finally ended up working in a pigsty, serving slop to the pigs. (To appreciate how bad that is, remember that Jesus was telling this story to a Jewish audience; pigs were forbidden, they were unclean; you couldn't eat them, touch them, or touch anything they touched. So here Jesus paints a picture of a young man who's truly hit rock bottom.)

Then one day the young man "came to his senses," Jesus explains. The son says to himself, "My father has workers, and he cares for them. They get paid well and have good housing and plenty of food. I will arise. I will go back to my father, and I'll tell him that I'm not worthy to be his son anymore, but I'll happily be a servant on his land, and get away from this place. Why would I ever stay here?" And so the young man set off for his home country.

Back on his father's land, his dad would go out every day and look toward the horizon, hoping to see his son whom he missed terribly. One day, he saw a figure walking toward his estate across the fields. From the way he walked, before he could even make out the walker's face he knew it was his son. The father hiked up his robe and ran out to his son in the field. (A man of stature never pulled up his robe to run, so this was a real statement of a man who didn't care at the moment about appearances or customs; he was happy to sacrifice his dignity to get to his son.)

The father reached the son in the middle of the field and threw his arms around him. The son started his well-rehearsed speech: "Father, I've sinned against Heaven, and against you. I'm no longer worthy to be called your son. Let me live and work here as one of your servants, and—" His father cut him off, calling out to his servants, "Bring my best robe and put it on my son! Bring my ring and put it on his hand. Go slaughter the fattened calf and make a feast!"

The father threw a party, with his son as the guest of honor. When the first son became upset at the treatment his waste of a brother was receiving, his father told him not to resent his brother, because "everything I have is yours, too. But we must celebrate, because it was as if your brother was dead, and now he is alive again. He was lost, and now he is found."

The Parable of the Prodigal Son is about the forgiveness of sins. It's a story of repentance and redemption, a beautiful picture of how flawed and fallen human beings can be restored to a right relationship with the living God who created us all in his image.

But it has an application to our current constitutional crisis. We have left our Founding Fathers' house. We have wasted our magnificent inheritance on self-indulgent lifestyles and an orgy of shameful spending (shameful because our children and grandchildren will pay the price for our disgraceful lack of self-control).

We can return to our Founding Fathers' house. We are still the heirs of what they intended for us, and we can go back to their home. It's possible that America is finally coming to her senses. If so, we can leave the pigsty that we're currently in and start the long, difficult trek home to our Founding Fathers' house.

We have to remember that—unlike the prodigal son—this is not just about us; it's about our children. Do we want our kids growing up and living in a pigsty, or do we want for them the comforts and joys of our Founding Fathers' house? If we return to that house, we will be welcomed with open arms, and our children will dwell there in happiness after us.

A REPUBLIC, IF YOU CAN KEEP IT

A portentous chance encounter sounds a somber note for where we are today. After the Constitutional Convention in 1787, the delegates left Independence Hall in Philadelphia. A lady stopped Benjamin Franklin on the street to ask him a question.

This is hardly surprising. First, Franklin was one of the most learned and well-known of the Framers. And second, he was a longtime resident of Pennsylvania; he represented Pennsylvania at the Continental Congress that declared independence, and was part of the Pennsylvania delegation to this convention. As one of the best-educated and most-experienced men in America—a statesman, a diplomat, an inventor, an entrepreneur, and many other things—it was a regular experience for someone to stop Franklin on the street.

The woman asked Ben Franklin, "Well, doctor, what have we got— a republic or a monarchy?" Everyone knew that the Articles of Confederation had failed. Everyone knew that the Constitutional Convention had been convened to create a stronger national government. She wanted to know what they had proposed to the American people.

Ben Franklin's answer is sobering: "A republic—if you can keep it."

That's where we are, 224 years later. We have a republic, but just barely; we're holding on to it by our fingernails. Can we keep it?

We can, but only through embracing constitutional conservatism. No time for half measures or half-truths. America is on the brink, and we need to save it now for our children's sake. We're like the Prodigal Son in the pigsty, and it looks like tens of millions of Americans may have finally come to their senses, perhaps enough to constitute a critical mass that forges a majority on Election Day 2012, if we can properly explain to them what policy options are best for the long-term interests of our nation.

That's what this book is about. If this resurgence of the Republican Party becomes more than a partisan resurgence, becomes a resurgence of *true* conservatism—not the modern pseudoconservatism promoted by some—and a resurgence of the Constitution itself, then we can keep our republic and restore its glory.

It's time to return to our Founders' house. It's time to come home to the wonderful place we should never have left. By returning to the Framers' constitutional conservatism of the past, we can lead America into a glorious future, illuminated by the blazing lamp of liberty.

1

DEMOCRATS AND REPUBLICANS HAVE BOTH FAILED AMERICA

"A pox on both your houses!"

—Mercutio, *Romeo and Juliet,* by William Shakespeare

"The nine most terrifying words in the English language are, 'I'm from the government and I'm here to help.'"

—Ronald Reagan

Most would expect that a book written by two Republicans—your authors—discussing the Constitution, history, politics, and policy would lambaste the Democratic Party, and especially President Barack Obama as the sitting Democratic president and as the most liberal president in American history. They'd also expect us to criticize Hillary Clinton, as the possible Democratic nominee in 2012. They're right; that's exactly what we do.

But we also do something that will surprise a lot of people (especially Republicans): We're pretty harsh with the GOP as well. The fact that we're loyal Republicans can't compel us to refrain from criticizing our party. To the contrary, we're deeply concerned about the state of the Republican Party, and as such we feel the need to sound the call that Republicans need to overhaul our party by returning to our core principles.

Some things are more important than politics. We're both Americans before Republicans. This book is about America; the U.S. Constitution, which is the Supreme Law in America; and what needs to be done to save the American Republic. This book is about Republicans only insofar as it shows what the GOP must do to be the political vehicle by which constitutional conservatism can bring America back from the brink of disaster.

As Americans who love this country, we take our fellow Republicans to task along with the Democrats. The country where we and our children live is in terrible trouble. Failed policies and ineffective leadership have left the United States in an unsustainable position, and hard choices confront the American people whether our leaders have the courage and strength to confront those dangers or not.

And the cold, hard reality is this:

Both Democrats *and* Republicans have failed the United States of America.

This is not to say that both parties are equally to blame. As you're about to read, the Democratic Party has done far more to damage America than the Republican Party. Democrats—especially now under President Obama, along with Hillary Clinton, Nancy Pelosi, and Harry Reid—have almost ruined the United States, driving us into bankruptcy, moral decline, and vulnerability to attack. The policies of the modern Democratic Party are not merely bad for America; they are disastrous.

But instead of being the solution, the GOP has too often been part of the problem. Republicans are too often watered-down Democrats. We grow an already-too-big government, we just grow it slower than Democrats in the name of being "moderate." We spend money we don't have, driving up the national debt; we just spend ourselves into bankruptcy slower than Democrats do, and embrace such "moderation" as a virtue. We pile debt on the heads of our children; it's just not the mountain range of debt that Democrats pile on our little ones. We make government more intrusive into people's lives while designating ourselves "in the middle"; we're just not micromanaging people's lives like Democrats. We go along with parts of a liberal social agenda and call it "moderate"; we just don't embrace a radical-secularist agenda like Democrats. We've not paid too much attention to the Constitution; we just don't ignore it like Democrats. We even sometimes appoint judges who don't consider themselves bound by the Constitution; we just don't appoint judges who feel free to completely rewrite it according to their own beliefs.

These are things to be ashamed of, not celebrate. Too many Republican incumbents deride their opponents in primaries as being "extreme," while bragging about how they themselves are "moderates" who are "in the middle" where "most Americans are." These assertions are ridiculous. Their "moderate" policies have placed us on the brink of bankruptcy and failed to address the serious and mounting problems facing America. In calling themselves "moderates," they admit that they've failed us all.

In fact, the reason we're currently grappling with the most radical president in American history, backed by a radical Congress (at least until last November, though it's now a divided Congress, not conservative), is that the voters ousted the Republican Party from power. They didn't embrace the Far Left; they just got sick of GOP hypocrisy, ineffectiveness, and lack of principle.

The rise of the Tea Party movement is a manifestation of voter rage against corruption and ineffectiveness in *both* parties. Not only is this rage justified, but those who don't share it must not understand the dangers facing America. Why do you think some Republican politicians won't show their faces at Tea Party rallies? Because Tea Partiers are protesting against some of them! That's why Tea Party–backed candidates trounced some well-established incumbents in their own primaries in 2010 and can expect more of that in 2012 and 2014. Too many Republicans have been part of the problem, helping Democrats drive America into a ditch, and possibly off a cliff.

It's time for the Republican Party to stop being the lesser of two evils half the time. It's time for us to stop being on track on one issue but dead wrong on the other issue debated that very same day. It's time for Republicans to be part of the solution by becoming the party of real and lasting solutions.

There's one point to make up front, however, because it's central to this chapter. The single most egregious failure of both the Democrats and the Republicans is that they've failed to protect the American family.

But here's the aspect of that argument that so many Washington leaders miss: *Restoring the family is more than a social values argument; it is an economic prosperity argument.* If you survey the broad scope of world history, you will find that government doesn't grow where families stay strong. Authoritarian and totalitarian regimes don't succeed in gradually enslaving a people through growing government in nations where families stay strong. Family is the basic unit of government. Where families are strong, government remains contained, and the family becomes a springboard from which economic freedom and prosperity vault to new heights.

Too many so-called conservative leaders fail to grasp this simple fact. To be pro–traditional marriage, pro-values, and pro-life is to be pro-business, pro–wealth creation, and pro-freedom. That is a central point of this book, which we lay out in detail in the following chapters. It's an essential key to restoring American freedom and prosperity, and any so-called conservative leader who doesn't embrace this truth is not leading America in a direction that will restore free markets and limited government.

Hypocrisy of Barack Obama and the Democrats

Let's start with the Democrats. There are plenty of unflattering words to describe how the Democratic Party has acted over the past four years, terms that would not describe the party a generation ago: *Leftist. Statist. Socialist.* But perhaps the best word—the one for which the America people are angriest—is *Hypocrite.*

Even children react to what they perceive to be hypocrisy. When Mommy or Daddy tells a little boy or girl not to do something, but then the child sees the parents do it, there are several results. First, the child is confused, because wasn't he just told that this thing was wrong? Second, the child becomes angry. And third, the child resents the parents' authority and is more prone to disobey them in the future. Hypocrisy destroys the hypocrite's moral authority.

American voters are not children, despite the fact that President Obama and his associates treat us as such. They are nothing short of paternalistic in how they treat the American people, as if we're too stupid to run our own lives. But arguing from the lesser to the greater, if even children detect and justifiably resent hypocrisy, tens of millions of grown adults are nothing short of outraged when they see it in their elected leaders.

This isn't to say all Democrats are hypocrites, of course. Nor does it say that American voters who happen to vote Democrat are hypocrites. Much of the time it's Democratic voters who are outraged most, because what they're seeing out of Washington is not what they voted for. This charge of hypocrisy is about the bulk of Democrats running the country at the moment, though as you'll see the so-called conservative Democrat who says he's not with those ruling elitists is a mirage that can't stand the light of day.

BROKEN PROMISES

One infuriating trait that has defined the Obama White House and the Pelosi-Reid Congress is broken promises.

Throughout this book, you'll read many examples of where President Obama and his lieutenants have promised one thing and done another. Here at the outset, though, we'd like to point out several notable examples that illustrate a recurring theme: a lack of character and trustworthiness.

It's important to keep in mind that there are at least three types of broken promises. One is something that you say you'll do and maybe you try—even if only halfheartedly—but the results don't materialize. That's a lie only if you didn't give it a serious effort. The second is something you promise, but once in office you learn critical facts you didn't know before, and realize that what you promised is bad, that following through would harm the nation's interests. It was a foolish promise, so you apologize, reverse yourself, and leave it to the voters to decide whether to forgive you. The third, though, is something you have complete power to do, and the facts haven't changed, and you just don't do it.

That last type is a bald-faced lie. It's a shameless lie, the sort that voters shouldn't let you get away with. It's an issue of character. Those who prove they are untrustworthy are not fit to serve as stewards of governmental power. Those are the kinds of promises we focus on here.

Start with the issue of transparency. A perfect example is when Senator Barack Obama promised that when Congress was debating healthcare legislation, instead of having secret meetings (which he decried), he would have all the hearings and negotiations broadcast on

C-SPAN.[1] Even though he'd have been morally bound by his promise even if it had been said only once, or said off-the-cuff, Obama made this promise no fewer than *eight* times.[2]

He broke his promise. President Obama flat-out deceived the American people about televising the healthcare negotiations. He promised, "That's what I will do in bringing all parties together, not negotiating behind closed doors, but bringing all parties together, and broadcasting those negotiations on C-SPAN." As the *Washington Examiner* reported, "As a candidate, President Obama repeatedly called for airing the health care reform debate on C-SPAN, but now that he's in office—and personally involved in negotiations—the White House says no cameras."[3] The chairman of C-SPAN, Brian Lamb, even wrote a letter requesting that the president's promise be kept, and asking for access for his cameras to carry the negotiations.[4]

What is especially troubling about episodes like the C-SPAN promise is what it suggests. This isn't the sort of promise that affects millions of people directly, so it's not likely to cost you much at the ballot box. In other words, this is the kind of false statement you can make deliberately, with every intention of deceiving people, because it sounds good at the moment, and you expect that you'll never pay a price for it. That makes it entirely about character; it's a dishonest act; it's dishonorable, and the American people should hold to account a leader who looks them straight in the face and willfully tells them falsehoods— *repeatedly.*

Another example may seem minor, but it's telling. President Obama promised that all legislation sent to him by Congress would be posted online for five days before he would sign it into law. Once again, he broke that promise. Obama gave his word that he "will not sign any non-emergency bill without giving the American public an opportunity to review and comment on the White House website for five days."[5]

This is routinely ignored. The credit card overhaul bill (which is raising your credit card rates, if you're generally responsible with credit cards) was signed on May 22, 2009, only two days after being passed by Congress. He did the same with expanding children's health insurance (which is a massive middle-class entitlement), and with a law expanding the time frame for women to sue when alleging gender discrimination at work. Despite the fact that none of these was an emergency that couldn't wait five days, the president broke his pledge.[6]

There are aspects of promises where we're willing to let President Obama off the hook. For example, as a candidate he criticized the Bush administration for using the state-secrets privilege to block our most sensitive classified information from being released in open court when prosecuting terrorists. However, since becoming president, Obama has invoked the state-secrets privilege. Using this privilege to protect national security secrets is vital for protecting America. Obviously President Obama has learned this. It was a foolish and wrongheaded promise not to use the states-secret privilege, which we chalk up to then Senator Obama's lack of experience in national security. We're glad the president reversed course to protect the United States.

But in most instances, the president broke his word without excuse. The administration that promised openness and transparency, along with the Speaker of the House who promised the same, has instead given America the most secretive government we've ever seen. First are President Obama's czars, which as we explained in our first, bestselling book, *The Blueprint,* are completely unconstitutional. One of the benefits that Obama reaps from these illegal czars is that those working inside the White House might be immune from congressional subpoenas.[7] This is a slap in the face to the American people, as these czars are running vast areas of national policy, czars such as Carol Browner, a socialist running cap-and-trade in an attempt to take over all of American industry,[8] and Elizabeth Warren, a statist who, despite being denied Senate confirmation, is building an agency that claims the power to control every loan made in America.[9] On top of those, on another front they've even made the SEC (Securities and Exchange Commission) exempt from requests under the Freedom of Information Act (FOIA), a law that exists solely to make government transparent and accountable to the voters by making them disclose their records and decision making to the public.[10]

Former Speaker Pelosi and her leftist comrades have followed the president's lead in this furtive attempt to keep the American people in the dark. When Democrats were scheming to ram through Obamacare, they started holding secret meetings with Democratic members of

Congress—no Republicans allowed—in order to substitute a new bill for the versions originally rammed through Congress. (How's that for transparency?) As public outcry was growing to open these meetings to public scrutiny, or at least to tell the public what was in the bill that would dominate a large part of every American's life, Pelosi defiantly waved off these demands, never opening the meetings to the public.

Then comes the issue of rules. Regarding Obamacare, Democrats made one of the most telling comments to summarize their tenure in office. Congressman Alcee Hastings—a Democrat who was Judge Alcee Hastings until he was impeached and removed by the U.S. House and Senate for taking bribes (whereupon the Democrats happily embraced him as a congressional candidate)—commented that "all this talk about rules—we make them up as we go along."[11]

Possible crimes also should be investigated. When Congressman Joe Sestak was running for the U.S. Senate in Pennsylvania as a Democrat in 2010 (he later lost to Pat Toomey), Sestak said someone from the White House offered him a job to drop out of the Senate race to protect the unprincipled Arlen Specter. Published reports state that former White House chief of staff Rahm Emanuel was personally involved, as was former president Bill Clinton. It's a federal crime for any federal employee to offer a candidate for federal office anything of value in an attempt to influence an election.[12]

Once Sestak reconciled with the Obama White House, he said he was offered only an unpaid advisory position. That's a joke so ridiculous that it insults the voters' intelligence. Sestak was a three-star admiral and U.S. congressman who had his eye on a Senate seat. It would probably take a highly paid, high-power job to entice him to give up his Senate bid. Sestak was offered something very important, meaning someone around President Obama may have committed a federal crime.

The same happened with Andrew Romanoff, when running against incumbent Senator Michael Bennet in Colorado. Romanoff claimed that Deputy White House Chief of Staff Jim Messina offered him a job in exchange for dropping his Senate bid.

Democrats came back with the saddest of defenses: "Everyone does this." First of all, no they don't. Second, who cares? It's a *crime*. If these

White House officials committed a crime, then they need to be held to account. (Conversely, if Sestak and Romanoff are liars, then the White House staffers should be exonerated.) One reason the American people have become so cynical about government is that they sense that a lot of corrupt acts go unpunished, and they're right to expect something better. Cities like Chicago have become so accustomed to corruption that it's become the way of doing business. Americans must reject the Chicago Way.

Also, there's a serious question as to whether President Obama was involved in these schemes. It's extremely unlikely that the White House chief of staff and deputy chief of staff could have offered Senate-confirmed presidential appointments of sufficient stature to bribe a U.S. congressman—appointments such as secretary of the navy or CIA director—without the president's approval. Given that offering these jobs would be a federal crime, if the president of the United States had knowledge of them, then it becomes a criminal conspiracy, where every coconspirator is liable to the maximum extent of the law as if that person had personally committed the crime alone.

Republicans should investigate these credible allegations of possible crimes committed by the White House. However, Republicans would make a damaging political error if they were to launch *every* possible investigation, and issues involving the president—*any* president of *either* party—should not result in impeachment hearings unless egregious felonies are involved. (We're quick to point out that offering a federal job to buy someone off from seeking a Senate seat is a misdemeanor, *not* a felony, so it does *not* meet the "high crimes" standard the Constitution sets for impeachment.) Nonetheless this is a public corruption issue that should be investigated one way or the other. If that means that the president needs to order White House staffers to cooperate with a criminal investigation, then so be it.

We would sternly warn the White House of the sobering political lesson that many administrations refuse to learn: The cover-up is usually worse than the crime. Offering to buy off a Senate candidate is a misdemeanor, but lying under oath is perjury, and *that's* a felony. If Republicans investigate this issue, then Rahm Emanuel, Jim Messina, and anyone else implicated in these possible crimes had better answer truthfully. If not, then there must be consequences. For that matter, Republicans should consider subpoenaing Bill Clinton as well, and see if the former president has learned his lesson, that saying things like "It all depends on what the meaning of the word 'is' is" is a poor substitute for telling the truth.

OBAMA IS SUBVERTING
CONSTITUTIONAL GOVERNMENT

A final issue is how Barack Obama has damaged the institution of the presidency. The office is bigger than any one person. Every occupant of that office has an obligation to protect its stature and prerogatives for future generations. Moreover, as our head of state and the most recognizable and authoritative person in America, every president must also be mindful of the other two branches of government, maintaining and building respect for our entire constitutional system of government.

Here, President Obama has failed miserably. He has demeaned the prestige of his office through attacks that are beneath the dignity of the presidency. One of countless examples that we could cite happened in the last days of the 2010 election, when Obama accused Republicans of taking illegal foreign money to influence the election.[13] As you'll read in Chapter 14, these comments launched a malignant campaign of deception and conspiratorial paranoia carried out by the vice president, the White House staff, and the Democratic National Committee, a campaign that even liberal pundits and the *New York Times* decried.

Moreover, President Obama insulted the American nation to foreigners. Speaking in Europe, Barack Obama apologized for America's greatness. He then went on to criticize the nation he leads by saying, "there have been times where America has shown arrogance and been dismissive."[14] Our president doesn't speak about us—his people—to *foreigners* in that way.

In the closing days of the 2010 elections, President Obama told Hispanic voters that Republicans are his "enemies," and that Hispanics should join him to "punish our enemies."[15] American statesmanship demands that every president accept that he is the president of our entire nation and temper how he speaks of even his political opponents, using broad and inclusive language. Rejecting more than two hundred years of presidential wisdom and dignity, President Obama calls Republicans his *enemies* and says that others should join with him to *punish* his enemies. Those are words expected from authoritarian statists or tin-pot dictators, not the president of a great freedom-loving republic.

And he has insulted his coequal branches of government in an unprecedented manner. On January 21, 2010, the U.S. Supreme Court handed down a landmark victory for the First Amendment in *Citizens United v. FEC.*[16] President Obama vigorously disagreed with this decision, for reasons you'll read about in Chapter 14 (all of which involve giving you, the American people, the right and power to speak your mind and hold your government accountable). So in January 2010, in his constitutionally mandated State of the Union address, with five justices of the High Court sitting in places of honor amid the gathered assembly, President Obama condemned the U.S. Supreme Court, saying that the Court's free-speech decision that we examine in Chapter 14 allows "American elections [to] be bankrolled by America's most powerful interests, or worse, by foreign entities."[17]

This disgraceful attack was patently false, leading Justice Samuel Alito to shake his head in disbelief and stately disapproval, muttering, "That's not true." It also compelled Chief Justice John Roberts to take the evidently unprecedented step of pushing back against the president, expressing the judiciary's disapproval of the "image of having members of one branch of government, standing up, literally surrounding the Supreme Court, cheering and hollering while the Court—according to the requirements of protocol—has to sit there expressionless, I think is very troubling."[18] Obama stirred up his congressional henchmen to act like a mob of brutish thugs to intimidate the third branch of government, in an appalling display of boorish demagoguery.

This reminds your author (Blackwell) of one of my experiences in the former Soviet Union when serving as U.S. ambassador to the United Nations Human Rights Commission. Assistant Secretary of State Richard Schifter led a delegation including me and Judge Danny Boggs of the U.S. Court of Appeals for the Sixth Circuit, to show them how to set up an independent judiciary. (Judge Boggs was born in Havana in Castro's Cuba, and understood totalitarianism.) It's the hallmark of authoritarian and totalitarian regimes that the courts are never free from political control and intimidation. Dictators denigrate courts of justice in other countries, and Assistant Secretary Schifter took me and Judge Boggs to educate the Soviets on how America holds its independent courts in the highest respect.

President Obama's actions were shockingly outrageous. Showing such disrespect for the Supreme Court is a grievous assault on our constitutional system of government. Even in the wake of the Court's most egregiously wrong decisions, like *Dred Scott, Plessy v. Ferguson,* and *Roe v. Wade* (all discussed in Chapter 6), the sitting president of the United States never humiliated the institution of the Supreme Court, especially not to the justices' faces before a national audience, surrounded by the president's political allies. It marks an utterly deplorable and shameful act that subverts our constitutional order.

President Obama is a marked contrast in this regard to President George W. Bush. Like his predecessor, President Obama is a credit to his office for being a faithful husband and a devoted father. However, the shameful examples discussed above could not be more different from the dignity and graciousness with which George W. Bush conducted his public affairs (as did President Reagan and President George H. W. Bush). Because so many presidents hold themselves to such an honorable and respectable standard, it's easy to lose sight of how petty and unseemly actions badly diminish the presidency. We cannot yet see the extent to which President Obama's tactics have weakened the stature of his office, an office that must endure so that it can serve future generations long after Barack Obama leaves the White House.

THE MYTH OF THE CONSERVATIVE DEMOCRAT

We could go on with countless examples of other issues, enough to fill a whole book.[19] We also want to note that we're somewhat uncomfortable dwelling on these points, because in a democracy it's better to give other people the benefit of the doubt regarding motives and character and keep disagreements focused on policy differences rather than personal issues. But if you assume high office, you open yourself up to a full and frank discussion of your integrity. When the president of the United States and his top congressional allies violate the public's trust, they must be called to account.

We conclude by pointing out that one of the things we've all learned over the past two years is the myth of the conservative Democrat. Anyone who supports President Obama for reelection, voted for Nancy Pelosi as Speaker, or supports Harry Reid as Senate majority leader is no conservative.

A number of Democrats in the U.S. House played their voters for fools. Bart Stupak called himself a pro-life Democrat, yet he sold out unborn babies at the end, voting for a version of Obamacare that includes funding for abortion (explained in Chapter 8). Others, like Brad Ellsworth and Joe Donnelly of Indiana, called themselves "Blue Dog" Democrats or even "conservatives."

The 111th Congress put the lie to all such assertions. Democrats conspired behind closed doors as to how many votes they could lose and still pass radical legislation such as Obamacare. Pelosi's office would put together a list of vulnerable Democrats according to how tough their reelection chances were, figure out how many votes they could lose (with any offsets from Republicans), and then give permission one at a time. This cynical approach allowed the most vulnerable Democrats to vote against a measure and then run for reelection touting their *opposition* to President Obama and Pelosi. But when the president or the Speaker needed their vote, or when it's time to decide whether to support Obama for a second term, these Democrats have been right where they are needed, doing exactly as they're told by their statist masters.

Nor were Democrats' losses limited to the House. Governors and senators who ran as centrists but were in reality liberal Democrats saw their political careers come crashing to an end in the 2010 midterms. Some, such as Indiana's Senator Evan Bayh, didn't even seek reelection. Others, such as Ohio's Governor Ted Strickland, were held to account by the voters.

The Failure of the Modern Republican Party

Although not as bad, Republicans have a lot to answer for, as well. The voters were right to fire the Republicans in 2006 and 2008 by expelling them from the White House and Congress, because Republicans betrayed their core principles and America suffered as a result. Although the United States would have been much better off over the past few years if Republicans had controlled Congress and the White House, GOP failures and betrayal of principles had grown to such an intolerable point that something had to be done. In short, the Grand Old Party had stopped being the solution to America's problems as a conservative party, becoming instead part of the problem as a moderate party.

The reality is that—unlike Ronald Reagan—George W. Bush was not a conservative. This isn't to say he was liberal; he was not. There are issues where President Bush was conservative. But overall, George W. Bush was a moderate Republican. The problem is that President Bush called himself conservative, and the media pushed that moniker like a slur because many of them despise conservatives, so too many people in the public eventually got the picture that if you want to know what a conservative looks like, take a look at President Bush. Anyone to the right of Bush—that is to say, a *real* conservative—was then called an extremist, a radical, or a nut.

BEWARE OF COMPASSIONATE CONSERVATIVES

We want to reiterate our respect for President Bush, and our strong support for many of his accomplishments. But our respect and personal affinity for the former president cannot be allowed to mute a frank discussion of how George W. Bush was a moderate, and yet what America now needs is a conservative head of state. Perhaps nothing sums up better how President Bush and his team were not conservative than the idea of the "compassionate conservative."

First, true conservatism is the most compassionate form of conservatism. The old adage is true: "Give a man a fish and he'll eat for a day. Teach a man to fish and he'll eat for a lifetime." True conservatism empowers individuals and families. It allows them to reach for the stars, using their God-given potential to the fullest extent that providence allows.

"Compassionate conservatism," however, is not conservative at all. It's all about moderate—not conservative—policies. It's a form of triangulation, used to play off the GOP base while peeling off a number of Democrats.

That's how a number of President Bush's signature legislative priorities won passage. Medicare Part D was a massive expansion of the Medicare program. Although fortunately to date this program has come in under budget, the reality remains that Medicare is on a path to bankruptcy, and new entitlements such as Part D only make the situation worse. Concerning another topic covered in Chapter 13, education, the No Child Left Behind Act was a monstrous expansion of the Education Department over the lives of Americans, supplanting the rightful place of states and local school boards. Although accountability is desperately needed in education, this is not the way to get it.

All this pales, though, against President Bush's last months in office. In addition to everything else, the president embarked on a massive government takeover of parts of the private sector. Although government action is needed during times of crisis, some ways of responding are worse than others. The president engaged in a massive intervention in the markets that gave the U.S. government a direct stake in some of America's most important companies. Beyond that, this gave tremendous political cover for Bush's successor—Barack Obama—to take these government controls to the next level. Although it's not surprising that President Bush would act in the face of a crisis, an action that empowers the federal government to control vast areas of our economy was a terrible idea, and was a final reminder of how long it's been since America had a conservative chief executive.

PREVIOUS REPUBLICAN TRANSGRESSIONS

Nor did these moderate policies start with President George W. Bush. Previous Republican presidents and Congresses likewise did not consistently adhere to conservative principles, and at times did even worse than that.

For example, the second President Bush was far more conservative on taxes than his father, President George H. W. Bush. The first President Bush partially doomed his 1992 reelection prospects by breaking a pledge. He had boldly proclaimed to the country that if the Democrats pushed him to raise taxes, he would defiantly tell them, "Read my lips: No new taxes!" He went on to raise taxes two years later, and millions of Americans never forgave him for it.

It's part of modern revisionist history to try to peg Bush 41's re-election defeat on economic issues, pushed by those who would like to redefine conservatism as a solely economic philosophy to the exclusion of social issues. This is yet another attempt—you'll see such attempts throughout this book—to falsely label "conservatism" as a philosophy that's exclusively concerned with economic and size-of-government issues.

Instead, Bill Clinton's defeat of George H. W. Bush was a perfect example of all three parts of conservatism, which we learn about in Chapter 3. President Bush appointed David Souter to the Supreme Court. Souter turned out to be an unabashed liberal, and showed that in spades just months before the 1992 election by preserving a consti-tutional right to abortion by reaffirming *Roe v. Wade,* and also voting to hold that prayers offered at high school graduations are uncon-stitutional. (Both cases were narrowly divided decisions.) The president also decided not to push to Baghdad in the Persian Gulf War. These decisions disappointed social conservatives and national security con-servatives, respectively. Coupled with a third-party candidate and the anger from economic conservatives, Bush 41 lost just enough votes from his base to allow a less-than-ideal challenger, Bill Clinton, to de-feat him for the presidency.

We don't want to sandbag the Bush family, which has done a lot of good for America through public policy in office, and also through developing and supporting candidates for countless offices over the past thirty years. (We also want to point out that former governor Jeb Bush of Florida has shown himself to be a committed conservative on many issues.)

Instead, we see that with the exception of Ronald Reagan (whose candidacy began as an insurgency) and 1964 nominee Barry Goldwater, who was also an insurgent, the Republican Party since the 1940s has been a moderate party, not conservative. John McCain was staunchly conservative on government spending and a hawk on national secu-rity, but aside from that was either seen as soft on issues (for example, he's pro-life but never outspokenly so) or moderate to liberal (such as his immigration and tax policies during the Bush years). Before that, Bob Dole was generically moderate on everything across the board, a throwback to the pre-Reagan GOP. In the 1970s, Gerald Ford was an unmitigated disaster of a president—every bit as much a failed president as Jimmy Carter. Ford supported abortion on demand, affirmative action, big government, and secularism. (Just a few years before his death, President Ford commented that appointing far-left justice John Paul Stevens to the Supreme Court was one of his greatest accomplishments.) And Richard Nixon became stridently moderate in his later years in office. For many years, every GOP *establishment* candidate has been moderate, not conservative.

The Republican Party has not fielded a unified conservative government since 1928, when Calvin Coolidge was still president. Few people alive today have ever seen a conservative Republican government.

Attack of the Fake Conservatives

In defining what it means to be conservative, we also need to take account of one other thing: There are some being billed as conservative who are anything but. While there's such a thing as an economic conservative who doesn't support the social conservative agenda, and a social conservative who doesn't support the economic agenda, there are also wolves in sheep's clothing. These people are not real conservatives, and to the extent that they're billed as such, they're an impediment to getting America back on the right track, or for the Republican Party regaining power in any lasting manner.

We're not talking about people who aren't even Republicans. For example, Matthew Dowd—who was Bush 43's pollster in 2000 and strategist for the 2004 campaign—was not a Republican; he's a Democrat who since leaving the White House continues to cast himself as an authoritative commentator on Republicans. Scott McClellan, one of Bush 43's press secretaries, and whose ineptitude rivals that of Robert Gibbs in the Obama White House, was also a Democrat, and wasted no time upon leaving the White House in betraying the former president and much of the White House staff. With those people, you should know what you're getting.

We're also not talking about those who make no pretense of being conservatives. Some economic or social moderates have a very sophisticated understanding of geopolitics and national security that can make them extremely useful in foreign policy. For example, General Colin Powell never claimed to be conservative, being completely up front that he favored abortion, affirmative action, and big government. But he's an outstanding soldier and a very thoughtful person, and as such was an excellent national security advisor to President Reagan and chairman of the Joint Chiefs of Staff for Bush 41 and a formidable secretary of state for Bush 43.

Instead, we're talking about those who are called conservative but are not. These people go on TV and radio to give a "conservative" view. They then misrepresent what conservatism is all about, and allow the media and Far Left to paint true conservatives as fanatics, as they're well to the right of these fake conservatives.

One example is Michael Gerson, who served as a Bush 43 speechwriter, and then became a senior domestic policy advisor. Gerson now works as a *Washington Post* columnist and a frequent ABC contributor. He's a brilliant speechwriter and respected public servant.

But he's no conservative. While billed by his leftist colleagues as conservative, ever since leaving the White House, Gerson has been relentless in his efforts to make the GOP more moderate and *less* conservative. He even wrote a book titled *Heroic Conservatism: Why Republicans Need to Embrace America's Ideals (And Why They Deserve to Fail If They Don't)*, which essentially is a treatise on how being a conservative is really all about being a moderate. That is to say, the kind of "conservatism" Gerson embraces involves massive government entitlements, an enormous regulatory government, and massive foreign-aid outlays. In other words, Gerson's "heroic" conservatism is what the rest of America calls "moderate." His book was even endorsed by such conservative luminaries as a former Democratic vice presidential candidate, Senator Joseph Lieberman (who supports abortion, gun control, Obamacare, tax hikes, gay rights, and "agenda" judges—explained in Chapter 6).

In August 2010, Gerson wrote a *Post* column ridiculing the "conviction that the federal government has only those powers specifically enumerated in the Constitution." He continues, "This view is logically inconsistent—as well as historically uninformed, morally irresponsible and politically disastrous. The Constitution . . . granted broad power to the federal government to impose taxes and spend funds to 'provide for . . . the general welfare.' . . ." He also says it's extreme to question birthright citizenship, and that Tea Party populism is incompatible with conservative principles, with Abraham Lincoln's "tone," and with Christian teaching.

The reality is that Michael Gerson's type is toxic to the GOP. We're regrettably going to be a little harsh. Setting aside numerous flaws in this column that would deserve a rebuttal if space allowed (such as the fact that there is a serious constitutional debate about birthright citizenship that we explore in Chapter 12), what Gerson doesn't realize (but would if he had the slightest training or education in constitutional law, or if he had bothered to read our first book) is that ever since the founding of the Republic, the Supreme Court has repeatedly emphasized, including as recently as this last term, in *U.S. v. Comstock*, with a liberal majority—a *liberal* majority—that "nearly 200 years ago, this Court stated that the Federal 'Government is acknowledged by all to be one of enumerated powers.'"[20] Even the most liberal Supreme Court justice knows and acknowledges this truth, and performs linguistic gymnastics to try cramming whatever he's trying to justify into a specific constitutional provision. Gerson didn't know it, but he casually discarded as trash the cardinal principle of the Constitution, which even judges on the Far Left respect because they understand it's the cornerstone of our whole form of government.

What's extremely troubling about this is that when Gerson was a commissioned officer of the United States, serving in a senior White House role, his oath of office was to "support and defend the Constitution of the United States." The problem is that too many Republicans have tried to take Republicans away from the Constitution, violating the core principles of the Founders (principles that Abraham Lincoln gave his life to save), all the while having the temerity to cite these giants as supporting preposterous and legally inaccurate positions. Although Gerson's misquotes are probably born of ignorance rather than deceitfulness, that's no excuse for misleading the American people.

Another example is Steve Schmidt, who served in a variety of political positions in the George W. Bush White House and 2004 campaign, and was manager of McCain's 2008 campaign. He's a talented and accomplished Republican strategist.

But again, he's no conservative. He's come out as a committed foe of social conservatives. He specifically blasts conservative people of faith, saying that no one should ever cite the Bible to support their beliefs, because "if you put public policy issues to a religious test, you risk becoming a religious party."[21]

Schmidt is outspoken on these social issues. He condemns the Republican Party for supporting marriage as the union of one man and one woman, calling for the GOP to embrace same-sex marriage.[22] He also regularly criticizes McCain's VP running mate, Sarah Palin. (We can't help but note that Governor Palin is an Evangelical Christian who is courageously pro-life and supports traditional marriage.)

Schmidt's ridiculous statements demonstrate a complete ignorance of America's history and a rejection of America's political theory. He may be a fantastic strategist, but that doesn't mean he understands anything about America's history or Constitution. When a person is elected, they're elected to make laws in accordance with their beliefs, and insofar as they have a religious faith, such faith will inevitably inform their moral beliefs, whether it's in regard to the death penalty, waging war, human cloning, or the more conventional social issues of abortion, same-sex marriage, religious liberty, and guns. For that matter, religious beliefs also influence countless public officials on economic issues such as taxes, education, welfare, and national security. Such religious sentiments dominate many of the most famous speeches or actions of presidents, and the Declaration of Independence was framed as an explicitly religious document.

For example, opposition to slavery was driven by Evangelicals in the Northern states. Read Lincoln's Second Inaugural address, which quotes repeatedly from the Bible. We challenge Steve Schmidt to condemn Lincoln's unapologetic Christian religiosity—which among other things informed his public policy stance on slavery, thereby violating Schmidt's test. The Republican Party was founded as a religious party in 1854, with a religiously driven mission to abolish the institution of slavery. (How's that for a religious test?) In fact, the GOP did not become an economic conservative party until 1896, more than four decades later.

These are just two examples among many. Gerson is a social conservative who flatly rejects economic conservatism, and Schmidt embraces at least some economic principles but rejects social conservatism with gusto. In both cases, they represent beliefs that contradict the Declaration of Independence, the Constitution, the Founders, and the creators of the Republican Party.

The media is very shrewd about using such fake conservatives to make real conservatives look bad. They put these fake conservatives on the air opposite unabashed liberals. The liberals give their leftist perspective, then the fake conservative gives a moderate opposing viewpoint that meets the liberals halfway. This frames the debate for the public as left-versus-right. Then, when a real conservative comes along and gives a truly conservative assessment of the matter, such an evaluation is of course to the right of the fake conservative. But since the moderate position has been labeled "conservative," the truly conservative perspective looks extreme. The media then labels the conservative an extremist and his position as radical, marginalizing conservatism in public debate.

We see this repeatedly on almost every issue. The Democrats used this tactic in this past election cycle to marginalize Republican Senate candidates. We saw this when genuine conservatives ran against moderates in the Republican primary, such as with Marco Rubio in Florida, Rand Paul in Kentucky, Joe Miller in Alaska, and Mike Lee in Utah.

Not only do they do this with politicians, they also do it with federal judges. They took a moderate like Justice Sandra Day O'Connor and called her a conservative once she announced in 2005 that she was retiring from the Supreme Court. Then Sam Alito—who judicially speaking is a real conservative—was nominated to replace O'Connor. Since they labeled O'Connor a conservative, and Alito was to the right of O'Connor, they screamed, "What an extremist! America is doomed!"

In doing so, whether with judges, politicians, or pundits, by calling moderates "conservative" they then are able to call real conservatives "extremists," to marginalize us and confuse the public. It's an old trick, but unfortunately it often works.

America Needs Conservative Government, Not Republican Government

Conservative government is what America needs, and we've not had a unified conservative government at the federal level for eighty-three years. During all eight years of our only conservative president during this long period—Ronald Reagan—the Democrats controlled the U.S. House, and even when the Senate was held by Republicans for part of Reagan's tenure, the Senate never had a conservative majority. During times of Republican control of both houses of Congress, spanning 1995 through 2006, there was either a Democrat or a moderate Republican in the White House.

Even during the years of a Republican majority, Congress never had a *conservative* majority. The House leadership was split, with some un-committed on social issues and others—while good on taxes—failing to ever tackle the cost and scope of government. In the Senate, as during the Reagan years, there were never fifty-one solidly conservative Re-publican senators, so there never were the votes for a conservative leg-islative agenda.

But as this book shows, the breathtaking challenges facing the United States and threatening to overwhelm us can be overcome only with sustained *conservative* policy. On all three policy fronts—economic, social, and national security—the conservative principles enshrined in the U.S. Constitution offer our only hope.

This is the one point on which libertarians often find traction with millions of voters. Libertarians often say, "Democrats and Republicans are taking us to the same big-government place, trashing the Constitu-tion along the way. It's just that the Republicans are getting us there in a car, while the Democrats are racing us there in an airplane." The reason this line gets traction is that too often it's true, because neither party has adhered to the Constitution. (And as libertarians correctly note, the Democrats have moved much further away from the Consti-tution than Republicans have in recent years.)

The modern Democratic Party is fundamentally incapable of em-bracing such conservative principles. It now elects presidents who run on promising to defy the Constitution, whether it's imposing unconstitutional mandates on the American people, or denying free speech to public interest citizens' organizations, or appointing government officers without congressional action or Senate confirmation. For the things President Obama cannot do through legislation or executive action, he's creating a Supreme Court that will declare what he wants, whether it's a constitutional right to healthcare or same-sex marriage, or that the Constitution does not mean what its plain words say, such as that the Second Amendment secures a right to keep and bear arms (we discuss this in Chapter 10).

The Republican Party is capable of embracing conservatism. But will it? There are committed constitutionalist members in the GOP in all the power centers. In the House, there's Mike Pence, Michele Bachmann, and Marsha Blackburn, as well as new faces such as Indiana's Marlin Stutzman and Todd Young. In the Senate, there are leaders such as Jim DeMint, who is now joined by new household names such as Marco Rubio, Ron Johnson, and Mike Lee. Among the governors, there are figures such as Tim Pawlenty and Rick Perry. And among other leaders, names such as Sarah Palin are quickly mentioned.

Many more full-spectrum conservatives are running in 2012. Already, former Texas solicitor general Ted Cruz is running for U.S. Senate in Texas. Another is former congressman David McIntosh of Indiana, expected to run for his former House seat (although national conservative leaders are asking him to run for Senate).

Will the Republican Party rally to principled conservative leadership, or will it revert to establishment figures who go along to get along and fail to address this nation's serious problems?

There are encouraging signs. For example, the new Republican House adopted a rule requiring all House bills to begin by specifying which constitutional provision(s) authorizes the legislation. This is a fantastic way to emphasize that the federal government has only those powers granted to it by the Constitution.

But more is needed. Continuing with this example, Republicans should fight for passage of the Enumerated Powers Act, which, as written by former Arizona congressman John Shadegg, would require all bills—House and Senate—to specify their constitutional justifications.[23] This law should further require that when the constitutionality of new statutes is challenged, courts must allow the Justice Department to base its defense only on the constitutional provisions named in the statute.

The split between the parties on this issue is growing. You'll read in Chapter 14 that President Obama's FCC voted that they have the power to seize control of the Internet. To this, Republicans are supporting a lawsuit by Verizon challenging this power. Likewise, the EPA has claimed the power to enact cap-and-trade through administrative regulations. Republicans are supporting a lawsuit brought by Texas challenging those regulations in a federal appeal led by David Rivkin, the Reagan administration lawyer who is also the architect of the national lawsuit challenging Obamacare in Florida, which we'll discuss in Chapter 8. In these and other instances, Republicans are rallying to the Constitution's text and separation of powers, while President Obama's Democrats are simply doing whatever they want without regard to this constitutional requirement. So there might be hope for the GOP after all.

America has suffered under ineffective government for too long. Both parties can boast of successes over the years, and as a country we've been blessed with strong leaders. But both parties have failed when it comes to adhering to the form of government given to us by the Founders in the Declaration and Constitution, a conservative framework for government that served us so well for the better part of two centuries, before some sought to change our form of government.

Both parties have failed America. The Constitution gives us the answer for how to make it right.

2

PARTY SPLIT IN 2012?
A REPEAT OF 1912 IS
OBAMA'S BEST CHANCE

"If we just stick together, and remain true to our ideals, we can be sure that America's greatest days lie ahead."
—Ronald Reagan, Message on Observance of Independence Day, July 3, 1981

A number of people are already writing the obituary of the Obama administration, as a failed, one-term presidency. They shouldn't. Republicans and conservatives indulge that idea at their peril.

Many are saying that President Obama could win reelection if Republicans don't deliver results. This is true in one sense, in that if Republicans fail to stand on principle and vigorously fight for the issues they ran on in 2010, we'll fail in 2012. It's not true in the sense—being advanced by certain pundits who we can't help but notice are either liberals or moderates, not conservatives—that Republicans need to be able to point to major legislative wins and policy accomplishments by 2012.

Not only is this false, it's a trap. Republicans control only the House. Democrats occupy the White House and still control the Senate. This gives Republicans partial negative control to block some things, but not the power to advance anything. The GOP has partial negative control because regulatory matters are done administratively, without Congress. Also, confirmation of federal judges and Supreme Court justices is a Senate matter, so Republicans can have a significant impact on confirmations, but there are limits to what you can do with even a large minority.

Therein lies the trap. President Obama remains a committed liberal. Although Republicans have a House majority, dozens of congressmen are moderates, not conservatives. Republicans have a large Senate minority, but that includes more than a half-dozen moderates. So the only way that congressional Republicans can get legislation passed will be if they sign on to *moderate* legislation. This talk about needing to pass legislation translates into saying that the only way the GOP can succeed is to act like moderates, not conservatives.

This would destroy the Republican Party. We were driven from power in 2006 and 2008 because the Republican congressional majority and Bush administration pushed moderate, go-along-to-get-along policies that didn't fix America's problems, instead making them worse. This was exactly what happened under moderate Herbert Hoover in the years 1929 through 1932. Republicans made historic gains in 2010 because candidates promised repeatedly that they would finally, at long last, push a conservative agenda. If they now act like moderates, many millions of voters will rightfully feel betrayed, and their vengeance will be swift and final.

As we explain in this chapter, a correct understanding of the American body politic leads to one conclusion, which goes to the heart of the current change happening in America: the Tea Party needs the Christian Right, the Christian Right needs the Tea Party, and the Republican Party desperately needs both. Without both Tea Party voters and Christian Right voters (and there is far more overlap between those two camps than many would lead you to believe—more on that later), the Republican Party cannot succeed.

How Barack Obama Could Win Reelection in 2012

There are three ways that Barack Obama could win a second term as president of the United States. Although it seems unlikely, presidents sometimes have a reversal of fortunes from apparently impossible situations. Republicans would be shortsighted fools—with equally short memories—to lose sight of this possibility.

(There's also a possibility that Hillary Clinton could be the Democratic nominee in 2012, which would be every bit as bad as Barack Obama, for different reasons. While we don't discuss Hillary in detail, the following discussion of how President Obama could win a second term would also be the way Hillary could beat the Republican nominee in 2012, so the following material is still relevant.)

One unlikely way that President Obama could be reelected is if he fundamentally changes course. Barack Obama could bring on a strategist who designs a two-year campaign of "triangulation," where Obama gives the Far Left half as much grief as he does conservatives, and in doing so persuades ten million voters that he's learned the error of his ways and wants to bring the country together. This is what Bill Clinton did by bringing on Dick Morris after suffering a wipeout in 1994, with Republicans gaining fifty-two House seats and eight Senate seats.

This, however, is extremely improbable.

First, we don't believe that President Obama is capable of fundamentally changing course. For one thing, Obama's DNA doesn't include the same pragmatic gene that Bill Clinton possesses. Clinton governed Arkansas—a moderate state with a conservative cultural streak—for more than a decade before becoming president. While Hillary Clinton is a militant ideologue, Bill Clinton wanted to be popular and was happy to drop liberal priorities whenever they became inconvenient. As such, Clinton had a lot of experience and skill at political compromise. Regardless of how liberal Clinton was personally, he had to do business with conservatives in Arkansas, and he had a pragmatic sense of wanting to get something done with a "half a loaf is better than no loaf" approach.

Second, Barack Obama is far more liberal than Bill Clinton (although Clinton has drifted left since leaving office). Clinton was an ordinary center-left liberal in the 1980s who gained national attention by being one of the original leaders of the Democratic Leadership Council (DLC), which advocated Democrats adopting some moderate positions to increase their mainstream appeal. When Clinton took two steps to the right in 1995, he became a moderate liberal for the final two years of his first term. Obama, by contrast, represented a far-left city in a liberal state, and then served only part of one term as a U.S.

senator. That was the sum total of his public experience before becoming president of a nation that's far more conservative than he will ever be. Even if he were to move two steps to the center, he'd still be liberal, not moderate. He'd have to move much further to the right to win back disaffected moderate voters, and we don't think he's got it in him.

A third reason we don't think a move to the center would help reelect President Obama is that our economic situation is the opposite of what it was in the 1990s. As we'll see more in the following chapters, when Ronald Reagan cut the top marginal tax rates and taxes on capital gains in the 1980s, this laid the long-term foundation for tremendous economic growth in the 1990s, as seen for example in Silicon Valley. When combined with Republicans moving toward a balanced budget after taking Congress in 1994, this made the remainder of the 1990s a period of robust economic growth. By contrast, with Obama we have record deficits and tax hikes to add to what was already a very troubled economy. So the odds of the vibrant economic growth that buoyed Clinton in his 1996 reelection campaign are slim. All things being equal, voters are happy with incumbents when the economy is good, and they blame incumbents when the economy is bad. The former helped Clinton in 1996; the latter will hang like a millstone around Obama's neck in 2012.

Setting aside the unlikely idea that he'll move to the center, a second, much more plausible possibility for Barack Obama to be reelected is Republicans nominating the wrong person. This is unfortunately a very real possibility. Since 1960, the GOP has tended to nominate whoever earns the backing of the party establishment from the previous election cycle or two. That won't be a problem if the establishment rallies behind a true conservative. But these days it's often the grassroots conservatives—found both in the Tea Party and in people of faith—who are at odds with establishment GOP players.

If the party leadership rallies to one of the more moderate Republicans positioning for a presidential run, then more than ten million energized conservative voters might not vote for the nominee in the general election. While it seems counterintuitive that any conservative would stay home when the chance comes to vote against Barack Obama, those grassroots voters are as fed up with Republicans as they are with Democrats. They have (correctly) come to the firm conviction that the Republican establishment is not solving the serious problems confronting America, problems that will bankrupt and ruin this nation if not aggressively and immediately tackled.

These grass roots see it as their mission to fundamentally refocus the electorate by supporting a candidate who will defiantly reject business as usual and face head-on the titanic issues facing us, issues that previously people would mention in campaign speeches but never actually do anything about because there was insufficient political will for major change. The 2012 election will be completely different in that regard. Any candidate who doesn't seriously address these issues will not get the support of these energized voters. Several candidates will compete to carry the banner of millions of freedom lovers in the Republican primary. If an establishment moderate beats those principled conservatives to win the nomination, then that moderate will likely lose millions of voters who would in other cycles be reliable Republican votes.

But there's a third possibility. It's usually not a serious risk in a presidential election cycle, but we're living in historic times, and so we could be facing a risk we've not confronted for a hundred years:

The Republican Party could split.

Three Fault Lines Where the Republican Party Could Split

Rush Limbaugh said shortly before the 2010 election that if the Republican Party doesn't fully embrace what people are crying out for in Tea Party rallies and among the grass roots, then the GOP could fall apart, never again having sufficient numbers to retake power.[1] That same week Sarah Palin said the GOP was finished if it couldn't keep Tea Party voters in the GOP fold. They're right.

The current situation for the Republican Party is more dangerous than losing the Tea Party, in that there are three different fault lines upon which a party split could happen. Any of these would give us eight years of Barack Obama in the White House, and possibly allow Democrats to retake the House in 2012 or 2014, as well as keep the Senate.

TEA PARTY COULD BOLT

The first split is the one many talk about: Tea Party people bolting the Republican Party. It's not hard to find someone at a Tea Party rally who says they're as fed up with Republicans as they are with Democrats, and swears they won't vote for anyone who isn't uncompromisingly committed to balancing the federal budget and reversing the socialist and statist policies of the past two years.

This possibility is fueled by the success of Tea Party–backed candidates in 2010. This goes beyond Marco Rubio's amazing come-from-behind bid for the U.S. Senate. Many pundits didn't think Rand Paul in Kentucky could possibly beat the handpicked candidate of Senator Mitch McConnell in the GOP primary, Trey Grayson, yet Paul did exactly that. Nor did anyone think Sharron Angle could grab the Senate nomination in Nevada. These were examples where establishment-backed candidates, with more money and party machine support, were swamped by energized voters.

But perhaps the biggest surprises came from Tea Party candidates unseating incumbents. Early on, Senator Arlen Specter switched parties to run as a Democrat. (It's a sign of providential justice that Specter then lost the Democratic nomination to Congressman Joe Sestak. So much for electability.) Then once the campaigns began, first came Utah, where incumbent moderate-right senator Bob Bennett was denied renomination. That nomination was instead won by Mike Lee, a spectacular conservative constitutional lawyer who's a member of the Federalist Society and a former law clerk to Justice Samuel Alito. Then came the most direct confrontation, with Alaska's Joe Miller opposing moderate senator Lisa Murkowski. Miller won the primary in an amazing upset, heralding what a profound change election 2010 would turn out to be.

The prospect that Tea Party voters could leave the GOP is buttressed by the reaction after 2010. Aside from being jubilant about the races they won, these grassroots activists are unapologetic about the races they lost. Sharron Angle, Ken Buck, Joe Miller, and Christine O'Donnell were all unsuccessful. But talk to Tea Party activists and they'll tell you that they'd rather lose a race on principle than win with a moderate who won't make the hard choices needed right now. These people will not back a moderate Republican for president, even if it means that Democrats could hold on to the White House as a result.

Every couple of cycles there's a senator defeated in his or her own primary. That's not surprising. But those defeats come when an incumbent is caught in some scandal, or has publicly turned against the party in some major way that becomes a national media focus.

What happened in 2010 is different. Neither Specter nor Bennett nor Murkowski was caught up in any scandal. And someone like Charlie Crist had such support behind him (including having been endorsed by the National Republican Senatorial Committee, which is not supposed to be done in a contested primary unless there is an incumbent GOP senator seeking reelection; your author Blackwell is pleased to say that he endorsed Rubio over Crist at the outset of the race) that Crist could almost have been regarded as an incumbent.

By the previous rules of the game, they all should have been shoo-ins. Normal political discussions would have focused on "electability": that we need to nominate candidates who can win the general election. The biggest factor in electability is incumbency. Another factor is being a moderate enough candidate to win over swing voters. And a third factor is having a major network of support, such as a sitting governor has.

These incumbents lost because many Republicans are hungry for a return to constitutional government, hungry enough to overcome all the typical factors. Republicans want to be the party of constitutional conservatism. They sense the profound danger America is in, and they're chomping at the bit to elect people who will save America. Alaska was a perfect example, where Murkowski ran bragging about how much money she brings to Alaska, and Miller fought by running on the idea that he would bring *less* money to Alaska.

The fact that Miller could win not only the primary with that message—but almost the *general* election—on the argument that all this "free" federal money was bankrupting the nation and harming our children, shows that the American people may finally be realizing that we must undergo a profound change in this country if we want to survive. Murkowski won denouncing constitutional conservatism as extreme, and promising to continue the policies that have buried our children with a horrific debt.

The Tea Party is not the only possible party split, however, and Republican leaders will make a fatal error if they assume there's only one way they can lose their own party.

SOCIAL VALUES VOTERS COULD BOLT

Remember the enormous success of Glenn Beck's "Restoring Honor" rally at the Lincoln Memorial on August 28, 2010? The entire event was about America returning to its moral principles through an acknowledgment that rights are not grants of government, they are gifts from God. It was a call to prayer, to faith, and to fidelity. Many of our friends were onstage with Glenn, such as Bishop Harry Jackson and Dr. Richard Land.

This rally was the largest of its kind in American history. When Martin Luther King, Jr., gave his "I Have a Dream" speech exactly forty-seven years before, on August 28, 1963, there were 200,000 people present. At the 2010 rally, there were at least 300,000. It was an enormous national event.

Restoring Honor was a *social* conservative event. It was not about taxes, or the size of government, or reforming entitlements. It was about prayer, about America's Judeo-Christian moral philosophy, and for most attendees and speakers it was about the Christian faith and the blessings that America enjoys with its rich biblical heritage.

When former Republican National Committee chairman and 2004 Bush campaign manager Ken Mehlman announced that he was homosexual (which both of your authors and many other political insiders had heard for years, so all the hype about his "revelation" was disingenuous), your authors wrote a column (which was published by the *Huffington Post*, of all places) about how the GOP would fall apart if it gave up on its commitment to traditional marriage.[2]

Tens of millions of Americans possess a devout religious faith that forms the basis of their conservative views. These millions are largely either born-again Evangelical Christians, committed Catholics, or dedicated Mormons. As a result of their faith, they are fiercely pro-life, hold marriage to be a sacred institution ordained by God as the union of one man and one woman, and believe in fully and freely living out their faith, raising their children in their faith, and sharing their faith with others.

As we discuss in Chapter 3, many Republican leaders regard social conservatives as "useful idiots" who are taken as much for granted as the black community is taken for granted by the Democrats. Many show contempt for social conservatives behind closed doors, calling us by such names as "fetus huggers" or "Jesus freaks." They assume that with certain catchphrases and code words, they can keep socially conservative Americans in line, without ever really pushing social conservative issues.

If GOP leaders are not careful, they will see millions of social conservatives bolt the party, with an end result every bit as disastrous as if Tea Party economic conservatives bolted. The success of Beck's rally shows there are millions of these voters, and their outrage is every bit as intense as what you find at any Tea Party rally.

MODERATES COULD BOLT

The third possible split could come in the middle. One perfect example of this is Charlie Crist, who despite swearing that he would run only as a Republican, showed his deceitfulness and lack of character when he broke his promise, ditching the GOP to run as an independent.

Congressman Mike Castle of Delaware considered a third-party candidacy when beaten by Christine O'Donnell in the Senate primary. Castle was not a moderate Republican; he was a *liberal* Republican. He was anti-gun and pro-abortion, supported tax hikes and cap-and-trade, and so on. He was a throwback to the pre-Reagan GOP, when he was first elected governor. Thankfully, he showed himself enough of a statesman in the end not to run as an independent.

Senator Lisa Murkowski ran as a third-party independent candidate for the U.S. Senate, and unlike Crist she won. This is the clearest proof that the threat of moderates leaving the party to run against the GOP is real. Had the Democrats fielded a strong candidate, that Senate seat might have become the only Democratic pickup in 2010. Senator Murkowski has rejoined the Republican Party in the Senate, but has since become a stridently moderate senator who regularly bucks the party. It's unclear if she will join GOP moves to uphold the Constitution. Murkowski's victory will encourage more third-party bids.

These instances show what the Republican Party could face from the "militant middle" if it's not careful. Crist harbored presidential ambitions. New York City mayor Michael Bloomberg—who was a Democrat, then liberal Republican—bolted the party to become an independent, and he too has contemplated a White House bid. Such a splinter party could never gain power. But it could siphon off 10% of the vote, guaranteeing consistent wins by liberal Democrats.

A FAILURE OF LEADERSHIP

It's possible to prevent this sort of a split. You manage the public discourse to be welcoming and inclusive. Allow everyone a seat at the table for a full and honest discussion. Make the debate civil and respectful, with genuine goodwill. Conservative principles don't need to drown out other voices; our policies are superior, so we'll win in an open debate. Politicians are people and respond according to ordinary human interaction principles: If someone can tell that you respect and appreciate them, that you're willing to hear them out even when you disagree, that you express disagreements pleasantly and diplomatically, and that you genuinely look for common purpose and common ground, they'll often stay on board with you.

Some things cannot be compromised. Taxes are too high, so you cannot agree to moderately raise taxes. Our out-of-control spending will cause an economic collapse if not reversed, so you cannot moderately reduce spending, stopping short of balancing the budget. The Constitution nowhere creates rights to abortion or same-sex marriage, so you cannot halfway support either and still support constitutional fidelity. America doesn't need moderate policies; they're bankrupting us fiscally and morally. We need conservative policies, but we also need to make the case as to why moderate Americans will benefit from them, and we need to welcome their political support.

This situation is the result of failed Republican Party leadership. The purpose of party leadership is to advance the party platform. You achieve what the party stands for by keeping it together, expanding its numbers, fund-raising, and rallying officeholders to enact policies embodying the party platform. The most basic formula for winning an election is to mobilize your base while persuading swing voters.

Some Republican leaders have completely failed at this basic task.

(Granted, it's easier said than done.) When the party chairman openly disagrees with major planks in the party platform; when the chairman of the National Republican Senatorial Committee picks favorites in a contested primary for an open Senate seat, selecting the "electable" candidate who openly disses the party base, then bolts the party; and when candidates decide to run third-party candidacies against the Republican Party, then the party is failing to do its job. And if a senator loses the primary and runs as an independent, that senator must be immediately stripped of all committee positions.

Party leaders must ensure that party positions faithfully represent the vast majority of party members. Candidate recruitment should focus on people who agree with enough of the platform, without any deal breakers, that the party faithful can enthusiastically rally around those candidacies. Primaries need to unfold in such a way that the conversation is constructive and productive in the face of what inevitably becomes a very emotional business. The party must build strong coalitions with public interest groups that support different planks of the platform, supplementing the organization and resources of various constituencies within the party. And the party must be organized at the grassroots level—precincts and counties—to ensure that statewide and national party leaders represent the party membership and platform.

Unfortunately, that's not what we've seen in the GOP. There have been deep and bitter divisions within the Republican National Committee and in many state parties. These unfortunate events have seen other groups sweep in to peel off donors and supporters, setting up competing organizations that can only complicate things. Some are trying to reinvent the Republican Party in terms of what we stand for, and in doing so they have exacerbated internal tensions.

Make no mistake: The extraordinary success of the 2010 elections did not come about through Republican leadership, but instead occurred despite a *lack* of leadership. Other Republicans stepped to the fore to fill the void, working with the American people to support the right candidates in a display of true political leadership. Republican leaders must step up and be worthy of the title.

The Last Time Republicans Split, the Democrat Won

If there is a third-party movement, it would almost certainly lead to a repeat of the last election in which the Republican Party split. In short, Barack Obama would be reelected, or another Democrat (Hillary Clinton?) would win the presidency. (It's also possible that Obama would recruit Hillary as vice president, since putting her on the ticket would be the best way to keep her from challenging him in the 2012 primaries.)

In 1900, William McKinley was reelected to a second term in the White House. He chose as his running mate New York's young governor, Theodore Roosevelt. (New York was the largest and most powerful state in America at the time, a distinction it continued to hold for another half century.) President McKinley was assassinated in 1901, marking only the third time such a tragedy occurred (the first was of course Lincoln).

Ascending to the highest office in the land at age forty-two, President Roosevelt became the youngest president in history. Roosevelt was energetic even beyond what his youth would suggest, emphasizing the merits of rigorous physical exercise and reveling in outdoor expeditions.

Everyone wondered what the future would hold for Roosevelt. Roosevelt ran for president in his own right in 1904, and won handily. There were no term limits written into the Constitution back then, but there was a consensus that no president should serve more than two terms. Our first president (Washington) retired after two terms. Our second president (Adams) was defeated after one. And the next three presidents (Jefferson, Madison, and Monroe) all left office after their second term. This established a pattern considered the ideal; if you serve well for one term and the people choose to elect you a second time, so be it. But after that, you go home. The American president is not a king.

But what about Roosevelt? He had been elected president only once, and before that had served out the last three years of McKinley's term. Did those three years count as one term? Could he run again without attempting to hold on to power longer than he should?

Finally Teddy Roosevelt said that he considered the partial term to count as a full term, and thus 1904 was his second term, so he would not run again in 1908. Instead Roosevelt supported the nomination of Republican William Howard Taft, who then went on to win the presidency. This era, 1896 to 1932, was dominated by Republicans—except for the brief period we're about to discuss.

President Taft was in many ways conservative. For example, he was solidly conservative as a constitutional lawyer. In other ways he fell into traps of the Left, such as supporting a graduated income tax.

But the still-young Teddy Roosevelt was restless in retirement, and so in 1912 he ran again for the Republican nomination. When the party convention instead renominated Taft, Roosevelt left the party. He ran in the general election as the Progressive Party candidate.

The result was a disaster. America had been solidly Republican during the thirty-six-year period from 1896 through 1932, but now the GOP split—conservatives voted for Taft and moderates voted for Roosevelt. In the end, the incumbent president received 23% of the vote, and the former president got 27%. As a result, Democrat Woodrow Wilson won the presidency with less than 42% of the vote.

Will 2012 Be a Repeat of 1912?

The consequences of the 1912 election are still with us today, nearly one hundred years later. President Wilson created the Department of Labor and made it a Cabinet-level agency. He also elevated the Department of Agriculture (USDA) to Cabinet status, making farming and food production and regulation a federal issue on an entirely new level. In 1913, he signed the Federal Reserve Act, creating a central bank with pivotal control over the U.S. economy. (The Supreme Court had upheld in 1819 the constitutionality of Congress chartering a central bank in *McCulloch v. Maryland*.[3]) In 1913, the Sixteenth Amendment to the U.S. Constitution was passed, empowering Congress to create a tax on income, which was then used to create a graduated income tax that has been with us ever since.

In addition to giving the federal government a massive role in regulating workers and businesses across the country, the Labor Department became a bastion of union power during Democratic presidencies, increasing burdens and mandates on hundreds of thousands of employers. The USDA's budget would become one of the largest in the federal government, with billions of dollars in subsidies. Taking advantage of the fact that moderate Teddy Roosevelt had increased severalfold the size of the White House staff,[4] Wilson began looking to see where a president could act unilaterally, without having to go through Senate-confirmed officials or congressional action.

Nor were these expanded presidential activities limited to domestic policy. Wilsonian foreign policy looked at America as having an unprecedented role in affecting the decisions of other sovereign nations across the globe. It was the beginning of interventionist foreign policy in this country. Wilson ran for reelection in 1916 promising to keep America out of the massive war in Europe, but once reelection was secure he took us into that conflict, which we now know as World War I. It was the beginning of America as the world policeman, projecting our power all over the planet with the idea that it is America's role to spread freedom by righting the world's wrongs.

Another aspect of Wilsonian foreign policy spawned the school of thought that America should sacrifice its sovereignty and submit to a world government. After World War I, Wilson campaigned to the point of exhaustion for the League of Nations. This was to be a world body—the precursor to the United Nations—where the world's nations would sit in council and act as one. But the American people understood the League of Nations as a permanent surrender of part of our sovereignty to nations that rejected our values and freedoms, and so the U.S. Senate refused to ratify the treaty.

Let's list the legacy of Woodrow Wilson: Centralized economic control through the Federal Reserve. Cabinet agencies governing two major areas of domestic policy considered local and state matters (labor and agriculture). America with a broad role regulating the world through military intervention and world government. And to feed this national machine, a massive new taxation system to extract whatever money the federal government needs from the American people. Although, to be fair, there are good things that can be said about the Wilson presidency—most administrations have accomplishments of which to boast—the aforementioned items were not in keeping with the Republican era of the time, nor the wishes of the American people for a limited government.

The period of Democratic governance was over. America had been governed by Republicans for sixteen years before Wilson was elected due to the Republican split, and it would resume Republican government for the following twelve years. In 1920, Republican Warren Harding won the presidency. Upon his death, conservative Republican Calvin Coolidge took the helm. Then, in 1928, moderate Herbert Hoover took office and set the stage for Democratic domination, beginning in 1932.

During this era, it should have been impossible for Wilson to win the presidency. America would have been a much different country otherwise, since Wilson—like Obama—was certainly a very consequential president. This is what happens when the Republican Party splits.

Will it happen again?

Realignments

While some issues facing every nation are ongoing—usually those rooted in human nature, human necessities, or features unique to a country's geography, climate, and natural resources—most issues change over time. When the major issues change, political parties either adapt to confront them or they do not. When one or both parties don't adapt, popular discontent grows until a political realignment occurs.

A political realignment happens when an electoral shift permanently changes a country's political equation. In a realignment, the organizing principles and issues of one party fall clearly and permanently out of favor (such as the Democratic Party being pro-slavery after the Civil War), such that the out-of-power party abandons its platform in favor of new issues or else fades into extinction. In a realignment the American people decide that there are certain issues with two sides, each with a broad following, and reach almost unanimous consensus on other issues that were previously contested, rendering this second category of issues nondebatable going forward. In short, it means that some major points of division have been closed, so rather than harp on those issues, both parties find common ground on them and fight over new issues.

In the very beginning, there were no parties in America. George Washington was unanimously elected president by the Electoral College, and took the oath of office on April 30, 1789. Washington was a towering figure, revered by Americans of every persuasion. He had unmatched fame from his success as the commanding general of the Continental Army, winning America's independence. Before that, he was also one of the delegates from Virginia supporting independence, which is why he had been commissioned as the commander in chief of America's army to fight for that independence. His stature was such that when delegates again gathered to replace the Articles of Confederation with a new Constitution, Washington was chosen as the president of the Constitutional Convention. Washington was perhaps the only major figure on the political stage whom all Americans embraced, the only person who could unite the people of the new nation, thereby claiming the mantle of Father of His Country.

But during Washington's presidency, two distinct camps emerged. One sought to develop a robust central government (especially on fiscal policy, such as establishing a national bank and assuming the debts incurred by the states during the Revolutionary War) and focused on developing commerce and merchant trade, establishing good relations with our erstwhile enemies the British, and building America's industrial base. They were the Federalists, and its emerging leaders included Vice President John Adams and Secretary of the Treasury Alexander Hamilton. The other camp sought to develop America as a local-economy country with a strong agricultural base and a small central government strictly constrained by the Constitution's text, and favored diplomatic relations with France instead of Britain. (France had allied with us in the War for Independence.) They were the Democratic-Republicans, whose most prominent leaders were Secretary of State Thomas Jefferson and Congressman James Madison.

This was the beginning of the party system. With few exceptions, from that time until now, and although some parties have declined and perished and others have arisen, there have been exactly two major parties in this country—no more, no less.

Realignment occurs when the two-party system breaks down. It's happened only five times in America's history. The first was in 1800, when President John Adams and his Federalist government were swept from power by the Democratic-Republicans, led by Thomas Jefferson.[5] The second was in 1828, when the one-party rule of the Democratic-Republicans split, Andrew Jackson's new Democratic Party took power,[6] and America transitioned from a country in which each of the two parties dominated different parts of the country, to one with two nationwide parties.[7] The third (and most violent) realignment was in 1860, when the new Republican Party, led by Abraham Lincoln, came to power in both Congress and the White House—followed by the Civil War.[8] The fourth was in 1896, when the Republicans became the party of economic growth and business, and, led by William McKinley, delivered Democrats their worst defeat in history.[9] The fifth was in 1932, when the Democrats, led by Franklin Delano Roosevelt, surged to take control of Congress and the White House.

LESSONS FROM REALIGNMENT

There are three lessons to take from the various realignments that America has experienced.

The first is why we've not had a realignment since 1932. A pattern emerged in which realignments occurred every twenty-eight to thirty-six years, with an average interval of thirty-three years.[10] Under that formula, a realignment could have been expected around the 1968 presidential election. It didn't happen.

Instead we saw what some call a "rolling realignment." In 1968, Republicans elected their only presidential candidate to run successfully on a right-leaning platform since 1924.[11] The American people chose a Republican president (Richard Nixon—who ran for reelection as a moderate in 1972) but Democrats retained control of the House and Senate. We then had unified Democratic government after Jimmy Carter's 1976 election. The political balance shifted again in 1980, when the American people elected the only truly conservative president since 1924—Republican Ronald Reagan—by a solid margin, and gave him a Republican Senate, but allowed Democrats to keep the House. In 1986 Democrats retook the Senate, but Republicans kept the White House in 1988 with George H. W. Bush. In 1992 the voters gave Democrats unified government when Bill Clinton became president, but they quickly reversed course in 1994 to give Republicans control of Congress—both the House and Senate—in a landslide. Then in 2000 Republicans gained the White House with George W. Bush but lost the Senate months later. Following this, Americans gave Republicans a unified government in 2002 with control of both the House and Senate, and built on those majorities in 2004. But serious GOP failures facilitated a Democratic takeover of Congress in 2006, which Democrats built on in 2008 when Barack Obama's election gave Democrats unified government once again. Then in 2010 voters again reversed course, giving Republicans their greatest House victory in more than a half century, and major gains in the Senate. These results conjure the image of water at a rolling boil in a pot on the stove, with different parties taking different power centers in each election only to lose others, without a durable majority holding all the elected bodies of government.

The first lesson this rolling realignment teaches us is the value of durable coalitions. FDR created the New Deal Coalition—millions of Americans who came to depend upon the federal government to provide a standard of living. Its cornerstone was Social Security. Americans consumed more and saved less for retirement. Instead of looking to retirement investments or a pension, Americans increasingly looked to government. (This shows the addictive power of entitlements, discussed in Chapter 13.)

Millions of Americans think they need government to give them food, shelter, and other necessities, and so they vote for whichever party promises these. President Lyndon Johnson built upon that addiction by creating Medicare and Medicaid in 1965, since healthcare is a necessity when illness occurs. The Democrats created these entitlements. And since these entitlements were never sustainable—always unaffordable and insolvent—Democrats always promised to increase them. When faced with the question of how to pay for them, they always said "the rich" would pay, through higher taxes. Enough Americans believed these empty promises that they kept voting for congressional Democrats, enabling them to control the House for forty years from 1954 to 1994. And even when Democrats were not in power, this big-government-entitlement rallying cry always gave them a large base of support, which they built upon to regain majority status in 2006 and 2008.

But the New Deal Coalition didn't endure just because entitlements are addictive. There's a second factor: True coalitions have staying power. Once groups develop relationships and build organizations that advance compatible policy goals, the key actors intertwine and cross-pollinate. (For example, you get the president of one organization serving on the boards of two other organizations in the coalition.) The coalition takes on a life all its own, where minor differences are overlooked and key leaders step forward when major differences occur to make the peace and keep the family together. (Picture the scene in *The Godfather* after Sonny Corleone is killed at the tollbooth, in which the heads of the Five Families gather for a meeting to make a truce.) Such coalitions can last for decades.

The third lesson here is the value of rewriting history. Sir Winston Churchill once said, "History is written by the victors." There's no better example of that than the enduring myth that Franklin Roosevelt got us out of the Great Depression. After Herbert Hoover created the Great Recession by abandoning conservatism in 1929, FDR's big-government policies transformed the Great Recession into the Great Depression and kept millions of Americans in need until we started mobilizing for World War II in 1939. Recent scholarship makes a convincing case that big government is what kept the economy from recovering,[12] but liberals contained enough channels of communication—in media and in academia—that most voters never heard the truth about the Great Depression for more than fifty years.

The fourth lesson is that although Americans rightly fear too much government control and a naïve foreign policy, realignments arise on changing paradigms of the ideal role of government in society. So Republicans cannot build a durable majority without becoming a truly conservative party, exemplifying government's proper role.

We see this in foreign policy. Americans wanted a Republican in the White House in 1968 because the Vietnam War–era Democrats had been taken over by the Far Left, with their unrealistic view of the world. The leftists' rejection of American exceptionalism (discussed in Chapter 11) and of a classical, biblical view of human nature led to the absurd idea that somehow America was to blame, and our opponents— whether atheistic totalitarians, communist dictators, or fanatical jihadists—were somehow misunderstood victims of oppression, instead of depraved enemies who must be defeated. The Far Left's romantic vision of humanity is a fairy tale, one that those of us who live in the real world understand cannot protect our children. The rejection of this leftist delusion by a majority of Americans is a big part of how we got Richard Nixon, Ronald Reagan, George H. W. Bush, and George W. Bush.

Likewise with domestic policy, Americans saw too much evidence to accept the laughable notion that government can solve problems better than the private sector can. Whether it's the daily frustrations with the department of motor vehicles or airport security, or occasional disasters like Hurricane Katrina or the BP oil spill in the Gulf of Mexico, Americans can't turn on their TVs without getting a fresh reminder that government is generally ineffective. While the private sector is greedy, wasteful, and filled with falsehoods, fraud, and self-promoters, it is vastly more efficient, effective, and ethical than government. Most people are too smart and too experienced to fall for the myth that government can provide what we need to live our lives, or that it can afford everything it promises.

That's why after LBJ's 1964 election, until 2008, the only Democrats to win the White House did so by claiming to be moderates. In 1976, Jimmy Carter was the governor of Georgia, a conservative state. He emphasized his conservative social values stemming from his Baptist religious beliefs (which he has long since repudiated). Then in 1992, the governor of another Southern state, Bill Clinton, ran while talking about how Democrats needed to pursue a "third way" of moderate policies both socially and economically.

That exposes the fallacy of the Bush years—that Republicans could out-Democrat the Democrats. The Medicare prescription drug plan has come in under budget thus far but is a potentially disastrous expansion of an entitlement program that has trillions of dollars in unfunded liabilities, and that unless overhauled will bring down a program upon which millions of senior citizens rely. The No Child Left Behind Act did several things to address serious problems in primary and secondary education, but at the cost of vastly expanding federal control in an area of government that the Constitution leaves to state and local governments. And President Bush's proposal for overhauling immigration was an amnesty plan for illegal aliens (discussed in Chapter 12). What do all of these moves have in common? Many political strategists calculated they would result in lasting political gains for the Republican Party.

But the problem with this approach is that these policies are bad for America. Some strategists are so focused on making sure Republicans win that they lose sight of the fact that we exist to serve and improve the nation, not just to be in charge. They understand how to win elections but not how to shape the destiny of a nation. We're not a conservative party when we pursue such policies. They may keep us in power, but they also keep us governing in a way that decimates our economy and shoulders our children with a crushing debt burden.

Republicans don't need moderate policies that poorly serve the voters in order to win elections. America is a center-right country. As such, we can build a governing majority by effectively addressing the needs of a majority of Americans, and making the case as to why those policies meet their needs. Conservative principles are winning principles when you explain how they make the lives of ordinary people better over the long haul, and how they deliver even greater dividends for your children.

The Republican Party, Tea Party, and Christian Right All Need Each Other

Conservative success comes from building (or rebuilding) a political party around constitutional principles. We'll explain in the next chapter how all three parts of America's modern conservative coalition need each other.

But one point should be made here. The vast majority of Tea Party members are also committed social conservatives, as are most elected officials who headline Tea Party rallies, such as Mike Pence and Michele Bachmann. Conversely, many social conservatives advocate low taxes, economic opportunities free from government control, and requiring people to accept responsibility for their own actions. We show in Chapter 3 how both of these philosophies can do more than peacefully coexist; properly understood, they naturally reinforce and enhance each other.

Both the Tea Party and the Christian Right are movements, not organizations. There is no recognized overarching authority structure. Both have local leaders and national figures to whom the rank and file look for inspiration and guidance, but members do not answer to them as binding authorities. Because so many Tea Party attendees are committed people of faith—and some Tea Party leaders seem oblivious to this fact and need to take this to heart—there are literally millions of Americans currently supporting the Tea Party movement who will denounce and leave that movement if Tea Party leaders ever say anything to support abortion, same-sex marriage, silencing religion, or gun control.

Conversely—and many Christian Right leaders need to lay hold of this—millions of Evangelical Christians, devout Catholics, Mormons, and Orthodox Jews are gravely concerned about how big-government policies are crushing our children and grandchildren under a mountain of debt, destroying jobs (or preventing job creation), and endangering the ability of families to stay together and take care of each other. Consequently, Christian Right leaders who express a lack of concern for these economic issues would see large parts of their organizations forsake them. There is so much overlap between these two movements that either would fall apart by alienating the other.

And the Republican Party is on the outs with both of these movements. If the GOP does not fully embrace an economic conservative agenda—which will involve bucking well-established interests and long-standing habits such as special tax provisions, earmarks, and "moderate" deficits—millions of enraged Tea Party voters will forever forsake the Republican label. Equally enraged by some Republican leaders expressing support for same-sex marriage, expanding the Education Department, and refusing to make judges a front-burner issue, millions of social conservatives—especially within the Christian Right—will leave the Republican Party. (This is all the more possible because while many Republican leaders are bending over backward to reach out to Tea Party groups, they are actively ignoring people of faith.)

The Republican Party needs both of these constituencies. Alienating either will cause a party split.

But it's not just that Republicans need to make sure they don't alienate either of these groups. Republicans should *embrace* them, and they should embrace each other. Not only is it true that their agendas do not conflict, they actually reinforce and enhance each other. So Republicans should do more than avoid a party split; they should encourage and welcome every part of the conservative movement.

As the next chapter explains, a revitalized conservative movement embracing every aspect of constitutional conservatism is the key for resurgence and renewal in America.

3

WE'LL HANG TOGETHER, OR
WE'LL SURELY HANG SEPARATELY

"We must, indeed, all hang together or, most assuredly, we shall
all hang separately."

—Benjamin Franklin,
on the need to work together to win the Revolutionary War

The American body politic is in a state of crisis and flux we
have not seen for decades, and have experienced only five or so
times in our nation's history. (These were largely the realignments we studied in the previous chapter.) The extraordinary strains on
our economy and culture generate profound levels of political unrest
and discontent, and with those come division. These in turn translate
into both extreme partisanship and to the rare phenomenon of millions
of Americans willing to renounce *both* major political parties if neither
of the parties adequately addresses their values and concerns.

For most of America's history, our political system has had two parties. Those parties are a result of tens of millions of citizens making a
choice as to which principles they are willing to fight over, versus those
they can tolerate disagreement on while still remaining allies.

It's essential to our democratic process that we maintain two vibrant
and healthy parties. We need more than one because it gives people a
choice, preventing a monolithic, unchallenged party from becoming
self-serving and apathetic. Such a political monopoly could even turn
into an autocratic government. With a two-party system, when one

party fails to deliver results that the voters consider acceptable, voters have the power to remove that party from power, giving majority control to a different governing philosophy.

But we must keep the number of major parties at two to allow one governing philosophy to attain majority status, making coherent and reliable policy for the nation. As explained below, violent changes to the political order in this country usually force political realignments. For perhaps only the fourth time in our history, the United States faces the realistic possibility of our two-party system fracturing. Should that happen, the major parties would split, leaving America with three parties and possibly more.

The end result of such fracturing is that no one governing philosophy can ever attain majority status. Thus a congressional majority could be achieved only by forming coalitions with two or more parties, and the possibility that U.S. presidents would often be chosen by the U.S. House, rather than by the voters through the Electoral College.[1]

Because no party has a majority, whoever comes closest to gaining a plurality has to form coalition governments with at least one other party, appointing Cabinet officials from the allied party and frequently offering the presidential candidate of that party a key position of power, such as secretary of state or defense. Consequently, a break with that allied party can cause the executive branch to fall apart. Such multiparty forms of government are inherently less stable than the form of government that the United States has known since 1789.

Coalition governments are also less able to respond to crisis. Because different parties have different philosophies about the role, purpose, and priorities of government, in times of crisis they may want to move in very different directions. If the controlling party doesn't have majority support, it can lead to disastrous delays or even gridlock at a crucial moment.

Danger of the Current System Breaking— Reflections of Attorney General Ed Meese

This isn't just our perspective. In March 2010, one of your authors (Blackwell) had coffee with Edwin Meese III, who was Ronald Reagan's principal advisor throughout his presidency: as counselor to the president in the White House during Reagan's first term, and as U.S. attorney general during Reagan's second term.

Attorney General Meese has a long-term perspective that few Americans can fully grasp. After graduating from two of America's finest schools—Yale, and the University of California at Berkeley for law school—Meese served his country as an air force officer, retiring at the rank of colonel. He taught at law school and served as an advisor to the chief executive of our largest state, Governor Ronald Reagan of California. Meese was a top leader in Reagan's presidential bid, and as just noted, served eight years under him. In the twenty-two years since Reagan's presidency, Meese has been involved in the leadership ranks of many of America's most prestigious conservative organizations.

General Meese's perspective is that of a true senior statesman, one who has for decades seen and worked from the vantage point of the pinnacle of power. Throughout, he's served with a love of country and commitment to principle that led President Reagan to say, "If Ed Meese is not a good man, then there are no good men."[2]

Ed Meese and I talked about our two-party system in March 2010. It was a Friday breakfast before a meeting of the executive committee of the Council for National Policy at the Ritz-Carlton in Naples, Florida. I was scheduled to give a briefing later that day on congressional redistricting. General Meese told me that conservatism is an intellectual defense against abrupt change. In the post-Reagan era, the challenge for conservatism remains how to forge a fusion of the three essential aspects of conservative thought: economic, social, and national security.

Meese added that the new challenge of the Obama era was whether conservatism could infuse a new sense of commitment to constitutional principles into the Republican Party sufficient to harness and channel the energy of the Tea Party. If not, the GOP would be part of the problem, working to protect incumbents who lacked constitutional fidelity and preserve the status quo. If that happened, the two-party system would fracture, leading to the party split we discussed in the previous chapter. That would allow Democrats to retain control of the government in a multiparty system, and European-style socialism could become irreversibly rooted in the American political order.

LOOKING AT FOREIGN PROBLEMS
THROUGH DOMESTIC EYES

As I (Blackwell) thought about these observations, what troubled me was that they rang true from my own experience. When it comes to economic policy, I coauthored a book with one of America's greatest minds on fiscal policy, the late Jack Kemp (under whom I also served as undersecretary at the Department of Housing and Urban Development), on taxes and spending, and also served on the Kemp Commission and as treasurer of Ohio. From a foreign policy perspective, I served as the U.S. ambassador to the United Nations Human Rights Commission, and have spent time in sixty-three nations around the globe. I've seen how economic turmoil leads to social unrest and political upheaval. At any given moment, such turmoil is taking place in dozens of countries around the planet. Such a thing can indeed happen in America.

Our economic prosperity is the reason scenes of widespread starvation, sick children, and deprivation do not occur in this country. Governments in dysfunctional countries promise to do all things for all people, so the problem isn't a lack of government. It's a lack of wealth and economic productivity. It's a lack of successful businesses where people can get a job or start a company of their own, with those workers and business owners then having money to spend on food, clothing, medicine, and a comfortable home. It's also being able to afford an education, and to accumulate wealth to fund retirements, safeguard against a rainy day, and enable capital formation for business investment. Economies with these characteristics, flush with money, are what take care of most people, and for those relatively few people in need, are what enable charitable organizations to amass the means to help the needy. This leaves a relatively small segment of the population in poverty, with a government possessing the means to help them.

But there are other reasons for American success, and other ways of measuring a society's worth.

Owing largely to our religious heritage, no country is as decent and honorable as America. We give more to charity and the poor—including foreign aid—than any other nation on earth. Despite the fact that our society is very competitive, has a well-armed population, and has millions of citizens trained in the use of force, we're a peaceful society with low crime rates. Children are safe walking down the street. The police are not corrupt. Government officials cannot simply seize things they want, or imprison or execute their critics. Consistent with the teachings of Christianity, our businesses are characterized by workers, managers, and owners who are honest, fair, trustworthy, and hardworking.

And we're a safe country. Despite the fact that we have deadly enemies, our citizens mostly live their lives in safety and tranquility. There are not regular shootouts or bombings. We suffered a single terrorist attack on our soil in the last decade, despite the attempts of some to launch many more attacks. Our military and national security system—while imperfect—works marvelously well.

The success in each of these three areas—economic, social, and national security—stems from cooperation between those who care about different policy areas. There are few natural majorities in a civilization; in order to get most things done in a democratic republic, you must form meaningful coalitions, building majority support to work for common goals and mutual benefit.

This cooperation is at the heart of the American experience, because it was essential to writing the Declaration of Independence and the Constitution. We'll study both of our founding documents in Chapter 5, but one important point must be made here.

Different authors conflict on the ideological beliefs that led to the Declaration of Independence. Many say it was the idea of natural rights, and that the British government ceased to have legitimate authority over the American colonists. Others say it was primarily economic, a social compact to protect property and contract rights, focused on building wealth and prosperity. Others say it was primarily legal, that the Framers were adhering to the English common-law system, understanding that many British government actions violated common law, and thus the Framers were merely acting as guardians and enforcers of their common-law rights. A fourth school of thought is that the revolution was primarily theological, that King George III and Parliament were no longer legitimate rulers, and therefore God did not require obedience to them and instead blessed the concept of empowering people to govern themselves.[3]

In reality, all four belief systems caused the revolution; each was a major factor. Although most scholarly emphasis is placed on the natural rights school, among the three million colonists at the time, all four of these schools were well represented, driving their adherents to support independence.

But the Founders understood that they needed each other to achieve their common goal of an independent, self-governing country. None of them individually had large enough numbers to achieve independence. To reach critical mass, they had to join forces. In doing so, they formed a federation, one large enough to pool sufficient resources to hold out against the mighty British military.

This federation approach was also seen in the Continental Congress and the new nation. Those pushing hardest for independence, from colonies such as Massachusetts (where John Adams and Samuel Adams were among the most outspoken advocates for independence), knew that they couldn't throw off British oppression without the central and southern colonies. They especially needed Virginia and Pennsylvania, the two most powerful colonies. Yet Pennsylvania's delegation included a committed opponent of going to war with Britain, and Virginia was a colony where slavery was widespread.

Despite their passionate opposition to slavery, they decided to work alongside the delegates of the slave-owning colonies, even while making clear that they opposed slavery and would at every turn seek to abolish it. Without sacrificing principle where they disagreed, they still joined forces fully and without reservation to fight as one on the issues where they did agree.

Three Parts of the Reagan Coalition

One of the things that made Ronald Reagan such a transformational figure in American history is that he built a new coalition. The Reagan Coalition stood in contrast to Roosevelt's New Deal Coalition, and enabled a Republican ascendancy in the 1980s. The legs of the Reagan Coalition gave America a conservative vision of government, one that can again be realized in modern America to tackle our current challenges.

President Reagan's coalition was a conservative coalition, which one of your authors (Blackwell) was honored to be a part of in the 1980s. It was the first time in years that a true conservative was on the national ticket and had a serious chance of winning. Reagan articulated a conservative vision of America that covered every area of policy.

THREE TYPES OF CONSERVATIVES

This conservatism could naturally be divided into three parts. Ronald Reagan defined and united all three types of conservative: economic, social, and national security. Each of these groups was able to define its objectives in a way that was compatible with the other two. Because Ronald Reagan's vision included their core principles, and his policy agenda embodied those principles, each of the three felt fully represented by President Reagan and was willing to follow his lead regardless of the other groups that were also following him.

ECons (Economic Conservatives)

The first type of conservative is an economic conservative, or "ECon" for short.

ECons care about three broad things. The first is the size of government, with its corresponding cost. This translates to being concerned about federal spending, where ECons demand a balanced federal budget and attacking our horrifying national debt. They're also concerned about taxes, which ECons want to keep low enough to maximize economic opportunities in the private sector for job creation and the accumulation of wealth. (This push for lower taxes isn't about cutting government revenue, however, because as discussed in Chapter 7, cutting taxes to a certain point actually causes the economy to grow so rapidly that it results in *more* tax revenue, not less.)

The second ECon concern is the intrusiveness of government into business decisions. They care about keeping government from regulating businesses in unproductive ways. This means avoiding needless regulations wasting countless man-hours of time and expense for excessive forms, permits, and reports. It also means preventing regulations that cause inefficiencies, redundancies, or impede providing good-quality products for which there is market demand. And ECons know it's impossible to eliminate downside risk; being free to succeed means running the risk of failure.

The final concern for ECons is allowing individuals to accumulate enough material wealth to be self-sufficient and able to make—and fund—their own decisions. They want people to be able to buy a nice house, have a couple of cars, and enjoy the fruit of their labors, such as a vacation or a TV. But more than toys or conveniences, ECons want families to be able to afford their own food, medicine, and education, provide for their own retirement, and hand down a solid financial foundation for their children and grandchildren.

ECons understand the need for both short-term economic gain and long-term economic prosperity. They understand that people must obtain an education that allows them not only to learn a skill set in order to obtain a good-paying job, but also to be able to update that skill set to remain competitive within the market.

We explore economic conservatism in Chapters 7 and 8.

SoCons (Social Conservatives)

The second kind of conservative is the social conservative, or "SoCon."

SoCons are "values voters." They are family focused, caring about family values issues.

These are typically thought of as marriage and abortion. SoCons promote sex within the context of a loving marriage, and also that people should accept the consequences for their actions. If people choose to have sex and a baby results, it's a tragic indictment of society that killing the child is considered an acceptable option to get out of the situation. While people come down on different sides of this issue in the extraordinary and terrible circumstances of rape, incest, or a danger to the mother—circumstances accounting for less than 1% of abortions—abortion cannot be used as a form of birth control. SoCons embrace marriage as the foundational unit of all of human civilization, and thus the union of one man and one woman, as found not only in natural law and as a sacred institution established by God, but also in the history and traditions of America.

SoCons are also champions of religious freedom, and many (though not all) are devout people of faith. They celebrate the fact that America was founded on religious freedom. As the Supreme Court declared, Americans "are a religious people whose institutions presuppose a Supreme Being. . . . When the state encourages religious instruction or cooperates with religious authorities . . . it follows the best of our traditions."[4] They believe that people should be free to practice and share their faith in every part of life, including the public square. So-Cons see sincere belief in peaceful religions—especially Christianity— as more than beneficial to American society; it's essential to America's long-term prosperity and happiness.

But it gives SoCons short shrift to define them solely in terms of abortion, marriage, and religion. SoCons believe that families need to have the freedom to make whatever decisions are best for them as a family. They believe that parents have the right to make decisions for their children, including the values those children will be taught and the kind of education they receive. They believe people should be able to make local laws supporting community values and embodying wholesome social principles. They believe that people should not be beholden to the government, should live their lives in a manner where they provide for themselves with enough left over to be able to help those in need or to support ministries or causes they agree with, and to be able to make arrangements to handle their own affairs.

Beyond that—and many politicians are learning this on Election Day—there is another social issue that politicians disrespect at their political peril: the Second Amendment right to own a gun. SoCons believe in the right to defend themselves, their families, their neighbors, their country, and liberty itself against those who seek to violate their rights. Gun ownership by law-abiding citizens is a positive good for society, protecting individuals, families, and communities and defending life, liberty, and property.

We explain social conservatism more in Chapters 9 and 10.

SafeCons (National Security Conservatives)

The third type of conservative is the national security conservative, or "SafeCon" in this book.

America's national security starts with a sense of American exceptionalism, that America is a singular beacon of light in a dangerous world, and that no country enjoys the light of liberty in all of its blazing glory as we do in the United States. As such, SafeCons understand that American sovereignty must be jealously guarded, both against foreign encroachment and against international and transnational organizations. In the United States, American law must reign supreme and American values must be upheld, no matter what any foreign countries think of such concepts.

SafeCons focus on protecting America against physical threats. This is usually thought of as keeping us safe from acts of terrorism, especially on U.S. soil. They understand the world can be dangerous. They also acknowledge that the U.S. Constitution draws a bright line between domestic policy and foreign policy, between law enforcement and protecting against foreign threats, and between peacetime maintenance of social order and wartime hostilities.

SafeCons understand that the Constitution is not a suicide pact. The Constitution gives the president extraordinary power where national security is concerned, and he's the exclusive voice of the United States in foreign policy. Moreover, when the United States is at war, the Constitution does not require Congress and the president to afford wartime enemies captured on foreign battlefields the same rights as U.S. citizens being investigated by local police.

The Constitution makes the top priority of the federal government securing the lives of American citizens. That is the single greatest difference between the role of the federal government versus state governments. SafeCons understand that this affects our foreign policy, such as our support for Israel and opposition to Iran's obtaining nuclear weapons. It gives the government broad powers to protect against terrorism here at home, though the Constitution commands that such powers never trump constitutional rights of U.S. citizens, especially those of free speech, holding elections, and the right to keep and bear arms.

A critical element of security is also found in private gun ownership by law-abiding citizens. Thus, although Second Amendment rights are a social conservative issue going to the heart of our cultural identity and heritage, nonetheless the role gun ownership plays in protecting our country against threats to security is enormously important, as discussed in Chapter 10. Beyond that, we consider what conservatism means when it comes to national security in Chapter 11.

THE THREE-LEGGED STOOL: EACH TYPE OF CONSERVATIVE NEEDS THE OTHER TWO

Constitutional conservatism holds that each of the three types of conservatives needs the other two. It's not that each should tolerate the other two, or that their goals are compatible and they can peacefully coexist. Properly understood, each one *needs* the other two.

That's why the Reagan Coalition is described as a three-legged stool. If you remove any one of those legs, the whole stool topples to the ground. You need the votes of ECons, SoCons, and SafeCons to win an election. And once in power, government isn't truly conservative unless it's conservative in all three areas.

SoCons need economic and national security conservatives

Social conservatives need economic conservatives.

Big government means higher taxes. That takes money out of the hands of working parents, making them dependent on government for education, where children can be ridiculed for their faith and not allowed to study certain subjects.

Government money always comes with strings attached, so big government undermines parents, empowering government to override parental rights and assume a parental role of instilling values in children. This taxing-and-spending burden pushes a stay-at-home parent to get a job, or a working spouse or parent to get a second job, reducing the amount of time that husbands and wives can spend together or with their children. Big government is hostile to moral self-government, leading millions of Americans to look to government for answers and providing for life's needs. It also undermines churches and ministries, as a growing government imposes ever-greater restrictions on these organizations' teaching, and crowds them out of the public square.

By contrast, a flourishing economy creates and protects good jobs. It allows for people to try starting their own business, which they can operate in a manner consistent with their values and beliefs, while encouraging their employees to consider such values. Good jobs help families stay together. When you have a job that pays well without too much taken out of your paycheck in taxes, it allows families to save, invest, and live comfortably. It also allows families to acquire their own home, which provides a level of security. It allows for families to be well fed and well clothed. It allows parents the flexibility to decide where to send the kids to school, and to spend quality time on trips and vacations. It allows a family to amass enough to provide for their future needs, as well as to be in a position to give generously to their church or to organizations and causes they support, as well as to those in need.

SoCons also need to support national security.

The threat of physical attack is profoundly destabilizing to families, leading to fear and anxiety. There are many nations where you cannot allow young women to go out at night for fear of what might happen. There are areas of certain cities where there's constant violence. Fear of assault, rape, robbery, or simply harassment profoundly disrupts the peace of a household. SoCons must support the government having the ability to detect threats at home and abroad and to decisively deal with those who would attack Americans.

To the extent that weak national security leads to compromising American sovereignty, that brings with it a host of additional dangers. In most countries, it's illegal to say the kinds of things that are protected here by the First Amendment, such as criticizing the government. In some countries, it's a crime to criticize other religions, or to speak against homosexuality. In others, it's illegal to spank your children, or to share the gospel of Jesus Christ. In others it's illegal to own a gun, or else firearm possession is heavily restricted. American values are rejected by most of the world, so allowing U.S. primacy to be undermined will facilitate foreign values flooding into this country and violate our core concepts of personal liberty.

SafeCons Need Social and Economic Conservatives

National security conservatives need economic conservatives.

A robust national security apparatus is amazingly expensive. We have the greatest military in the history of the world. But a B-2 bomber costs $1 billion. An F-22 Raptor stealth fighter costs $100 million. And it takes only one glance at a *Nimitz*-class nuclear-powered aircraft carrier to realize that it costs billions of dollars. Our troops are well fed, well paid, and well housed, with good benefits and high-quality, advanced weapons and equipment. The ongoing cost of maintaining our current military commitments alone exceeds the gross domestic product of many countries around the world.

However, that's not even close to the total cost of American safety. The reason we have advanced weaponry and equipment is that we invest countless billions of dollars in long-term research and development, and new weapon systems and defensive technologies can take decades to develop and deploy. Beyond that, our massive military is only part of our vast national security and homeland security structure. There are a dozen intelligence agencies such as the CIA, and domestic law enforcement agencies such as the FBI.

We wouldn't have the faintest hope of maintaining the Arsenal of Democracy without an enormous and robust economy. That's how Ronald Reagan won the Cold War: He kept ramping up our military, prompting the Soviets to try matching us (with their much smaller economy), until the expense broke the Soviet government. Thus Safe-Cons must support job creation and productivity gains, because they're the economic engine that allows our nation to invest so heavily in safety and defense.

The money isn't enough, however. SafeCons also need social conservatives.

The other vital aspect of us having the finest military, security, and intelligence forces is our citizenry. In most countries, soldiers and police are corrupt. A few well-greased palms gets you anything you want, while government officials all too often shake you down if you don't pony up. Countless soldiers and officers are willing to sell out their own country for the right price, or moonlight as hired thugs for crime syndicates or wealthy elites. Compared to Americans, most nations' soldiers are undisciplined and disorganized, and can be routed on the battlefield.

Not so Americans. Our country is full of patriotic men and women. They're willing to risk their safety and even their lives. They make enormous sacrifices and ask their families to sacrifice as well. They work long hours, often to the point of exhaustion. They act honestly and honorably, unwilling to take bribes or kickbacks, and never willing to give up or give in.

American soldiers, sailors, airmen, and marines are a great force for good in this world. Lieutenant Colonel Oliver North of *War Stories* fame tells the story of when he was with our troops in Iraq. There was a firefight on April 6, 2003, and North—a Vietnam combat veteran who earned Purple Hearts for being wounded in battle—was in the fight, reporting for Fox News Channel. As the medics were retrieving the wounded to be transported to safety for medical care, one of our navy corpsmen (that's pronounced "core-men," not "corpse-men" as commander in chief Barack Obama said twice in *prepared* remarks) was carrying a wounded combatant to safety. A Reuters reporter embedded with our troops shouted to the U.S. medic, "Hey, what did you do that for? Didn't you notice he's not a marine?" Because in fact, the wounded person was an enemy Iraqi soldier. North says that at that moment our corpsman gave the reporter a one-fingered salute and shouted back, "Didn't you notice? He was *wounded.* That's what *we* do. We're Americans!"[5]

Few if any nations have troops who would show such compassion and mercy, helping someone who minutes before had been an enemy. North adds that this was the third time that medic had rushed into the firefight. His first two times he carried wounded marines to safety. What bravery and selfless courage! No country is blessed with finer guardians than the United States. The same can be said of our police, our firefighters, and our intelligence agents.

Why? North says that he's struck by how many Bible studies start up among our troops, and how many attend worship services in forward areas by the battlefield, and will gather together in prayer before going into the fight. It is the faith of our soldiers and our police and emergency responders—that we answer to a higher authority, that we all stand accountable to God, that there are things worth fighting for, and there are things worth dying for—that gives us such a safe and secure nation.

Faith, honor, integrity, and bravery—they are the code of the millions of Americans who serve to keep us safe both here and abroad.

ECons Need National Security Conservatives

Economic conservatives need national security conservatives.

We are a safe, stable, and secure country. Despite all that's been done to damage us as a job creator and wealth generator over the past couple of years, there's no better nation than the United States in which to invest long-term. As a result, we're a magnet for investment dollars from all over the world.

A critical element to America's prosperity is that we are a nation under the rule of law. In this country, the courts and police will enforce and uphold property rights, contract obligations, and criminal penalties for malicious or deceptive acts. There are civil courts available for all manner of torts, whether it's theft, destruction of property, or fraud. Our laws are stable and predictable. Regulations are evenly enforced, even if they've become much less predictable over the past few years. You can start and operate most forms of business with minimal obstacles and red tape.

Many Americans take this business-friendly environment for granted. When you work with foreign governments, you see the dark underbelly of how things work in many other countries, where deals are routinely broken, property is stolen or damaged, or the government can summarily seize your life's work. By comparison, America is a wonderful place to invest.

THE REAL CONFLICT: ECONOMIC CONSERVATIVES
NEED SOCIAL CONSERVATIVES

The foregoing material on how different types of conservatives need each other is important, but all the combinations we've looked at thus far are, in a way, just conversation. In reality, there's only one big conflict. And it's a serious conflict, one that could conceivably even split the Republican Party—or at least cause millions of voters to vote for a third party—and doom the American Republic to another few years of far-left dominance by Democrats that would end our country as we know it.

If there's one thing people need to realize right now, it's that economic conservatives need social conservatives.

Too many Republican leaders in Washington consider social conservatives "useful idiots." A politician shows up, does a "Jesus dance" of talking about going to church and of praying, says "my faith is important to me," and expects thereby to receive the support and votes of SoCons.

Too often that's exactly what happens. The politicians glad-hand SoCons at town hall meetings and in public places and give a big smile in district offices or at the state fair. As a result these politicians give SoCons just enough to keep them from revolting outright, and then they huddle with their urban-elite, Ivy League friends to talk about taxes and regulation and other "real" conservative issues.

Those are indeed conservative issues, of course. But they're no more important than social issues. That's why when ECon leaders justify their support when talking about a gay-marriage group or an anti-gun group by saying, "This group is basically conservative," they're signaling their rejection of social issues of abortion, marriage, religious liberty, or gun rights as having any core relevance for public policy.

The reality, however, is that ECons need a socially conservative culture to maximize America's economic potential. Strong traditional families are the fundamental building block of the U.S. economy (or any economy, for that matter). As our friend Congressman Mike Pence said recently, "We must realize there's a direct correlation between the stability of families and the stability of our economy."[6]

Married families with children tend to have more productive economic characteristics. Such people tend to purchase a house and pay it off. They purchase durable consumer goods. They think long-term, saving more, investing more, and planning more. They are less likely to waste untold sums on illegal drugs, excessive drinking, heavy smoking, or other self-destructive behavior. They are likely to live longer and healthier lives.

Regarding faith, the economic benefits are tremendous. Economic prosperity requires honesty and morality. One of the reasons that America has such a strong economy is that—relative to other countries—Americans are remarkably honest and hardworking. We're more likely to be at work on time, to work our assigned hours, and to put in a full day's work before quitting for the day, even if unsupervised. Americans derive a sense of dignity from having a job and doing it well. As a society we condemn theft and embezzlement, whereas many cultures don't. Most Americans also deride those who slack off on the job, while in many cultures it's considered commonplace. Millions of Americans are honest and trustworthy in their job and have a sense of loyal obligation to their employer and coworkers. A great deal of our work ethic is derived from the religious beliefs of our people, whether they personally hold such a faith or simply adopt and apply our cultural values derived from that faith.

By contrast, there's an enormous cost to the lack of stable families. Divorce and out-of-wedlock births cost the U.S. economy at least $112 billion per year.[7] This is absolutely breathtaking; that's well over *$1 trillion* a decade. And that's just direct economic loss. The total cost of divorce is $175 billion every year.[8] That includes the result of many formerly united households having to dispose of major assets like houses and cars at fire-sale prices, resulting in ridiculous loss. They have enormous additional costs such as shuttling children back and forth. They also set up redundant expenditures, such as duplicate housing.

There are additional damages that these figures do not capture. While they reflect the cost of treating children for the trauma of a broken family and the increased odds of juvenile delinquency, they don't measure the child's divided ambitions, going for a high school diploma instead of a college degree, or a job that pays $30,000 after one year of preparation instead of a job that pays $80,000 after four years of preparation. It also doesn't count the value of the example that a loving married couple gives to young people. Or when a young couple is going through a rough time, it doesn't count the impact of having an angry young wife talk to her mother and father who have been married for forty years, who encourage her to get through that tough time with the result of a stronger marriage, versus the twice-divorced mom who tells her daughter it's time to look someplace else for a new man.

Strong families make better workers and better long-term consumers. Such families raise the next generation with better consumption and investment habits. Their children tend to be better adjusted and more disciplined, which leads to more education, which in turn leads to better-paying jobs.

Why Don't ECons Like SoCons?

Among each type of conservative, there are some who don't want to make common cause with those belonging to the other two conservative camps. The reality, however, is that nine times out of ten, it's social conservatives who get thrown under the bus. The sad truth is that many small-government people share the disdain of the Left for churchgoing people who make moral judgments. The Christian Right found a welcome seat at the table in 1980 because Ronald Reagan shared with them a belief that the Bible is the Word of God. Reagan respected Bible-believing Christians. He included people who read it and talked with people about it, who had biblical views on the sanctity of life, moral issues, and the wholesome influence of Christian beliefs in society.

Why do so many economic conservatives dislike social conservatives? There are several reasons.

One has to do with the fact that Ronald Reagan welcomed people of faith. The 1960s and '70s saw the Supreme Court, after taking a hard turn to the left, embark on a campaign of radically secularizing the country, and Republican leadership was mostly unconcerned about these things. But Reagan believed that religious expression was a key part of maintaining a virtuous and honorable people. While many elected officials met this description, it marked a turning point for one to become leader of the party and then leader of the nation. This is what led to leaders such as Jerry Falwell and Pat Robertson organizing the Christian Right, followed years later by others such as Chuck Colson, D. James Kennedy, and Jim Dobson. Millions of Americans of faith—mostly Evangelicals, but also devout Catholics and Mormons (and increasingly Orthodox Jews)—were drawn to this Republican Party that honored and respected faith and the values accompanying such faith.

Many Republicans who were part of the GOP before this shift were never comfortable with these "holy rollers." These "faith voters" spoke a different language and they cared about different things. Some Republicans were perfectly content with the lack of religiosity in the Republican Party, and all things being equal they would have preferred it was that way again.

Stemming from their own nonreligious affections, many of these GOP insiders believed that talking about abortion, public prayer, or homosexuality would alienate swing voters. In other words, they thought it would cost them elections, so they tried to bury these issues. (Interestingly, during this time many of these insiders also had disdain for the other big social issue, the Second Amendment. But the astounding success and massive political clout of organizations like the National Rifle Association over the past thirty years have now made disrespect for guns a nonstarter in the GOP.)

It goes deeper than that, however, to the question of absolute truth versus moral relativism. Many ECons consider SoCons intolerant. They often use phrases like "Faith is a personal matter, as far as I'm concerned," or "I don't think those sorts of issues belong in public debate." These people bifurcate faith and reason, such that they believe you can speak about the economic consequences of a change in tax law with firm matter-of-factness, but when it comes to spiritual issues or values, you can speak only in terms of your personal *opinions*. In other words, "That may work for you," or "I'm glad your faith brings you peace." Or the utterly nonsensical "Well, that's true for you, but something else is true for me."

Of course, when SoCons speak of such things, we speak of them in objective terms; we state them as matters of fact. We state them as truth, meaning that which agrees with reality, regardless of whether anyone agrees with it. As theologian R. C. Sproul says, if the God we speak of does not exist in reality, then all of our praying and attending church and Bible reading and talking about him with others does not have the power to create him. Conversely, if the God we're talking about does exist, then even if the world rejects him and refuses to acknowledge him, it doesn't have the power to kill him.

This sense of absolutism is what makes so many ECons without firm personal faith uncomfortable with SoCons. They don't like the certitude, and they reject the proposition that you can truly know God in a personal way just as you know your spouse or your best friend. With that they also reject the idea that you can know right and wrong, or moral and immoral, as certainly and clearly as you know that increasing marginal tax rates impedes economic growth, or that imposing healthcare mandates on employers inevitably leads to higher healthcare premiums and a net increase in the number of uninsured people. Some freely call SoCons fanatics, zealots, or even bigots. One D.C. Republican insider we're thinking of likes to call pro-lifers "fetus huggers."

A third reason has to do with personal lifestyles. Nobody's perfect. But many people with the right education or experience to make them well-grounded ECons or SafeCons reject all sorts of personal morality. While we understand that, sadly, many marriages fall apart, and we all have good friends who made unfortunate mistakes—or sometimes deliberate choices—many of those people nevertheless accept and respect that there are certain moral ideals, even if we fall short of them. But others—including many Republicans—who reject these values for themselves also feel profoundly uncomfortable around those who hold such beliefs. These people are uncomfortable around values-oriented people; they feel that they can't drink too much in front of them, cuss in front of them, or tell the jokes that they want to tell, that those people are killjoys around whom you can't "be yourself."

Part of this is because of the values of many otherwise conservative leaders. Washington, D.C., is full of people who claim to speak and act for Christian conservatives but would not be accepted into membership in many serious Evangelical churches. Nor would they attempt to join such churches. Others like to cast themselves as leaders of the Christian Right but are not accepted by Evangelicals because of their personal lifestyles.

Marriage is hard work, and so is being a parent. All of us know and love many wonderful people who've been divorced or don't have children. This isn't about them. Instead it's about those who claim to speak for Bible-believing Christians (who make up roughly 20% of the presidential electorate, with 24 million such voters).

Many people in Washington feel uncomfortable with committed Christians who practice what their faith teaches because, frankly, some people's lifestyles are characterized by willful or ongoing moral failings, and they feel uncomfortable dealing with people who make moral judgments.

For example, one top official in the Bush White House called one of your authors (Blackwell) a "religious fanatic" because I'm an Evangelical Christian who was chairing the effort to amend the Ohio Constitution to protect marriage. I've always stood for marriage as between one man and one woman, and believe the biblical standard that sexuality is ordained as part of the marital relationship, despite the fact that countless people don't accept that standard, and millions more believe in this standard yet fall short in living up to it. My standing up for marriage as chairman of the 2004 Ohio marriage amendment initiative, and my personal belief in the Bible as the Word of God, earned me opponents within the GOP, simply because of my religious beliefs. It doesn't matter that I never tried to impose my personal beliefs on anyone; the very fact that I sincerely held those beliefs made me an ignorant bigot and a religious fanatic in this person's eyes. (I don't lose any sleep over it, though.)

The irony here is that marriage is a winning issue, and a perfect example of the split between true conservatives versus Republican establishment figures. It's a common misperception that the Bush White House ginned up marriage as a wedge issue to drive turnout in 2004. In reality, top White House people joined every other Republican holding statewide office in Ohio in opposing me and my friends in getting the marriage amendment on the ballot and passing it; those who didn't openly oppose us stayed quiet. So the president and many closest to him publicly supported marriage only with reluctance, and now that the social dynamic on this issue has shifted, we're seeing many of those top Republicans announce that they have supported same-sex marriage all along. We weren't pushing this issue to help the Bush reelection effort; instead supporters of marriage had to fight the establishment GOP just as they did the Democratic establishment.

A fourth reason is elitism. Many otherwise conservative leaders are coastal, urban elites. Many aspects of international finance, tax policy, trade agreements, and long-term foreign policy require a great deal of education or experience to master. As such, many of the leaders in these fields are very well educated and/or wealthy and spend much of their time in cities or on the coasts. But social issues are matters of the heart, not only the head. As such, those who hold these issues dear are spread across all educational, socioeconomic, and demographic brackets. This means that many of them aren't well educated, or don't have much money. Frankly, many ECon and SafeCon leaders see most SoCons as country bumpkins or simpletons.

For all four of these reasons, many ECons would prefer that SoCons would just "vote for the right person" on Election Day, and aside from that just go away. These ECons don't see anything wrong with a secular society, or same-sex marriage, or (for some of them) a society where only the criminals have guns. They don't think of abortion as killing a human being.

In short, they think of SoCons the same way as liberals think of SoCons.

That's why it's so important to examine the underlying economics of these social issues. Although that can't completely rectify the situation because—again—social issues are largely issues of the heart, it can work to build bridges of understanding to maintain a robust electoral coalition that can continue winning elections. The Reagan Coalition still has three legs; all three kinds of conservatives are necessary for lasting victory, which in turn produces lasting solutions to America's problems.

Some Conservatives Get It, and Republicans Are Starting to Catch Up

The good news is, conservatives are starting to wake up to the fact that different types of conservatives need each other, and also—more important—millions are waking up to the idea that these three conservative legs naturally reinforce each other. Over the past year, two documents have come to public prominence, especially in political and policy circles, that are very important in building and solidifying a lasting conservative coalition.

There's a good chance you've never heard of these two very important documents. The fact that the media did nothing to cover the signing and sharing of them frankly shows where the media lines up on these issues. The liberal mainstream media has a vested interest in creating conflict between ECons and SoCons. These documents have also been buried by those we've previously mentioned who are trying to marginalize social issues and redefine conservatism as being strictly about limited government and economic issues. They're also being ignored by those seeking to drive SoCons out of the Republican Party, which, as we saw in the last chapter, would be the ultimate act of self-destruction, resulting in a party split that would keep Barack Obama (or Hillary Clinton) and congressional Democrats in power.

Fortunately, a growing number of leaders in the Republican Party embrace the importance of social issues. Senator Jim DeMint says, "It's impossible to be a fiscal conservative unless you're a social conservative because of the high cost of a dysfunctional society." Governor Mike Huckabee adds, "We need to understand there is a direct correlation between the stability of families and the stability of our economy." And Congressman Mike Pence declares, "Those who would have us ignore the battle being fought over life, marriage and religious liberty have forgotten the lessons of history."

MOUNT VERNON STATEMENT

On February 17, 2010, more than one hundred conservative leaders—including both of your authors—gathered south of Washington, D.C., at Mount Vernon, Virginia, the home of the Father of our Country, President George Washington. The meeting was convened by the Conservative Action Project, an organization chaired by former attorney general Ed Meese and dedicated to building bridges of understanding and cooperation between the three different legs of the conservative coalition. It's an organization we both work with. On that day, we all signed a document titled "The Mount Vernon Statement: Constitutional Conservatism: A Statement for the 21st Century."[9] It begins:

> We recommit ourselves to the ideas of the American Founding. Through the Constitution, the Founders created an enduring framework of limited government based on the rule of law. They sought to secure national independence, provide for economic opportunity, establish true religious liberty and maintain a flourishing society of republican self-government.
>
> These principles define us as a country and inspire us as a people. They are responsible for a prosperous, just nation unlike any other in the world. They are our highest achievements, serving not only as powerful beacons to all who strive for freedom and seek self-government, but as warnings to tyrants and despots everywhere.
>
> Each of these founding ideas is presently under sustained attack. In recent decades, America's principles have been undermined and redefined in our culture, our universities and our politics. The self-evident truths of 1776 have been supplanted by the notion that no such truths exist. The federal government today ignores the limits of the Constitution, which is increasingly dismissed as obsolete and irrelevant.

The Mount Vernon Statement embraces natural law and acknowledges that rights and rightful governmental power come from God. It proclaims that free enterprise and individual entrepreneurship can thrive only when government is strictly limited. And it declares that American liberty is endangered by tyranny abroad and the threat of terrorism at home.

Some of the signatories evidently do not agree with everything in that document. Several who signed the Mount Vernon Statement embrace aspects of the gay agenda. Others refuse to take a stand protecting life. Some have taken stands regarding national security that are inconsistent with constitutional principles.

This serves to remind us that we're a coalition, and as such we must follow a federation model. While a majority of Americans might not embrace every part of conservatism, a supermajority embraces at least part of it. So building a federation of these allies is critical, and we should gratefully take the hand of those willing to stand with us in advancing a common agenda.

THE MANHATTAN DECLARATION

The other document is an important indication that people of faith understand they've been thrown under the bus, not only by the Left and the media, but by plenty of Republican leaders and those who call themselves leaders of the conservative movement. It's called the "Manhattan Declaration: A Call of Christian Conscience." It begins, "Christians are heirs of a 2,000-year tradition of proclaiming God's word, seeking justice in our societies, resisting tyranny, and reaching out with compassion to the poor, oppressed and suffering."[10]

Roughly one-half *million* Americans have signed the Manhattan Declaration, almost entirely Evangelicals and Catholics. It's a call for civic engagement to rally people of faith to fight for the protection of life and marriage, and for the advancement of religious liberty. It's a proclamation that these issues matter.

The signatories of the Manhattan Declaration represent tens of millions of voters. These are Americans who believe in absolute truth, moral principles, family, and that no right is more important than the right to worship and obey Almighty God in accordance with the dictates of conscience and revealed truth. This document and its signers are a sobering reminder that those seeking to drive people of faith out of the public square will be met head-on with fierce determination and uncompromising opposition. Those who try to silence people of faith—and especially conservative Christians—had better remind themselves that we can never be bought off. We're here to stay, and those who oppose us had better decide whether they want to work with us, or instead to fight against us year after year in a conflict that will never end.

Yet the many millions of Americans represented by the Manhattan Declaration are open to being part of a broader conservative coalition. There is great energy and enthusiasm among the ranks of people of faith, and that energy can be channeled in collaboration with other constituencies to move America in the right direction.

This is especially true since, as we've noted several times already in this book, the greatest single defense against runaway government is strong families. Stable, traditional families are tremendous engines of economic growth and free enterprise, and committed families drastically lessen the role—and thus the demand for—large government. No statist agenda can succeed in a democracy where families are growing, thriving, and caring for each other. So the natural alliance between So-Cons and ECons presents a historic opportunity.

The Path to a Durable Majority

Taken together, ECons, SoCons, and SafeCons can form a coalition capable of establishing a durable majority that could enjoy a critical mass of support to hold Congress, the White House, and the vast majority of state governments long-term across the nation.

TURNING THEORY FROM ACROSS THE CENTURIES INTO REALITY

The Greek philosophers perceived a dilemma to forming a durable government. Plato wrote of this in *The Republic*, and Aristotle then expanded upon his thinking in *Politics*. They saw three different governmental forms.[11] The first was a monarchy—a king or other such single ruler. The second was an oligarchy (the *aristoi*)—meaning nobles or elites—from which we get our word *aristocrat*. The third was a democracy (the *demoi*)—meaning government by the people.

Observing the history of governments across the world, they believed that any of the three would eventually become complacent, then apathetic and corrupt. The government would then collapse from within, in a revolution. After that revolution, one of the other two types of government would be the new order that would restore first principles. And so it would happen again and again, in a circular pattern—hence the term *revolution*. Aristotle theorized that one possible way to break this would be by creating a "mixed government" of these three.

Political philosophers over the centuries examined and debated these ancient Greek works. They also studied how the Roman philosopher Polybius argued that the Roman Republic was a mixed government with the consuls as monarchs, the Senate as an oligarchy, and the popular assemblies as democracy. These ideas were then picked up by Cicero during the time that the Roman Republic transformed into an empire.

The Framers were all educated men, and devoted students of these great political philosophers such as Montesquieu, Locke, Berkeley, Hobbes, and Rousseau. Those philosophers in turn were devoted students of Plato, Aristotle, and Cicero. The Framers believed that they could break this historical pattern of revolution by improving upon the Roman model to create a truly mixed government. The president would be a form of monarch (though with strictly limited powers). The House would be a form of democracy. The Senate would be a form of oligarchy or aristocracy. By dividing their powers and setting them against each other in ways that we'll examine in Chapter 5, the Framers believed that they could build a form of government that could break the cycle of revolution to continually endure by constantly renewing first principles of freedom and virtue.

A WINNING COALITION

Those principles are the precepts of constitutional conservatism. Rebuilding a coalition dedicated to conservative principles is the key to a resurgence of constitutional conservatism, which we unpack and explain in the next chapter. And as we said in the Introduction, whether the Republican Party can be resurgent over the long term will turn on whether conservatism is resurgent, which can happen only if the Constitution is resurgent. The Supreme Law of the Land must again take primacy in American politics, policy, and culture.

Constitutional conservatism is a unified view of government, which manifests itself in terms of economics, society, and security. A constitutional conservative understands that each of these three types of conservative—properly understood—reinforces and augments the other two.

As we wrote early in this chapter, successful governments are built as coalitions. Think of it as three overlapping circles forming a triangle, one for each of the three types of conservative. Those who embrace all three aspects of constitutional conservatism form the heart of this co-alition at the center. Beyond that, millions more will share two of the three, forming overlaps between two circles. And finally, many millions more focus on one kind of issue; they're either single-issue, or they care about several related issues that are all part of one type of conservatism.

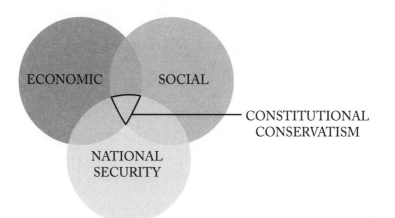

With those in the center acting as interlocutors and ambassadors between the various camps, the three legs of the Reagan Coalition—the parts of constitutional conservatism—can establish a majority coalition that could govern America for generations. Our children can then inherit the freedoms that we have enjoyed for more than two hundred years.

4

THE EIGHT KEYS OF CONSTITUTIONAL CONSERVATISM TO CREATE A SOVEREIGN SOCIETY

"A constitution founded on these principles introduces knowledge among the people, and inspires them with a conscious dignity becoming freemen; a general emulation takes place, which causes good humor, sociability, good manners, and good morals to be general. That elevation of sentiment inspired by such a government, makes the common people brave and enterprising. That ambition which is inspired by it makes them sober, industrious, and frugal."

—John Adams, *Thoughts on Government*, 1776

We saw in the Introduction how our constitutional crisis and the enormous economic and social dangers we face have created the possibility of a profound shift to regain our Constitution and founding principles for the first time in generations. We saw in Chapter 1 how both political parties have utterly failed America. As discussed in Chapter 2, Republican failures could even split the GOP into two parties. And in Chapter 3 we learned that all three types of conservative—economic, social, and national security— need each other, that instead of being in tension, each can realize its full potential only if the other two also succeed.

Now we identify and lay out the keys for a conservative America. The United States of America can regain its economic, social, and security supremacy only by embracing and restoring *constitutional conservatism*. This is the conservatism envisioned by our Founders and embodied in the Constitution. Constitutional conservatism—and nothing less—must be the policy of the Republican Party and must be what every candidate for public office embraces to be accepted as conservative. Only then can the Republican Party become a conservative party.

Constitutional conservatism is the path to creating a *Sovereign Society*. A Sovereign Society is one where individual Americans are truly sovereign in their own lives. It's where Americans have the means and ability to run their own lives in a fashion that causes them to prosper individually, as well as all together as a nation. A Sovereign Society is what will enable our republic to last for centuries, with strong and self-sufficient individuals and families, a flourishing free-market economy, good-paying jobs, and a military and security apparatus second to none, protecting us from threats while respecting our civil rights.

America was designed to create a Sovereign Society. We must grasp this truth and what it means, and achieve it in our day by embracing constitutional conservatism.

What Is Constitutional Conservatism?

The term *conservative* is thrown around these days in ways that can mean all sorts of things. Evidently its only meaning is whatever the speaker wants it to be. Beyond that, it's regularly redefined for political ends. President George W. Bush was called a conservative, though as we've already seen, the former president was not. Justice Sandra Day O'Connor was called a conservative, though likewise, she was not. Same for Justice Anthony Kennedy. Same for Senator John McCain.

This isn't to say that those individuals aren't conservative on certain issues. For example, John McCain is more committed to spending restraint than many Republicans. And George W. Bush was conservative on taxes. Many people may be conservative in several specific areas but shouldn't be called "conservative."

True conservatism is *constitutional conservatism*. That's the system of conservative government derived from the principles of freedom enshrined in our Constitution, erected within the philosophical framework arising from the Declaration of Independence. The Constitution includes many specific limits on the scope of government power, some of which limit the power of the federal government specifically and others of which limit the power of all governments (including state and local). The Constitution also secures many specific rights that Americans possess; some can be asserted only against the federal government and others can also be asserted only against state and local government.

Taken in the context of the Declaration of Independence and coupled with the history and traditions of the American people, a clear set of principles emerge. These principles form a cogent argument as to what the ideal government looks like. As we saw in the previous chapter, the Framers settled upon those principles after a lengthy study and energetic debate over the lessons of world history, as well as over the writings of the acclaimed philosophers, theologians, and historians who had studied the lessons of those earlier years. The Framers embodied those lessons in the Declaration and the Constitution.

Looking at more than two centuries of experience since those founding documents were adopted in this country, eight keys emerge. They are the principles of constitutional conservatism for re-creating and restoring a Sovereign Society in the United States.

There is some overlap between these eight keys. That's because they're not separate concepts; they're an integrated whole. Like eight different facets on a single sparkling precious gem, the Sovereign Society envisioned in constitutional conservatism is an overall picture of individuals who are truly free; thus all eight of these keys must exist together.

KEYS 1, 2, AND 3: ECONOMIC KEYS TO A SOVEREIGN SOCIETY

The first three keys are economic. A Sovereign Society is one wherein a person has the material means to provide for themselves and their family, both for the short term and the long term.

This means providing for daily needs like food and shelter. It also means being able to supply contingent needs such as healthcare. It means being able to obtain long-term capital assets that are used over a long period of time, such as a home and transportation. Finally, it also includes long-term individual personal needs such as retirement, as well as long-term needs for children, such as an education.

Key 1: Jobs

The first key to a Sovereign Society is a job. Whether as an employee, an independent contractor, or a business owner, everyone needs a way to make a living.

This doesn't mean that every *person* needs to earn a paycheck; it means that every *family* needs to bring home income. This is one aspect of how family stability is critical for economic prosperity. Obviously a single adult needs a job, unless he has some sort of disability that makes him completely unable to participate in economic production. (Such instances are rare, as many people with severe physical or mental challenges are still able to work certain jobs, and with it enjoy the dignity and respect that accompany such work.) Some people have more than one job. In some marriages both people work, while in others one works for a paycheck and the other works by raising children, keeping the house, or philanthropic or charitable work. For children or young adults, it might be their job to go to school or college to get an education and skill set. And for retired persons, they may no longer need to work for a paycheck, but there's still plenty of worklike activity to productively use their time, such as mentoring young people, volunteering at church, or helping the community.

No one is entitled to the basics of life. Every person must either make enough money to provide for themselves, or be part of a family structure where someone else brings in that money. As we'll read about in Chapter 9, some leftists and socialists even hijack Christianity to say that it's each person's moral duty to partner with government to redistribute income to care for those with less. That's what President Obama means when he speaks about how his vision for America is one in which "each of us is his brother's keeper."

But while the Bible encourages cheerful and merciful *voluntary* (not government-ordered) giving to help others, it also teaches a message very different from that of Barack Obama and Hillary Clinton. It says, "Make it your ambition to . . . mind your own business and work with your hands, . . . so that your daily life may win the respect of outsiders and so that you will not be dependent on anybody."[1] Moreover, "He who has been stealing must steal no longer, but must work, doing something useful with his own hands, that he may have something to share with those in need."[2] Beyond that, Scripture also instructs, "If a man will not work, he shall not eat."[3] So far from mandating vast government entitlement programs, the Bible calls for personal responsibility and hard work, to the point of denying welfare to those who refuse to work. While the Left will call that merciless and coldhearted, you're fighting a losing battle when you call the Bible unchristian.

Not only is no one entitled to government handouts, it's also true that no one has a right to a job. One day in 2010 the *Drudge Report* featured a picture of a young woman sitting despondently on a curb, holding up a sign (she appeared to be part of a protest) that read, "I deserve a job." I don't want that person working for me. An employee who thinks she is entitled to the job is likely to show up late, leave early, take a long lunch, take frequent breaks, and basically be unproductive. Don't ever try asking her to stay late or come in on Saturday when there's some urgent need. Don't expect her to look proactively for ways to improve the business or her performance. And don't expect her to honestly admit mistakes and offer to fix them on her own time. In short, you should expect her to do only the bare minimum to avoid getting fired each day. And when the time comes that you need to fire her, since she feels entitled to the job you run the risk of a lawsuit.

In a Sovereign Society, no person has a right to a job. Instead people have the right to compete for a job. They have the right to agree to work under whatever reasonable and safe conditions they choose, and to be paid according to those agreed terms for all the work they perform. They also have the right to start their own business, and if it succeeds to be able to create jobs for others.

It's not the proper role of government to create jobs. Government jobs are burdens on the taxpayers, as government does not produce revenue, to say nothing of profits. Some taxpayer burdens are absolutely necessary. Service in the military or law enforcement, for example, is not only vitally important but also honorable and worthy of great respect. Other government jobs, such as in important agencies, might not carry the same level of respect because they don't exact the same sacrifice and risks, but are still worthwhile. We need federal prosecutors and U.S. Customs inspectors. But we must recognize the reality that every government job consumes resources that could otherwise be put to productive use, and takes out of the workforce a person who could otherwise be involved in economically productive activity. And many government jobs, such as education policy analyst or human genome mapper, either infringe upon state sovereignty or perform tasks that the private sector handles perfectly well.

Second, to the extent government has a role in job creation, that role is primarily filled by state and local governments, not the federal government. While government doesn't create lasting jobs, it has a vital role in creating an environment that fosters job creation and wealth creation. But most of that role is filled by state employment, corporate, and labor laws as well as state licensing boards, local building codes, and local zoning.

There is a role for the federal government, but it's minimal. The Constitution empowered the federal government to regulate *inter-state* commerce, not local commerce. As you'll read in the Obamacare discussion in Chapter 8, in 1937 the Supreme Court vastly expanded the scope of the Constitution's Commerce Clause, reaching its modern extent in the 1942 case *Wickard v. Filburn.* Even under these expansive limits, though, the federal government's constitutional role is limited, largely involving patents, copyrights, and racial discrimination.

All that said, government can still be held accountable for high unemployment or—worse—rising unemployment, because although government is lousy at creating jobs, it's marvelously effective at destroying jobs. Raising taxes, imposing employer mandates, and increasing regulation all kill job creation. Not only that, but it can also keep unemployment high by making it hard for employers—especially small businesses—to create jobs.

Fostering the view that government provides jobs and welfare plays into the hands of the Left in four ways. First, it makes millions comfortable with the idea that they don't have to work or be part of a family that works, that they're entitled to have someone pay for their food, housing, and other needs, and that there's nothing wrong with government providing such things permanently. Second, it lends itself to millions voting for more government handouts, paid for by higher taxes on workers and families, because those voters see such programs as the proper role of government. Third, it undermines confidence in American workers and businesses, eroding reliance on the hard work of millions of productive citizens to create wealth and opportunity. And fourth, it elevates government into the place of family, supplanting the family and degrading family values.

More on jobs in Chapter 7.

Key 2: Balanced Budget—
Ending the Culture of Debt

The second principle of constitutional conservatism to create a Sovereign Society is a balanced budget. Individuals must balance their own personal budget. Families must balance their collective budget and teach this key to the next generation. And the government must have a balanced budget, which can be reliably achieved only through a Balanced Budget Amendment to the U.S. Constitution.

CULTURE OF DEBT

One aspect of this is debt. Scripture says that "the borrower is servant to the lender."[4] In other words, the Bible makes clear that those living in debt are never truly free. Yet we have become a culture consumed by debt, and worse, a culture where living in debt with no plan for getting out is no longer frowned upon. The biblical admonition to limit and avoid debt is paid no mind.

Only a generation ago, the national consensus was that a person pays his or her own way. It was universally accepted that people should live within their means, and only irresponsible people got into excessive debt. Credit was hard to come by and carefully evaluated. Large lines of credit were generally available only to successful businesses or to individuals with a proven record of income generation and sound financial judgment. People who lived beyond their means went hungry until the next paycheck or went hat in hand to friends or family, and so were motivated not to make such a mistake again. The only thing for which it was considered acceptable to take on massive, long-term debt was purchasing a home.

Now we've become a culture of debt. Beyond just houses, everything is purchased on credit: cars, jewelry, TVs, you name it. People make decisions based on how much credit they can get their hands on, not their income or how quickly they can pay off the balance. Instead of being embarrassed about debt and paying it off as soon as possible, people pay the bare minimum so that they can keep spending as much as possible on a monthly basis. As your author Blackwell wrote in early 2009, coupled with such behavior America's current public policies "are a Trojan horse creating not only a mentality of government reliance, but also a mindset where a lifestyle of permanent debt is acceptable."[5]

We've lost sight of the fact that living debt-free is essential to personal freedom, and so have abandoned the principle in two ways. The first is in buying things that we don't need—luxury items—and that we also can't afford. The second is in buying too much of the things that we do need. For example, a person who could responsibly handle a $200,000 house instead gets a $400,000 house that he can't possibly afford.

What are the consequences of this culture-wide recklessness? Total consumer debt currently stands at a horrifying $11.7 trillion.[6] Home foreclosures are on the rise, and the number of personal bankruptcies is up a frightening 34%.[7] Most people are in a position of debt that would take them many years to get out of even if they went into a radical repayment plan. As a result, so much of their income is consumed in interest payments that it cuts their true purchasing power by 70% or more, and once you add interest payments the overall purchase price can be as much as three times the sticker price.

This is a problem that must be addressed at the family level. Parents must teach their children about delayed gratification. They must fight the culture of instant gratification in which we live, where people act on whatever their impulses are right now, without heed to future consequences.

Children do a great job of sensing hypocrisy, though. If parents are to teach these principles to children, the biggest part of that instruction must be through practicing those principles in their daily lives.

BALANCED BUDGET

We tend to tolerate in our leaders what we tolerate in ourselves. It's only because we're such a debt-laden society that we don't vote out by the dozen the members of Congress—or a president—who vote for deficit spending on anything other than a temporary wartime emergency that threatens our national existence. If we all balanced our checkbooks and didn't live off credit cards, we would send packing any politician who votes for spending that exceeds our tax revenues.

This gives politicians a perverse incentive for not teaching our children sound financial principles. Members of Congress can't give hometown speeches about teaching our children to provide for themselves if those congressmen go back to Washington and vote to spend us into bankruptcy.

This also makes the government more inclined to bail out irresponsible companies that make reckless corporate decisions that put them in danger of going under. If voters better minded their own financial houses, then they would react in absolute outrage at the idea of bailing out reckless corporate executives. They'd throw their congressman or senator out of office if he voted for such a bailout, and so those members would vote against bailouts.

People get the government they vote for, and as a result usually get the government they deserve. If we get right on this issue individually, then we'll have enough of the right people in office to stop the madness.

The surest way to end the madness is through a Balanced Budget Amendment to the U.S. Constitution. The political will rarely exists to truly restrain spending, so to the extent there are any loopholes for deficit spending, you can count on enterprising politicians exploiting those loopholes. So we must amend the Constitution to save America from bankruptcy.

More on a Balanced Budget Amendment in Chapter 7.

Key 3: Ownership

The third key of constitutional conservatism to create a Sovereign Society is ownership. It's not enough to have a job to make money and live debt-free so that you retain enough of that money. Beyond those two keys, the third economic key is to be able to direct your money over time into those assets you need—both tangible and intangible—to be self-sufficient.

On its most basic level, private ownership of property is something without which no one can be truly free, because a person without property must rely upon another for food, shelter, and basic necessities. But beyond daily needs, a person cannot be sovereign unless he owns the means to provide for his own future.

It's worth pointing out that socialism violates property rights, and that communism denies the very concept of private property altogether. Ownership is an essential aspect of personal sovereignty, and so nations in which the government is dedicated to denying its citizens true freedom must undermine ownership of wealth and property.

THE BASICS OF LIFE

Property ownership has always been part of the fabric of American society. It was a leading cause of the American Revolution, as the colonists cried, "No taxation without representation!" No person can be secure without the means to feed and clothe himself and his children, a place where they can be safe together, and the means to obtain medicine and other contingent necessities, as well as other things that—while they may not be literally necessary to live—provide comfort or dignity.

Property in the sense we're speaking of is wealth. Wealth is a measure of your total purchasing power. It is a way to quantify that which you possess, and that which you can buy.

Yet private property—your wealth—is being assaulted in three ways, depriving people of their property rights. Any one of these keeps an American citizen from enjoying his full status as a sovereign. Taken together, they leave many people in a state of de facto serfdom.

We've already seen as part of Key 2 that debt is antithetical to ownership. Beyond that, there are two other points to consider.

Taxes

The first is taxation. To the extent that government taxes something, it is taking part of your wealth. Government lives off taxes, so we would have no government (no military, no police, etc.) if there were no taxes. But the trade-off is that the more you're taxed, the less you have. Taxes can get so high that they become confiscatory. Fifty years ago the highest marginal tax rate was 91%, where people at that rate were keeping next to nothing. Taxes need to be kept low to allow people to amass enough wealth to care for themselves.

Taxes should encourage growth and investment. That's why we support a Family Flat Tax in Chapter 7. We also support abolishing the Death Tax, as it results in the destruction of family farms and family businesses, and zero tax on capital gains, as such a tax impedes capital formation, asset appreciation, and funding of retirements.

Regulation

The second is regulation. Simply possessing your property isn't enough if you can't enjoy it. Both families and businesses need the freedom to make productive and effective use of their property.

The biggest impact of regulation is on business. Government exerts power on every aspect of a business, from whom it can hire, to the hours they work, the workplace, its products or services, to its obligations to the customer and the community. Government mandates—especially recent mandates such as environmental regulations and the Obamacare employer mandate—can break a company.

When you take a semester on property law in your first year of law school you learn about total regulatory takings. The Fifth Amendment provides that if the government takes your property, it must be for a public use and the government must give you "just compensation," with that compensation generally considered fair market value. Government actions like rezoning affect property values, depriving you of uses of your property. If government regulation becomes so comprehensive that you can't make any meaningful use of your property, then it becomes a total regulatory taking, triggering the Taking Clause protections, and the government has to pay you fair market value.

Through regulation, government can influence where you live, what you can do in your house, what sort of permits you need for your home or your car, what you can build, and what sorts of chemicals or materials you can use. But if you can still meaningfully use the property, you can't make the government compensate you for it.

PLANNING FOR THE FUTURE

Ownership as part of a Sovereign Society goes beyond daily matters and low taxes, nonexcessive regulation, and living debt-free. Those measures are all about playing defense. Beyond that, constitutional conservatism is about going on the offense to acquire things that you need over a lifetime.

You must own your own retirement. Unless you drop dead while still able to work, at some point you'll be alive but unable to bring in a paycheck. Beyond not being strangled by debt, you need to be able to save and invest enough money to live comfortably after you're no longer working. You need to have compound interest working for you, not against you. Although millions of people are understandably grateful for the safety net that Social Security provides to seniors today, the serious downside is that the majority of seniors rely upon Social Security for the majority of their retirement income. As we discuss in Chapter 13, Social Security as we know it will not exist a generation from now. Unless we fundamentally reorient ourselves on a nationwide level to fund our own retirements, millions of elderly Americans will be left destitute.

Each family must own its own home. Shelter is a necessity not just for individuals, but even more so for a family to be together. You need the psychological security of a place to call your own. This is especially important for children, to give them a feeling of calm and safety. People prove to be better stewards of property that they own, deriving a sense of self-respect out of managing and tending their home.

Each family must own its own healthcare. Each of us gets sick at some point. Although better nutrition, sanitation, and shelter allow people to live longer, the main reason the average life expectancy today is 78, versus only 47 in the year 1900, is advances in medicine. There are countless maladies that would kill so many people each year were it not for modern methods of detecting, diagnosing, and treating illnesses. Both of your authors have experienced health episodes that could have killed us a century ago, and either you or someone close to you can surely say the same. You must be in charge of your own healthcare and be able to make medical decisions for you and your family. You can never be sovereign over your government if it holds the strings to your health.

Each family must own its own education, meaning both your own education as well as your children's. Education is the doorway to opportunity, to develop an understanding of the world and a marketable skill set to make a living. It is the path to finding a job that pays well, that you enjoy, and that you can do well. It's what equips you to make sense of those things that affect you, to inform you as a voter and a citizen, to work within your community to benefit society, and to help raise your children and provide for their needs.

You must own all of these things. If the government controls your retirement, then you are enslaved to government in your older years. If you rely upon the government for a home, then you are always at the mercy of the government choosing to tell you what you must do if you want to have a place to sleep. If government controls your healthcare, then your life—or the lives of your children—could be at risk if you get on the wrong side of the state. And if government controls your children's education, then government will control how your children are trained to think of themselves, their world—and their government.

You can never be sovereign—never be truly free—unless these key economic principles in the Constitution keep you from being dependent on your government. You or a family member in your house must have a job, you must not live in debt, and you must own your retirement, home, healthcare, and education.

KEYS 4 AND 5: SOCIAL KEYS TO A SOVEREIGN SOCIETY

As we've noted before, one of the greatest mistakes of many Republicans and so-called partial conservatives is seeking to redefine conservatism as an exclusively economic philosophy. But as we saw in Chapters 2 and 3, true economic conservative policies cannot succeed in the long run without stable and flourishing families. In other words, economic conservatism cannot endure without social conservatism.

Two principles of constitutional conservatism, and keys for a Sovereign Society rooted in social conservatism, are as American as Mom and apple pie: faith and family.

Key 4: Family

A fact that liberal cultural and media elites bury is that America isn't just about individual freedom. America is about the freedom and rights of individuals *and* families.

There's an old saying, "As goes the family, so goes the nation." It's an old saying because you don't hear it anymore. That's because the Far Left doesn't want you thinking about it.

To build on what we said in Chapters 2 and 3: A liberal socialist agenda cannot succeed in America if American families stay strong, but a liberal socialist agenda cannot be stopped if America's families fail or fall apart. Therefore traditional families are one of the keys to a resurgence of constitutional conservatism; conservatism cannot endure without them.

This is true in terms of occupations and income. It's easier for a single adult without children; that's a one-person family. But raising children and managing a household is a full-time job in its own right, one that doesn't come with a paycheck. It is a lie of the Left to say that every adult must have a job. It's rather the case that every family must be free to figure out its own division of labor. Many decide to be two-income families. Others decide to be dual income until they have children, and then have one parent stay home or work part-time. Others decide to have a grandparent live with them. Thus on matters of employment—such as the income taxes that a family must deal with—we need to regard families not as individuals, but as the fundamental units of society, with individuals treated as one-person families.

It's also true in terms of ownership. Society encourages spouses to keep separate property, money, etc. That's a recipe for separation and divorce. If you choose to get married and have children—a choice that you freely make in this country—then you have an identity as a family as well as an individual. Every house should be in the name of both spouses, or in some form of family trust. Bank accounts and investment accounts should be joint. Major assets such as cars should have both spouses on the title. Ownership should be at the family level, not split up like a business partnership, of individuals who can just walk away at will.

This is important for marriages. Both of your authors know stay-at-home mothers who, after raising their children, saw their husbands leave them for a young, attractive woman; the abandoned mother had to fend for herself. Ownership means owning what you need to be sovereign—home, healthcare, retirement, etc.—on a *family* level to make sure *everyone* is cared for. That's how you help avoid people suddenly being foisted on welfare at society's expense. As children grow up and start working, then of course they start to accumulate their own assets. But once they get married, they need the example of loving and giving parents who care for each other and share all things in common with themselves, rather than hoarding important assets for exclusively personal use.

The law should recognize the value of family. It should be recognized in the tax code, which is why in Chapter 7 we argue in favor of a Family Flat Tax, which among other things eliminates the marriage penalty. Although divorce is an unfortunate reality in every culture, divorce laws should encourage reconciliation and protect children as much as possible, and protect stay-at-home spouses. In the event of death, laws should protect spouses and children, and protect family businesses by abolishing the Death Tax. Laws must protect the rights of parents to make decisions for educating their children, practicing their religious faith, and raising and disciplining their children. The law should protect the weakest among us, the unborn, as human beings with the right to live. It should protect marriage as the sacred union of one man and one woman. Laws should be family friendly.

Key 5: Faith

The fifth key to a Sovereign Society arising from constitutional conservatism is faith. America was founded as a nation of faith. Although most Americans with a personal faith profess to be Christians, we have a rich diversity of faith in this nation.

That faith drives and sustains us as a nation. The teachings in countless churches across the country serve as a moral foundation for America, informing the consciences of countless millions. People should not murder or steal. People should be honest and trustworthy.

People should be compassionate, caring, and giving. People should be faithful to their spouse and love their children. Family and country are things worth fighting for, and if necessary, dying for. People will be held accountable by an all-knowing, all-powerful, all-present God for everything that they say and do.

The majority of Americans claim to be Christian, but the underlying numbers show a much more diverse religious environment. Many millions believe basic biblical teaching, but millions more do not. Many who call themselves Christian do not believe core historical doctrines of the Christian faith, such as the virgin birth and divinity of Jesus Christ, his sacrificial death on the cross, bodily resurrection from the grave, ascension into Heaven, or eventual return in glory to judge all of humanity.

The diversity is also found within the various camps of Christendom. Within Protestant circles—and even among some who call themselves Evangelical—millions don't believe the basic doctrines that every person is a sinner in need of a savior, and that a person is saved by grace alone, through faith alone in Christ alone. Within Catholic circles, millions do not believe in one or more sacraments of the Church.

Outside Christendom, there's even more variety. Among millions of Jews, Muslims, Hindus, Buddhists, and people of every faith there are countless variations. In fact, our official policies of religious tolerance and free practice—policies that you'll see in Chapter 9 are under attack—make us a very diverse nation on matters of faith.

The bottom line is that in America you have the constitutional right to be theologically wrong. While God may not give you the right to be wrong about him, that's an issue between you and your Maker, not something for the government to decide.

American society benefits nonetheless from well over 200 million of our fellow citizens sincerely holding some sort of defining faith from which they derive moral principles that inform their daily actions. That's why in this country the police don't beat people or extort them for money. That's why our soldiers don't rape good-looking women walking down the street or kill people who owe them money. That's why most business deals take place with both sides keeping up their end of the bargain, and with courts ready to enforce legal compliance by those few who deceive or defraud. That's why people work hard: They're looking to the future, working for something greater than themselves. That's why Americans give more to charity and the needy than does any other nation on earth.

This is not to say that a person without religious faith can't be a great American. Many Americans—whether as secular humanists, spiritualists, or holding on to basic principles like karma—live their lives in an honorable and productive fashion. A person can hold to Judeo-Christian morality without the accompanying Christian faith. It's just harder for them to explain why they believe as they do.

To look at the result of a lack of faith, just look at Europe. These countries are similar to us in many regards, as being intelligent, cultured, high-tech, and having access to considerable wealth. Yet their economies are in the dumps, unemployment is high and doesn't improve, adultery rates are high, and there are fewer stable marriages, which, combined with their high rates of aborting their unborn, results in a low birth rate. Europe is a spiritual vacuum, a vacuum that is being filled by a flood of Islamic radicals, decadent existentialists, nihilists, and people who are unwilling to fight for themselves, their children, or their way of life. Although rich and beautiful and with many fine people, Europe suffers from a lack of faith.

One critical aspect of how faith makes us different from most other countries is our allegiance to transcendent truths. Some things are objectively right and true, regardless of popular opinion or current trends. As we'll see in the next chapter, it begins with the second paragraph of the Declaration of Independence: "We hold these truths to be self-evident." Some things are so true that we don't need to explain them, much less apologize for them. We proclaim the truth, and we boldly act upon that which we know to be true and right.

The greatest Republican president since Abraham Lincoln, President Ronald Reagan, explained it this way:

> The truth is, politics and morality are inseparable. And as morality's foundation is religion, religion and politics are necessarily related. We need religion as a guide. We need it because we are imperfect, and our government needs the church, because only those humble enough to

admit they're sinners can bring to democracy the tolerance it requires in order to survive.

The state is nothing more than a reflection of its citizens; the more decent the citizens, the more decent the state. If you practice a religion, whether you're Catholic, Protestant, Jewish, or guided by some other faith, then your private life will be influenced by a sense of moral obligation, and so, too, will your public life. . . .

Without God, there is no virtue, because there's no prompting of the conscience. Without God, we're mired in the material, that flat world that tells us only what the senses perceive. Without God, there is a coarsening of society. And without God, democracy will not and cannot long endure. If we ever forget that we're one nation under God, then we will be a nation gone under.[8]

America's faith and devotion is what makes us a Shining City on a Hill, as one of the first sermons preached in America called us. We have riches and power like no nation has ever seen. We have limitless opportunities. It makes us a land that millions are willing to leave everything to travel to and make their home. And it makes us a country where our countrymen are willing to go to another country to fight and die for freedom. We seize none of their land, instead respectfully asking for just enough land to bury our dead.

More on faith and family in Chapter 9.

SECURITY

The next key has to do with security. The paramount function of any national government is security. A nation-state exists in large part to protect the lives of its citizens. If it fails to do that, little else matters.

The concept of security is perhaps the most dangerous governmental concept, in that it's the one most subject to abuse. Authoritarian and totalitarian regimes maintain their draconian oppression over their people in the name of "internal security."

The fact that something that can be so abused is also essential to freedom is what makes a conservative concept of security a principle of constitutional conservatism that is necessary for a Sovereign Society.

Key 6: Security

The sixth key to a Sovereign Society derived from constitutional conservatism is security. This security is divided between federal and state levels of government, and is profoundly different depending on whether we're talking about foreign threats to national security or about domestic threats to individual citizens, as we examine in Chapter 11.

Constitutional conservatism holds that the federal government has little law enforcement power. Law enforcement is mostly a state and local issue. Under our federal system of government—explained in the next chapter—public safety and punishing crime is mostly an issue over which the Framers did not want the central government to wield power over the people.

In those aspects of law enforcement where there is a federal role, the Constitution draws a bright line between national security and law enforcement. Law enforcement is a domestic policy issue, while national security involves foreign policy. Congress is in the lead for making provisions for law enforcement under Article I of the Constitution, while the president as commander in chief is in the lead for national security under Article II. The courts are the central decision makers in law enforcement under Article III, but Article III gives them almost no power to be involved in national security issues. In law enforcement the targets are criminal defendants who are presumed innocent and given the full range of constitutional rights. In national security against foreign threats, the targets are military, to whom we give certain rights by federal statutes but who are entitled to no constitutional rights.

When many people think of security, they specifically think of national security. A conservative foreign policy is one predicated upon strength. It's one in which we do not project force abroad unnecessarily or unwisely. But nonetheless it's one in which we have power that's terrifying in its sheer magnitude, as a stern and silent message to the world that if threatened, we can respond with unfathomable force.

A perfect example was shortly before the Persian Gulf War, when Secretary of State James Baker sat down across from his Iraqi counterparts. Knowing that we were on the verge of war, Baker told the Iraqis that if they used weapons of mass destruction against American troops, we were willing to utterly annihilate them. They got the picture, and Iraqi nerve gas and mustard gas never showed up on the battlefield.

Constitutional conservatism requires us to make the necessary investments to ensure we have the best-trained, best-equipped military in the world. We also make those investments in our intelligence agencies, to know what's going on in the world and detect threats, and to respond with precision on the battlefield. And we invest in all the parts of our national security apparatus to provide the necessary support for these military and intelligence capabilities.

Constitutional conservatism also understands the critical role that private gun ownership plays in a free society. As we show in detail in Chapter 10, the Supreme Court and lower judicial tribunals recognize that the Second Amendment plays three roles in our republic. The first is to enable every law-abiding citizen to protect his life, family, and property against criminal elements in society. The second is to ensure that the entire citizenry is able to hold our land against any foreign invader that overcomes our armed forces; the United States is thus made unconquerable. And the third is to protect the American people against their own federal government in the event of a tyrannical regime's trying to seize power after the people have voted that government out of office. The right of peaceable and law-abiding private citizens to own and keep firearms is one of the most distinctive rights enjoyed in America, and James Madison noted that almost all other nations fear their people holding them accountable by an ultimate check against government oppression.[9]

Security is therefore a key to a Sovereign Society. A truly free people must have a strong military for use abroad, and effective law enforcement and counterterrorism forces to protect ordinary people in their daily lives. In such a free culture, there's a strict separation between how we regard foreign threats to our security versus how we deal with our own citizens in law enforcement, where the latter possess all sorts of rights not held by the former. And as the Second Amendment to our Constitution declares, the bulk of our citizens well armed, "being essential to the security of a free state, the right of the people to keep and bear arms, shall not be infringed."[10]

PHILOSOPHICAL

The two final principles of constitutional conservatism are philosophical. They're derived entirely from the structure of the Constitution, as part of the separation of powers built into the fabric of how our government is designed.

That design is to keep the government from being able to direct all of its power against us as American citizens. In *The Federalist* No. 51, James Madison explains that the multiple parts and levels of our government are set in tension with each other because "ambition must be made to counteract ambition." In other words, if you split governmental power between various power centers in such a way that no one part of government can expand without threatening or diminishing another part, then that other part will push back in its own self-interest. With the government thus effectively limiting itself, the people will remain free.

One of the greatest victories of the Left over the past fifty years has been to get the American people to the point where they don't even know the governmental philosophy behind our form of government. They're not even taught what the Constitution is all about. Your author Klukowski has a recent story that illustrates this point.

I was talking with my friend Mitch while driving to lunch in Hawaii. We were there with our wives for a wedding, who were with the bride as she was getting ready. Mitch lives in California and wanted my take on the California same-sex marriage decision.

Trying to make the case for same-sex marriage, Mitch (a businessman who's liberal on social issues) said, "For me, it comes down to this: What's the Constitution all about? Equality. It says all men are created equal. So there it is. If you can get married and I can get married, why can't someone who's gay get married?"

It makes perfect sense, except that it profoundly misunderstands the Constitution (as well as the definition of "marriage"). First, as discussed in the next chapter, the phrase "all men are created equal" is found in the Declaration, not the Constitution. Second, the Constitution is *not* about equality.

The Constitution is about creating a central government of strictly limited powers. It's about taking only certain narrow areas of policy—such as foreign diplomacy, the military, interstate commerce, and copyrights—and putting a national government in charge. Even then the Framers didn't trust the idea of a unified federal government, so the Constitution split governmental power into three categories— legislative, executive, and judicial—and assigned each to a separate branch of government. Aside from those narrow areas, each of which is explicitly mentioned in the Constitution, the individual states were to remain completely sovereign in terms of what they do.

Seen in that light, the California same-sex marriage case is a perfect example of why America has gotten so far off track: It violates the Constitution. As we'll see in Chapter 9, marriage is mentioned nowhere in the Constitution. Although the Supreme Court declared an implied right to marriage decades ago, such a right is protected only if it's rooted in our national history back to the founding of the United States, showing that such a liberty is essential to an American scheme of liberty. No one can argue that same-sex marriage is deeply rooted in American history; same-sex marriage has been around only since 2003, not since 1787. So every American's gut reaction should be that a federal judge has no business telling the people of any sovereign state that they need to create same-sex marriage.

My friend is an intelligent, well-informed citizen. He thinks through issues, and discusses them to understand them better. Our conversation shows how successful the Left has been at deceiving whole generations of Americans as to what our Supreme Law is all about. There cannot be a resurgence in conservatism and a return to constitutional government unless we educate the next generation as to our form of government, and its proper role in our lives.

Key 7: Federalism

The seventh key to a Sovereign Society derived from constitutional conservatism is federalism. That's the principle that the Constitution vests the federal government with power to act in certain specified areas, and that outside those areas the fifty states are sovereign republics with complete autonomy to make laws reflecting their values and priorities.

THE REAL FOURTEENTH AMENDMENT

You can't understand federalism without understanding the Fourteenth Amendment. After the Civil War, the American people adopted the Thirteenth Amendment to ban slavery. Realizing that didn't go far enough, in 1868 they adopted the Fourteenth Amendment to remake the federal-state balance of power in the Constitution.[11]

Constitutional conservatism doesn't make sense outside understanding several parts of the Fourteenth Amendment. It declares that people born in the United States and subject to our national jurisdiction are American citizens. (We discuss this in Chapter 12 on immigration.) It declares that no state may violate the rights of U.S. citizens, and that all people in the United States must receive due process and equal protection of the laws whether citizens or not.

This completely changes the federalist system in two respects. First, the Fourteenth Amendment empowers the federal government to enact legislation to carry out the purposes of enforcing federal issues in the states.[12]

Second, the Bill of Rights originally gave American citizens rights only against the federal government; you couldn't enforce those rights against the states.[13] The Fourteenth Amendment extended federal rights that are deemed *fundamental rights* to also be rights against the states.[14] Fundamental rights are those that are "deeply rooted in this Nation's history and tradition . . . such that neither liberty nor justice would exist if they were sacrificed."[15] These are rights rooted so deeply in our history and tradition that they're "necessary to an Anglo-American regime of ordered liberty."[16] These fundamental rights include most—but not all—of those enumerated in the Bill of Rights.[17] The Supreme Court over the past century has also recognized several rights that are not found in the Constitution—called *implied rights*—as also enforceable against the states, such as the right to get married or the right to raise your children.[18]

But there are limits to these expansions of federal power and federal rights. Congress's laws to enforce the Fourteenth Amendment are constitutional only so long as they are congruent and proportional.[19] And federal rights are enforceable against the states only if they are fundamental, and must be narrowly and carefully defined if the right is an implied right not found in the Constitution's text.[20] So even while enlarging the federal government against the states, the Constitution works to protect state sovereignty.

THAT'S A CRIME

A second aspect of federalism, one which is a virtually unknown part of the explosion of federal power, is *overcriminalization*. That's the federal government creating so many new crimes, and defining them so broadly, that the government has a hook to prosecute and even imprison almost anyone it wants.

The number of federal crimes has exploded in recent years. In 1980 there were around 3,000 criminal statutes in the U.S. Code, meaning 3,000 separate crimes. Today there are over 4,500. What's worse, many statutes also give administrative officials the power to declare many more things to be crimes, and the best government estimate is that federal crimes now number in the tens of thousands.[21] (We congratulate our friends at the Heritage Foundation for their groundbreaking work on this issue.)

Two aspects of overcriminalization are especially alarming. Many of these criminal laws are worded so broadly and vaguely that government officials have broad and dangerous latitude to bring charges on a whole host of things. A conservative view of government never allows government such power. The second is that although an essential element of most crimes is mens rea—some kind of intent to commit a crime, or at least a knowledge that what you're doing is wrong—most of these new federal laws have no mental component.[22] Simply doing something as mundane as buying fish for your restaurant that you didn't even know had been harvested from protected waters can land you in federal prison.[23] Between those two aspects, if the federal government wants to charge you with a crime entailing jail time, it can. If you're innocent you might beat the rap after years of litigation, but it could bankrupt you and cost you your sanity as well.

The power to declare and punish crimes has always been a state issue, not a federal issue. In the next chapter you'll learn that states have police power, which enables them to make laws for social order and public safety and morality, among other things. That's the basis for most criminal laws; they are moral value judgments by society. The state has police power, but the federal government does not. Thus historically the only federal crimes were those pertaining to the issues the Constitution commits to the feds, such as copyright infringements or tax evasion. It was a check on national power to have most criminal issues be state issues.

Although it's often said that the power to tax is the power to destroy, it's equally true—or even more true—to say that the power to prosecute is the power to destroy. The power to take someone's liberty by putting them behind bars, or to take someone's life, is a power that can motivate like no other. On civil charges and penalties, what can they do? Fine you ten thousand dollars? Maybe take your house? Terrible things, but you can make it through. But tell someone that you're going to put them in prison for twenty years, that they'll never see their children until their children are middle-aged, that they'll lose their spouse, that they'll lose all they care for, that's *real* power to coerce. It's frightening, irresistible power. That's what the federal government does through overcriminalization. It violates federalism, and it's unconstitutional.

THE BENEFIT OF LIBERTARIANS, AND
THE DANGER OF RADICAL LIBERTARIANS

When Republicans have strayed from constitutional principles in marching toward big-government programs, but programs that weren't as big as Democrats wanted, libertarians (whether or not they were part of the Libertarian Party) have often provided a helpful voice to return to the text and meaning of the Constitution.

Many libertarians have been helpful in that regard. Andrew Breitbart has helped advance free speech through his series of websites such as Breitbart.com, BigGovernment.com, BigHollywood.com, BigJournalism.com, and BigPeace.com. (Both of your authors are contributors to these outlets.) Judge Andrew Napolitano provides a valuable voice on Fox News Channel and Fox Business Network. Curt Levey is a helpful voice on judicial nominations and judicial restraint through his Committee for Justice. David Kopel is a leading authority on the Second Amendment, at the Independence Institute and Cato

Institute. The Competitive Enterprise Institute has been a very positive contributor to public debate on economics and regulation, with friends such as Fred Smith and Christine Hall focused on building coalitions to expand freedom. Many of the patriots at the Club for Growth and the National Taxpayers Union are libertarians; your author Blackwell serves on the boards of both organizations.

These and many other people have been helpful and productive advocates for looking to the Constitution and ending the insanity. Many aspects of constitutional conservatism are so fully embraced by libertarians that they would claim these issues as their own, and we welcome their help and support. These people are part of the solution.

Radical Libertarians

Then, however, there are the "radical libertarians." They haven't been part of the solution; they're instead often part of the problem. They endanger the Constitution on all three fronts we discuss in this book: economic, social, and national security.

The social record of radical libertarians matches that of the Far Left. Partial-birth abortion is a hideous form of infanticide, yet the Cato Institute (where there are many fine and helpful libertarians, especially on economic issues like Social Security) filed a brief calling for the U.S. Supreme Court to strike down the federal partial-birth abortion ban. Arguments that that is the principled constitutional stand are nonsense. The Supreme Court wrongly declared a federal constitutional right to abortion, and until the judicial disgrace of *Roe v. Wade* is overturned, the principled constitutional argument is that the federal government can place restrictions on abortion just like the states, while we look forward to the day when we protect human life.

Another social issue is marriage, where Cato chairman Robert Levy joined forces with ultra-left authoritarian John Podesta to call for the U.S. Supreme Court to declare a constitutional right to same-sex marriage and strike down every state law across America defending marriage as the union of a man and woman. They called laws protecting traditional marriage "wrongful discrimination" that "serve[s] no purpose."[24] Similarly, David Boaz, who is executive vice president of Cato, ridicules not only those who stand for traditional marriage, but also those who are pro-life, concluding an op-ed on this topic by saying, "social conservatives point to a real problem and then offer phony solutions."[25] The principled constitutional approach for libertarians is to say that since the Constitution is silent on marriage, every state in America should be free to define marriage as they see fit without federal interference.

On economics, radical libertarians in *McDonald v. Chicago* called for the Supreme Court in 2010 to overrule the *Slaughter-House Cases*. In *Slaughter-House*, some Louisiana butchers challenged a state law giving a monopoly for slaughtering animals within city limits, arguing that this statute violated the "privileges or immunities" guaranteed by the Fourteenth Amendment.[26] The Court rejected this argument,[27] noting that states have police power to regulate public health.[28] The Court held that the Privileges or Immunities Clause secures rights that come from the U.S. Constitution,[29] and held that no federal right was implicated by the Louisiana law.[30]

The principled position is that the Supreme Court holding Louisiana's law unconstitutional would have been gross judicial activism. The Constitution is silent about butchering animals; there's no constitutional provision against state laws regulating butchering within cities. The plaintiffs in *Slaughter-House* were asking the Court to judicially invent a right out of thin air, and to use it to strike down an important public health law adopted by the people's elected legislators.

Overruling the *Slaughter-House Cases* would empower federal courts to declare countless new economic rights found nowhere in the Constitution. Every state labor law, employment law, corporate law, tort reform law, and minimum wage law, as well as every county or city zoning ordinance or building code, could be struck down by an *unelected* federal judge. The fact that striking down such a law would enhance individual freedom is irrelevant; where the Constitution is silent, the courts should be silent, too.

All this has two things in common with the Far Left. The first is that this form of judicial activism is the end of federalism. Instead of fifty states free to act and experiment as they see fit, it's calling for federal courts to declare universal national standards on everything.

Living by the will of unelected judges would effectively eradicate state governments, rendering states insignificant subdivisions of the national government. The second is that it's a form of condescending paternalism, that millions of ordinary people are too stupid to make their own constitutions and laws, have no right to make laws embodying their values, and need a law-trained elite to use the courts to declare national standards for all of us to create a fair and just society.

Well-meaning principled libertarians should not be confused with these radical libertarians.

THE SPIRIT OF REAGAN TO REVIVE
FEDERALISM FOR THE FUTURE

We need to revive the spirit of Ronald Reagan when it comes to federalism. President Reagan issued Executive Order 12612 in 1987. This order called for preempting the states only when authorized by Congress, maximizing state discretion on implementing federal programs, restraining the feds from creating national standards in programs, and not proposing legislation that interferes with state autonomy. It also required an officer in every department to oversee compliance with this order.[31] Not surprisingly, this order was revoked by Bill Clinton in 1998.[32] The next president should reissue that order, and put real teeth in it to enforce federalism.

Federalism allows America to have fifty separate "laboratories of democracy," to famously paraphrase Justice Louis Brandeis.[33] Fifty different economies, fifty different sets of commercial, corporate, and labor laws. Fifty different educational systems. Fifty different sets of social values and moral laws. It allows the states to compete, and for the American people to have an option of fifty different republics in which to live while still living in America. It gives every American either the right to make their state a place that reflects their values and provides the best place to live for them and their family, or the freedom to move to a state that better embodies that family's understanding of liberty and the pursuit of happiness.

As Governor Rick Perry of Texas recently wrote, "In short, it is not America that is broken; it is Washington that is broken."[34] When the

Constitution does not make something a federal issue, the more governmental powers we can devolve from the federal government to state and local governments, the better.

Key 8: The Judiciary

The eighth key to a Sovereign Society derived from constitutional conservatism is the federal court system.

We won't spend much space on this now; Chapter 6 tackles the courts (especially the Supreme Court). But two points need to be made here about what is necessary to restore true freedom in America.

JUDICIAL RESTRAINT

The first is judicial restraint. It's the simple principle that where the Constitution or federal law speaks, judges are obligated to uphold them. Where the Constitution or law is silent, then the courts must be silent, too, and allow the people to work their will through the democratic process of holding elected officials accountable for their actions.

Justice John Paul Stevens—a strident liberal—wrote for a unanimous Supreme Court, "State legislation which has some effect on individual liberty or privacy may not be held unconstitutional simply because a court finds it unnecessary, in whole or in part."[35] Even liberal Supreme Court justices have to admit that it's not the job of a judge to do whatever is "right" or "just" or "fair." They must be bound by what We the People have decided to enshrine in our Constitution, and they do not have power to act where we do not give them license to act.

ORIGINALISM

The second is originalism. Although discussed more in Chapter 6, there is only one permissible way to interpret the Constitution or any law. The Constitution should be interpreted according to the original meaning of its terms. This is not original intent, because that allows creative lawyers to quote just one Framer and argue that his words represent what all the Framers intended. Instead, originalism restricts constitutional interpretation to discovering the original meaning of each word and phrase, as that meaning was understood by the voters of the time.

As the Supreme Court itself has declared, "The Constitution was written to be understood by the voters; its words and phrases were used in their normal and ordinary, as distinguished from technical, meaning; where the intention is clear, there is no room for construction and no excuse for interpolation or addition."[36] We the People adopted the Constitution as a sovereign act. We voted on certain exact words written on paper that the voters could read and understand. Therefore the only legitimate way for the courts to interpret the Constitution is according to the meaning that the voters understood when they voted to approve those words.

Judges usurp the sovereignty of the people and the role of the elected branches when they abuse their power to reinterpret the Constitution according to their own personal or political agenda. Originalism is the most effective way to restrain judges from ruining our democratic republic.

Courts are the prism through which actions of the political branches—legislative and executive, both federal and state—are examined. They are the branch empowered to take what our leaders do, hold those actions alongside the Constitution, and ensure that our politicians adhere to the Supreme Law of the Land. For constitutional conservatism to give rise to a Sovereign Society, we need courts that are faithful to the U.S. Constitution.

The eight keys of constitutional conservatism can liberate the American people. By creating a Sovereign Society, We the People can restore constitutional government as it existed two hundred years ago, laying a solid foundation of liberty for our children for the next two hundred years.

5

THE TENFOLD PROMISE OF AMERICA

"Ours was the first revolution in the history of mankind that truly reversed the course of government, and with three little words: 'We the People.' 'We the People' tell the government what to do; it doesn't tell us. . . . Almost all the world's constitutions are documents in which governments tell the people what their privileges are. Our Constitution is a document in which 'We the People' tell the government what it is allowed to do."

—Ronald Reagan, Farewell Address to the Nation, January 11, 1989

O f all the nations on earth, the United States of America is a land of promise. We truly are the land of the free and the home of the brave. For more than a century, the Statue of Liberty in New York Harbor has served as a symbol the world over for a land of liberty and opportunity, as millions immigrated from the Old World through Ellis Island.

The first Europeans to visit North America after Columbus were traders. The British sent expeditions during the 1500s to our eastern shore to develop and harvest agricultural products, and also to search for gold and other treasure. Settlements such as Jamestown (founded in 1607) and at other locations in Virginia, Maryland, and North Carolina were established for commercial purposes.

But in November 1620, a group of Separatist Puritans came to the New World to build exactly that—a new world. They did so to create a God-honoring society, one free from centuries of European decadence that would uphold ideal principles of morality in civil life. Their first charter of government, the Mayflower Compact, begins as follows and reads in part:

> In the name of God, amen. We whose names are underwritten, the loyal
> subjects of our dread sovereign lord King James . . . Having undertaken,
> for the glory of God and the advancement of the Christian faith and
> honour of our king and country, a voyage to plant the first colony in the
> northern parts of Virginia . . .

They considered themselves lawful subjects of the British Crown, but wanted to establish a semi-independent colony where they could start over. (They also didn't fully appreciate at first how far north they were from Virginia, landing in modern-day Massachusetts.)

As others came to America during those colonial days, they did so for various reasons. Many more likewise came for religious liberty, such as the Quakers settling Pennsylvania.[1] As noted, many came for economic reasons. Others settled here for political freedom. Everyone was looking for a land of opportunity, one where they could pursue whatever was profoundly important to them and had been denied to them in their homeland.

Over time the British government became oppressive. Petitions to change course were met with scorn and derision.[2]

Just as things reached a boiling point, there came the Shot Heard Round the World on April 19, 1775. British general Thomas Gage ordered his redcoat soldiers to march to the armory at Concord, Massachusetts, to seize the colonists' firearms and ammunition. (The British understood that you need to disarm a population if you wish to subjugate the people, as we discuss later.) Colonists went out fully armed, not to spark a confrontation but instead to make a statement. British soldiers opened fire on colonists—both men and their sons, still boys. Having been forced into a situation where we were to be subjugated, America declared its independence from Great Britain and went to war to fight for freedom.

But the Founders understood that antigovernment action is just rebellion leading to anarchy unless you take positive steps to affirmatively create a governmental structure when you throw off the existing structure. As we explained in the Introduction, the Founders all held to the classical view of humanity. They knew that people needed government because "men are not angels," but also that government must be strictly limited because any government is run by those same nonangelic people.

So the Founders began constructing a government. During this time the Founders put forth two documents embodying the promise of America. They are the Declaration of Independence and the Constitution of the United States. The first of these embodied fundamental principles regarding our founding philosophy and political theory, enshrining these principles in our founding charter, the Declaration. And through trial and error, the Framers began an experiment that lasted eleven years, exploring different aspects of how to create an enduring republic, the end result of which was the Constitution.

The Founders embraced the vision of the Puritan Pilgrims of 1620, that America is a Shining City on a Hill—the same vision revived by Ronald Reagan two centuries after the Founding. They recognized the profound and unprecedented promise of America. The two governing documents they gave embody the tenfold promise of America for all generations—including our current generation, if we will only embrace it once again.

The Fivefold Promise of the Declaration of Independence

In declaring independence, the Founding Fathers wanted to publish a principled statement whose scope was broader than the immediate conflict with Britain. Thomas Jefferson (the primary author) wanted a document that would go far beyond itemizing the long list of abuses that King George III and the British Parliament had inflicted on the colonies, instead invoking natural law and proclaiming the underlying principles that make any government just and legitimate.

The Declaration begins:

> When in the course of human events it becomes necessary for one people to dissolve the political bands that have connected them to another and to assume among the powers of the earth, the separate and equal station to which the laws of nature and of nature's God entitle them,

a decent respect for the opinions of mankind requires that they should give the reasons which impel them to the separation.

Our Founders understood that they were doing something unprecedented. For the first time in human history, a nation-sized body of people with a preexisting economic system and shared legal philosophy and basic religious faith were seeking to learn from all the lessons of human experience over the centuries to design the best governmental system ever created. For the first time in known history, a people were going to choose their own form of government.

They invoked laws higher than the laws of men. There are natural laws that justified what they did. Even higher, the laws of God entitled them to be independent.

"We hold these truths to be self-evident." That is a very genteel, polite, colonial way of saying, "Any knucklehead ought to be able to figure this out." That in itself flies in the face of postmodern relativism and political correctness. Modern culture would expect something like, "We're currently inclined to think that the available evidence leads us to the following opinions, though we concede that other opinions could be equally valid, and we don't want to go out on a limb." The Founders believed in transcendent truth, that some things are objectively true and can be discerned from the world around us, and that we can proclaim such things to be true and oppose those who reject these truths.

THE CREATOR WHO MADE US ALL EQUAL

"That all men are created equal." The Declaration's first promise is that all people are created equal. We say it so often that it's a cliché, but in 1776 it was a profound statement. According to the European model (seen on every other inhabited continent on earth), some people were considered inherently worth more than others. The Founders instead proclaimed that every human being is made in the image of Almighty God, possessing an immortal soul and a rational and thoughtful nature.

In that regard every human being is equal. Look around you. We're not equal in terms of height, or weight, or wealth, or athletic ability, or intelligence. But we're all equal in the ways that really matter, in that our worth comes from those attributes that are inherent in our human dignity. No matter what disability you have, no matter that you don't have a family, no matter that you don't have a job, or a car, or even a home. You are worth every bit as much as the president of the United States or any famous person you can think of. All men are created equal.

INALIENABLE RIGHTS

"That they are endowed by their Creator with certain unalienable rights."[3] The second promise is that we have a Creator and our rights come from that Creator, and can never be taken away by government. Some rights are alienable rights, meaning that they can be taken away. A right to drive at a certain speed on the road, or a right to health-care benefits, or a right to perform surgery on a sick person, is a right granted by government, and it can be taken away by government.

Other rights are inalienable. When we speak about "rights," without any adjective, we're referring to inalienable rights. "Inalienable" means no one can take them away. Our rights are not grants from government, they are gifts from God. The Founders understood that and en-shrined it in our founding charter.

"That among these are life, liberty, and the pursuit of happiness." These rights named in the Declaration are given in that specific order for a reason. Life, then liberty, then the pursuit of happiness. Because you can't be free if you're dead. And you can't pursue happiness if you're a slave. Each right can exist only if built on the foundation of the previous one.

From that we see first that the highest reason for the existence of government is to protect innocent life. Some on the Left immediately throw up their guard at this, seeing a natural segue to abortion. But the reality—both historically and philosophically—is that the single great-est purpose for government is to protect innocent people from those who would otherwise kill them. That's why we don't walk around in daily fear that someone who's bigger or stronger will just decide on a whim to kill us to take our wallet, car, or house. The power of govern-ment is ideally a benevolent guardian to protect every innocent human being, especially those who cannot protect themselves.

GOVERNMENT EXISTS TO PROTECT RIGHTS

"That to secure these rights, governments are instituted among men." The third promise is that the purpose of government is to secure your rights. Government doesn't exist to tell us how to live our lives. It doesn't exist to redistribute wealth. It certainly doesn't exist to coerce us to serve the state in the name of the "collective good." It doesn't exist to give you a basket of handouts paid for by someone else or to tell you whom to blame for whatever makes you unhappy at the moment.

It exists instead to protect your personal rights. It does this through passing laws that respect your rights. It also does it through faithfully administering and enforcing those laws that have been passed for your benefit. And it does it through courts that faithfully interpret and apply those laws.

GOVERNMENT BY CONSENT OF THE GOVERNED

"Deriving their just power from the consent of the governed." The fourth promise is that the American government continues to have lawful authority over us only by our consent. The definition of a free society is one where government rules by consent of the governed; conversely, tyranny is where government forces its rule upon the people.

We express our consent through the democratic process. The primary way we express consent is through voting. When we vote, we join together to speak as We the People. In that moment we act as the sovereign, choosing to whom we shall temporarily give the power to serve us by ruling our land, and ready to replace on the next Election Day those who fail to justify our confidence. We also express ourselves through speaking, writing, protesting, carrying signs, and many other activities. But all that is primarily designed to affect the way others vote on Election Day, so again we find that we grant our consent—for a limited time—when we go to the polls.

THE RIGHT TO ALTER OR
ABOLISH THE GOVERNMENT

"That whenever a government becomes destructive of these ends, it is the right of the people to alter or abolish it, and institute new government." The fifth and final promise is that we can change the government whenever it becomes destructive of our rights.

We have to be especially careful about this, because it's easy to misinterpret (or for opponents to mischaracterize). As we'll read in Chapter 10, the Supreme Court has recognized that the Second Amendment was put into the Constitution to enable the American people to cast off a tyrannical regime, if any should ever come to power in the United States, by force of arms. However—and this is key—even passionate opposition to the current government never justifies a Second Amendment response. The Second Amendment comes into play only if a president is voted out of office, but then refuses to leave office—holding on to power through fear and military might. So long as we have the right to vote for our rulers, we have the right to throw them off only if we vote them out of office and yet they refuse to relinquish power.

These five guarantees are what the Declaration of Independence promises to the American people. It's America's founding charter. Our country doesn't date its birth from the adoption of the Constitution. We were born when our forebears—chosen by the people—voted to create an independent nation based on these simple, self-evident truths. And from that birth arose the greatest nation the world has ever seen.

The Fivefold Promise of the Constitution

For all the promise of America and the sublimity of the Declaration of Independence, our first national government proved lacking.[4] We were to be one new nation, not thirteen allied nations. The Founders adopted the Articles of Confederation in 1777 to provide a federal government that would orchestrate cooperation between the states, but within a decade it became clear that the states were incompatible in crucial ways. A new charter for government was needed if we were to survive as one nation.

The solution was the Constitution. Delegates from each state gathered in Philadelphia at Independence Hall—the same place where the Declaration of Independence had been signed. Working for months, these delegates to the Constitutional Convention created the magnificent governing document that still reigns as the Supreme Law of the

Land today. It was ratified two years later, in 1789, and the Constitution of the United States established our new federal government, and forever with it our identity as a nation.

This was an inconceivable concept at the time. There had been precursors for a limited government, such as the Magna Carta in 1215 or the English Bill of Rights of 1689. But this amounted to a comprehensive charter of a national government—a written constitution.

No one had ever seen such a thing in 1789. Today in 2011, the U.S. Constitution is the oldest written constitution in the world.

Like the Declaration, the Constitution also contains promises for the American people. It makes five promises, which we seem to have lost sight of as a people. The principles in those promises come up repeatedly throughout this book; they are the essence of constitutional government.

A GOVERNMENT OF ENUMERATED POWERS

The first promise is that the federal government is a government that has only *delegated powers*. We the People vested certain powers in the federal government. It has only the specific powers mentioned in the Constitution, which is to say that the federal government is a government of *enumerated powers*.

This was considered such a crucial point that the Constitution would never have been ratified without an explicit constitutional provision to that effect. That's why the Tenth Amendment was added at the end of the Bill of Rights. It reads, "The powers not delegated to the United States by the Constitution, nor prohibited by it to the states, are reserved to the states respectively, or to the people."[5] Even though voters were assured that they didn't need a Bill of Rights because everyone would understand that the feds could do only what the Constitution said they could do, the American people were not willing to accept any charter of government that did not explicitly make the promise that the new national government would have only specific, delegated powers.

That's why we have a written constitution. The British Constitution was unwritten, philosophically composed of various acts of Parliament and royal decrees. The colonists considered the fact that there was no document definitively setting forth the British Constitution as one of the excuses used by Parliament to do as it pleased. So when it was time for a U.S. Constitution, the American people demanded that our leaders put it in writing.

In the most important and consequential case in American history, *Marbury v. Madison*, the Supreme Court declared, "The powers of [Congress] are defined, and limited; and that those limits may not be mistaken, or forgotten, the constitution is written."[6] Just a few years later, the Court added in another landmark case that the federal government "is acknowledged by all, to be one of enumerated powers. The principle that [the government] can exercise only the powers granted to it . . . is now universally admitted."[7]

The point of a written constitution is so that everyone can see exactly what it says, and also what it doesn't say. It gives all of us exact words, written in plain English, that we can examine and study. And it was given to the voters, so that they could hold accountable any public officer who failed to fulfill his oath of office to support and defend the Constitution.

A GOVERNMENT OF LIMITED JURISDICTION

The second promise is that the federal government's power is limited to certain national issues. Not only does it have only delegated and enumerated powers, they also cover only certain narrow areas of policy.

As noted, the main driver for adopting the Constitution was to replace the failed Articles of Confederation. Specifically, the Articles failed to address all the issues that a functioning nation needed to handle. So the Constitution was designed to deal with the issues that needed to be handled at a national level, and to give the federal government only those powers necessary to achieve these national priorities.

That's why the Constitution is so short, around 4,400 words. (You can read it in thirty minutes.) It creates three branches of government—legislative (Congress), executive (the president), and judicial (the Supreme Court), and specifies how the officers in each branch obtain these offices (either elected or appointed). It specifies the areas of policy where the feds can act, the three main ones of which are regulating interstate commerce, foreign policy, and the military.

Thus the federal government is what the law calls a government of *limited jurisdiction.* Only certain narrow areas were committed to the feds, mainly regarding the three issues we just mentioned, plus an assortment of narrow issues such as patents and copyrights, the establishment of a postal service, and the making of immigration laws. The Framers intended that the states should still be sovereign republics, with authority over most areas of life.

The states are therefore governments of *general jurisdiction.* This means that states have authority to make laws in every area of life, except for those narrow areas where the Constitution says the states cannot act. (For example, states are not allowed to declare war on a foreign country, so Indiana can't declare war on Venezuela.[8]) This means that states have *police power,* which is the power to make laws for public health, safety, morality, and social welfare.[9] Despite what some on the Left will tell you (or what radical libertarians say—see Chapter 3), the states are sovereign to make all these laws, according to the will of the people in each of those states. The federal government—including federal courts—has no right to interfere with the people's sovereignty to control their own local communities.

THE SEPARATION OF POWERS

The third promise is that the federal government has a *separation of powers.* It was not enough for the Framers to limit the jurisdiction of the federal government, and delegate to it only specific, enumerated powers. Beyond that, the Framers wanted to break up governmental power to prevent a monolithic federal government.

The Framers divided government power into three parts. First is Article I's legislative power, which is the power to make laws. That's vested in Congress. Even then, the Congress is split into two houses, with seats in a House of Representatives assigned according to population, and a Senate where each state gets two seats regardless of population. Second is Article II's executive power, which is the power to administer and enforce laws. That's vested solely in the president, though Article II also lays out the framework for government officers serving under the president. Third is in Article III's judicial power, which is the power to interpret and apply the law in lawsuits. That's vested in the Supreme Court, as well as in any lower courts that Congress creates.

By dividing government power into three parts, the Framers created a system where the government would never be a unified structure. For example, in the British system we were escaping, Parliament was supreme; the prime minister and his Cabinet were part of Parliament, and the House of Lords (one of the two chambers of Parliament) was similar to our Supreme Court, acting as the highest court of appeals. In many other countries, there is one supreme ruler, with authority over all aspects of government.

The Framers separated powers to ensure that no one branch of government would have enough power to tyrannize the American people. Each branch would have enough authority to do its duty in serving the American people, but not enough for the servant to become master.

THE SYSTEM OF CHECKS AND BALANCES

The Constitution's fourth promise is the system of *checks and balances*. After dividing the federal power into legislative, executive, and judicial branches, the Framers did something else: They set each of those three branches against the other two to hold them in check. It wasn't enough to break up government power; the Framers wanted the three branches to constantly be in tension with each other.

To Congress, they gave the power to override a president's veto by a two-thirds vote, and no money could be spent by the executive branch unless appropriated by Congress. Between the House and Senate, Congress has the power to impeach and remove any executive officer (including the president) or any federal judge. Only the House can introduce a tax bill. Only the Senate has the power to confirm or reject senior executive branch officers and all federal judges (including Supreme Court justices), as well as the power to ratify or reject treaties signed by the president.

The other two branches have fewer checks, but they're enough. To the president, his check of the legislature is the power to veto bills by Congress. The president's check over the courts is that he's the only person who can nominate federal judges. And the courts' check is the power to declare unconstitutional any law passed by Congress or any action of the president.

THE SOVEREIGN POWER OF WE THE PEOPLE
TO REIGN SUPREME OVER OUR GOVERNMENT

The fifth and final promise is that the people are always sovereign, trumping the federal government. The Constitution includes three provisions to make sure the American people will always be the ultimate sovereign in the United States.

The first is given by Article IV of the Constitution, requiring every state—and with it the United States—to always have a republican form of government. That means a representative government where law-abiding adults have the right to vote. Each state makes its own voting laws. Under those laws, voters have the right to choose at regular intervals—whether that means every two, four, or six years—every legislative officer, the chief executive officer (the governor), and other top government officials.

That means that we get to decide who has power to rule over us. At fixed intervals, those people must stand before us, and we decide whether to allow them to keep governing, or to replace them with someone else.

The second is the power to remove tyrannical rulers who refuse to leave office when we vote them out, as discussed elsewhere in this book. Intended as a last resort, the Second Amendment secures the right to bear arms primarily to ensure that if the government ever completely abandons the Constitution and attempts to retain power after the rulers' terms of office have expired, the American people will never be powerless to hold them to account.

The Supreme Court recognized this anti-tyranny principle in 2008 when it declared that the Second Amendment right to bear arms was written into the Constitution as a "safeguard against tyranny."[10] As Judge Janice Rogers Brown of the D.C. Circuit (whom we discuss more in Chapter 6) explained when she was a justice on the California Supreme Court, "Extant political writings of the [Founding] period repeatedly expressed a dual concern: facilitating the natural right of self-defense and assuring an armed citizenry capable of repelling foreign invaders and quelling tyrannical leaders."[11] The best judicial explanation of the Second Amendment, however, comes from Chief Judge Alex Kozinski of the Ninth Circuit, who wrote:

The Second Amendment is a doomsday provision, one designed for those exceptionally rare circumstances where all other rights have failed—where the government refuses to stand for reelection and silences those who protest; where courts have lost the courage to oppose, or can find no one to enforce their decrees. However improbable these contingencies seem today, facing them unprepared is a mistake a free people get to make only once.[12]

The third is the power to change the Constitution, found in Article V. The Framers knew that any man-made system would be imperfect, so the American people have the power to amend it anytime they choose, with amendments either proposed by Congress or by a Constitutional Convention called by the states. Either way, these amendments must then be ratified by the states. Although this process is difficult in order to prevent amendments from being adopted lightly, the American people are always free to change the Supreme Law of the Land.

Between these three tools, the American people would always be sovereign in this country. As such, government would always be our servant, never our master.

Liberty Promises a Land of Opportunity, Not Results and Entitlements

The common theme throughout the ten-part promise of America found in the Declaration and Constitution is that people are free only to the extent that government is limited. The bigger that government looms, the more it consumes the lives and limits the choices of the people. The American people have the ability to live and act freely only to the extent that government does not constrain them. Therefore the Founders wanted a strictly limited government, so that the sky would be the limit for Americans to live their lives.

The impetus behind these limitations on government power is a profound distrust of all governmental power. The Founders did not share the romantic view of humanity that humans were inherently good and benevolent. Instead they held to the classical view of humanity, that each of us is an imperfect sinner. Each of us has bad impulses and impure motives, and as such none of us can be trusted with un-checked power over our fellow man.

So America is about promising a level playing field where people are free to succeed or fail according to their ability and resources as op-portunities present themselves.

Thus the United States is a country that relies upon rugged indi-vidualism. No one has a right to a job, or healthcare, or housing, or an education. We have government programs in place to help people obtain such things, but those are benevolent acts to help in tough times, not entitlements that a person can sit there and demand. Sadly, too many in America have this sense of entitlement and resent whatever politician has the courage to say that such government handouts are in-consistent with the American ideal. As an unfortunate result, too many politicians are craven and morally decrepit demagogues who pander to the entitlement-minded segment of society, assuring them that they are indeed entitled, slandering those who oppose such entitlements as greedy, selfish, and coldhearted, and promising ever-larger entitlements if reelected. They have embraced the big-government socialism of many countries in Europe and other places around the globe, and have abandoned what it is that makes America different—and better—than other countries.

That's why we're now bankrupt as a nation. Too many politicians lack any fidelity to the principles of the Declaration and the Constitu-tion. They've lost sight of what America is all about. They've tried to make us more like Europe, more like the Old World that we delib-erately chose to leave behind. They try to take the easy road, focusing on the politics of the present without a thought of the horrible conse-quences those policies are inflicting upon our children and grandchil-dren.

It seems that the American people are returning to the tenfold promise of America, to these great truths in the Declaration of In-dependence and the U.S. Constitution. Millions of Americans are embracing the founding principles of our nation. Economically this country is about providing a level playing field, where you can go and do whatever your time, talent, and passion enable you to, as providence presents opportunities. America willingly embraces the possibility of failure with bravery and daring, knowing that in such a wide-open field of liberty, you can shoot for the stars.

The Ultimate Power of We the People: Amending the Constitution

Although both parties have failed the American people, failures have been worse at the federal level than the state level. We must address the sad reality that a dysfunctional government in Washington, D.C., has ill served the American people.

The Founders understood the tendency of government to fail. As discussed in this book, a key part of the solution is limiting the power of the central government. Part of that is done through federalism—keeping the national government narrow in its scope and powers, and empowering state and local governments (which are more responsive to the people) to handle most aspects of governing.

But what do we do when an issue of national significance arises but the national government fails? Even more challenging, how can the American people—We the People—force the national government to address an issue it cannot or will not address?

Not only did We the People adopt the Constitution as our Supreme Law in 1789, we've amended it twenty-seven times. The first ten amendments were enacted together, ratified in 1791 immediately after the Constitution was adopted, and called the Bill of Rights. Also three amendments—the Thirteenth, Fourteenth, and Fifteenth—were passed in rapid succession after the Civil War to end slavery and the denial of civil rights and voting rights to people of color. Aside from those two brief windows, the Constitution has been amended only fifteen times in the 222 years that it's been in force.

There are two reasons why there have been only a handful of amendments made to the Constitution, despite more than one thousand amendments having been proposed over the centuries. Both reasons arise from Article V of the Constitution, where the amendment process is spelled out. The first is that it is extraordinarily difficult to amend the Constitution, which since our founding has been done only through the first method allowed in Article V. Under this method, an amendment can be proposed by a two-thirds supermajority vote in both the U.S. House and the U.S. Senate. The proposed amendment then goes to the states, where it must be ratified by an ordinary majority of the legislatures of three-fourths of the states in the Union. In modern terms, it takes 290 congressmen and 67 senators to propose an amendment, and then 38 states must vote to ratify the proposed amendment to make it part of the Constitution.

That's an extremely high hurdle. But given the stakes, the Founders wanted to make sure that the Constitution couldn't be changed unless there was overwhelming support among the citizens for such a change, so that it would carry the imprimatur that We the People amended the Constitution as a sovereign act of self-government.

The second option allowed under Article V is that the states can propose an amendment through a convention. A Constitutional Convention can be called if the legislatures of two-thirds of the states (currently thirty-four states) pass a resolution calling for such a convention. This convention could then propose amendments by a simple majority vote of the convention delegates, and—as in the first method—those proposals become amendments to the Constitution if they get ratified by three-fourths of the states.

We've never had a Constitutional Convention since our current form of government was adopted in 1789. The reason is simple: the fear of a "runaway convention." A Constitutional Convention can do more than propose constitutional amendments; it can entirely scrap the U.S. Constitution and write a completely new one. It's true that the new Constitution wouldn't take effect unless thirty-eight states ratified it, and that's obviously a tremendous check on the process. But fear over what a Constitutional Convention would do is the primary reason that we've never had one.

Think this fear is unfounded? Don't, because a runaway convention is how we got the Constitution we have today. When the constitutional delegates first arrived at the only Constitutional Convention America ever had, it was to amend the Articles of Confederation that had been the charter of government since America declared independence from Great Britain in 1776. Even though the convention was called to amend the obviously failing Articles, the end result of that process was that on September 17, 1787, at Independence Hall in Philadelphia, the Constitutional Convention proposed an entirely new governmental system for America. That proposed charter was ratified in 1789 as the Constitution of the United States.

FEAR OF CONSTITUTIONAL CONVENTIONS
CAN FORCE CONGRESS'S HAND

One of the amendments proposed through the usual fashion came about as a result of fear of a possible Constitutional Convention. In the original Constitution, U.S. senators represented the states, not the people. As such, state legislatures voted for senators; the people did not vote directly to fill Senate seats.

There was significant populist unrest about senator selections in the late 1800s and early 1900s. First, the Progressive Era was under way, fueled by the spread of socialism and a nonviolent form of Marxism in popular literature. (This era gave us such things as a graduated income tax, a central bank, a Cabinet-level Department of Labor, and elevation of the Department of Agriculture to Cabinet status.) Direct democracy was all the rage in political circles, as seen by the fact that state constitutions adopted during this time—such as that of Arizona, which became a state in 1912—included ballot initiative provisions, where the voters directly vote for specific laws on Election Day, which trump actions of the state legislature. Many Senate seats were given away as political spoils, and many people had the sense that most senators got their seats as part of a corrupt bargain.

There was also plenty of alleged corruption over Senate elections. Over a half-dozen bribery cases involving Senate seats were brought during this period, and deadlocks frequently caused prolonged delays in filling Senate seats. For example, one Delaware seat was vacant for four years. By the time it was filled, the other seat was vacant as well.[13]

Like so many things, one particular scandal became a popular illustration of the problem. William Clark was a wealthy Montana businessman elected to the U.S. Senate by the Montana legislature. In 1899 it was discovered that Clark—who was one of the richest men in America, not just Montana—had bribed legislators. This scandal became a national story that for many people confirmed their cynical view of senatorial elections.

There were widespread calls for direct election of senators. But Article I of the U.S. Constitution specifies that state legislatures make the choice, so a constitutional amendment would be necessary. Needless to say, it was hard to find two-thirds of the Senate to vote in favor of changing the system; doubtless some senators were good inside players in politics but knew they'd be outperformed in a traditional popular election. Not many politicians are keen on giving up a game they know they can win to try a new game they might lose.

Fed up with the current situation, states began calling for a Constitutional Convention so that they could change the manner for electing senators. By 1910, the number of states calling for a convention had almost reached the two-thirds needed. Knowing that a convention would immediately propose the direct election of senators—and fearing what else could be changed in our Supreme Law during a convention—the Senate voted by the necessary supermajority margin, along with the House, to propose an amendment for direct Senate elections.

In 1916, this became a reality when the Seventeenth Amendment was ratified.

THE MADISON AMENDMENT: A POSSIBLE WAY
FOR A LIMITED CONSTITUTIONAL CONVENTION

There might be a third way. We call it the Limited Convention Amendment, one version of which is promoted as the Madison Amendment.

In this book, we will discuss several proposed constitutional amendments that different leaders or groups have called for, some of which we support, and some of which we don't. These span everything from marriage to taxes. They cover economic, social, and national security issues. The Madison Amendment is supported by our friend and conservative leader Colin Hanna and his organization Let Freedom Ring.

As in previous times of crisis, there is enough political will right now in America—if we can only channel it—to enact amendments to the Constitution to address the major structural failures in our national governmental policy. Amending the U.S. Constitution should be done only with the greatest care, because each amendment permanently changes this nation—often in profound ways beyond what the framers of these amendments could have imagined.

There's a legal theory out there that it's possible for the states to call for a "Limited Constitutional Convention," which would consider only the matters specified in the state resolutions calling for a convention. This idea has led some leaders, such as former lieutenant governor André Bauer of South Carolina, to call for such a convention.[14] But the theory of a limited convention is untested, and stands on shaky grounds both historically and legally. The odds are that any convention called would be a general convention with plenary power to propose changes to the Constitution in any manner it wishes, subject to ratification by the states.

What some suggest might work instead is a constitutional amendment that would amend Article V to create a third way to change the Constitution. This amendment would explicitly allow for the states to call a Constitutional Convention to consider constitutional amendments limited to certain subjects. Each state resolution calling for a convention would specify what issues the convention was to consider. A Constitutional Convention would be called to consider whatever subjects are proposed by two-thirds of the states; everything else would be off-limits.

A Limited Constitutional Convention would propose only specific amendments, taking the place of a two-thirds vote in the House and Senate. Those proposed amendments would then go to the states, where the legislatures of 38 states (three-fourths of 50) would have to vote to ratify those proposals.

As opposed to well-meaning but ineffectual state resolutions asserting Tenth Amendment state sovereignty, the Limited Convention Amendment is something that Republicans may consider rallying around. It would install a new check that the states would possess to limit federal power.

The Founders would never have imagined that the federal government would become as all-consuming as it has, especially over recent decades. They would have thought that federal elected officials attempting a socialist takeover of whole parts of the U.S. economy or redefining the American family would promptly be kicked out of office by the voters, and that the prospect of the voters' wrath would ensure that federal officials would never attempt such things. But now that they are attempting just that, it might be time for a Limited Convention Amendment.

Of course, Congress would need to propose the Limited Convention Amendment (or Madison Amendment). For that reason, the GOP needs to debate making this an issue for the national platform, getting people on record and putting Democrats on the spot. If that still doesn't get it to two-thirds, then states could start passing resolutions calling for a general Constitutional Convention. As with the Seventeenth Amendment for the direct election of senators, watching states pass resolutions for a full convention should light a fire under Congress's seats.

The failure of both Democrats and Republicans at the federal level is intolerable, and the voters cannot let it stand. In this book we'll be laying out what we as Americans need to do on many fronts to restore the Constitution and rebuild the American Dream.

As we said, amending the Constitution should be done only with the greatest of care. As we've seen in this chapter, the Founders were extremely careful in dividing and balancing governmental power. They wanted the people to have democratic participation in government, but they wanted to make the government a republic, not a democracy. They also wanted a federal government that had only enough power to fulfill its role.

But the federal government has grown to a level beyond the wildest imaginings (or the wildest fears) of the Framers. It's grown into an all-consuming leviathan, feeding upon our freedoms and crushing our children under mountain upon mountain of debt. If this continues, drastic measures such as constitutional amendments likely will be considered to reenergize and reinvigorate the people to act through their states to restore the Framers' balance.

6

GOD SAVE THIS HONORABLE COURT

"The powers of the legislature are defined, and limited; and that those limits may not be mistaken, or forgotten, the constitution is written. . . . Certainly all those who have framed written constitutions contemplate them as forming the fundamental and paramount law of the nation . . . that an act of the legislature, repugnant to the constitution, is void. . . . It is emphatically the province and the duty of the judicial department to say what the law is."

—Chief Justice John Marshall,
Marbury v. Madison, 5 U.S. (1 Cranch) 137, 176–177 (1803).

The Constitution of the United States is a firm foundation for freedom because it's a written document specifying all the powers of the federal government, denying the government any other powers, and going the extra mile by also specifying certain rights that the American people enjoy. But millions overlook one critical fact:

The U.S. Constitution is only as good as the Supreme Court that interprets it.

In this time of people flocking to the Constitution, laying hold of its promises to regain its blessings, it's shocking that the federal courts have been discussed so little. Part of it goes back to what we've seen before about economic conservatives trying to marginalize social conservatives, and thinking of the courts as a social issue.

But as you'll see here, nothing could be further from the truth. The courts are taking an active role in setting policy on economics and national security, overriding laws they don't like.

The federal judiciary—both the Supreme Court and lower federal courts—are essential to constitutional conservatism. The Constitution cannot be resurgent without good judges, which means that neither the Republican Party nor the conservative movement can succeed unless the courts become a front-burner issue that drives elections and politics. It must be a deal breaker for any candidate for the White House or Senate if that candidate is not committed to appointing originalist judges.

The Courts That Democrats and the Left Gave Us

The Left came to understand by the 1960s that an activist judiciary was essential to their agenda. If the American people were generally center-right, and over time would not vote for the Left's agenda, then what liberals needed were leftists on the bench who would abuse the power of constitutional interpretation to declare that the Constitution commands whatever the Left wants.

It is a lie of the Far Left, enthusiastically parroted by many in the media, that the Supreme Court is conservative. The heck it is. The Court used to be far to the left. It became more moderate in the 1970s and '80s, and finally became a right-leaning moderate Court in 1991 with the appointment of Clarence Thomas. Then it became left-leaning moderate after Ruth Bader Ginsburg's appointment in 1993, then again became right-leaning moderate with Samuel Alito's appointment in 2006. That's the Court as it stands today.

ROBERTS COURT NOT CONSERVATIVE

While we have great respect for the Roberts Court—and for the Supreme Court as a whole regardless of the Court's membership—it is in fact a moderate Court, not a conservative Court.

Take for example the whining of one leftist. Senator Tom Harkin of Iowa complained, "Why do the conservatives always get the conservatives but we don't get to get the liberals [onto the Supreme Court]."[1] Excuse me? We have no idea what planet Senator Harkin lives on, but on our planet, called "Earth," the opposite is true.

The last time a liberal justice failed to get confirmed to the Supreme

Court was 1968, with the nomination of Abe Fortas to be chief justice. Fortas was already an associate justice on the Court, but ethical questions emerged, scuttling Justice Fortas's bid to be elevated to the chief's seat. Since several Republican nominees have gone down to defeat after Fortas, any suggestion that liberals never get their judges is plainly absurd. The same is true for the lower federal courts.

Instead, the record shows the Roberts Court with its current membership to be moderate.[2]

In 2010, by a 5–4 vote the Court held that a Christian organization can be denied equal status on a college campus just because the organization officially believes that sex outside the context of marriage is immoral, since such a belief would exclude someone who's gay from holding a leadership position in that Christian organization.[3] Also that year the Court held 6–3 that giving a seventeen-year-old life in prison without parole violates the Eighth Amendment's ban on cruel and unusual punishment.[4]

In 2008, the Court held 5–4 that foreign terrorists held by the U.S. military on a base in Cuba could petition a federal judge in civilian court for release, despite the fact that the writ of habeas corpus has never extended to foreigners held on foreign soil.[5]

In 2007, the Court held 5–4 that states have standing to sue the Environmental Protection Agency to force the EPA to regulate so-called greenhouse gases, throwing out two hundred years of precedent under which Massachusetts and the other states lack standing to file suit. The states lack standing both because it's unproven that global warming is man-made (and thus Massachusetts might not have been injured by the EPA's refusal to regulate CO_2 emissions) and because American courts cannot stop the alleged harm, since our courts cannot control foreign polluters.[6]

Such decisions are not the product of a right-wing judiciary. These are liberal decisions.

The reality is that America has not had a conservative Supreme Court since 1936. When FDR came to power, he started appointing liberal justices. But the Supreme Court still had a solid majority of justices committed to the Constitution's text, so FDR threatened to expand the Court by six new justices (for a total of fifteen), giving him the votes to uphold anything he wanted. (The number of justices is set by statute, not the Constitution, so Congress can add new seats to the Court.)

In 1937, FDR had appointed justices who solidly supported his New Deal. Then two older justices got nervous that FDR's court-packing scheme might pass Congress, so in the "switch in time that saved nine" these two justices reversed their earlier opposition to the New Deal, voting to uphold a massive expansion of federal power, as we'll read in Chapter 8 discussing Obamacare. Despite the fact that the justices had misread public opinion (the American people passionately opposed FDR's court-packing scheme; it was a major factor in Republicans picking up eighty-one seats in a 1938 landslide to provide a check to FDR's power), the Court never recovered from this huge leftward shift. We've not seen a conservative Supreme Court since that day.

Obama's Courts

President Obama has an unusually informed perspective on the crucial role that courts have in fundamentally transforming America. As president of *Harvard Law Review* and a lecturer (*not* a professor) at University of Chicago Law School, Obama understands how interpreting the Constitution can change the course of the nation.

President Obama has an intense focus on changing the Supreme Court, and he knows what he's looking for. When asked for justices from history he'd use as a model for judicial appointments, he named Chief Justice Earl Warren.[7] That answer is revealing, in that of the seventeen chief justices in U.S. history, Earl Warren is the most liberal.

When asked to name a current justice serving on the Court who would be a model for the justices he would appoint, Barack Obama said Ruth Bader Ginsburg. That's also telling, but again not surprising, in that Justice Ginsburg is likely the Court's most liberal member.[8] So Obama couldn't be clearer in saying he's committed to appointing the most liberal judicial nominees he can find.

DOUBLE STANDARD ON SUPREME COURT
NOMINEES—THE OBAMA RULE

That seems to be what President Obama has done with Justices Sonia Sotomayor and Elena Kagan, though to be fair, his nominees haven't been on the bench very long at the time of this writing. But they're clearly committed to interpreting the Constitution in accordance with what they believe makes a better society, regardless of the text and original meaning.

The best example regarding Justice Sotomayor comes from the dissenting opinion she joined in *McDonald v. Chicago*. During her 2009 confirmation hearings, Sotomayor said that she accepted as settled precedent the Supreme Court's 2008 decision in *D.C. v. Heller*, where the Supreme Court held that the Second Amendment secures the right to own a gun. Yet in *McDonald*, Sotomayor joined a dissent saying she saw "nothing in the Second Amendment's text, history, or underlying rationale that could warrant characterizing it as 'fundamental' insofar as it seeks to protect the keeping and bearing of arms for private self-defense. . . . why would the Court not now reconsider [overruling] *Heller* . . . ?"[9] Just in case we missed this, the dissent adds, "In sum, the Framers did not write the Second Amendment in order to protect a private right of armed self-defense. There has been, and is, no consensus that the right is, or was, 'fundamental.'"[10] (We discuss *Heller* and *McDonald* in Chapter 10.)

Thus, precedent or no precedent, assurance or no assurance, the Constitution doesn't say what it plainly says, if the justice doesn't like the result. There's every reason to believe that Justice Kagan approaches the Constitution the same way, and is even further to the left than Justice Sotomayor. From her disregarding the Solomon Amendment in order to bar military recruiters from Harvard Law School, to working to bury scientific conclusions in order to prevent a ban on partial-birth abortions, to her opposition to the Second Amendment, the obviously brilliant and charismatic Justice Kagan is committed to the idea that judges should use their power to promote certain values that achieve liberal social goals.[11]

However, by the standards of Barack Obama, Hillary Clinton, and the rest of the Democrats, Supreme Court nominees who might be conservative can be blocked at all costs. Obama and Clinton both voted against John Roberts's 2005 nomination to the Supreme Court.[12] They voted against Samuel Alito's 2006 nomination, and even voted to filibuster the nomination to prevent an up-or-down vote.[13] The simple fact that a Republican—and not an especially conservative Republican at that—nominated the justice meant he had to be stopped.

Regarding Roberts's nomination, Obama said:

> There is absolutely no doubt in my mind Judge Roberts is qualified to sit on the highest court in the land. Moreover, he seems to have the comportment and the temperament that makes for a good judge. He is humble, he is personally decent, and he appears to be respectful of different points of view. It is absolutely clear to me that Judge Roberts truly loves the law.[14]

Yet after going on to praise Roberts with many other words, Obama then said, "I ultimately have to give more weight to his deeds and the *overarching political philosophy* that he appears to have shared with those in power than to the assuring words he provided me in our meeting. The bottom line is this: I will be voting against John Roberts' nomination."[15]

In voting against Roberts, Senator Obama gave us the Obama Rule. That rule is that a senator will vote against a nominee if he doesn't like the nominee's "political philosophy." In other words, he voted against Roberts because Roberts was a Republican. He even voted to *filibuster* a nominee because of politics, as he did to Justice Alito. (Obama and Hillary Clinton were two of only a few senators to filibuster Alito, as Alito won that vote 73–25. They were two of even a smaller number of senators to vote against Roberts's nomination, being on the losing side of a 78–22 vote.)

The Obama Rule—also used by Hillary Clinton—is unconstitutional and outrageous. It's a recipe for gridlock and obstruction. It violates the Constitution by making the Senate a co-appointer of judges, which it's not. Under the Obama Rule, you vote against nominees you admit are perfectly qualified, just for the petty partisan reason that they're members of the other party. It ignores the fact that elections have consequences, and that Democrats whine like spoiled little children if a Republican talks about applying the same standard to the nominee of a Democratic president. This insufferable hypocrisy must end.

SAME DOUBLE STANDARD FOR
ALL FEDERAL COURTS

Unfortunately it doesn't end with the Supreme Court, as liberal Democrats—again including President Obama and Secretary Clinton—apply the same unconstitutional standards to judicial nominees to the lower federal courts. Realizing that many judicial nominees rightly have majority support for their confirmation even when the White House and the Senate are held by different parties, Democrats decided to do something that had never been done before: filibustering judicial nominees to the circuit courts of appeals. As Tom Jipping wrote in *Human Events,* the Democratic Senate majority leader in 2002 said that Democrats would "use whatever means necessary" to stop a Republican president from appointing conservative judges.[16]

Some of the time, this obstructionism worked. Many fine nominees never received their up-or-down vote, including two nominees to the D.C. Circuit whom we're about to discuss in detail—Miguel Estrada and Peter Keisler.[17] Others finally got through after years of obstruction, notably another nomination we're about to examine in detail—Janice Rogers Brown to the D.C. Circuit.[18] In fact, John Roberts's nomination to the D.C. Circuit was originally blocked by the Democrats for two years. Had not Republicans retaken the Senate after 2002 and confirmed Roberts to the D.C. Circuit, he would never have even been considered for chief justice of the United States.

The importance of the U.S. courts of appeals cannot be overstated. Each encompasses several states, and together they decide more than 20,000 cases each year. There are less than two hundred federal appeals judges assigned across the country. Of the 8,000 cases offered to the Supreme Court each year, the Court takes only about 80—roughly 1%. So out of 20,000+ circuit cases, more than 99.7% of the time they are the last word on an issue. America needs our federal appeals courts working properly, staffed with all the judges they need to do their extremely important work.

The Democrats clearly understood this with the U.S. Court of Appeals for the Fourth Circuit, one of the most important appellate courts in the country. There are fifteen seats on that court. Having blocked several Bush 43 nominees to keep an increasing number of seats vacant, President Obama had several vacancies on this closely divided court. As of this writing, he's had four nominees confirmed, and there's one more recently vacated seat he'll be able to fill. Consequently, Democrats have transformed this center-right court to a center-left court, in less than two years.

TALE OF DISCRIMINATION FOR THREE JUDICIAL NOMINEES—BROWN, ESTRADA, AND PICKERING

Three circuit court nominations embody everything that's wrong with the modern judicial confirmation process, thanks to the Far Left.

Christian Persecution: The Unconstitutional Obstruction of Charles Pickering

In a modern case of religious bigotry, Senate Democrats perpetrated a shocking outrage in blocking the nomination of Judge Charles Pickering to become a federal appeals judge on the Fifth Circuit. Judge Pickering was obstructed for only one reason: He's an Evangelical Christian.

Judge Pickering was a judge on the U.S. District Court for the Southern District of Mississippi.[19] Before that he served as a prosecutor who went after the Ku Klux Klan during the years when the Klan had great power in the Deep South, and when whites who stood with blacks against the Klan faced threats of physical danger. This courage earned him the support of various civil rights leaders, including former leaders of the Mississippi chapter of the NAACP when President Bush nominated Pickering to the U.S. Court of Appeals for the Fifth Circuit on May 25, 2001. This civil rights support came at the same time that the Democrats' gold standard for judicial nominees—the far-left American Bar Association (ABA)—gave Pickering its highest rating of "well qualified" to be confirmed to the appeals court. Add to this bipartisan support, such as from current and former Democratic governors of Mississippi.[20]

The Far Left tackled him with force. Two of the Senate's most aggressive liberals on judges—Charles Schumer and Dianne Feinstein—
came out blasting Judge Pickering, saying that his "right-wing views,
both politically *and personally*," were unacceptable.[21]

What personal beliefs? Pickering is an Evangelical Christian. He
had served as president of the Mississippi Baptist Convention and
was active with the Southern Baptist Convention. Judge Pickering is a
Bible-believing Christian. For that, liberal Democrats wanted to prevent his elevation to the circuit bench.

The Constitution forbids any federal official to discriminate on
the basis of religion. Under the Religious Test Clause in Article VI of
the Constitution, "no religious test shall ever be required as a qualifi-
cation to any office or public trust under the United States."[22] It's
noteworthy that the Framers included the word *ever* in that clause. That
means that no federal official—including a Democratic senator—can
ever oppose confirming a nominee because of that person's religious beliefs. Voters can use whatever criteria they choose when deciding whom
to vote for, but those sworn to uphold the Constitution in the performance of their public duties must be blind to the personal religion of
every nominee.

Regardless of your personal faith, this bigotry perpetrated by Senate
Democrats should infuriate every patriotic American. Every person has
a religious faith. Even atheists, as they firmly hold to the religious belief
that God doesn't exist. In America you have a constitutional right to
be theologically wrong. That respect and protection for matters of faith
and conscience goes to the heart of American liberty. Such discrimination by U.S. senators must be fought without compromise.

Pickering's nomination should also have been a serious wake-up call
to Evangelical Christians in America. To their credit, Roman Catholics
do a good job of rallying to protect their own when religious discrimination rears its head. The same is true of Jews, Mormons, and, increasingly, Muslims. But Evangelicals have been pathetically apathetic about
rallying to support prominent Evangelicals who are attacked for their
Christian faith and testimony. They're taught to turn the other cheek
and accept mistreatment on account of their faith. But that ignores
the fact that our Constitution explicitly demands that one's faith be

respected, and so Evangelicals have a firm foundation from which to assert their rights and demand an equal place in the public square.

In the end, President Bush gave Judge Pickering a recess appointment to the Fifth Circuit. But when that temporary appointment expired, Judge Pickering retired, as it appeared likely he still wouldn't be confirmed.

The religious persecution of Judge Pickering for his nomination has not yet been repeated, but it will. This time the church must rally to the nominee's defense.

Killing Supreme Court Justices in the Cradle

The outrageousness of obstructing judicial nominees reached a different type of low point—but one also driven by discrimination—with the nominations of two jurists who are, like John Roberts, considered Supreme Court caliber, but who also happen to be minorities.

Janice Rogers Brown is an African-American, a single mother born in 1949 in the Deep South, the daughter of a sharecropper in Greenville, Alabama. She put herself through law school, earning her J.D. from the University of California at Los Angeles (a top-twenty school) in 1977. She worked in various positions in California government and the private sector, and became the legal advisor to the governor of California. She became a California appellate judge in 1994 and was appointed as a justice on the California Supreme Court in 1996. While serving on that court, she also earned an LL.M. (a graduate law degree) from the elite University of Virginia School of Law in 2004.

Justice Brown was nominated to the nation's second-highest federal court, the U.S. Court of Appeals for the District of Columbia Circuit, in 2003. Even though Democrats had narrowly lost the Senate majority, they spent the political capital to filibuster Brown's nomination. Justice Brown is extremely intelligent and well-spoken, writes excellent opinions, and consistently adheres to principled judicial restraint in interpreting the law according to its original meaning. In short, she was a perfect candidate for the U.S. Supreme Court, so Democrats made it a mission to keep this well-respected and well-qualified candidate off the federal bench.

Their obstruction lasted two years, until the American people had enough of this subversion of the Constitution and handed Republicans four additional Senate seats in 2004. Janice Rogers Brown was finally confirmed in early 2005 to the D.C. Circuit, where she has continued to distinguish herself.

Although Judge Brown ultimately succeeded, another well-qualified minority candidate didn't fare as well.

In 2001, Miguel Estrada was also nominated to a seat on the U.S. Court of Appeals for the District of Columbia Circuit. Estrada was another American success story, an immigrant from Honduras who didn't speak English when he first arrived as a teenager. Estrada mastered the English language and became an outstanding student. He was a top graduate from Columbia, then attended Harvard Law School, where he was an editor on the *Harvard Law Review*. Estrada clerked for a federal appeals judge, then for Justice Kennedy on the Supreme Court. Afterward he served under the U.S. solicitor general in both Democratic and Republican administrations. He's currently a partner at Gibson, Dunn & Crutcher, one of America's top law firms.

As Klukowski can attest, anyone who's seen Miguel Estrada argue before the Supreme Court can tell you he's one of the best appellate lawyers in the country. He smoothly parries the toughest questions put to him by the justices, and does so with wit and ease.

When he was nominated to the D.C. Circuit at age thirty-nine, Democrats quickly realized that Estrada was being groomed for the U.S. Supreme Court. (Four of the nine current justices were previously D.C. Circuit judges.) Another Hispanic who was a Senate staffer, Manuel Miranda, saw a Democratic strategy memo wherein Senate Democrats wrote that they must filibuster Estrada to make sure a Republican president wouldn't have the opportunity to nominate the first Hispanic to the Supreme Court.

Senate Democrats' plan to keep down Hispanics unfortunately worked. Miguel Estrada never got an up-or-down vote despite the fact that he had the votes to get confirmed. Then several years later Democratic president Barack Obama appointed the first Hispanic to the Court, Sonia Sotomayor. Estrada's nomination was never confirmed, despite the fact that Estrada is manifestly well qualified. Even Justice Elena Kagan testified during her own confirmation hearings that

Estrada would make not only an excellent federal appellate judge, but more than that would make an excellent Supreme Court justice.[23]

It's an absolute disgrace that Democrats would try to block individuals because of their skin color. They would rather see a minority who's not a liberal Democrat go down to defeat than see a minority who opposes the liberal agenda succeed.

Senator Marco Rubio

We saw this racial discrimination on the part of liberal Democrats more recently in another area of politics, in the 2010 U.S. Senate race in Florida.

The story broke that the Obama White House was trying to beat Marco Rubio to keep Hispanic-Americans from having a conservative Republican in high office. This was proof yet again that the Left is willing to take down a minority candidate solely on account of race, showing that it's Democrats, not Republicans, who are trying to keep minorities down in America today.

With the approval of the Obama White House, Hillary Clinton's husband, former president Bill Clinton, pressured Congressman Kendrick Meek—an African-American Democrat—to drop out of the U.S. Senate race in Florida and publicly throw his support to independent (and former liberal Republican) governor Charlie Crist.

The Democratic Left did this for one reason: They want to deny minorities a choice, deceiving minorities into thinking that only the Democrats offer them anything of value. Obama and Clinton are happy to take out minority candidates—even Democratic candidates—to perpetuate this lie.

That's what Democrats tried to do with Marco Rubio. The son of immigrants, Rubio's final campaign ad, about the generational choice Americans must make, telling his own inspiring personal story, was magnificent. Senator Rubio is the perfect picture of the American Dream; the victory of this thirty-nine-year-old conservative Republican senator is an awesome example of how you can achieve anything in America, regardless of background, skin color, or heritage.

The fact that the Obama White House and the Clintons would push a Democratic black man to drop his own Senate bid shows where they truly stand on empowering minorities. Democrats wanted the black man to drop out and support a white man who's not even a Democrat, in order to stop a Hispanic just because that Hispanic-American happens to be Republican. They'd rather a minority fail than succeed without them. Any way you cut it, that's just another form of racism in all its un-American ugliness.

Obama's Judges: Goodwin Liu and Robert Chatigny

In contrast, two specific nominations show the American people what kind of judge President Obama thinks should sit on our federal courts. They are Goodwin Liu and Robert Chatigny.

Goodwin Liu is a law professor at the University of California at Berkeley who has been nominated to the U.S. Court of Appeals for the Ninth Circuit. He has admittedly impressive academic credentials.

But he's nothing short of radical. If confirmed to the Ninth Circuit, there would not be a more leftward judge in all the United States than Goodwin Liu. For example, Liu holds to the extremist position that there are constitutional rights to "health insurance, transportation subsidies, job training, and a robust earned income tax credit."[24] That last one is the biggest, because it's saying that low-income people have a *constitutional right* for the government to just give them money from other people. That's stunning. In other words, more than just believing in socialist policies, Goodwin Liu believes that the Constitution *commands* socialism.

Robert Chatigny is a U.S. district judge in Connecticut who has been nominated to the U.S. Court of Appeals for the Second Circuit. Judge Chatigny ruled that killer-rapist Michael Ross's "sexual sadism" was a mental illness that must be considered a "mitigating factor" that made that felon *less* responsible for murdering and raping. Beyond that, after sentencing this criminal, it was discovered that before Chatigny was appointed to the bench, he had done private work reviewing defense motions for this murdering rapist. His refusal to disclose this shocking fact resulted in ethics complaints filed against the judge, and a congressman called for his impeachment. Instead President Obama wants to promote him to a higher court.[25]

These nominations are extraordinarily telling. Supreme Court nominees receive so much scrutiny that presidents are often cautious about whom they nominate. But appellate court nominees often slip under the radar, so when you see nominees like this, they're a window into what sort of judicial philosophy the president favors. It's disturbing to see that President Obama wants far-left extremists like Liu and Chatigny on the bench.*

NEW JUDGESHIPS

President Obama and the Left are not merely content to fill judicial vacancies with nominees who share their view of the Constitution. They want to create new judgeships. Although federal judges are appointed for life, the number of judges on each court is set by federal statute. Congress can create new judicial seats anytime it wants, and does so from time to time as our country grows and the number of federal laws increases. (Congress can also eliminate judgeships, although all current judges continue to hold their offices until they retire, at which point their seat on the bench ceases to exist.)

The Judicial Conference of the United States, which is chaired by the chief justice and includes the chief judge of each federal appeals court as well as other select judges, makes various recommendations and assessments to Congress. Recently the Judicial Conference stated that the courts are overburdened and recommended that Congress should create twelve new circuit judges on the courts of appeals, and fifty new judges in the district courts.

Democrats tried using the judgeship bill for partisan advantage. In early 2008, Senator Pat Leahy, then Democratic chairman of the Senate Judiciary Committee, and Senator Orrin Hatch, Republican former chairman of the committee, cosponsored a bill to expand the courts. The bill specified that the new judgeships would not actually come into existence until January 21, 2009, one day after the next presidential inauguration.[26] (No one knew which party would win the presidency in November 2008.) The bill stalled and never became law.

*As this book was being edited after the 2010 midterms, President Obama chose to re-nominate several controversial figures from 2009 and 2010. Liu was among those to be nominated again, but Chatigny was dropped.

But after President Obama's election, Leahy introduced another bill. This one was almost identical to the bipartisan bill from 2008, with only one major difference: The new judgeships would be created the day the bill was signed.[27] With a Democrat in the White House and a Democratic majority in the Senate, the bill was designed with the sole purpose of guaranteeing that a raft of liberal judges could be appointed immediately, with no chance to stop them. Fortunately—and surprisingly—Democrats never brought that bill to a final vote. Since the House changed hands in 2011, Democrats may have lost their chance if Republicans hold firm.

The Left understands the value of the courts, and Barack Obama and his allies are doing everything they can to stack the courts and remake America.

Republican Courts

Although not the unmitigated disaster that President Obama and the Democrats are giving us, the Republican record on the judiciary has been mixed, rather than laudable. President George W. Bush gave America many good judges. But there are enough problems to make the case that the GOP must do better if we're to have courts that uphold constitutional conservatism.

Many allies and aides to former President Bush say, "We gave you Roberts and Alito, so quit complaining." They evidently think we have short memories, or that we don't know what a conservative judge looks like.

George W. Bush wanted to give us Alberto Gonzales and Harriet Miers, not John Roberts and Sam Alito. When the first Supreme Court vacancy was announced in July 2005, a number of short-list names were leaked to the press.[28] One recurring name was that of Attorney General Alberto Gonzales. This was a White House trial balloon, but many stakeholders knew that Gonzales was no conservative. The pushback was enough that Gonzales never made it to the final round of consideration.

When it came to Harriet Miers, the White House didn't get the hint. For reasons that defy understanding, the president nominated

Harriet Miers in what can best be described as a shocking instance of "What the heck was that?" President Bush nominated someone who most lawyers would regard as manifestly unqualified for the Supreme Court. President Bush explains in his memoirs that he wanted a woman to replace Sandra Day O'Connor, and that he trusted Miers would reflect his philosophy.

That's understandable, but unacceptable. Miers demonstrated her ability as a manager and a leader by running law firms and bar associations, but she had no accomplishments to suggest that she could handle the extremely sophisticated theoretical issues decided by the High Court. The conservative backlash to her nomination was quick, clear, and well deserved. After the Miers nomination crashed, President Bush made a perfect course correction with Sam Alito.

Even then, Roberts and Alito are not what the American people were promised. During the campaign, then governor Bush said he would appoint justices in the mold of Antonin Scalia and Clarence Thomas. Alito is to the left of both Scalia and Thomas, and Roberts is to the left of Scalia. While they're both conservative, it would be fairer to say they're in the mold of late Chief Justice William Rehnquist, not Scalia or Thomas. In terms of intellect and skill, Roberts and Alito are both among the best justices the Court has ever seen—they're brilliant and their credentials are stellar. But already in a number of cases they've taken a more moderate approach, especially Chief Justice Roberts. Both Roberts and Alito have broken with Scalia and Thomas on several important constitutional cases in the past four years.

Bush 43 also gave us a number of outstanding judges on the lower courts. Judges like Priscilla Owen to the Fifth Circuit, Jeffrey Sutton to the Sixth Circuit, Diane Sykes to the Seventh Circuit, and William Pryor to the Eleventh Circuit all appear to be as good as any of the judges whom Ronald Reagan appointed with the counsel of Ed Meese.

But again, rightly or wrongly, almost the only thing the public focuses on when it comes to the judiciary is Supreme Court picks. That said, some previous Republican presidents have not done as well as George W. Bush when it comes to Supreme Court appointments.

George H. W. Bush gave us both Clarence Thomas and David Souter. While Justice Thomas is the most conservative jurist on the

Court, Justice Souter was an unmitigated disaster as a straight-out liberal. And the first President Bush truly deserves credit for Thomas, but not unlimited credit. The president was looking for a qualified African-American to take the seat of Thurgood Marshall, and Thomas—who was serving as a judge on the D.C. Circuit and was a graduate of Yale Law School with an impressive résumé—was the only black Republican with enough legal gravitas to ascend to the Court in 1991.

It's not that Bush 41 was trying to appoint moderate judges, because although a number of Bush 41 appointees were moderate or even slanted to the left, he also appointed many conservatives to the lower courts. These included several justices and justice-caliber judges, such as Sam Alito on the Third Circuit, J. Michael Luttig to the Fourth Circuit, Alice Batchelder on the Sixth Circuit, and A. Raymond Randolph and Clarence Thomas to the D.C. Circuit. So the former president's record was fairly good.

Not surprisingly, President Reagan was the most successful president in nominating judges who interpret and apply the Constitution as it is written—even if he wasn't the most successful in getting them confirmed. He appointed Antonin Scalia to the Supreme Court and elevated William Rehnquist to chief justice. Reagan also nominated Robert Bork, whom we are about to look at closely. When Bork's nomination failed, Reagan nominated Douglas Ginsburg. When Ginsburg went down Reagan nominated Anthony Kennedy, who everyone at the time mistakenly thought was a solid conservative. Reagan made a mistake in nominating Sandra Day O'Connor in 1981 and again with Kennedy in 1987. Both were understandable in that both were considered conservative, but they were Reagan's choices nonetheless, so he must be held responsible for those decisions. But most of his Supreme Court nominations were among the best ever.

Reagan's success was also seen on the circuit courts. Advised by Ed Meese, President Reagan appointed a constellation of constitutional conservative judicial stars, many of whom you read about in this book. These include Antonin Scalia, Robert Bork, Ken Starr, Douglas Ginsburg, and David Sentelle to the D.C. Circuit, Edith Jones to the Fifth Circuit, Danny Boggs to the Sixth Circuit, and Diarmuid O'Scannlain to the Ninth Circuit. Judges such as these marked a sea change in

American law, as it brought the courts back to the original meaning of the U.S. Constitution as the cornerstone of judicial action.

The Bork Nomination of 1987

No discussion of this issue is complete without a hard look at the failed Supreme Court nomination of Judge Robert H. Bork in 1987. Chief Justice Warren Burger—a moderate who voted for *Roe v. Wade* and many other things condemned by conservatives—called Bork as well-qualified a nominee as the Court had ever seen.[29] Bork was U.S. solicitor general, acting U.S. attorney general, a professor at Yale Law School (the top-ranked law school in America), and then a judge on the U.S. Court of Appeals for the D.C. Circuit. Bork may be even more brilliant than Scalia, having written some of the most famous legal works in modern law, from the seminal treatise on antitrust laws to explaining how the law requires neutral principles. Bork is also certainly more conservative than Scalia, more in line with Clarence Thomas.

Judge Bork was nominated in 1987 to fill the seat vacated by Justice Lewis Powell. Senator Ted Kennedy defined the Bork nomination by giving his infamous "Robert Bork's America" speech, in which he trotted out an absurd parade of horrors, in which women would die in back-alley abortions and black Americans would have to sit in segregated seating at restaurants. The White House was caught flat-footed, and White House chief of staff Howard Baker—a moderate—did not mobilize an effective defense for Bork. Also, Judge Bork did himself no favors, with an unapologetic demeanor in his confirmation hearings that eroded Senate support. In the end, with Democrats having taken the Senate majority in 1986, Judge Bork's nomination was rejected.

One lesson from this sad episode is that the Left will not allow a Republican president to compromise on a Supreme Court nomination. No matter if the American people elect a Republican president, if that president nominates someone whom a liberal Democrat would not have appointed, then Democrats believe that any means available— even a filibuster—is okay to stop that nomination. A second lesson is that it's not enough to have a Republican nominee; it must be a truly conservative nominee to restore the Constitution.

Constitutionalist Judges vs. Agenda Judges

What America needs are *constitutionalist judges*. This should be the public label to describe *originalist* judges. Constitutionalist judges are the opposite of agenda judges, which is what Barack Obama, Hillary Clinton, and the Left are pushing on America.

Some conservatives call for judges who are strict constructionists. There are four problems with this label. First, that's a layman's term, not a legal term. Lawyers do not speak of "strict constructionism" as a school of legal thought, so it has no clear meaning. Second, it's often considered code for someone who will overturn *Roe v. Wade*. But that's a simplistic understanding that gives short shrift to dozens of other critical constitutional issues, and it taints the term "strict constructionist," hindering confirmation efforts.

Third, it caves in to the Left in terms of defining judicial philosophy as one that delivers certain results. Nothing could be further from the truth. A principled judicial philosophy is one that focuses on how to interpret the Constitution regardless of the outcome, not one that focuses on results regardless of methodology.

And finally, the Constitution is to be construed neither strictly nor broadly. It should be construed according to the original meaning of its words, regardless of how broad or narrow that meaning is. For all these reasons, *strict constructionist* is not a useful term to use in the ongoing debate over judicial appointments.

We need to have a term that's easy to explain to the voters regarding what they want in a judge, one that's not corrupted by the Left. We need to frame the debate in a way that cuts through the rhetoric and explains the choice to the American people.

ORIGINALISM

Judges must be originalists. As we saw in Chapter 4, originalism is the belief that any law—including the Constitution—must be interpreted according to the original meaning of its words, as those words would have been understood by a reasonably well-informed and educated voter at the time those words were adopted.

The Constitution was adopted by the American people—*not* the states, as some are fond of saying. The federal government was created by the people of the United States, not the states of the United States. We the People acted as the ultimate sovereign in adopting the Constitution. When the people voted for it, what did they understand it to mean?

That's the only legitimate way to interpret the Constitution. Anything else allows judges to act according to what they personally believe, rather than what the American people actually said. So America needs judges who uphold originalism.

Constitutionalist is a helpful term not polluted by misuse or redefinition. A constitutionalist judge is an originalist judge. That's the kind of judge that constitutional conservatives must demand.

AGENDA JUDGES ARE ACTIVIST JUDGES

We also need to clarify the language on the other side of the judicial debate. We need a new term because—once again—the Left has corrupted the term that we've been using.

That term used to be *judicial activism.* A judicial activist is one who substitutes his personal policy and political preferences for the words in the Constitution. A judicial activist is a judge who does whatever he thinks is right, and interprets the Constitution to mean whatever he thinks it should mean, instead of what it actually says.

The Left has hijacked this term to smear conservatives. They say that whenever the Supreme Court strikes down a law, it's an "activist" Court. (Of course, this is a hypocritical lie. When the Supreme Court strikes down a restriction on abortion, or a law defining marriage as one-man-one-woman, or gives terrorists the Bill of Rights, then the Court is a sublime institution of enlightened humanity.) So if the Supreme Court strikes down a law that provides that the federal government cannot ban guns in your home if you live there, because the Second Amendment promises you the right to own a gun, then somehow this is judicial activism.

The opposite is true. Whenever a court has a case properly brought before it challenging the constitutionality of a law, the court's choice should be simple. It must hold the law alongside the Constitution. If the law does not violate the Constitution, then the court must say so, and it would be activism to strike it down. Conversely, if the law violates the Constitution, then the court *must* strike it down, and it would be judicial activism *not* to do so.

Because the term *activist* is so misunderstood, it's better to refer to "agenda" judges. An *agenda judge* is one who declares that the Constitution means whatever he or she wants it to mean—a judge who uses judicial power to push his own agenda.

A constitutionalist judge, by contrast, is someone who accepts the role that the Framers assign to courts in Article III of the Constitution. It's the role of interpreting the Constitution according to its original meaning, and letting the chips fall where they may.

This is the debate we face. Constitutional conservatives need to understand that America cannot restore the Constitution without constitutionalist judges, and they need to make the case that agenda judges subvert the Constitution, no matter how beneficial their decisions in individual cases may seem.

Agenda Judges Changing America for the Worse

Overwhelmingly, agenda judges change the United States for the worse, not the better. Many unfortunate changes in this country can be traced to an incident where some judges decided that they knew better than the people and acted to declare their preferences in the Constitution.

We looked at some recent activist decisions earlier in this chapter, but they're not the worst. We'll survey just a few of the truly awful cases to make this point. Although many of such cases focus on social issues, we're skipping major activist decisions that we cover elsewhere in the book, instead discussing some major economic and national security judicial outrages under different headings.

Each case shows a different way that agenda judges are eroding the Constitution's system of government in our republic.

The worst Supreme Court case of all time is *Scott v. Sandford*, better known as *Dred Scott*, the most egregious instance of judicial activism ever. It's the epitome of what agenda judges can do, determined to reach a particular outcome in a case, no matter how many rules of constitutional law must be trampled underfoot in the process.

Dred Scott was a slave. He traveled with his master, Dr. John Emerson, to Illinois, which was a free state, and also Wisconsin—which at that time was a territory under the Northwest Ordinance, which did not allow slavery. Years later Scott moved with Emerson to Missouri and then Louisiana. When his master died, and Emerson's widow rented Scott to another man, Scott tried to buy his and his wife's freedom. When his offer was refused, he sued in federal court, arguing that when he was in Illinois and Wisconsin he was a free man, and nobody's slave.

His case went all the way to the Supreme Court. By a 7–2 decision, the Court denied Scott's claim. Writing for the Court in 1856, Chief Justice Roger Taney wrote that no person of African descent—such as Dred Scott—was a U.S. citizen.[30] Since Scott was not a citizen, no federal court had jurisdiction to hear his case: It did not fall within any federal jurisdictional categories found in Article III of the Constitution. The Court then went on to hold that it would violate a slave owner's property rights to allow him to lose his rights to his slave by moving to a free state.

This is judicial activism on three fronts. First, when a federal court lacks jurisdiction, the only thing the Constitution permits that court to do is declare why the court has no jurisdiction, and then to dismiss the case.[31] (Limiting the jurisdiction of the federal courts is one of the best ways to prevent judicial activism.) The way agenda judges are subverting this country is perhaps best seen in *Dred Scott,* showing courts exerting judicial power where they have no constitutional authority to do so.

Second, there's no right to own a slave mentioned in the Constitution. The Court here was saying that this "property right" was implicit in the Fifth Amendment's Due Process Clause. But like the rest of the Bill of Rights, the Fifth Amendment gave rights only against the actions and laws of the federal government.[32] It wasn't until the Fourteenth Amendment was adopted years later that any part of the Bill of Rights applied to the states. So the Court declared a right that didn't exist and applied it to the states at a time in which the Bill of Rights didn't apply.[33]

Third, it was the worst form of revisionist history to suggest that a black man is not a "citizen" as that term is used in Article III of the Constitution. It was ignoring the original meaning of the term, doing so to achieve a particular predetermined result.

Finally, the *Dred Scott* case set the ball to be spiked in a follow-up case. If having a slave was a constitutional right, then no state could forbid it. That would mean that the Missouri Compromise was unconstitutional, allowing for free states to remain free but slave states to have slaves. We were one Supreme Court case away from having slavery declared nationwide, including in hotbeds of abolitionist sentiment in the North such as Massachusetts. The Court was on the verge of profoundly remaking the United States.

Although no case reaches the outrageous heights of *Dred Scott*, another of the all-time worst cases is *Plessy v. Ferguson*.[34] With *Plessy*, we see the second way agenda judges harm America; it showcases how one terrible decision can create a judicial doctrine that haunts America for decades.

Louisiana had passed a law in the 1800s, after the Civil War, requiring trains to provide separate quarters of "equal" quality for blacks. A man of mixed racial background bought a first-class ticket and took an empty seat in the first-class car. When he refused the conductor's order to go to a "black" car, a policeman helped the conductor physically eject him from the train and took him to jail. The passenger sued.

In *Plessy*, the Court in 1896 declared the "separate-but-equal" rule. Racial discrimination was okay so long as you provide equal-quality facilities for use by nonwhites. (Of course, such facilities were never equal.) The Court thus allowed government-regulated entities to ignore the clear meaning of the Fourteenth Amendment. Agenda judges create bad precedent, saddling America with bad rules of law.

Plessy was the law of the land until 1954, when the Court overruled *Plessy* in *Brown v. Board of Education*. In *Brown*, the Court held that separate-but-equal school systems—that is to say, racially segregated schools—are unconstitutional. Thus we see that the remedy for agenda judges is good judges, to undo the damage of terrible decisions in the past. (It must be noted, however, that in reaching the right result in *Brown*, the activist Warren Court did not go to the original meaning of the Fourteenth Amendment, as it should have to firmly root its holding in the Constitution's text. Instead the Court resorted to social science and policy-making material, setting the stage for many future decisions where such an unprincipled approach led to terrible outcomes.)

Although the Court has held for almost a century that the Constitution includes *implied rights* (that is, those not explicitly found in the constitutional text), it's terrifyingly easy for the Court to use this as an excuse to alter American society by declaring new rights. The third way in which agenda judges are dismantling America is by declaring constitutional rights where none exist. There is no better example of this danger than *Roe v. Wade.*

In *Roe,* the Supreme Court in 1973 declared a constitutional right to abortion.[35] All states had laws in the 1970s restricting abortions in various ways. But in 1965 the Supreme Court had declared a previously unnoticed right to privacy,[36] which somehow had gone undetected for almost two centuries. The predictable next step came when a woman named Norma McCorvey tried to get an abortion in Texas, where abortion was illegal except in special circumstances such as rape.

In declaring a right to abortion, the Court created a bizarre pregnancy-trimester framework, under which the types of abortion restrictions the Constitution allows depended on how far along the pregnancy was.[37] It embarked on a meandering exploration of ancient cultures, talking about what the Greeks and Romans thought about pregnancy. It was a grotesque perversion of what constitutional interpretation involves. And it ended with its foreordained result: The Constitution decreed that a mother could have someone kill her unborn child. The Framers would be nauseated at such a preposterous suggestion—and they would be enraged.

Two more examples of egregious activism illustrate the fourth way in which agenda judges eviscerate our Constitution. The Court can abuse its power by imposing its own moral judgments on Americans, instead of allowing states to make their own moral judgments, as is their right as sovereigns.

The first of these is *Lawrence v. Texas,* where the Court struck down, 6–3, a Texas law forbidding homosexual sodomy.[38] In *Lawrence,* the Court in 2003 held that the Constitution protects a right to homosexual conduct. In doing so, the Court overruled a fairly recent case, *Bowers v. Hardwick,* which had upheld a state's sovereign right to make laws for public morality as part of the police power.[39] The Court took the power to make moral judgments away from local elected officials whenever the Court decided those decisions were wrong.

The second case is even more recent: *Graham v. Florida,* decided in 2010.[40] In *Graham,* the Court struck down, 6–3, a rarely imposed Florida law by which some crimes were so heinous that someone under the age of eighteen could be sentenced to life in prison without parole if the jury thought the facts were extreme enough to justify that punishment. The Court said that if no homicide was involved, then life in prison was unconstitutional for a teenager.[41]

The fifth way in which agenda judges are imposing judicial activism is by invoking foreign law to override U.S. law when the courts don't like the laws the people of the United States choose to enact here in our own country. Ironically, *Graham* also falls into this category, as it examines foreign law and culture in striking down Florida's law.[42]

The Court has invoked foreign law at least three times in the past decade. All of these cases were challenges to the death penalty. On the basis of foreign law the Court held 5–4 that the death penalty is unconstitutional when applied to someone under the age of eighteen even if they've committed murder.[43] The Court held the same 6–3 for someone with low intelligence,[44] and again 5–4 for someone who raped a child.[45] On questions of justice and interpreting our Supreme Law, several justices on our highest court have set aside American law, history, and values to impose foreign laws on the American people.

Another reason these decisions erode the Constitution is what we discussed back in Chapter 4, that defining and punishing crimes is a state issue. That also makes these decisions part of the sixth and final way that agenda judges undermine the Framers' constitutional system: These decisions destroy federalism.

As we saw in Chapters 4 and 5, federalism is one of the keys of constitutional conservatism to create a Sovereign Society. It's one of the five structural promises of the Constitution. And the courts have been destroying federalism, eroding state sovereignty.

Part of this occurred when the Court invented what is called the Dormant Commerce Clause. Although Congress has authority to regulate interstate commerce, the Court went the extra mile, laying down the rule that an action by a state violates a negative corollary of the Commerce Clause if it impedes or burdens interstate commerce, even if Congress never says so. This is a massive federal intrusion into the states' authority, not allowing them to pass laws for business and economic development. It has stifled economic creativity among the states.

Eroding federalism has only gotten worse in recent years, as the Court declares new rights, upholds overly broad federal criminal statutes, and invokes the Dormant Commerce Clause. Add in cases like *U.S. v. Comstock,* where a majority of the Court upheld a federal police-power law allowing the feds to keep locked up "sexually dangerous" people once they had finished prison sentences for any crime (including those not involving sexual activity).[46] *Comstock* is especially dangerous because it rested on the Necessary and Proper Clause. As we discuss in Chapter 8, this provision of the Constitution is extremely dangerous to our liberty if incorrectly interpreted, as it was in *Comstock.*

It's clear that federalism cannot be restored without a president appointing justices who respect federalism. Agenda judges have caused terrible damage to our constitutional order. We never impeach judges simply because we disagree with their rulings; the courts cannot be independent unless they are shielded from such backlashes. Instead we must focus on filling each judicial vacancy with a constitutionalist judge until we replace every agenda judge on the bench. Originalism must trump judicial activism.

Judicial Confirmation Pledge for 2013

The greatest problem currently facing the third branch of government is that the judicial confirmation process is broken. Good nominees cannot get confirmed to the federal courts, and it affects who can even be nominated.

In his 2010 annual report on the judiciary, Chief Justice Roberts denounced the current state of judicial confirmations. He called on the president and Congress "to find a long-term solution to this recurring problem." His report is an indictment of Democrats *and* Republicans.[47]

Judicial confirmations should be overhauled to restore a workable system delivering the same sort of dependable results we had from 1789 until as recently as 1987. It needs to be a standard under which there shouldn't be filibusters, where the entire process from nomination to confirmation does not exceed 120 days, and in which the U.S. Senate uses only four criteria in deciding whether to confirm or reject a nomination. Such a system can never be created, however, unless Democrats actually bind themselves to it along with Republicans.

Regardless, this system cannot be allowed to go into effect until January 21, 2013, the day after the next presidential term begins. This process must not be used to give one party an advantage over the other. As this book comes out in 2011, no one knows whether the president will be a Democrat or Republican. Also, no one knows which party will control the Senate, or how big a margin the majority will enjoy.

Not only that, but Democrats cannot be rewarded for breaking the confirmation system. They did this to stack the courts with judges who reinterpret the Constitution in a leftist fashion. Let *both* parties run on this issue in 2012. Present it to the American people, and let the voters factor this issue into their voting decisions for president and for senator.

For this reason, every candidate in both parties for the U.S. Senate must take a pledge. Make them sign a "Judicial Confirmation Pledge" that incorporates the terms below. Then once the American people have spoken, and have determined which candidate for president they want nominating federal judges, as well as which senators they want to confirm or reject those nominees, America can get back on track with the kind of judges we need to uphold the Constitution and the rule of law.

120 DAYS FROM NOMINATION TO UP-OR-DOWN VOTE
Starting in 2013, if *and only if* Democrats commit to abide by this new system, the confirmation process should work on a 120-day time frame. (If the Senate is in recess when the person is nominated, then the clock should begin on the first day that the Senate is back in session.) When

the president nominates someone to fill a judicial vacancy, the Senate should be given at least thirty days before a committee hearing is held, out of respect for the Senate's critical role in judicial appointments, giving senators ample time to fully vet the nominee. When the Senate receives a judicial nomination, it's referred to the Senate Judiciary Committee. This thirty-day minimum gives the Judiciary Committee staff time to evaluate the nominee's record and study all of the nominee's writings and work.

As part of this, a nominee must agree to respond to requests for information within thirty days, except for those kinds of information that are privileged. Privileged information is anything covered by attorney-client privilege, or by the work-product privilege. The former covers any advice—whether written or verbal—given by the lawyer to a client. The latter covers all substantive legal work done in connection with that legal advice, including research, legal analysis, and discussion with experts or other lawyers. If the nominee served as a lawyer for the government, such as in the White House Counsel's Office or the Justice Department's Office of Legal Counsel or Office of the Solicitor General, all those documents remain confidential.

All other information is fair game. To keep the process moving, immediately upon receiving the nomination the Senate Judiciary Committee should dispatch that same day a standard form requesting whatever documents are required of all nominees, such as tax returns, any law review articles or essays they've written, any speeches they've given, or any leadership role they've played in an organization. Also on that first day, the committee should send out its standard questionnaire for the nominee, giving that nominee a full month to answer the many questions that are put to them.[48]

In that timeline, the senators will receive all of this information by the end of the sixty days, and must promptly have a hearing and then a vote. The information requested immediately will have been reviewed by day 30, and any follow-up documents will have been received by day 60.

The committee must take a final vote on the nomination by day 90. By that time the committee has had the nomination for months, and committee members have all the requested information. There's no reason to delay any longer. The committee should hold a hearing early in this third thirty-day window. Committee members should give the nominee written follow-up questions within the next three days, and give the nominee seven days to answer. Then the committee should promptly take a final vote on the nomination.[49]

It's unacceptable for the chairman of the Senate Judiciary Committee not to have a committee hearing for someone whom the president of the United States has nominated for a federal judgeship. Congress determines by statute how many federal judges should sit on each court in the United States to uphold the Constitution and federal law, and to ensure that justice is speedily done. The president should nominate in a timely manner someone for every single vacant seat. The Constitution then requires the Senate to act on judicial nominations to fill those seats on the bench, and it does not authorize a committee chairman to lock up the gears. The committee must vote and then report the nomination back to the full Senate. There are no circumstances under which ninety days is not enough to make this happen.

The full Senate must then have whatever floor debate the majority chooses to allow, and then must have a final vote by day 120. That means the Senate has thirty days to schedule any floor debate on a nominee, and then have either a recorded vote or voice vote.

Most judicial nominees are not controversial in the slightest. Most are quickly and easily confirmed. But the unprecedented obstruction we've seen from the Democrats since 1987 has been used to keep some of the most promising judicial nominees off the bench, and almost stopped the rest of those promising nominees.

No Filibusters

This means there shouldn't be filibusters, an ideal that can become reality only if both parties faithfully play by the same rules. The filibuster is not found in the constitutional text, and is instead derived from Senate Rule 22 (pursuant to the Constitution's provision that each house of Congress can determine the rules governing its own proceedings). Instead of filibustering, the Senate should reject unacceptable nominees.

Democrats argue that Republicans were the ones who started the filibuster of judicial nominees, but that's not true. When President

Johnson nominated Associate Justice Abe Fortas to succeed Earl Warren as chief justice in 1968, the nomination was blocked by Republicans on account of serious character allegations made against Fortas.
But Fortas never had majority support (even with a large Democratic
majority to support the Democratic president). Had the nomination
been brought to a final floor vote, it would have been voted down. In
retrospect, that's exactly what should have happened.

There was never a Supreme Court nominee who had majority
support to get confirmed and was blocked by a minority of senators
filibustering the nomination. In other words, it's never been the case
that there were fifty-one votes to confirm a nomination but the opposing minority blocked that nomination on account of the fact that the
majority didn't have a sixty-vote supermajority. The Constitution does
not require a supermajority.

Although the Senate is perfectly free to filibuster whatever legislation it likes, the same should not be true for judicial confirmations. The
Constitution allows the Senate not to act on proposed legislation. It
does *not* allow the Senate to keep the federal bench empty.

This doesn't mean the Senate must confirm a president's nominee.
Not at all. If the Senate doesn't approve of a nominee, they should reject him or her. Then the president will nominate someone else, and the
process will begin anew. The president makes his choice and the Senate
either gives a thumbs-up or a thumbs-down. This was the rule for exactly two hundred years, and it must be again.

The Senate is not only a legislative body; it's also a quasi-executive
body, modeled after the Privy Council in the British system of government. The Constitution requires that all legislation pass both the House
and Senate in exactly the same form, and then be signed by the president. But nominations are obviously not legislation, both because the
House has no role in nominations whatsoever and because nominations
start with the president and then go to Capitol Hill, not the other way
around.

The Senate calendar reflects this. The Senate has two calendars. One
is the legislative calendar, on which it handles all bills and resolutions.
The other is the executive calendar for confirmation of presidential appointees and the ratification of treaties that the president has signed.

However, this no-filibuster deal cannot go into effect until after the next presidential election. Democrats created this atrocious mess. And as a senator, Barack Obama was part of this problem, voting to filibuster Justice Alito. Obama has no right to expect he should receive any treatment better than what he's given.

Republicans are correct in saying that the Senate is a body of precedent. Democrats established the precedent that it's okay to filibuster a president's judicial nominees for any reason or no reason. Now that the shoe is on the other foot, Republicans are perfectly justified in holding to the same standard the judicial nominees of a Democratic president.

We need to start over and hit the reset button on judicial confirmations. But it should be when the whole system resets. The current system can stay in place until the next presidential and senatorial election, but after that we all need to get back to the Constitution when it comes to judicial nominations. If the Democratic Party commits to returning to how things used to be, then the Republican Party might do the same.

Keisler Rule for D.C. Circuit Until 2013

Until the next election happens, however, there is a special rule that should be in place for our nation's second-highest court, the U.S. Court of Appeals for the District of Columbia Circuit. It should be called the Keisler Rule, and it too should expire on January 21, 2013.

Senate Democrats—largely at the instigation of Chuck Schumer, with plenty of willing accomplices (including the erstwhile junior senator from Illinois, Barack Obama)—filibustered nominees to the Fourth Circuit to be able to remake that important court in their image.

They also tried to keep top nominees off the D.C. Circuit. We've already seen what they did with Miguel Estrada and tried to do with Judge Brown. But that wasn't all. When they held the majority from May 2001 until after the 2002 midterms, they succeeded in keeping John Roberts off, who was then confirmed in 2003. They stalled Thomas Griffith, who made it in 2005. They stalled Brett Kavanaugh (for having worked in the Bush White House), who was finally confirmed in 2006.

But we also have one other nomination on the D.C. Circuit. Peter

Keisler was the assistant attorney general in charge of the Civil Division at the Department of Justice, making him the number 5 in charge of the department.[50] Keisler was nominated to be a judge on the D.C. Circuit back in June 2006, and the Democrats filibustered him. Then once the Democrats took the Senate in the 2006 elections, they didn't allow a single confirmation to the D.C. Circuit for a full two years. They just shut the process down—in a way that must never be allowed to happen again.

All in all, that means Peter Keisler was denied a confirmation vote for thirty months. Then a new Congress and new president were sworn into office, and the Keisler nomination died. Even though there's no reason to believe that Harry Reid, Dick Durbin, Chuck Schumer, and Pat Leahy would have allowed a confirmation vote on Keisler the following day, let's give them the benefit of the doubt.

Until January 2013, the Keisler Rule is that any nomination to the U.S. Court of Appeals for the D.C. Circuit must wait thirty months before a final confirmation vote occurs on the Senate floor.

To be fair, judicial nominees to the D.C. Circuit sometimes stall. Chief Justice John Roberts, who as we've noted was confirmed to the D.C. Circuit in 2003, was originally nominated to that court by the first President Bush in 1992. But several months later Bill Clinton was elected, and the Roberts nomination was withdrawn. Similarly, Justice Elena Kagan was originally nominated to the D.C. Circuit by Bill Clinton in July 1999. But she never received a committee hearing, so eighteen months later, when George W. Bush took office, her nomination also failed.

Thus both parties have been guilty of not allowing nominations to move forward. But the Keisler nomination marked a new low. He didn't wait eighteen months. He waited thirty months—almost twice as long—until a new president took office. That's just absurd. This obstructionism must end. The course of action we set forth above is a call to both parties to commit to an orderly process and return to the constitutional standard on judicial nominations.

This is not about revenge, either for Peter Keisler or for other nominees like Miguel Estrada (or Charles Pickering). This is instead about fixing the system. By holding to this system until 2013, Republicans can help bring Democrats to their senses, calling them to return to the Constitution when it comes to judicial confirmation standards. Make it clear that these are the consequences for hijacking the judicial appointment process, and maybe we can move forward as a country to return to the wise system that our Founders gave us.

What we find surprising about this D.C. Circuit conversation, however, is the fact that we can have it. Why are there *any* vacancies on the D.C. Circuit?

President Obama has nominated one lawyer for the D.C. Circuit, Caitlin Halligan; he did so in September 2010. Why did he wait almost two years? And more to the point, with two vacancies on this extremely important court, why hasn't Obama nominated someone for the second open seat?

Regardless, Republicans should hold the line that Halligan must wait thirty months for a vote. This will push us past the next presidential election. If Obama wins reelection, then he can renominate Halligan and expect a vote in March 2013. But Republicans should not allow a vote before then.

FOUR CRITERIA FOR CONFIRMING
A JUDICIAL NOMINEE

There should be only four criteria for vetting judicial nominees.

The first is education. The reality is that not all law schools are equal. The higher-ranked schools, like Harvard, Stanford, Columbia, or the perennially top-ranked school, Yale, teach law on a more philosophical level, seemingly assuming that you figure out basic rules of law when you study for the bar exam after graduation.

There's nothing wrong whatsoever with lawyers whose careers are spent on the nuts and bolts of the law. Everyone needs a will; every person arrested needs a defense lawyer; every crime committed needs a skillful prosecutor to see justice done.

Federal judges often deal with extremely complex issues. A nominee for a district judge or circuit judge position needs a good education. At the U.S. Supreme Court, nine justices have to navigate impossibly complex legal waters. Getting it wrong has consequences for the whole nation, consequences that history shows can last for decades. Those are the only sort of cases that get to the High Court. If it's not a case like that, then the federal appeals court or state supreme court that decided the issue will be left alone; the Supreme Court rarely takes it if it's an easy case. A deeply philosophical training in the law is extremely helpful to getting those cases right.

The fact is that only a few lawyers are cut out for this kind of work. That's not elitism; it's just reality. A candidate needs to have done well in school, and it's fair to consider the institution he or she attended.

The second is experience. A great education is only the beginning. For a district judge—who handles trial-level work—you need a great legal career as a practitioner.[51] For a circuit judge on a court of appeals, the job is more about mastering legal doctrines and understanding not just countless rules of law, but also having a principled judicial philosophy. It's helpful to have clerked for a federal judge—usually a circuit judge. For Supreme Court justices, these days it's often going on from a circuit clerkship to then clerk for the Supreme Court. Either way, after those clerkships, it's usually a number of years of impressive achievement with established firms, or in top government positions, or as a professor. And for a Supreme Court justice, it often involves first serving as a lower federal judge.

The third is character. Criminal convictions are problematic, though not always a disqualifier. Crimes—or even noncriminal actions—that involve deceit or dishonesty tend to be deal breakers. Actions that show a person to be less than honest, or to be dirty, or prone to dishonorable behavior, will scuttle a judicial nomination. Abe Fortas, whom we referenced in the filibuster section, was denied confirmation as chief justice because of such concerns regarding his finances.

But in recent years, something unthinkable to the Founders has happened: Some people openly say that judges should just do whatever they think is right, regardless of what the Constitution says. They say that being a judge is about "doing justice" or reaching a "fair" result in a case, regardless of what the law says.

The New Test: Fidelity to the Constitution

So the fourth factor must be fidelity to the Constitution.

Attorney General Ed Meese sees fidelity to the Constitution as being what John Roberts described in his confirmation hearings: that a judge has the job of an umpire, calling balls and strikes according to the rules of the game, without regard to which side is advantaged by those decisions. As then Judge Roberts said, "Umpires don't make the rules, they apply them. The role of an umpire and a judge is critical. They make sure everybody plays by the rules, but it is a limited role."[52] In other words, the chief says he must "remember that it's my job to call balls and strikes, and not to pitch or bat."[53] Sam Alito said much the same thing.[54]

Any way you look at it, the principle emerges that a judge must be bound by the written Constitution. The reason this factor wasn't clearly spelled out in the early years of this country is that it was taken for granted, just like it's not a factor that a judicial nominee must love America, because it goes without saying that someone who doesn't love this country shouldn't hold a lifetime appointment as an officer in this country's government.

From the Constitution's drafting in 1787, until the early years of the twentieth century, everyone understood the role of a judge. As Alexander Hamilton wrote in *The Federalist* No. 78 when explaining to the American public why they should ratify the proposed Constitution, "nothing would be consulted [by federal judges in deciding cases] but the Constitution and the laws."[55] That is to say, federal courts were designed to be "bound down by strict rules and precedents, which serve to define and point out their duty in every particular case that comes before them."[56] For some 140 years, judges acknowledged that their role was to apply the clearly defined rules set forth in the law to the facts before them.

However, we then went through three stages of increasing abandonment of the Constitution. First, "legal realism" began to emerge in the 1920s and '30s, where some judges began to argue that they could take a step away from the words of the law and "look beyond ideals and appearances" to instead decide what is "really going on."[57] By the 1950s and early '60s, liberals moved another step away from the Constitution's text by promoting the "legal process" school, which argues that every law has a "purpose," and so judges should imagine themselves as legislators passing that law, imagining what those legislators were intending to do through this law, then applying those supposed reasons to the specific case before the court.[58] In other words, judges started thinking that it was their job to be mind readers and decide cases according to this legal clairvoyance, a channeling of the Framers or Congress.

But it's gotten worse. Some judges have taken a third step away from the Constitution to become superlegislators.[59] Instead of guessing what Congress or the Framers intended to do, and declare their guesswork law, liberal judges now instead proclaim what Congress or the Framers would have tried to do if they were as enlightened as the judge and had such a superior sense of fairness. As one of the most liberal members of the federal bench from the Ninth Circuit said, "the 'guiding principle of the judicial branch' should be 'concern for social justice and individual rights.'"[60]

No More ABA

We also must remove the American Bar Association (ABA) from the judicial confirmation process. The ABA does not represent the legal community; it's a far-left political organization that advances liberal causes, and it has no business playing a role in judicial confirmations.

Many people don't realize that the ABA is not an official organization. Only a fraction of the lawyers in America belong to the ABA, just as only a small fraction of doctors in the United States are members of the American Medical Association (AMA). There's no official national organization for lawyers. Each state has a state bar, which is part of the supreme court of that state. A person is a lawyer if they are licensed to practice law as a member of the bar of any state, not if they are part of the ABA.

The ABA has repeatedly shown its leftist bias when it comes to judicial nominees. While even the ABA could not deny a "well qualified" rating to John Roberts and Sam Alito, because doing so would have reduced the ABA to a laughingstock, they've selectively used their ratings against Republican nominees to the circuit courts. For example (and there are many), the ABA rated Judge Brett Kavanaugh of the D.C. Circuit "qualified" despite the fact that this graduate of Yale Law (and Yale College) clerked for one of the most demanding circuit judges in the country, then Justice Kennedy on the Supreme Court, and then had an impressive career as an associate White House counsel and staff secretary. What's more, the ABA originally rated Kavanaugh "well qualified," but then downgraded him (and another judicial nominee as well) after a couple of additional leftists joined the ABA's evaluating committee.[61]

One thing that the Bush administration did well when it comes to judicial nominees was to say that ABA ratings would no longer be a factor for considering a nominee's fitness to sit on the bench. The ABA has become a nest of left-wing hackery, on everything from same-sex marriage to gun control, and shouldn't have any role in assessing candidates' fitness. The next Republican president should promptly jettison the ABA from the confirmation process.

Federalist Society to the Rescue?

At minimum, the Federalist Society for Law and Public Policy Studies should have exactly the same role as the ABA.

The Federalist Society (Fed Soc) is an organization of conservatives and libertarians created to debate liberalism head-on. Founded in 1982 by David McIntosh, Steven Calabresi, Lee Otis, and Spencer Abraham, the Federalist Society has grown to almost fifty thousand judges, lawyers, law professors, and law students, with a chapter in every law school in America. Fed Soc serves as a counterweight to the ABA and works to provide an organizing structure in legal academia for those seeking to uphold fidelity to the Constitution.

The Federalist Society has its own challenges, to be sure. Despite the fact that it was founded to offer an open forum where all viewpoints could be expressed, increasingly radical libertarians (largely within the Beltway) are working to ensure that only libertarian—not conservative—viewpoints are expressed, especially on social issues such as same-sex marriage. Fed Soc will have to continue to work hard to welcome conservatives—especially Christian conservatives—if they don't want to see a rival organization arise that represents a broader cross section of America's political spectrum.

But the Federalist Society's leadership—which includes conservative stalwarts such as former attorney general Ed Meese—is committed to maintaining a broad appeal and a big tent to provide an intellectual defense for a view of the law that calls for judicial restraint and adherence to original meaning. According to David McIntosh—a conservative former congressman expected to return to public office in Indiana—Fed Soc's focus is to be an organizing force for constitutional fidelity in America and it understands that there are far more conservatives than libertarians in America. Although its membership rolls are not public, Justice Sam Alito, Senator Mike Lee, and former attorney general Michael Mukasey are among its members. The Federalist Society continues to be a growing presence that ties in nicely with the reawakening of the American people to constitutional conservatism, and can provide an invaluable tool to help educate millions of Americans on how to understand the intricacies of the Constitution and what it means for all the challenges we face today.

Ed Meese, Godfather of Originalism

Further perspective on this comes from Attorney General Edwin Meese III, who has an unparalleled perspective on the U.S. Constitution and the role of the U.S. Supreme Court.

Aside from U.S. presidents, Ed Meese has had more impact on the direction of constitutional law in the United States than any other person in our history. (And even among presidents, perhaps only seven have had a greater impact on constitutional law:[62] George Washington,[63] John Adams,[64] Thomas Jefferson,[65] James Madison,[66] Abraham Lincoln,[67] Franklin Roosevelt,[68] and Ronald Reagan.[69])

In this context, Meese is best understood as the godfather of originalism. On July 9, 1985, shortly after making the transition of being counselor to the president for Ronald Reagan to becoming Reagan's attorney general, Meese gave a speech to the American Bar Association. In it, General Meese said:

> The belief in a jurisprudence of original intention also reflects a deeply rooted commitment to the idea of democracy. The Constitution represents the consent of the governed to the structures and powers of the government. The Constitution is the fundamental will of the people. . . . To allow the courts to govern simply by what it views at the time as fair and decent is a scheme of government no longer popular. . . . The

permanence of the Constitution has been weakened. A constitution that is viewed as only what the judges say it is no longer is a constitution in the true sense.[70]

In a speech to the Federalist Society several months later, General Meese clarified that by "original intention" he meant exploring the original meaning of the words the Framers agreed upon by their vote to adopt them. Speaking for President Reagan on behalf of the administration, Attorney General Meese said:

> Our approach to constitutional interpretation begins with the document itself. The plain fact is it exists. It is something that has been written down.... Indeed, judicial review has been grounded in the fact that the Constitution is a written ... document.... The presumption of a written document is that it conveys meaning.... And the meaning can be found.... Our approach understands the significance of a written document and seeks to discern the particular and general principles it expresses. It recognizes that there may be debate at times over the application of these principles. But it does not mean these principles cannot be identified.[71]

The ascendancy of originalism is essential to the resurgence of constitutional conservatism. You can't be faithful to the Constitution if you don't know what it means. And you cannot restrain government power unless you confine its application of the Constitution within a fixed and objective meaning that can't be reinterpreted on a whim.

That's why originalism is the sole legitimate way to interpret the Constitution. It makes the Constitution mean what We the People adopted as our Supreme Law. And the Constitution cannot be upheld as our Supreme Law unless we have judges who faithfully apply our Constitution in the courts today.

Split the Ninth Circuit to Create the Twelfth Circuit

We need to proactively shape the courts in the direction of constitutional conservatism.

The United States is divided into twelve federal appeals courts.[72] The country is geographically divided into the following appeals circuits, listed with the number of authorized judges for each court:

Circuit	Judges	States and Territories
1st	6	Massachusetts, New Hampshire, Maine, Rhode Island, Puerto Rico
2nd	13	New York, Connecticut, Vermont
3rd	14	Pennsylvania, New Jersey, Delaware, Virgin Islands
4th	15	Virginia, Maryland, North Carolina, South Carolina, West Virginia
5th	17	Texas, Louisiana, Mississippi
6th	16	Ohio, Michigan, Kentucky, Tennessee
7th	11	Indiana, Illinois, Wisconsin
8th	11	Arkansas, Missouri, Iowa, Minnesota, Nebraska, North Dakota, South Dakota
9th	29	California, Arizona, Nevada, Oregon, Washington, Idaho, Montana, Alaska, Hawaii, Guam, Northern Mariana Islands
10th	12	Colorado, Wyoming, Utah, New Mexico, Kansas, Oklahoma
11th	12	Florida, Alabama, Georgia
D.C.	11	District of Columbia

Which of these doesn't look like the other? It's the goliath two-thirds of the way down the list. The Ninth Circuit includes roughly one-third of the population of the United States, and has twelve more judges than the next-biggest circuit court.

For years, the U.S. Court of Appeals for the Ninth Circuit has been the most liberal federal appellate court in the nation. It's time to split the Ninth Circuit. Every couple of years someone introduces a bill to do just that.

The Constitution empowers Congress to create new courts. Only the Supreme Court must exist per the Constitution. Beyond that, Article III of the Constitution authorizes Congress to create inferior courts as Congress sees fit, as well as set the number of judges on each court. Congress should split the Ninth Circuit into two new circuits, and create a new court called the U.S. Court of Appeals for the Twelfth Circuit.

Court splitting happened as recently as 1981. That's how we got the current Eleventh Circuit. If you look at the graph above, all the states now in the Eleventh Circuit were formerly in the Fifth Circuit. But since the Fifth Circuit had become too large, Congress passed and Jimmy Carter signed a law creating the new Eleventh Circuit, which has its courthouse (or "sits") in Atlanta.[73] Not only that, but the new Ninth Circuit and Twelfth Circuit under our proposed plan would both be larger than the Fifth Circuit and the Eleventh Circuit under previous law. The Eleventh Circuit plan to split the Fifth Circuit, by the way, was passed by a Democratic House and Senate and signed by a Democratic president in 1980, before a presidential election. But this law did not go into effect until October 1, 1981, when it was not clear which party would hold the White House. Democrats and Republicans cooperated in doing this because they knew that it was the right thing for the courts and country, even if it meant that a Republican president might have an opportunity to appoint new judges.

Jimmy Carter should have split the Ninth Circuit, instead of adding ten new judgeships to it. Instead he took the opportunity to pack that court with far-left judges, as we saw earlier. But later Carter signed the 1980 law to create the Eleventh Circuit. The next president should follow Carter's court-splitting example, not Carter's court-packing example.

The Ninth Circuit would continue with California, Hawaii, Guam, and the Northern Mariana Islands. The other states—Arizona, Nevada, Oregon, Washington, Idaho, Montana, and Alaska—would become the new Twelfth Circuit. This court would sit in Phoenix, Arizona, as the largest city within the new circuit. Current judges would be reassigned according to the states wherein those judges reside.

This Judicial Reorganization Act has stalled for far too many years. The Ninth Circuit is a massive, unwieldy court, and it doesn't serve the interests of justice to create such a clogged system. All the circuits should be roughly the same size, and if the Ninth Circuit is split and a Twelfth Circuit created, it would restore parity among the federal appeals courts.

All Conservatives Must Focus on the Courts

The courts are not just an issue for SoCons. ECons and SafeCons must be every bit as focused on getting constitutionalist judges on the bench. Beyond abortion, same-sex marriage, and gun control, the courts are now weighing in on issues across the policy spectrum.

ECONOMY ON THE CHOPPING BLOCK IN COURT

These include economic issues. In Chapter 8, most of our discussion on Obamacare focuses on the legal challenges to the law's constitutionality. (Klukowski is involved with these lawsuits.) There are also various lawsuits involving the Clean Air Act and EPA findings with huge implications for the economy.

This is one issue where radical libertarians are as dangerous to constitutional law as the Far Left. As mentioned in Chapter 4, one of the hallmarks of radical libertarians is that they want the courts to decide economic issues by declaring new economic rights and striking down laws that run afoul of these nonexistent rights. They write of returning us to the era of *Lochner v. New York,* where the Supreme Court struck down a New York labor law under which bakeries couldn't allow employees to work more than sixty hours a week.[74] The Court corrected course in 1937, rightly holding that the Court is completely unqualified to decide matters of economic policy, and that it's judicial activism for judges to try such a thing.

Both the Far Left and radical libertarians want the Supreme Court to return to *Lochner.* Constitutional conservatives must fiercely oppose such a wrongheaded idea. Most judges would be completely inept at evaluating business decisions or corporate management. Many radical libertarians are ivory-tower elites who themselves would never be trusted with running a business, to say nothing of imposing those judgments on business leaders who by contrast *do* know what they're doing. Conservatives must remain united against the courts taking over businesses.

Standing

One particular aspect of one of these recent economic cases bears discussing here. In 2007, the Supreme Court held that Massachusetts had standing to sue the EPA and force it to create a cap-and-trade system. The Bush EPA was rightly trying not to claim this power, and Massachusetts (joined by other states) sought to force the EPA to seize control of part of our economy. Ignoring two hundred years of precedent, the Court held 5–4 in *Massachusetts v. EPA* that a state has standing to force the federal government to exert power on questions of global warming.[75]

EPA therefore turned on what is called "standing." Article III of the Constitution limits judicial power to "cases or controversies."[76] That means the lawsuit papers filed in a federal court must meet certain requirements to be a "case" where the court can properly exert its power. One element of Article III's case-or-controversy requirement is standing. To have standing, a plaintiff must show that he has suffered a concrete, personal injury that's different from the public at large, an injury that can be traced back to the defendant, and one that a court can fix by granting the relief that the plaintiff requests in his lawsuit.[77]

In *Massachusetts v. EPA*, the Supreme Court got it wrong. The science doesn't support that global warming is a man-made injury. The science does not support that it's traceable to the United States. And even if the Court gave Massachusetts what the state asked for (cap-and-trade in America), it wouldn't redress the injury, because 80% of CO_2 emissions come from foreign sources. In finding standing, the Court bought into the global warming debate, took a side in this political issue, and handed down a ruling with critical implications for the U.S. economy.

The reason we're talking about standing is that it's a jurisdictional issue. Although "jurisdiction" sounds unimportant, the reality is that jurisdiction defines the scope of power of the federal courts to act. Where a court lacks jurisdiction, it lacks power to do *anything*. So if a court doesn't find that a plaintiff has standing, it has to leave the people and their elected leaders free to decide issues themselves.

In one of the Supreme Court's most recent commentaries on standing, Justice Kennedy's controlling opinion explained, "Relaxation

of standing requirements is directly related to the expansion of judicial power."[78] While completely true, it's ironic that Justice Kennedy would say that, given that he was the fifth vote to find standing
in *EPA*.

The stakes are tremendous when a case involves striking down a law
adopted by the people's elected leaders. As William Rehnquist wrote
for the Supreme Court:

> The exercise of the judicial power . . . is, of course, most vivid when a fed-
> eral court declares unconstitutional an act of the Legislative or Executive
> Branch. While the exercise of that "ultimate and supreme function" is
> a formidable means of vindicating individual rights, when employed
> unwisely or unnecessarily it is also the ultimate threat to the continued
> effectiveness of the federal courts in performing that role. While the
> propriety of such action has been recognized since *Marbury v. Madison*,
> it has been recognized as a tool of last resort on the part of the federal
> judiciary throughout its nearly 200 years of existence.[79]

Discussing standing in particular, Rehnquist went on to explain:

> Those who do not possess Art. III standing may not litigate as suitors in
> the courts of the United States. Art. III, which is every bit as important in
> its circumspection of the judicial power as in its granting of that power, is
> not merely a troublesome hurdle to be overcome if possible so as to reach
> the "merits" of a lawsuit which a party desires to have adjudicated; it is
> part of the basic charter promulgated by the Framers of the Constitution
> at Philadelphia in 1787, a charter which created a general government,
> provided for the interaction between that government and the govern-
> ments of the several States, and was later amended so as to either enhance
> or limit its authority with respect to both States and individuals.[80]

As shown above, ignoring standing requirements is what made possible
the worst judicial travesty in American history, *Dred Scott*. Nothing
should be a higher priority for economic conservatives than pushing for
judges who strictly adhere to the Constitution's limits on the jurisdiction of the federal courts.

FEDERAL JUDGES IMPERILING
NATIONAL SECURITY

SafeCons should also focus on the judiciary. Courts are taking an un-precedented role in deciding national security issues, and conservatives must shove the courts out of this area of government, where judges are completely unqualified to make decisions.

In 2008, the Supreme Court made an unprecedented move, ignor-ing centuries of Supreme Court decisions to weigh in on how America was waging the War on Terror. By a 5–4 vote, the Court held in *Boume-diene v. Bush* that foreign terrorists held at the U.S. naval base in Guan-tánamo Bay, Cuba—which is foreign soil—are entitled to the writ of habeas corpus to challenge their detention in federal civilian court.[81]

Writing for all four dissenting conservative justices in this 5–4 deci-sion, Justice Antonin Scalia says:

> America is at war with radical Islamists. . . . The game of bait-and-switch that today's opinion plays upon the Nation's Commander in Chief will make the war harder on us. It will almost certainly cause more Ameri-cans to be killed. . . . [This] decision is devastating. . . . Astoundingly, the Court today raises the bar, requiring military officials to appear before ci-vilian courts and defend their decisions under procedural and evidentiary rules that go beyond what Congress has specified. . . . And today it is not just the military that the Court elbows aside. A mere Two Terms ago . . . four Members of today's five-Justice majority [said]: "Nothing prevents the President from returning to Congress to seek the authority [for mili-tary commissions]." . . . Turns out they were just kidding. . . . the Court blunders in nonetheless. Henceforth, as today's opinion makes unnerv-ingly clear, how to handle enemy prisoners in this war will ultimately lie with the branch that knows least about the national security concerns that the subject entails.[82]

But that's not the only case where courts are ignoring the Constitution in overriding the political branches of government on national security these days.

By now everyone's heard of Judge Vaughn Walker's decision from the U.S. District Court for the Northern District of California, declaring a federal constitutional right to same-sex marriage in *Perry v. Schwarzenegger* and striking down part of the California Constitution defining marriage as between a man and woman. (We discuss marriage in Chapter 9.) The Ninth Circuit heard arguments in the case on December 6, 2010, and a decision may have come down by the time you're reading this, with the case now heading to the Supreme Court if it wasn't dismissed for a procedural reason.

However, fewer people have heard of Judge Virginia Phillips from the U.S. District Court for the Central District of California. In the case *Log Cabin Republicans v. United States,* on October 12, 2010, Judge Phillips struck down Congress's Don't Ask, Don't Tell law (DADT).[83] This decision is shocking and outrageous, far worse than the California same-sex marriage one. It was on appeal to the Ninth Circuit when Congress repealed DADT and rendered this case moot.

That's not to say that this district court decision in *Log Cabin Republicans* has more of an impact on society than redefining marriage. After all, marriage is the fundamental institution of human civilization, so overhauling marriage obviously has a greater effect on our nation.

What makes *Log Cabin Republicans* worse is the judicial interference in the military. As Judge Phillips acknowledges in her decision, the Supreme Court has repeatedly held that courts must give special deference to the president and Congress when it comes to the military. This rule stems from the fact that judges have no training or experience in national security and lack access to classified information that informs the decisions of Congress and the president on questions of military readiness.

But then she completely ignored that rule by declaring DADT unconstitutional. Even though President Obama and Hillary Clinton opposed that law, it was still the law unless Congress repealed it.

There's no constitutional right to serve in the military. Someone who is blind or hearing-impaired cannot serve in uniform. In fact, having foot problems or allergies will disqualify you from being able to serve in the military.

So it's utterly outrageous—a level of judicial activism rarely seen in America—for a federal judge to invoke a supposed right to homosexual conduct, declare it a fundamental right (which the Supreme Court *never* did when it legalized sodomy in the 2003 case *Lawrence v. Texas*, which we examined earlier), and use it to strike down a *military* law.

ALL AMERICANS SHOULD DEMAND
CONSTITUTIONALIST JUDGES

An agenda judge doesn't change his spots. A judge who's willing to ignore the plain meaning of the Constitution in one case doesn't think twice about doing it in another.

This covers every issue voters care about. Obamacare is unconstitutional. But a judge who's willing to declare a constitutional right to same-sex marriage or right to serve in the military is also willing to declare a constitutional right to healthcare. The same goes for denying rights the judge doesn't like that are expressly mentioned in the Constitution, such as free speech when it comes to laws such as McCain-Feingold in the recent *Citizens United* case. Or the right to bear arms as a fundamental right guaranteed to individual citizens, as in the recent *Heller* and *McDonald* cases.

You cannot compartmentalize how you interpret the Constitution. A judge either believes he or she is bound by the words of the constitutional text, and interprets those words according to their original meaning, or that judge does not.

If you care about anything in the Constitution, you need to be outraged whenever an unelected, unaccountable, life-tenured judge overrides the will of the people in the name of the Constitution, when in fact the Constitution never speaks on that issue. Judges must strike down laws that violate the Constitution, but must strike them down only when the Constitution demands it.

Nothing should be more important to constitutional conservatives than the federal judiciary, and especially the Supreme Court. More than any other factor, whether our Constitution is resurgent will depend on whom the next president appoints to our Supreme Court.

7

A BALANCED BUDGET
AND FAMILY FLAT TAX

"It's time Congress cut the federal budget and left the family budget alone."

—Ronald Reagan, March 19, 1987

I f there's one thing Americans are outraged about right now, it's that the government spends too much. If anything, though, this issue is far worse than most people realize. We are facing a tsunami of federal spending obligations that could literally destroy our republic as we've known it. Our situation is so dire that it could easily become catastrophic, so we must pass the Balanced Budget Amendment to the U.S. Constitution.

The Left tries to focus the debate on "debt" and "deficits." If that's the problem, there are two ways to fix it: One is to cut spending, and the other is to raise taxes.

Constitutional conservatives need to ensure that the Republican Party doesn't fall into this trap. We don't just have a problem with deficits. We have a problem with spending too much. It's not that taxes are too low, it's that spending is too high. We need to cut spending until the budget is balanced, and then lock spending levels within what the government takes in.

At the same time, we need to fix America's broken tax code. Also as we explain here, we need a fundamental overhaul of the federal income tax to create a Family Flat Tax.

It has taken the United States decades of irresponsible and unrestrained spending and counterproductive taxes to get into the terrible mess we're in today. With a Balanced Budget Amendment and a Family Flat Tax, America can begin to climb out of the fiscal pit that we've dug for ourselves over the past seventy years.

This is going to be a very painful process over the coming years. It will require genuine sacrifice from the American people, and a new way of living and doing business. But we have no choice. If we care about our children as much as we claim to, we must finally fix this terrible problem for their sake, or they will inherit a bankrupt country where millions are in need, families struggle just to find food and work, and we're in constant danger of foreign invaders that could topple our nation.

As apocalyptic as this description may sound, it's not hyperbole. Without exaggeration, we face a fiscal meltdown like nothing we've seen in our national existence. We'll either conquer this problem, or it will destroy us. Although we talk about the biggest part of this fiscal monster in Chapter 13—the entitlements of Social Security, Medicare, and Medicaid—we now turn to the big picture of fixing our taxing and spending problems.

BALANCED BUDGET AMENDMENT TO THE U.S. CONSTITUTION

When Republicans took Congress in 1994, part of the GOP agenda was to pass a constitutional amendment requiring a balanced budget. It failed. As we've discussed, constitutional amendments require two-thirds of the House and Senate to propose amendments, and then three-fourths of the states to ratify. While there was a lot of political will for change when 1995 began, it wasn't enough for such a monumental effort for structural reform of America's finances.

Today may be different.

Americans are more outraged about the size and cost of government than they've been in many decades, if not ever. The Tea Party has proven a potent political force, especially in Republican primaries. If a national campaign is properly structured, then over the next four years it's possible that a constitutional amendment could be adopted to forever rein in government expenditures.

The American people know we need to balance our budget. Recent polls show that 85% of voters understand that these deficits will hurt future generations. And voters prefer cutting spending to raising taxes by almost two-to-one.[1]

Text of the Proposed Amendment

Two versions of the Balanced Budget Amendment were considered in the aftermath of the 2010 midterm elections. One was written by the senior senator from Utah, Senator Orrin Hatch, which attracted support from some of the more established members of the Senate. The other was written by the junior senator from Utah, Senator Mike Lee, and was the favorite of a dozen unapologetic conservatives, including most of the newer senators backed by the Tea Party.

They represent two different groups. Hatch was elected to the Senate in 1976, is tied with one other member as the most senior Republican senator, and was chairman of the Senate Judiciary Committee. Lee was elected as part of the constitutional conservative wave of 2010 and is one of the youngest members of the Senate at the time of this writing. Despite being a junior member of the body, as the only former Supreme Court clerk in the Senate, Lee has quickly become a top constitutional scholar in the Senate, and is touted as a potential future Supreme Court justice. This pairing shows a new consensus—both between generations and across a broad swath of the political spectrum—that our national debt is a top national priority requiring extraordinary and unprecedented action by addressing it at the constitutional level.

Senators Hatch and Lee chose to work together, and wrote a composite version of the BBA introduced as Senate Joint Resolution 10 on March 31, 2011, with all forty-seven Republican senators signing on as cosponsors. This shows that the BBA has now become a priority of the entire Republican Party, creating hope that after decades of failure on this issue, the GOP may finally be facing reality. This version has eleven sections tackling every aspect of America's fiscal disaster.

Section 1 provides that for every fiscal year, total monetary outlays for the federal government cannot exceed total receipts. The former must be less than the latter. There can be no spending items that are "off-budget," meaning that we pay for them, but they don't get counted on the balance sheet. There's no way to get around it. In comparing these top-line numbers, government must spend less than it collects. It also provides that the only way this cap can be exceeded—except for the emergencies explained in Sections 6 and 7—is if a two-thirds supermajority of both houses of Congress vote to do so for one year.

Section 2 caps total government spending at 18% of our gross domestic product (GDP). Government spending is a major economic factor. After a certain point, government spending pulls so much money out of private commerce that it hampers business innovation and economic growth. In other words, when government becomes too big, it hurts the economy even if the government budget is completely balanced. Persuasive research shows that when federal spending exceeds 18% of GDP, it begins to have this negative effect.[2] Thus 18% of GDP may be the optimal size of government for economic growth and stability in a modern economy. Given that America has a $14 trillion economy—and an economy that can become far larger if we enact the right policies—18% of $14 trillion still allows us to afford a massive government, far larger than the entire GDP of many nations around the world. Such a government has all the money it needs to perform all the functions assigned to it by the Constitution. So Section 2 is a second limit on federal spending—this one on the overall size of spending relative to America's economy—to ensure that the size of our government doesn't harm economic growth.

Section 3 tasks the president of the United States with submitting a balanced budget to Congress before the beginning of each fiscal year. Although Article I of the Constitution gives Congress exclusive power to appropriate money (and includes no role for the president aside from signing or vetoing a spending bill), for many decades the president has proposed a budget that Congress uses as a starting point. This section does two things. First, it requires presidential leadership, putting the president on record for spending levels he's willing to stand by that give us a balanced budget. Second, it increases political pressure on Congress in that they can't say "We can't figure out a way to balance the budget" if the president has already given them a book-size document showing at least one way balance can be achieved.

Section 4 requires that any increase in federal taxes can be enacted only through a two-thirds vote of Congress. This new supermajority requirement is the best possible check on excessive taxation, especially when coupled with the Family Flat Tax discussed later in this chapter. Recognizing that cutting taxes can lead to increased government revenues, this section also explicitly excludes calling any cutting of marginal tax rates an increase in taxes.

Section 5 requires a three-fifths vote to raise the debt ceiling. That's a crucial issue, in that as of 2011 it has become a potent political issue in the fight against runaway spending creating crushing intergenerational debt. By raising the threshold needed to increase the overall debt of the country—which is at a horrifying $14.3 trillion at the time of this writing—we may finally be able to force government to live within its means by empowering even a large minority in Congress to impose a limit on aggregate federal debt.

Section 6 allows an escape valve as a contingency to handle a true emergency during a war. Congress can suspend Sections 1, 2, and 5 for one year. In the event of a *declared war* (not some unilateral presidential action or some vaguely authorized conflict) against a *nation-state* (not international terrorism or some other amorphous enemy), a simple majority (50% plus one) can vote to suspend it, but only if Congress specifies exactly which spending items can exceed revenues.

Section 7 allows Congress to suspend for one fiscal year Sections 1 and 2 only with a three-fifths vote of Congress, and only in the event of a military conflict that threatens national security but is short of an actual, declared war. The conflict must be specified as such by a joint resolution of Congress, and again this provision does not lift the debt-ceiling requirement of Section 5.

Section 8 specifies that no court—federal or state—can order a tax increase in any lawsuit brought to challenge a supposed violation of the

BBA. So if there is a violation and a lawsuit results, all a court can do is stop spending, not raise taxes.

Section 9 defines "total receipts" and "total outlays" to make sure no one can find creative wording to get around the BBA. It specifies that "total receipts" means every dollar coming in except borrowing (which is held in check by the debt-ceiling provision). And "total outlays" means every dollar spent except for paying down the principal on our national debt.

Section 10 empowers Congress to pass legislation to enact the BBA. This language is found in various other amendments such as the Fourteenth and Fifteenth Amendments. It makes sure that Congress can act to fill in the gaps if someone tries to get around the BBA. It also specifies that Congress can rely on estimates regarding GDP and making a budget.

Section 11 declares that the BBA will take effect on October 1 five years after being ratified by the states. This allows the government time to massively cut spending without a catastrophic cutoff, but no longer.

The BBA represents the most comprehensive, most aggressive attempt in American history to tackle our out-of-control spending since our gross excesses began in the 1930s. The mushrooming of the size and scope—and thus the cost—of the federal government spun completely out of control during the presidency of FDR, and now both political parties have been gripped by an insanity concerning spending, strikingly similar to a drug addiction. Congress has refused to check into rehab, so We the People must force them to permanently change their ways through a constitutional amendment.

There are still concerns to be addressed to make the BBA truly effective at balancing the budget. For example, one provision that was in Senator Mike Lee's BBA that didn't make the final cut would have empowered an individual member of Congress to bring a federal lawsuit to enforce the BBA if that member filed the case with a petition signed by one-third of the members of either house of Congress. The purpose of this was, in the event that the political branches of government failed to abide by the BBA, wherein a president and a majority (but not a supermajority) of Congress decided to spend too much money, to enable an uncompromising constitutional conservative to appeal to the courts to enforce the BBA.

Without this section, it's possible no one would have standing to bring a lawsuit to enforce the budget limits. In Chapter 6, we saw how Article III requires a plaintiff to have standing, which in turn requires his suffering a distinct injury that is traceable to the defendant and that the court can redress. The Supreme Court correctly held in 1923 in *Frothingham v. Mellon* that being a taxpayer doesn't confer standing; you must suffer an injury that can be distinguished from the public at large.[3]

The congressional standing provision would create an exception to the prohibition on taxpayer standing. Otherwise who could sue? The BBA is all about how taxpayer money is spent, so there's no injury except for the one suffered by 300 million people. Requiring a member of Congress to get a petition signed by one-third of the members of either chamber would prevent the possibility of a lone congressman getting angry that his pet program is on the chopping block, and attempting to use a lawsuit as retaliation. If you don't have two-thirds to suspend BBA for a year, then you should have at least one-third willing to sign a petition to enforce BBA.

But there were downsides to this provision. One is that courts can take a long time to resolve issues. Even if you passed a statute sending any case directly to a three-judge district court, with an immediate appeal to the Supreme Court, with strict time limits (weeks, not months), it's possible that the fiscal year could be over before a case could be resolved. Also, once you involve the courts in something, there can be exasperating, unintended consequences. So it was a mixed proposition, and the drafters ultimately decided against it.

The BBA that remains, though, represents an extraordinary achievement. Every constitutional conservative in America needs to demand that every candidate for the U.S. House and Senate, as well as state house and state senate, sign a pledge promising to vote for S.J.R. 10, the BBA.

Making the Amendment a Reality

To pass this constitutional amendment, your author Blackwell has taken the position of national chairman with an organization started after the 2010 elections, called Pass the Balanced Budget Amendment (website http://www.passthebba.org). This is a grassroots organization exclusively devoted to enacting the Balanced Budget Amendment, and Blackwell is working closely with Republican members in both the House and Senate—as well as leaders in the states—to help see the BBA become the Twenty-Eighth Amendment to the Constitution of the United States.

Political will to do this exists that has previously been lacking. As of this writing, several Republican candidates and possible candidates for president have endorsed a constitutional amendment. Increasingly more members of Congress support the idea.

To make it happen, Blackwell's organization is focused on recruiting ten thousand volunteers in every one of America's 435 congressional districts to demand that any candidate for office in that district support passing the Balanced Budget Amendment.

This is a perfect project for the Tea Party to tackle in force. Tea Party members should take a copy of the pledge to every county party meeting and town hall event, making sure every candidate for the U.S. House and U.S. Senate signs the pledge to vote for the BBA, and do the same for every candidate for state house or state senate to vote to ratify the amendment.

This is no time for malleable punch lines like "Cut wasteful spending" or "Stop the spending." Everyone will say they're for that, and nothing will change. To get results, we need clear, unbreakable commitments to something with a concrete, objective meaning.

It's not enough to cut spending in order to merely *reduce* the deficit. We must cut spending however much is necessary to completely balance the budget. We applaud both the senators on the Hatch-Cornyn BBA and the Lee BBA for their principled leadership on this extraordinarily important issue. We need a BBA. Nothing less is acceptable.

TAXING AND SPENDING

The Balanced Budget Amendment is only part of the larger picture of the size and cost of government. Although it balances the equation of taxing and spending, we also need to completely overhaul both how we tax and how we spend.

This is an issue where I (Blackwell) have a great deal of experience. I served as one of the fourteen members of the National Commission on Economic Growth and Tax Reform. These members were appointed by House Speaker Newt Gingrich and Senator Bob Dole. It was chaired by the famed Jack Kemp, and cochaired by Ed Feulner. I was state treasurer of Ohio at the time and had previously served under Jack Kemp as an undersecretary at the U.S. Department of Housing and Urban Development. With Jack I edited and coauthored *The IRS v. The People,* published in 2004 by the Heritage Foundation and with a foreword by Rush Limbaugh. This book then became the initial blueprint for the flat tax book by Steve Forbes discussed below. In fact, it was Jack who years earlier introduced me to Steve. And when Steve ran for president in 2000, I was the national chairman of his campaign.

Taxing and spending—the size and cost of government, ending deficit spending, and repaying our entire national debt—are issues I've worked on for much of my public life. Now is a moment unprecedented in my lifetime to do something about it.

Family Flat Tax

America's tax system is broken. It must be replaced.

Growing awareness of how dire our economic predicament is has resulted in the public being willing to accept higher taxes.[4] One independent quoted by the *Wall Street Journal* said politicians should say, "You know what? It's going to be horrible for the next few years, but you've got to shut up."[5]

But we cannot allow politicians to exploit that willingness by proposing a "grand compromise" of tax hikes coupled with spending cuts. Why? Because higher taxes will make our economic situation worse. It may bring in more revenue in the first year or two, but our problem is a long-term structural spending problem. Thus tax hikes will increase revenue in the first year or so (making it politically attractive) but will result in *less* revenue coming into government coffers in subsequent years, worsening an already terrible situation.

There are problems with our tax system. First, it's a graduated income tax, which punishes success and kills growth. Second, it's riddled with countless special carve-outs, each one designed to help a particular constituency under certain facts, but in so doing it passes along the tax burden to those lacking a high-powered lobbyist. These are the tax equivalent of earmarks, special set-asides reserved for those who can afford expensive lawyers and lobbyists, paid for by everyone else.

The mantra of the Left is to get rid of the "Bush Tax Cuts." That's disingenuous. After President Bush cut taxes, a new baseline for taxes was established. If President Obama allows those taxes to go up, they will be the Obama Tax Hike.

However you define the term, the reality is that we're taxed too much, and we're also taxed badly. While maintaining current tax levels is better than raising taxes, constitutional conservatives must support a bold tax solution.

That solution is a Family Flat Tax.

THE LEFT TAXES JOB CREATION,
NOT "THE WEALTHY"

But first, we need to debunk the myths being parroted by the media about what the Left is trying to do about taxes right now.

Even according to the Tax Policy Center, a joint venture of the liberal Brookings Institution and the Urban Institute, the Obama-Left tax hikes would hit 900,000 small businesses, and 50% of total small business income.[6]

Some on the Left latch on to the point that the Tax Policy Center report says this tax hits only 3% of small businesses, but that misses the point entirely. Most small businesses in America are one-man operations. They're consultants or independent contractors making $30,000 or $60,000 a year. They're independent salesmen, people with a shoe-shining business, or a home repair service. They're independent electricians, plumbers, or house cleaners. These people are not going to get hit directly by this tax increase, but they're also not job creators.

It's the small businesses in that 3% that get hit by the tax—as the report says, 900,000 businesses—that are the job creators. These are the convenience store owners whose store employs five people and makes a $400,000 profit, who can afford to hire a sixth worker as a manager for $50,000 a year. It's the local florist who makes $350,000 a year and employs four people, who wants to hire on a fifth at $32,000 a year. It's the restaurant owner who employs ten people and makes $600,000 a year, who's willing to take a risk and hire a new cook and two new table servers, creating three new jobs at a total cost of $120,000 a year. These job creators are the ones who will get hit by the tax, and hitting them will prevent them from being able to afford to create those new jobs.

Only thriving businesses are able to create new jobs. These jobs would be destroyed by raising taxes, whether by Barack Obama or anyone else.

But that only stops a new problem from being added to the mix. It doesn't solve the current problem.

THREE PRINCIPLES TO KEEP IN MIND

Several tax ideas are being proposed by conservatives. While space doesn't permit exploring all of them, three principles deserve mention here.

First, the ideal tax code in a democracy is a *participatory* tax system. The percentage of Americans paying no federal income tax is growing. Last year, 47% of taxpayers had no federal income tax liability.[7] This may seem like good news for some families, but it's bad news for the country.

The key to keeping taxes low is to give everyone a reason to want them low. If you want people to vote for low taxes, you need to make it in their interest to do so. If they no longer have to pay taxes, then they might not care about voting for someone else to pay higher taxes. And if you promise to a nonpayer that you'll create a new program if someone else pays for it, you can persuade many of them to vote for it. After all, it's no skin off their back.

So to keep taxes low, you need a solid majority of voters paying taxes. When 60% or 70% of voters have to pay taxes, suddenly there's plenty of electoral pressure from the voters for Congress to keep *everyone's* taxes low.

The other principle is that the more provisions you put in the tax code, the more potential there is for government control. Tax credits act as carrots. Tax penalties act as sticks. If you create enough carrots and sticks, you can manipulate the behavior of millions, as they constantly run toward various carrots and away from various sticks. This reduces human beings to Pavlov's dogs, seeking to control the smallest details of their lives. Government control grows proportionately to the size of the tax code.

The lesson from this principle is obvious: You should want as few tax provisions as possible. The shorter the tax code, the more free you are to make your own decisions without government enticements or coercions. So instead of seeking your own pet tax provision, you should seek to have provisions eliminated.

The third principle is that graduated taxes increase government power by progressively punishing success. That's why a graduated income tax is an essential part of a socialist system. By placing an increasingly heavy burden on productivity, the state can increasingly redistribute income to others.

The application of this principle is that the flatter the tax rates are, the more that spurs growth, investment, innovation, and business start-ups.

THE RYAN ROADMAP

These principles also apply to a plan rightly getting a lot of focus these days, the Ryan Roadmap. This plan, put forward by the new House Budget Committee chairman, Paul Ryan of Wisconsin, cuts the number of income tax rates to two, and gets rid of most exemptions, deductions, and credits to drastically simplify the tax code.

This tax system would be far better than what we have today. It does much less to punish success and manipulate behavior, and it does a great deal to simplify an out-of-control tax code. Also it shrewdly focuses on keeping the most popular and most beneficial adjustments in the tax code while scrapping the rest.

While this system would be good, it's important to also understand its remaining drawbacks. First, there's no objective principle upon which to have two tax rates. Why not three? Why not four? Two seems like an arbitrary number. Second, choosing certain tax deductions or credits while getting rid of the rest reflects policy judgments. Although these choices might make sense, they still concede that the government has a role in attempting to influence people's behavior.

The problem with both of these drawbacks is that ten or twenty years from now, there's nothing to keep a future Congress from gradually going back to five or six tax rates. There's also nothing to prevent each new Congress—after the current national mood has passed—to start adding back tax deductions one at a time, starting with the most popular ones. Over a half century, we could find ourselves back where we are today.

While the Ryan Roadmap is a great start, we should go the extra mile to fix this problem once and for all on principles that can be adhered to without exception going forward.

QUESTIONS ABOUT THE FAIRTAX

One plan talked about in conservative circles these days is instituting a national sales tax, called a FairTax. This tax would be a 30% tax (not 23%, as some are incorrectly saying) on almost all goods and services in the United States. To offset the crushing burden this would place on low-income or no-income Americans, the government would send a "prebate" of money calculated to cover food and other life essentials.

There are a number of concerns about this system, although its advocates are completely sincere and they are understandably energized. But there are some questions that we've not yet seen answered. Most of these arise from *The FairTax Fantasy* by Hank Adler, who is a professor of accounting, and Hugh Hewitt, who aside from being a national talk radio leader is also a professor of constitutional law.

The concerns raised by Adler and Hewitt are interesting, though we don't know whether there might be a good answer for each one from the FairTax crowd. One concern is that it could violate a number of U.S. trade treaties, which would carry the consequence of causing a trade war in which American-made exports would drop and foreign goods would be more expensive. The second is that it punishes home ownership in favor of renting a home. The third is that it may not be revenue neutral, in which case it could be a massive loss of revenue to the country (since our models on this issue are unreliable, lacking a frame of reference). And there are many other concerns.[8]

Regardless of those, there are five problems with a FairTax that there might be no way around. The first is that it could be unconstitutional by imposing a taxing regime on the states, which is barred by the Tenth Amendment, since the states are coequal sovereigns. You might need a constitutional amendment to enact the FairTax, not merely a federal statute.

The second is that for the "prebate" to work, the government needs to accurately calculate the cost of living for every household in America and get the checks to every taxpayer on a regular basis. This shows far too much faith in the government, and trusts them with too much information. We're trying to get the tax monkey off our backs, not teach it new tricks. Will the prebate be adjusted for cost of living? Every community has different costs, and even within relatively small areas like a midsized city, some areas are much more expensive to live in than others. Every county has its own taxes. How could government factor all of that into its prebate? And given that many people tend to spend too much of their paycheck within the first few days of getting paid, what about the people who blow through the check right away? Will these checks come monthly? Weekly? Will there be a bailout fund for people going hungry because the prebate is gone for the month?

The third is that the government could manipulate the tax level. If there would be enough public outcry, the government could introduce a lower FairTax rate on certain basics like groceries, or on child-friendly products like schoolbooks. During times of class tension and envy, it could introduce a luxury surcharge to create a higher FairTax rate for certain expensive goods such as sports cars or luxury cars. We could in time have another graduated tax system that's every bit as complex and manipulative as the current system.

The fourth is that it could make tax revenues to the government too unpredictable, making chaos out of an attempt to balance the budget. Consumer purchases are much more volatile than income. During good times people tend to spend a lot more (often more than they should) and during bad times people can pull back sharply. Paychecks, by contrast, are relatively stable. So making all federal dollars contingent on how much people are spending may suddenly leave the government with a large deficit, which under a Balanced Budget Amendment would trigger sudden and drastic cuts to all sorts of programs.

The final challenge with the FairTax is that we would have to repeal the Sixteenth Amendment to the U.S. Constitution, which authorized the income tax. If not, then this could become the worst of all tax systems, where the FairTax would become a European-style VAT (value-added tax). Then our economic candle would be burning at both ends, from an oppressive income tax on one hand and a tax on everything we buy on the other. We see very little chance that the political will exists to repeal the Sixteenth Amendment, so we fear that the enthusiasm for a FairTax will be used by the Left as a foil to trick people into supporting a VAT.

Those pushing for a FairTax do so for all the right reasons and they make many good points. Perhaps there are answers to all of these concerns, and if so, FairTax supporters should make their case in scholarly, peer-reviewed journals. But until someone can dispel each of these concerns, we must consider the possibility that the cure would be worse than the disease.

Family Flat Tax Is the Solution

The solution is the Family Flat Tax, which is essentially the Flat Tax proposed by financial giant and business genius Steve Forbes in *Flat Tax Revolution*.[9] We'll set forth the basics, and leave it to interested readers to peruse a copy of Forbes's book to get a very detailed understanding of this brilliant idea that is sweeping Eastern Europe and fueling prosperity.

This tax would have one large, very generous standard exemption, around $16,000, which would then be indexed for inflation. Like the current system, it could be claimed either by an individual, a head of household (single parent), or a married couple. A married couple's deduction would be exactly double the individual deduction (in this case, $32,000); no penalty for being married. Unlike the current system, though, it would be a refundable exemption instead of a deduction.

To this would be added a generous refundable exemption for every child living at home to a certain age, as well as a credit. You would have a $4,000-per-child exemption, plus a $1,000 refundable credit for every child to age sixteen. Again, both indexed for inflation. Because these provisions are refundable, you would actually get money back if you were low-income or perhaps working-income, instead of just a zero tax liability.

All income beyond this amount would be taxed at 17%. No deductions. No credits. No government interference with your decisions or your life. Also no tricks and gimmicks, or ways for the wealthy to escape most of their taxes through elaborate foreign or offshore structures or charitable vehicles.

Low-income people would not only have no income tax; they would get money from the government. Working-income families would see their taxes drop, not increase. Middle-class families should also see their taxes drop. Upper-middle-class family taxes should be about the same. Some upper-class taxpayers might pay a little bit more. And extremely wealthy individuals—not the small business owner or typical job creator—would see their taxes increase.

This tax would also get rid of all double taxation. No taxes on savings, dividends, or capital gains. This would especially help retired couples and those living on a fixed income. In that vein, no taxes on Social Security, either.

The Family Flat Tax would also get rid of the Death Tax and the Alternative Minimum Tax (AMT). The tax code would be simple and predictable. It would also be eminently fair, in that it would not punish success but the rich would always pay more, because 17% of rich is more than 17% of middle-class.

And here is the kicker: Consistent with Steve Forbes's design, the Family Flat Tax would be *voluntary*, not mandatory. If you prefer, you could stick with the current Tax Code. Predictably, over a few years, the vast majority of Americans would freely choose the easier, simpler, fairer flat tax. But the choice would be yours.

The Family Flat Tax exemplifies the best of the three principles we considered above. It is participatory, in that more than 60% of Americans would pay into it each year (some paying very little). It is completely simple, robbing the government of any control or influence over your decision making. And it's completely flat, fostering maximum economic growth and family wealth creation.

We think it's important to call this a Family Flat Tax. Going back to Chapter 4 and the economic keys of constitutional conservatism for a Sovereign Society, this recognizes that we are a nation of families, not individuals. This policy will encourage family decisions and long-term planning. It will tax the family as the basic unit of our civilization, instead of individuals. (A single adult, of course, is a family of one.)

Many more details can be found in Steve Forbes's excellent book. The Family Flat Tax is the way to go if we are to completely overhaul taxation in America in a way that helps the American people and fosters economic growth to actually *increase* government tax revenues over the long term.

Spending

With all that done, we need to also fix government spending. On that topic we're not going to list countless wastes of your tax money, because the list of waste from Republicans alone would fill this book. The GOP has been a disgrace in their ridiculous spending for many years now.

But if the Republicans were bad, the Democrats were nothing short of contemptible. The numbers bear this out. In the last year of unified Republican government, Fiscal Year 2007, federal spending grew by 2.8%. The next year, with the same Republican president but a Democratic Congress, spending grew 9.1%.[10]

Every president is to blame for signing these bills. But as much blame—if not more—must be laid at the feet of members of Congress. As Thomas Sowell wrote:

No President of the United States can create either a budget deficit or a budget surplus. All spending bills originate in the House of Representatives and all taxes are voted into law by Congress.

Democrats controlled both houses of Congress before Barack Obama became president. The deficit he inherited was created by the Congressional Democrats, including Senator Barack Obama, who did absolutely nothing to oppose the runaway spending. He was one of the biggest of the big spenders.[11]

The reason is that many of President Obama's policies and programs—happily rammed through by Nancy Pelosi and Harry Reid—are socialist policies. Socialism is expensive. As British prime minister Margaret Thatcher once said, "The problem with socialism is that eventually you run out of other people's money."

To restrain such spending, it's extremely helpful not to let politicians grab the money at all. For example, Governor Mitch Daniels is proposing that in Indiana: When the government collects more revenue than the budget requires, the government is to stop collecting after a certain cushion is built up. He tells us, "I would just like to establish the principle that at some point the state should stop collecting money and should leave those dollars with the people who earned them. When the state gets its hands on them it's liable to spend them." Governor Daniels is proposing legislation to create such a system.[12]

STIMULUS? ARE YOU KIDDING?

To all the routine disgraces, the past few years have seen a new type of shameful spending: stimulus. The reality is, the stimulus plan was a complete waste. Christina Romer, President Obama's former chairman of the Council of Economic Advisers, testified under oath to Congress that most of the job-creation effect of the spending stimulus would be seen in 2009, with minor additional effects in 2010. If 2010 is what the stimulus was all about, then America got ripped off.

President Obama's team says we shouldn't be too critical, because aside from creating jobs, the stimulus was designed to surge economic growth. On the unemployment front, President Obama's big-government policies actually have the opposite effect. "One of America's great advantages has always been its flexible, private-sector labor markets. From 1985 to 2008, U.S. unemployment averaged 5.6%. For the six largest economies in the European Union, the average was 34% higher, at about 7.5%."[13] On the economic growth front, the after-action examinations of the stimulus led to headlines such as "Economists: The stimulus didn't help."[14]

Such "stimulus" amounts to no more than political wish lists, an orgy of spending for every worthless idea that an individual member of Congress had, but that others laughed at the thought of funding. When the stimulus came along, all these bad ideas were crammed into a ridiculous bill.

Steve Forbes mentioned one part of the stimulus as an example: railroads. The stimulus included $8 billion to build high-speed railroads in several places in the country. While it sounds interesting, in reality it's a loser. The railway that's been slated to connect Tampa and Orlando replaces a ninety-minute car ride with a sixty-minute train ride. However, those sixty minutes don't count driving to the station, waiting for the train, or how you'll get around sprawling Orlando once you get there. Another between Chicago and St. Louis would reduce travel time by only 10%. Another, to connect four California cities, has seen its cost estimates go from $25 billion in 2000 to now over $80 billion.[15]

Forbes goes on to say of these rail projects, as can be said of these stimulus programs generally, that they "couldn't pass the laugh test in the private sector, yet they will soak up capital that otherwise could be used for productive purposes. And it's not just the capital. Almost all high-speed rail schemes around the world operate at a loss."[16] Beyond that, experts explain that freight train systems operate better under a different set of track factors than passenger trains, so if we retool our track system for these high-speed systems, we will degrade what is currently the most effective system in the world for moving large amounts of goods nationwide.[17]

BAILOUTS

A close cousin of the stimulus outrage is the concept of taxpayer-funded bailouts. If you can't succeed in the marketplace, then you need to find a new job. You can't be free to succeed unless you run the risk of failure. In the free market, businesses go under all the time. But it's a system that creates more wealth for more people than any other system in the history of humanity.

The basic theme of the national dialogue on bailouts over the past three years shows just how deeply flawed the whole approach is. The White House showcases statements like the idea that many economic leaders (including some Republicans) agree that we lost far fewer jobs in 2008 and 2009, and did much better in terms of GDP with the stimulus than if we had done nothing.[18] One study says that with the bailouts, employment maxes out at 10% and in 2011 we'll have a GDP of $13.8 trillion, whereas without the bailouts we'd have 16% unemployment and a $12 trillion GDP.[19]

However, the correct question is: What if instead of passing the bailouts, we did the *right* things to fix the economy?[20] The economy was in shambles. Yes, something had to be done. It's a false choice to say we must either do the bailouts or do nothing. There were dozens of different approaches we could have taken. The bailouts were the wrong choice, because that put a Band-Aid on a growing tumor, giving us months of a respite but not fixing the problem. Instead it made a grave problem even worse and stole precious time that could have been used to enact a true solution.

Nothing would stimulate the economy more than a massive cut in federal deficit spending, coupled with broad-based, permanently low taxes. Yet despite the fact that keeping taxes low at the top marginal rates is the one thing that will create jobs, it is the one thing that President Obama seems congenitally unable to do. Going into the midterms, he promised that the one thing he would not do is stop the massive tax hike that's coming for everyone making $250,000 or more a year.[21]

After getting humiliated in the midterms, President Obama caved to Republican demands to extend those tax cuts, thereby alienating his base. But he extended them for only two years, evidently not understanding that real businesses (as opposed to "community organizing" and other shakedown scams) make investment and employment plans on five-year or ten-year plans, so while it was extremely important to keep tax rates from increasing, we won't see major business expansion as a result.

What do you do with the companies on the edge of failing? You let them go into bankruptcy reorganization. They would not have needed to go into Chapter 7 bankruptcy. Chapter 7 is liquidation, where the company is broken up, dissolved, and ceases to exist. Instead they would have gone into Chapter 11 reorganization, where everyone is brought to the table before a federal bankruptcy judge.

What's killing companies like American automakers are unprofitable and unsustainable labor agreements with the unions. Had those companies gone into Chapter 11, a bankruptcy judge would have had the power to open up all contracts with the companies and adjust all of them in a way to save the company. Instead stockholders and bondholders got completely ripped off by the government, and the unions came away with a far better deal than they would ever have gotten. So the unions got a windfall, paid for by a terrible bite on those who invested or lent money to the company, including millions of ordinary Americans in their 401(k)s and IRAs.

Jobs must be sustainable over the long haul, as do retirement plans. One other failure of governments (and some private industries, such as the automakers) is that they've devised retirement plans that are unsustainable. For example, one New York City police officer making $74,000 a year retired at age forty-four with an annual pension payout of more than $101,000.[22] Such jobs in New York are common, where employees are promised far more than pension funds can possibly deliver, given the actuarial reality that people are living longer. New York City's pension system has increased its payouts 900%—that's almost *tenfold*—just since the year 2000.[23] One of two things are certain: New Yorkers will get smacked with a crippling tax increase that will chase businesses out of Gotham, or New York City will face bankruptcy—again.

What will happen is predictable. New York City will cry to the federal government for a bailout, aided by the incessant pleading of most of its congressional delegation, which will alternate between pitiful whining, saying that it's all about the children, and self-righteous indignation that "after all they've done for us" in this country, somehow the rest of us owe them.

That's a classic example of this country's bailout mentality, which must end. There's only one entity that's truly "too big to fail" in terms of something that we cannot allow to collapse, and that is the United

States itself. The problem is, unless we stop these bailouts, it's in fact the United States that faces the growing prospect of financial collapse. So everyone else must put their own house in order, or be left to suffer the consequences of their profligacy if they don't.

All this talk about losing jobs and saving a historic company is ridiculous. Chapter 11 should have saved companies like the automakers and made them stronger. If one of them can't survive Chapter 11, then that company is so profoundly unworkable that it should be dissolved, with other automakers stepping in to grow in its place.

No company is too big to fail. We're a nation of people, not companies. Any company so unprofitable that after reorganization it still cannot survive should not survive, because it's a drag on the American economy and thus on the American people.

Finally, some suggest a shocking idea: that we should bail out cities and even whole states that are drowning in debt. California's far-left politics have caught up with it, and now the state is insolvent and barely floating each debt from one month to the next. Its budget deficit is now at least $25 billion,[24] an amount it can't possibly raise. New York is also in critical condition, as are Illinois and other states.[25]

We call on every reader to call their congressman and their two senators and tell them not just no, but "Heck no!" (By the way, a majority of voters oppose bailing out California, so Congress would do itself a favor by voting down such a proposal.[26]) States are sovereign entities, with their own government and constitutionally separate taxing and spending systems. If voters in a state are foolish enough to elect reckless leaders who drive their state off a fiscal cliff, we must unapologetically hold the line in making them reap what they have sown, rather than drive our whole nation deeper into debt.

FAULTY COMPARISON TO 1938

In the *New York Times*, far-left economist Paul Krugman compared our current situation to 1938. Just when it looked like America was emerging from the Great Depression, 1937 saw us fall back. With polls showing that Americans in 1938 supported ending deficit spending, FDR pulled back on his out-of-control government expansion. The U.S. economy continued to decline until we mobilized a couple of years later for the largest global war the world has ever seen so far. Krugman writes:

> The economic moral is clear: when the economy is deeply depressed, the usual rules don't apply. Austerity is self-defeating: when everyone tries to pay down debt at the same time, the result is depression and deflation, and debt problems grow even worse. And conversely, it is possible—indeed, necessary—for the nation as a whole to spend its way out of debt: a temporary surge of deficit spending, on a sufficient scale, can cure problems brought on by past excesses.[27]

This is vintage Krugman. He often criticizes President Obama for not spending enough money, and seems to think the solution for everything is a government takeover. We give him credit for consistency and predictability.

There are two problems with Krugman's analysis of 1938. First, it ignores an alternative theory of the Great Depression as a whole. That analysis is presented in a number of excellent books, such as Burton Folsom's *New Deal or Raw Deal? How FDR's Economic Legacy Has Damaged America* (Threshold Editions, 2009). Folsom's book presents a cogent argument that New Deal economic controls strangled the economy and prevented economic recovery. What enabled the American economy to recover was our national mobilization for World War II, which put millions of Americans in uniform and millions more in factories producing weapons and military assets to defeat a deadly threat to our nation.

The second fatal flaw in Krugman's analysis is that it ignores a fact we study in detail in Chapter 13: America has over $100 *trillion* in entitlement liabilities—a number so large that it's impossible to conceive of its vastness. Social Security was brand-new in 1938. There were sixteen workers for every beneficiary, and less than half the population ever became Social Security recipients, because the minimum eligibility age was set slightly past the national life expectancy. Medicare and Medicaid didn't even exist. We are now in a completely different world from the one to which Krugman refers.

BACK TO SCHOOL ON ECONOMICS

The profoundly misguided policies of the Obama administration come about as a result of two schools of economic thought, and we had better fully escape from both of them if we're going to survive as a country.

The first is Keynesian economics, the school of economic thought named for its pioneer, John Maynard Keynes. Keynesian economics argues that in an economic downturn, the government should both cut taxes and increase spending even if it means running a deficit, both of which are expected to stimulate demand, growing the economy. History proves Keynesian economics is a failed fiscal policy, as demonstrated by the results of three recent presidents who attempted to implement Keynesian policies: Nixon, Ford, and Carter.

So has the Obama administration learned its lesson after almost three years of a struggling-to-failing economy? Do the president and his team understand that his economic plan has failed, and that long-term economic factors will continue to worsen as this plan continues to fail?

No. Just a couple of months before she left the Obama administration to return to academia, Chairman of the Council of Economic Advisers Christina Romer said that the only way to improve our current economic condition is to "spend more and tax less."[28]

But even though Keynesian economics fails, President Obama's policies aren't Keynesian. Under the Keynesian school, deficits must be both *small* and *temporary*. They must be small so they don't swamp the overall budget. And they must be temporary so that you quickly get back to surplus, at which point you take the surplus tax revenues to pay off the debt you just incurred. Obama's budgets, by contrast, run deficits of hundreds of billions of dollars (and often over a trillion dollars) every year for as far as the eye can see. That's neither small nor temporary. Instead, it's a recipe for bankruptcy.

The second school of economics that's infecting the federal government's current economic policies is socialism. This is not to say that everyone (or even most) in the Obama administration is a socialist. But some of the most prominent members of President Obama's team are socialist, such as energy czar Carol Browner, discussed in Chapter 1.

And President Obama himself has made socialist comments. Saying that it's better for everyone when you "spread the wealth around," or that some people make too much money, is a socialist statement. So is saying that out of basic "fairness" you'd enact a tax increase, even though it would not raise more money for the government.

That's the way rulers think in countries such as communist Cuba. Born of Cuban immigrants, Senator Marco Rubio explains why such authoritarian or totalitarian countries don't have their own version of the American Dream. Rubio says, "In those countries, the employee never becomes the employer, the small business can never compete with a big business, and no matter how hard your parents work or how many sacrifices they make, if you weren't born into the right family in those countries, there's only so far you can get." [29]

That can never be allowed to happen here. Perhaps President Obama is not a socialist, and out of the greatest respect for the president and the office of the American presidency we hope he is not, but some of his statements and policies clearly are.

DEBTS AND DEFICITS

These bailouts and falsely labeled stimulus bills are just the latest chapter in the growth of America's insane financial debt.

As *Forbes* describes our current situation, "This year [2010] the U.S. fiscal deficit is projected to be about $1.3 trillion, or 9.1% of GDP. This is the largest it has been for 65 years save for the fiscal 2009 deficit that was 9.9% of GDP. . . ." [30]

At the time of this writing, the most recent mid-session review released by the White House Office of Management and Budget was on July 23, 2010. That's important because July 23 was a Friday, and the report was issued late in the afternoon. It's an old rule in White House politics that whenever possible you release bad or embarrassing information late on a Friday, because the opposition leaders in Congress are gone, media people are leaving the office for the weekend, and the Sunday talk shows are all booked. By the time Monday comes around, the White House spokesman says, "What? That story's three days old."

Commenting on this particular report, one expert says, "Next year's [2011] budget deficit is projected by Mr. Obama's own analysts to be $1.4 trillion, up from $1.3 trillion projected in February. Over the next decade, under his own policies, the cumulative deficit would be $10 trillion. And the national debt would rise from $6 trillion in 2008 to $19 trillion in 2020." These are Mr. Obama's numbers, not those of his Republican critics.

> [The Obama White House] report forecasts real GDP growth to be 3.6% in 2011, in contrast to the . . . Congressional Budget Office forecast of 1.9%. GDP growth rates are projected [by the White House] to be above 4% for 2012 through 2014 and 3.6% in 2015.
>
> This is a five-year average of 3.9%, a pace our economy has rarely met over the past 40 years. One exception was the five years from 1996 to 2000, not coincidentally, the last time the federal budget was balanced.[31]

In other words, the White House estimates are ridiculously optimistic. We don't need Pollyanna planning our future, but that's what OMB's rose-colored glasses amount to.

The reality of politics, though, is that you can deceive the voters only for so long. At some point the truth comes out, and when it does there's no fooling people. When America doesn't enjoy 3.9% economic growth in 2010, 2011, and 2012, Democrats will have to answer for it when Election Day arrives.

THE DEBT CEILING

The one barrier that everything else leads to is the debt ceiling. Deficits, tax revenues, price tags for stimulus packages, bailouts, and Obamacare—it all leads to one aggregate number: our national debt. Our short-term problem is deficit spending. Our long-term problem is debt, and the reason a deficit is a problem is that it means we're adding to the national debt.

The only workable solution to our debt is to balance the budget by radical spending cuts. Alan Greenspan said, "I'm in favor of tax cuts, but not with borrowed money."[32] By that Greenspan meant that the threat the debt poses to our national health is so severe that he'd prefer to let taxes rise than to add to the deficit (and thus the debt). So the only way to prevent a massive tax hike without heaping new debt onto our current situation is to cut spending in a way we've not seen in decades.

This issue is coming to a head, as Congress will have to vote in early 2011 on the "debt ceiling." That's the amount of debt the United States is authorized to issue. Only Congress can authorize incurring debt. The debt ceiling is the aggregate total of allowable debt. When we're running deficits, we're adding to our debt and moving toward the ceiling.

Once that ceiling is reached, one of three things happens. The first is that Congress votes to authorize additional debt, raising the ceiling to permit more deficit spending. The second is that Congress institutes immediate spending cuts—including *rescission* legislation to cancel already appropriated funds—to bring the budget into complete balance. The third is that the United States defaults on its current debt. This would result in our credit rating immediately dropping, devaluing all U.S. debt held worldwide, causing millions of retirement accounts and pensions to become insolvent, and possibly sparking a worldwide financial crash. We know that sounds alarmist, but that's seriously what would happen if $14 trillion in debt instruments were to suddenly lose creditworthiness.

In early 2011, the United States will reach its debt ceiling. That's a moment of truth. Some committed constitutional conservatives like Jim DeMint and Mike Lee in the U.S. Senate have already said they won't vote to increase it without a clear commitment to balance the budget through a constitutional amendment.

The fact that we've reached such an unimaginable number in national debt itself poses a serious risk to this country. Although Congress is almost certain to end up raising the debt ceiling, we should expect that every debt-ceiling vote from this point on will become a serious political event that involves a heated discussion on deficit spending until our budget is balanced. Only then will we stop digging the impossibly deep hole we're in, and start the long climb out of it.

Social Issues at Stake

The issues discussed in this chapter are not just for ECons. Social conservatives, too, have every bit as much at stake when it comes to balancing the budget and overhauling taxes and spending.

This is a moral issue. We are committing intergenerational theft. Every single child in America today is born with a debt burden of $50,000 at the moment they come into this world. Since of course most people don't owe taxes (children, stay-at-home parents, etc.) the personal share of every taxpayer is $120,000. That's a mortgage on a house . . . with no house.

We're doing a terrible thing to our children. As Governor Mitch Daniels of Indiana says, "We are practicing child abuse in a literal sense. . . ."[33] It's unconscionable that parents and grandparents would be so selfish and self-indulgent to allow politicians to run up such horrifying debts on our children. It's time to fight back for our children's sake.

Debt is a burden that those in debt feel every day. It places stress on marriages, and living in it teaches the wrong lesson to our children. It will take us many years to get free of our national debt, and it may take you years to get free of your personal debt. But the time to start is today. That's why America needs a Balanced Budget Amendment, and we need it now.

SoCons should support the Family Flat Tax. It focuses our national domestic policy where it belongs: on the family. Because of its exemptions and credits, the Family Flat Tax doesn't penalize marriage, and it doesn't penalize having children. By getting rid of all the special carve-outs and provisions, it maximizes family autonomy to allow you to make whatever decisions are best for you and your family. The only credits and exemptions are based on the number of people in the family.

SoCons should also support ending stimulus bills and bailouts. These are grossly irresponsible, rewarding failure, self-indulgence, and foolishness. Those who run businesses in such a way must be allowed to fail so that capital and resources will flow to responsible companies and states. Only then can the latter create sustainable jobs that will provide for families for the next generation.

National Security Danger

The government's out-of-control spending is a threat to national security as well (a topic we'll also discuss in Chapter 11).

In fact, the chairman of the Joint Chiefs of Staff has identified the debt as a threat to national security. Noting that by 2012 we'll be paying a dizzying $600 billion a year in interest on the national debt—just interest on current debt, not counting the debt we continue to pile up every single year with our record deficits—Admiral Mike Mullen sounded the alarm at this interest amount: "That's one year's worth of defense budget."[34]

Taken in context, Chairman Mullen's comments seem unbelievable. We have over a million people in active military service, not counting reserves. We have billion-dollar B-2 bombers, fighter aircraft that cost $100 million each, multibillion-dollar aircraft carriers, countless other immensely expensive battleships, destroyers, submarines, tanks, tankers, and carriers. That doesn't even consider the costs of missiles, rockets, munitions, ammunition, gear, fuel, food, housing, salaries, healthcare, and everything else that our military requires.

And according to the highest-ranking officer in the U.S. military, our interest *alone* on our federal debt equals that vast sum. A towering mountain of American wealth, wasted every single year as interest payments on debt.

This situation gets worse every single year. We have the best military in the world. But we won't have it forever if we can't afford the finest equipment and training for our troops, massive investments in researching next-generation weapons technology, good pay and benefits to recruit the best people and provide for their families, and the care our veterans deserve for their service.

The Left incessantly whines about how much we spend on the military, and is blithely ignorant of America's singular role in maintaining some semblance of peace in a dangerous world—a peace predicated on instilling in certain nations around the globe a sobering awareness of what the United States can do when stirred to wrath. Although there are countless ways in which the military procurement process must be improved, it's nonetheless a fact that massive annual outlays for national security programs are a necessity for American safety.

Democrats claim to love employees. The problem is, you can't love employees while hating employers. If those employers go under, then the employees are left without a job.

Republicans need to love both employees and employers. A constitutional conservative economic policy will help employers grow and thrive, enriching their employees in the process.

But government employees are different from private-sector employees. As we'll see in Chapter 13, this has profound implications for government unions. While private unions bargain for higher wages and benefits out of company profits, every dollar of government money comes from the taxpayers. Thus the massive pay and benefits of government union workers—federal, state, and local—is one of the reasons that government debt is crushing our children. Yet unions fight for every penny in states such as Wisconsin, Ohio, and Indiana. When it's government unions versus our children, we must stand strong for our children.

The quintessential Tea Party candidate, Senator Rand Paul, said that the entire Tea Party agenda can be summed up in one word: *debt*.

This book explains how constitutional conservatism encompasses economic, social, and national security issues. Debt is not the only problem that threatens our republic. But make no mistake: The debt we face is a horrifying monstrosity that could bring down our country. Lesser nations could not have survived nearly as long as we have under this crushing burden. Despite our might, though, we are not unbreakable. This debt can break us.

We must reverse course now. Pass the Balanced Budget Amendment. Enact the Family Flat Tax. These two steps will get us on the path to addressing our other pressing needs.

8

OBAMACARE

"It would be a radical departure from [precedent] to hold that Congress can regulate inactivity ... If it has the power to compel an otherwise passive individual into a commercial transaction ..., it is not hyperbolizing to suggest that Congress could do almost anything it wanted. It is difficult to imagine that a nation which began, at least in part, as a result of opposition to a British mandate ... imposing a nominal tax on all tea sold in America would have set out to create a government with the power to force people to buy tea in the first place. If Congress can penalize a passive individual for failing to engage in commerce, the enumeration of powers in the Constitution would have been in vain for it would be difficult to perceive any limitation on federal power, and we would have a Constitution in name only. Surely this is not what the Founding Fathers would have intended."

—Judge Roger Vinson, *Florida v. U.S. HHS,* Jan. 31, 2011

(citing *United States v. Lopez,* 514 U.S. 549, 564, 592 (1995))

(internal quotes and citations omitted).

Of all the areas where President Obama and congressional Democrats have damaged the U.S. economy, the most visible example is healthcare. What they have done is also unconstitutional.

The Far Left finally got one of their longest-standing dreams. In 1993 and 1994, Hillary Clinton pursued an authoritarian socialist government takeover of healthcare. Despite having a Democratic Congress, there were enough moderates in the Democratic Party at that time—and Republicans held enough Senate seats as the minority—that they managed to defeat Hillarycare. But in 2009 and 2010, President Barack Obama—with the support of an ultraliberal Democratic Congress led by Nancy Pelosi and Harry Reid—just barely had the numbers to force it through. Obamacare became law on March 23, 2010.

As we explained in 2010 in *The Blueprint,* key parts of Obamacare are unconstitutional. One of your authors (Klukowski) brings a particular expertise to this issue. Klukowski is one of the lawyers involved in challenging Obamacare in federal court, and was one of the first constitutional lawyers to write about why the Obamacare mandate is unconstitutional, as early as October 2009 in *Politico.*[1] Then, in January 2010, we wrote a column for the *Wall Street Journal* with Senator Orrin Hatch (Republican of Utah) to frame the debate as Obamacare moved toward final passage. Klukowski lectures and debates at law schools across the nation on the unconstitutionality of President Obama's signature legislation. And in the landmark win in the biggest federal case challenging Obamacare—the case in Florida involving twenty-six states—the judge cited Klukowski *twice* in holding Obamacare unconstitutional.[2]

Obamacare is a legislative monster, both in terms of its size and reach, with tentacles spreading into people's private lives and the private sector. Out of its many provisions, the centerpiece of Obamacare is the individual mandate: the requirement that every American—unless you fall within some narrow exception such as belonging to one of a few recognized religions that morally object to any form of insurance or medicine—must purchase federally approved health insurance.

We'll look at its worst provisions here, as well as discuss at the end of this chapter what conservative healthcare reform looks like. But at the outset, we want to note that Obamacare has a critical weakness. It lacks a *severability clause.* If a court finds the individual mandate unconstitutional, and possibly certain other parts of the law unconstitutional, then a court can strike down the *entire* law with a single court decision.

This is what happened in Florida's major Obamacare federal court case. In fact, the amicus brief Klukowski wrote was on severability. Of that brief, Judge Roger Vinson wrote, "In considering this issue, I will at times borrow heavily from one of the amicus briefs filed in the case for it quite cogently and effectively sets forth the applicable standard and governing analysis of severability."[3] The brief persuaded him that the individual mandate could not be severed from the rest of the Obamacare statute. Should this ruling be upheld on appeal, Obamacare will be entirely swept away.

Leftists Call for National Takeover of Healthcare, Say Challenges Not Serious

Evidently sensing the serious danger a constitutional challenge to Obamacare would pose, White House supporters jumped to its defense. Erwin Chemerinsky, an ultraliberal law professor and law school dean, wrote a rebuttal to Klukowski's op-ed in *Politico,* saying, "Klukowski's argument is flawed."[4] Other liberal professors also jumped to defend Obamacare, with Yale's Akhil Amar (whom some tout as a conservative but who's firmly on the left) saying Obamacare "easily passes constitutional muster."[5] Bill Clinton's former acting solicitor general Walter Dellinger said, "This issue is not serious."[6] Harvard's Laurence Tribe and Yale's Jack Balkin struck the same note.[7]

The key here is not whether such a challenge would succeed or fail. The key is found in the breezy phrases they use. There "is no doubt" that Obamacare is constitutional. Obamacare "easily passes" constitutional muster. Such talk isn't even "serious." In other words, these challenges are ridiculous. In their left-wing world, it's absurd to think that the Constitution actually limits the power of the federal government. They think government should do anything it wants. They also truly think of government-run healthcare as an unmitigated good—the civil rights issue of our generation—and so it's inconceivable that the Constitution would not let them create such a thing.

As the healthcare fight was heating up, Speaker Nancy Pelosi gave us a glimpse of what the modern Democratic Party and the Obama White House think of the Constitution. After David Rivkin (a top lawyer on Florida's multistate Obamacare lawsuit, along with Michael Carvin and Gregory Katsas) coauthored a piece in the *Washington Post* on why the individual mandate is unconstitutional,[8] and I (Klukowski) published my *Politico* piece making similar points, a reporter told Speaker Pelosi on camera that some constitutional lawyers were saying the mandate was unconstitutional, and asked her which provision of the Constitution authorized the mandate. To this Pelosi responded, "Are you serious?" Then she refused to answer the question, going on to the next reporter.

Happy that we might have gotten her attention, I then wrote an open letter to Nancy Pelosi and the White House which Fox News carried, saying, "Yes, Madame Speaker, I am serious," and explaining in more detail why the core provision of Obamacare should not survive a court challenge.[9]

The Speaker never responded to my letter, but her reaction to the question tells us everything we need to know. What follows is what you need to know about why Obamacare is unconstitutional, and the best way to get rid of it.

Individual Mandate Unconstitutional

This individual mandate—the heart of Obamacare—is unconstitutional.

Back to what we discussed in the Introduction and Chapter 5, one of the Constitution's promises is a government of specific, delegated powers (called "enumerated powers"). Unlike state governments, the federal government must cite a specific provision in the Constitution that gives it the power to do anything. If there's no specific provision of the Constitution authorizing the federal government to do something, then the Tenth Amendment automatically renders it unconstitutional.

Contrary to what the Obama administration argues, nothing in the Constitution authorizes the individual mandate.

NOT AUTHORIZED BY THE COMMERCE CLAUSE

The Obama administration lawyers' first argument in court is that the individual mandate is authorized by the Commerce Clause.

Article I, Section 8 of the Constitution gives Congress power to regulate interstate commerce.[10] One of the problems with the original Articles of Confederation, which provided America's first government once we declared independence, was that the laws of various states differed so drastically—they even had their own currency—that they were incompatible. As such we weren't able to develop a national economy.

When the Constitution was later written, the biggest domestic policy concern for the Framers was providing this interstate commerce authority, enabling Congress to ensure that Virginia's economy could effectively interface with Maryland's economy. It was to provide certain standards, facilitate and encourage people from one state to do business in another, and allow different states to specialize in products for which each state was particularly blessed with abundant resources, and for the whole country to benefit by being able to freely trade and purchase across state lines.

Although the power to regulate interstate commerce is broad, it is by no means absolute. That's why when FDR implemented his New Deal in the 1930s, the Supreme Court struck down major parts of it for exceeding Congress's power under the Commerce Clause.[11]

But then, as we saw in Chapter 6, the Supreme Court took a huge step to the left in 1937. FDR appointed new pro–New Deal justices to the Supreme Court as vacancies arose, and two previously conservative justices got nervous about FDR's court-packing scheme. So in the 1937 *Jones & Laughlin Steel* case the Court announced that the Commerce Clause allows Congress to also regulate commerce within each state, as long as whatever Congress wants to regulate has a "substantial relationship" to interstate commerce.[12] The Court expanded on this concept in 1941,[13] and then in 1942 stretched the concept to absurd lengths in *Wickard v. Filburn,* where the Court upheld federal authority to fine a farmer for growing too much wheat (he grew twenty-three acres, when the government told him he could grow only eleven).[14] Even though this extra wheat was exclusively for his family and farm, the Court upheld the fine on the idea that if one person's commercial actions were repeated by other people who would buy less wheat because they were growing their own, and if the aggregate impact of these actions would "substantially affect" interstate commerce, then Congress could regulate those individual actions.[15]

This "aggregation principle" was then used to uphold more such laws in 1964, during the height of the Warren Court (although it should be noted that those laws were trying to secure equal treatment for blacks during the civil rights era).[16] The consensus in the legal community was that the Commerce Clause was a "dead letter," meaning essentially it was a joke to say anything violated the Commerce Clause. Apparently Congress could do anything if it claimed that whatever it was doing had a "substantial effect" on interstate commerce.

But then the Supreme Court brought the Commerce Clause back to life. First was *U.S. v. Lopez,* where in 1995 the Court struck down the Gun-Free School Zones Act, throwing out the conviction of a student who brought a gun to school because, although gun violence at school is a serious issue, it has little to do with interstate commerce.[17] Then in 2000 the Court struck down the Violence Against Women Act in *U.S. v. Morrison,* because even though the statute was full of congressional statements about how violence affects interstate commerce, the Court held that the economic impact of such violence is too tenuous to be considered part of interstate commerce.[18] Such violence is despicable, but nonetheless it's up to local and state authorities to prosecute people for these felonies (which they readily do), because the Constitution does not entrust Congress with the power to act on domestic and other gender violence, as they are not economic actions.[19]

There are limits to this revitalizing of the Commerce Clause. For example, when a self-described radical libertarian pushed the Court in *Gonzales v. Raich* (2005) to declare federal laws regulating marijuana unconstitutional, the Court choked, with five justices voting to sustain the law under the very broad rule that Congress merely needed to have a "rational basis" for believing that growing and using marijuana was related to interstate commerce. This decision was a serious blow to federalism.[20]

Nonetheless, from these cases a clear argument arises as to why the Obamacare mandate is unconstitutional: The Commerce Clause cannot be invoked unless a person voluntarily chooses to engage in commercial activity. Once that person has chosen to make an economic action, then it becomes a question as to whether that economic activity can properly be called "interstate," such that it would be part of "interstate commerce" and thus something that Congress can regulate. All the liberal Supreme Court cases, beginning in 1937, require that a person be engaged in commerce before Congress can claim that it's interstate commerce. That's why the Court was able to strike down the laws at issue in *Lopez* and *Morrison* without overruling any of these earlier cases; the actions involved in *Lopez* and *Morrison*—carrying a gun in school or striking a woman—are not commercial in nature. And *Raich* doesn't pose a big problem to this argument, as *Raich* was essentially *Wickard* again—a person was growing an economically valuable "crop" that could have been sold (as an illegal drug) for personal use.

So the Commerce Clause argument that can beat Obamacare is that the individual mandate does not wait for you to first engage in commerce, such as by visiting a doctor's office or buying medicine at the pharmacy. (It would still be unconstitutional if it did, but that would be a closer case.) Instead, it commands you to spend money. It tells you that you must go buy something, and then it tells you what you must buy (health insurance) with your own money. No such law has ever been enacted by the federal government in America, and no Supreme Court decision gives a green light to do so.

This is the difference between regulating commercial activity versus coercing someone into commercial activity. Put otherwise, it's the difference between regulating action versus regulating inaction. It's a difference in kind, not in degree. This mandate crosses the line, and the courts have never sanctioned anything on the other side of that line.

The key to beating Obamacare in the Supreme Court is to give the Court a way to do it that doesn't involve overruling any precedent. This is especially true for Chief Justice Roberts and Justice Kennedy. Roberts is the biggest adherent on the Court for stare decisis (which is the doctrine that precedent should be upheld unless there's a special justification—a truly compelling reason—to overturn it). Kennedy is to the left of moderate former justice Sandra Day O'Connor when it comes to the Commerce Clause. (In *Raich*, O'Connor voted the right way to strike down the law as being beyond the Commerce Clause; Kennedy voted to uphold it.) This is no time for radical legal theories, and no time to reinvent the legal wheel. We need to make an argument that is consistent with the entire body of current Commerce Clause jurisprudence—as messed up as that jurisprudence is—and if so, we can win.

NOT AUTHORIZED AS A TAX
UNDER THE GENERAL WELFARE CLAUSE

President Obama's primary alternative argument in court is that the individual mandate is authorized by the Taxing and Spending Clause (sometimes referred to as the General Welfare Clause). Republicans rightly went ballistic over this, because Barack Obama promised repeatedly as a candidate and as president that no one making less than $250,000 per year would have their taxes increased.

His hypocrisy on this count proved too much for two federal judges hearing cases on the constitutionality of Obamacare. When applying Supreme Court precedent to hold that the individual mandate is not a tax, in striking down the individual mandate in *Virginia v. Sebelius* (currently on appeal to the Fourth Circuit), Judge Henry Hudson rebuked the president and Congress by writing that his "analysis begins with the unequivocal denials by the Executive and Legislative branches that [the mandate] was a tax."[21] And in *Florida v. HHS*, when denying the Justice Department's motion to dismiss the case, Judge Vinson likewise took Congress's emphatic denials that the mandate was a tax as evidence of congressional intent that courts should not uphold it as such.[22]

Individual Mandate Is Not a Tax

The Obamacare individual mandate is indeed not a tax.

A tax is when government takes money from you to put into the public treasury. It can do this through withholding from your paycheck, or a tax on things you buy, such as beer or wine, or making you pay on April 15 of each year. The government then spends that money (often on things that are a complete waste). The Supreme Court has long recognized this fact, holding, "A tax, in the general understanding of the term, *and as used in the Constitution,* signifies an exaction for the support of the Government."[23]

The individual mandate isn't government taking money from you; it's the government commanding you to give your own money to another private entity, not to the public treasury. You don't send any money to the government, so it's not a tax. Every federal judge to rule on the constitutionality of Obamacare—both liberal and conservative, appointed by a Democrat or a Republican—has rejected the Justice Department's argument that the mandate can be upheld as a tax.

If you don't obey the mandate, you pay a penalty, and that penalty does go to the Treasury. That might look like a tax, but the Supreme Court has held that penalties aren't taxes.[24] If you get caught speeding and a policeman gives you a ticket, that's not a tax. It's a penalty for breaking the law. The same is true if you get a ticket for an expired parking meter. When farmer Roscoe Filburn had to pay his fine for growing more wheat than the government allowed in *Wickard v. Filburn,* the Supreme Court didn't call it a tax; they called it a penalty, and upheld it as coming from the Commerce Clause. A tax must have the primary purpose of raising money to support government, not regulating or penalizing people.[25]

The individual mandate is legally separate from the penalty. The mandate must be constitutionally justified by a specific provision in the Constitution.[26] If the mandate falls because it's unconstitutional, then the penalty falls with it.

If the Mandate Were a Tax, It Would Still Be Unconstitutional

The Taxing and Spending Clause in Article I of the Constitution gives the federal government broad power to tax the American people. But while broad, that power isn't unlimited. The Constitution originally allowed only three types of taxes, each mentioned in Article I.

The first two were indirect taxes. These are taxes that could be passed on to consumers, which means they are usually on goods or services sold to the public, where you can increase prices to cover the taxes put on the seller. One of these indirect taxes is duties, which are taxes on imports.[27] The other is excise taxes, which are taxes for the privilege of doing something. Excise taxes include "sin taxes" on buying something considered either a luxury or unhealthy, such as alcohol or tobacco. Excise taxes also include fees for engaging in certain types of business that are restricted because they involve the public trust. These include business or professional licenses, such as a yearly license to practice law or medicine.

The third tax allowed by Article I is a particular type of a direct tax. Direct taxes can't be passed on to someone else; the person against whom the tax is assessed is the person who must pay it. Originally the only type of direct tax permitted by the Constitution was a "capitation tax" (that is, a "head tax"). Every person, or at least everyone with a head, could be required to pay a tax. (Some people in D.C. might be exempt from this tax.) But any capitation tax must be apportioned among the states, meaning that every person in each state has to pay exactly the same amount. New Yorkers might have to pay $800 per year while Ohioans pay only $500 and Hoosiers pay only $490 (because taxes are always higher where Democrats are in office), but every person within each state must pay exactly the same amount. There are no exceptions or exemptions from a capitation tax.

So when the federal government created an income tax in the late 1800s, the Supreme Court found that an income tax was none of these. It was a direct tax, but not apportioned. The Court in 1895 struck down the income tax in *Pollock v. Farmers' Loan & Trust*. In doing so, the Court rejected the concept that there was some generic taxing power outside the specific taxes allowed in Article I, such as some catchall tax for the "general welfare" (described below). The Constitution didn't authorize a tax on incomes.

That's why Congress proposed an income tax amendment to the Constitution, and in 1913 three-fourths of the states ratified it as the Sixteenth Amendment, which authorizes a tax on incomes without apportionment among the states. A tax on incomes is the fourth and final type of tax that the federal government can impose.

The problem for President Obama is that the individual mandate fits into none of those four categories. It's not an imported product, so it's not a duty. It's not tagged onto any purchase, and it doesn't involve engaging in any sort of privilege, so it's not an excise tax. Certain people are exempt from it and different people pay different amounts for insurance, so it's not a capitation tax. And although people below a certain income level are exempt and the IRS is involved, it's not a tax on income, so it's not authorized by the Sixteenth Amendment.

Therefore it's unconstitutional for the federal government to impose the individual mandate as a tax. Even if it were a tax, it would be every bit as unconstitutional as an income tax prior to the Sixteenth Amendment.

The only way this scheme could be done constitutionally would be to set up a national healthcare-welfare system, and impose a massive income tax on everyone to pay for it. That kind of socialism is so blatantly at odds with Democrats' promises, and would be a crushing tax on middle-income and working-income families, that it would be political suicide for Democrats to push it. So the one way this could be done legally cannot be done politically.

NOT AUTHORIZED BY
THE GENERAL WELFARE CLAUSE

The next argument Obamacare's supporters make to justify the individual mandate is that even if it's not authorized by the Commerce Clause or as a tax, it's authorized by the General Welfare Clause. Again, they're wrong.

The General Welfare Clause is also called the Taxing and Spending Clause, reading in total, "The Congress shall have power to lay and collect taxes, duties, imposts and excises, to pay the debts and provide for the common defence and general welfare of the United States...." [28] This can be confusing, since that's the same clause where we get taxing and spending. This new argument refers to the second part of the clause, as if the government has a freestanding power to act for the "general welfare."

But the Supreme Court has held that the General Welfare Clause gives no power to the federal government at all. All it says is that any tax must be for the general welfare, and any spending must be for the general welfare. "General welfare" means national welfare, as opposed to just the welfare of one particular state or one particular region. If something is a tax, it means that in addition to being one of the four constitutionally approved federal taxes (duties, excises, capitation, or income) it must also be for the general welfare. For example, if the government imposed a $1-per-pack cigarette tax as an excise tax, it could not impose that tax for the purpose of paying for all healthcare in the state of Indiana. Whatever the taxing or spending is must be for the national benefit.

The Supreme Court faced this issue in the 1930s, when a massive expansion of federal power was under way. The Court responded in the 1936 case *U.S. v. Butler,* and again the following year in *Helvering v. Davis,* by holding that the General Welfare Clause gives no new power to the government.[29] The Court quoted the leading treatise on the Constitution from the 1800s, by the foremost constitutional scholar of the early republic, Joseph Story, who also served on the Supreme Court. Justice Story served from 1811 to 1845, and was appointed by President James Madison (the primary author of the Constitution). The Court quoted Justice Story, who explained that the General Welfare Clause must not and could not be a source of federal power, since "it is obvious [from] the generality of the words, to 'provide for the . . . general welfare,' the government of the United States [would become], in reality, a government of . . . unlimited powers. . . ."[30]

Instead, the Framers gave us a Constitution that created a federal government of strictly limited powers.

NOT AUTHORIZED BY
THE NECESSARY AND PROPER CLAUSE

Finally, the Obama Justice Department argues that if the individual mandate is not authorized by the Commerce Clause, or the Taxing and Spending Clause, or the remainder of the General Welfare Clause, then it's authorized by the Necessary and Proper Clause. That clause says simply that Congress has power "to make all laws which shall be necessary and proper for carrying into execution the foregoing powers, and all other powers vested by this Constitution in the government of the United States, or in any department or officer thereof."[31]

When you're studying for the bar, you're taught that there are two questions in the constitutional law section of the multiple-choice part of the exam that are perennial trick questions. The first is that any time one of the choices is the General Welfare Clause, that's the wrong answer. The other choice that, if offered, is always the wrong answer is—the Necessary and Proper Clause.

All the Necessary and Proper Clause provides is that for each of the enumerated powers given to the government in the Constitution, the government has with it whatever other authority is implicit in being able to carry out the enumerated power. For example, if the government has the power to make copyright infringement a crime, then it has the power to build federal prisons in which to incarcerate those convicted of copyright infringement.

We saw in Chapter 6 that as recently as 2010 the Court continues to read the Necessary and Proper Clause very broadly. In *U.S. v. Comstock* last year, Justice Stephen Breyer wrote for the Court that "in determining whether the Necessary and Proper Clause grants Congress the legislative authority to enact a particular federal statute, we look to see whether the statute constitutes a means that is rationally related to the implementation of a constitutionally enumerated power."[32]

This language might seem problematic. And it must be noted that if in the end the Supreme Court upholds Obamacare, it will be through a combination of the Commerce Clause conjoined with the Necessary and Proper Clause.

But *Comstock* doesn't need to be a problem. The Necessary and Proper Clause carries with it the power to do only things that are implicitly necessary to effectuate an *enumerated* power. If there's no healthcare provision in the Constitution, and if it's not covered by the Commerce Clause, then the Necessary and Proper Clause can't be used to save the mandate. Since the Commerce Clause reaches only actions, the Necessary and Proper Clause can reach only *activities* that are related to interstate commerce. Again, here there's no activity. It's inactivity instead, putting it beyond the reach of Congress.

President Obama's Justice Department is also arguing that the mandate is necessary and proper to pay for the enormous costs and subsidies in the rest of the bill. This is the first time DOJ has argued that a new law creates a problem, and then an otherwise-unconstitutional mandate is necessary to fix the problem the law just created. DOJ argues that this, coupled with regulating the interstate healthcare market under the Commerce Clause, authorizes the individual mandate.

Yet even this argument should not be enough. For all the reasons above, the individual mandate is unconstitutional. Although it will be close, it's likely that the individual mandate will be struck down by a 5–4 vote.

Other Constitutional Challenges to Obamacare

Even though most of the public focus is on the individual mandate, there are a number of other provisions of Obamacare being challenged in court.

One is the sweeping changes to Medicaid, which was created as a federal-state partnership. Obamacare makes Medicaid much larger and more expensive for the states. The Obama administration argues that since Medicaid is a voluntary program from which a state can withdraw, the administration can attach whatever conditions it wants. But Florida and the states in the multistate Obamacare lawsuit argue that Medicaid consumes such a large part of their budget that the states cannot simply walk away. If any state were to refuse Medicaid, it's possible that every American worker in those states would still pay for it in their payroll deductions, except now that money would go to other states. Thus, they argue, Obamacare's transformation of Medicaid is coercive, and as such that it violates the Tenth Amendment.

This argument—developed by the lawsuit's architect, David Rivkin—is correct, though it faces an uphill climb with the current Supreme Court. There was a time when the Court struck down a federal law that interfered with payroll taxes on state employees, on the grounds that it violated the Tenth Amendment for the federal government to interfere with state government functions.[33] Unfortunately, the leftward trend of a couple of activist justices (agenda justices, as described in Chapter 6) resulted in this case being overruled just nine years later.[34]

Since then, the Supreme Court has struck down only two laws for violating the Tenth Amendment outside the context of simply exceeding the Constitution's enumerated powers. The first case was *New York v. U.S.* in 1992, because the law in question commanded state legislatures to enact certain legislation.[35] The second was the 1997 case *Printz v. U.S.*, where the Court extended the doctrine in *New York* to hold that the federal government cannot commandeer state or local officials by tasking them with performing any duties or implementing federal laws.[36]

But as weak as the Supreme Court has left the Tenth Amendment, there's still hope of reviving it. For example, in modern times the Court has acknowledged that if conditions on federal funding to the states amounted to undue influence, then it could rise to the level of coercion, which would violate the Tenth Amendment.[37]

If there's ever been a case that would cross that threshold, this is it. While it's clear that the federal government cannot commandeer any part of state government, it's far from clear how far the current Court is willing to go in giving any additional teeth to the Tenth Amendment. These changes to Medicaid are coercive. The question is whether the Court stands by the idea that the states can step away from Medicaid anytime they want, or instead if they think it's an "offer you can't refuse," and strike it down.

There's also an employer mandate, under which any company with more than fifty employees is subject to a heavy fine if it doesn't offer health insurance to its employees. (This is a sop to the labor unions, to punish small businesses since they're often not unionized, and push workers to go to large, union-shop companies.) Liberty University—a Christian university where both of your authors are faculty at the law school—self-insures for healthcare coverage in a way that may not meet federal requirements. So Mat Staver, dean of Liberty University School of Law, is pursuing a legal challenge to the employer mandate pending before the U.S. Court of Appeals for the Fourth Circuit as of this writing.[38]

Winning this case turns on the individual mandate. If we win on a Tenth Amendment claim or on the employer mandate as well, those would be wonderful surprises.

The Silver Bullet: Severability

The individual mandate is only one intolerable aspect of the legislative monstrosity known as Obamacare. Not all other provisions are innocuous (and sometimes comical) irritations, such as the tax on tanning beds. We've discussed another authoritarian provision, the employer mandate, imposing draconian penalties on every employer with more than fifty employees who does not offer health insurance. We've also discussed the coercive Medicaid overhaul. Obamacare includes myriad such mandates, taxes, and administrative burdens.

There are also other objectionable parts of Obamacare that don't lend themselves to a constitutional challenge. For example, it funds abortion, notwithstanding President Obama's executive order to the contrary. (At least one federal appeals court has held that the White House cannot attach conditions on funding that Congress does not impose in the statute's language.[39]) Other provisions drive up premiums, like requiring insurers to keep young adults on their parents' policies until their mid-twenties.

There is a way to nullify all of these provisions in one stroke.

Obamacare lacks a *severability clause.* A severability clause provides that if any part of the statute is found invalid or unenforceable, then the remainder of the statute continues in full force and effect. Severability provisions are so common that they're almost boilerplate. (If you look around your home at any sort of lease, license, or other contract, you'll probably find such a clause toward the end of the document.)

The earlier version of Obamacare had a severability clause. It was found in Section 255 of H.R. 3962. But after all the careful negotiating to buy off exactly the number of votes needed to pass the bill, the final version of the bill (H.R. 3590) contained no such provision.

This doesn't mean that if you take down one part of Obamacare, you automatically take down the whole thing. Even without a severability clause, a court will apply a presumption of implied severability. So the fact that there's no severability provision doesn't make all the parts of a statute stand or fall together. Under severability doctrine, a court will surgically remove an unconstitutional provision from a law if possible. However, if the court finds the invalid provision to be an essential part of the legislation, then the court can strike down the entire statute.

Thus, if a court finds the individual mandate unconstitutional, and that the mandate is an integral provision that goes to the core of the legislation, then the entire 2,700-page law could be struck down with a single court decision.

As Klukowski explains in his court briefs in the Obamacare cases—the brief cited by Judge Vinson in the Florida case—and also in a law review article, courts look to two things when figuring out severability. The first is whether the law no longer makes sense grammatically or logically with the unconstitutional provision gone, such that the law is reduced to gibberish.[40] That's not the case with Obamacare, where it would be removing only one provision (Section 1501) of the statute, while leaving the other 450 sections in place.

But the second part of a severability analysis in court is determining whether the law cannot function in the *manner* Congress intended without the unconstitutional part.[41] The question becomes if Congress would have passed the bill without the unconstitutional provision, and if not, then the whole thing goes down.[42] That's where a severability clause becomes important, because it announces Congress's intent that a law survive even if part of it is unconstitutional. Courts sometimes strike down a whole law even if there is a severability clause, but without it courts have more of a free hand in deciding whether the political will existed to pass the bill without the bad provision.

These cases make about as strong an argument as you could imagine for holding the individual mandate nonseverable from the rest of the statute. The Obamacare law itself says the individual mandate is essential to Obamacare functioning the way Congress intended.[43] And the Justice Department conceded the same thing during arguments in district court, where the Florida judge noted and accepted this admission.[44] While the Virginia judge declined to take the extra step to strike down all of Obamacare when he held the mandate unconstitutional, in his very short treatment of severability in the district court, he didn't even address the facts discussed above.

There's no evidence that Congress intended the mandate to be severable, and lots of evidence to the contrary. That's why when Judge Vinson did a full severability analysis in *Florida v. HHS,* he correctly concluded that the individual mandate could not be severed from the rest of the statute, and thus that all of Obamacare is unconstitutional. If this issue is properly presented on appeal (and Klukowski will continue as part of the legal effort to strike down Obamacare), there's a solid chance the entire law will be struck down by the Supreme Court.

The documentary film *I Want Your Money* quotes Speaker Pelosi's infamous Obamacare comment that "we have to pass the bill so that you can find out what is in it." Well, Madame Speaker, a severability clause is one thing *not* in the bill. And that should prove to be its undoing.

Why did Congress take out the severability clause in the final version? Democratic aides insist it was an oversight. Our best guess is that Congress removed it to protect the mandate. When this legislation started, Democrats didn't appreciate the constitutional problems with it, which is why the severability clause was in the first version. But as time passed and some of us started writing about why the mandate was illegal, Democrats knew the mandate might be vulnerable to a constitutional challenge. So they took out the severability clause to try to protect the mandate. Democrats figured that there was no way that the Supreme Court would strike down the entire law. Thus they decided to up the stakes on striking down the individual mandate by making it an all-or-nothing deal for the Court.

It makes little difference why they excluded it, though. What matters is there's no severability clause. Without it a court has more freedom to strike down the whole law.

The Far Left considers government-run healthcare to be an unmitigated good. While they paternalistically believe that many ordinary Americans don't support Obamacare (like Hillarycare before it) because the Left thinks you're too stupid to know what's good for you or to make your own decisions, they think educated and sophisticated people all accept the righteousness of what Democrats are doing to healthcare. Thus they just can't imagine that the nine justices on the Supreme Court—brilliant, Ivy League–educated legal scholars—would ever be willing to strike down entirely something the Left considers the Civil Rights Act of our generation.

Make the individual mandate stand or fall together with the rest of the bill, and Democrats think they are protecting the mandate. It never occurred to them that they might doom the entire statute.

NO PARTIAL REPEALS OF OBAMACARE—
DON'T RUIN SEVERABILITY

This also means that Republicans must be careful not to push any legislation that would negate severability as an issue in court. The Congress elected in 2010 rightly pushed a full repeal of Obamacare, but Democrats managed to defeat it. (And President Obama would have vetoed such a repeal anyway.) Now Republicans are trying to decide how best to erode Obamacare, and are trying to repeal parts of it.

One such partial repeal would repeal the individual mandate. This would doom all the major legal challenges to Obamacare, and possibly preserve 99% of this leviathan forever. As we discussed in Chapter 6, Article III of the Constitution gives federal courts power only over "cases." One of the elements of the case is that there must be a live controversy—meaning an ongoing injury for the court to address. If the injury over which the plaintiff is complaining goes away, then the lawsuit becomes moot. It is no longer a "case," and so the court must dismiss it. The individual mandate is the "injury" these lawsuits are challenging, an injury that doesn't even go into effect until 2014. If the mandate is repealed, then there's no injury. If there's no injury, there's no lawsuit. If there's no lawsuit, then it becomes irrelevant that the mandate can't be severed from the rest of the law. The other 450 sections of Obamacare would come back to life, and cause terrible damage to America's healthcare system.

Another proposed change that would save Obamacare is proposed legislation to allow states to opt out of Obamacare. Under the doctrine of exhaustion, a plaintiff has standing to bring a federal lawsuit only if he has exhausted whatever remedies the law gives him to fix his injury through an administrative process. This bill would provide a new administrative remedy, one that all twenty-six states in the lawsuit could use to get out of the mandate. If so, then they can no longer ask a federal court to stop the mandate. This would definitely destroy the Virginia case. Although other plaintiffs in the Florida case include the National Federation of Independent Business (NFIB) and a couple of individuals, and perhaps a court would allow the case to continue with only those plaintiffs, it nonetheless presents an unacceptable risk to a case that could result in Obamacare's abolition.

The same is true of various other proposals. Although it's likely that provisions of the law that are incidental to Obamacare could be repealed without endangering the lawsuits, all of them carry some level of risk. Besides, Democrats could try to retroactively insert a severability clause into Obamacare. This defies legal logic, since a severability clause must be part of a specific bill, and once that bill is signed, there's no way to change the words that are printed on the paper. But there's no Supreme Court decision that squarely rejects such a theory, so as crazy as the idea is, if five justices on the Supreme Court decide to buy it, this too would save most of Obamacare.

There are legislative ways to oppose Obamacare before the Supreme Court strikes it down. Many provisions require federal funding, and conservatives can work to ensure that Congress denies any funds for those provisions. Other provisions require hiring new federal employees, and Congress can refuse funds to pay them. Others must be administered by federal employees, and Congress can insert into annual authorizing legislation for the various agencies doing such work that no funds shall be spent on carrying out any part of Obamacare.

All of these could help mitigate the harm caused by Obamacare as we work to get rid of this legislative nightmare. But legislative efforts must be confined to those things. No partial repeals of Obamacare. We don't want to give the courts any excuse not to strike it all down.

Striking down the Obamacare individual mandate would be monumental. But if the Supreme Court agrees with Judge Vinson in Florida and holds that the mandate is not severable from the remainder of the statute, then it could wipe clean the entire slate of healthcare reform. That would return this issue to a new Congress—and, God willing, a new president—to devise reform legislation that will actually improve healthcare costs. Maybe we can get that, instead of an unprecedented invasion into the lives and liberties of American citizens.

Unlimited Power

Never before has Congress presumed the power to tell you how to spend your own money. Our greatest hope for winning the Commerce Clause argument (and defeat the Obama administration's other arguments as well) on the individual mandate is that there's no limiting principle to the government's argument.

As Klukowski has gone around the county debating at law schools against liberal (and very intelligent) constitutional law professors, they tend to make one of three arguments for the individual mandate. Each of these arguments is fatally flawed, but they're coherent arguments that are presented well by some of the best (liberal) constitutional lawyers in the country.

The first is that the point of decision of whether to buy insurance is what affects interstate commerce, and so Congress can regulate your decision. The second is that the Framers considered adding to the Constitution that Congress can act whenever the states are incompetent to act, so Congress need only declare an issue to be beyond the states' ability to handle (such as healthcare). The third is that everyone uses healthcare at some point, so we can assume they will eventually substantially affect interstate commerce, and preemptively regulate them.

The Obamacare mandate cannot be sustained on any of these. In *U.S. v. Lopez*, Chief Justice Rehnquist wrote, "Under the theories that the Government presents ... it is difficult to perceive any limitation on federal power, even in areas ... where States historically have been sovereign. Thus, if we were to accept the Government's arguments, we are hard pressed to posit any activity by an individual that Congress is without power to regulate."[45]

This is far worse. If government can make you buy health insurance because your decision whether to do so substantially affects interstate commerce, they can command you to do anything. The food you eat affects your health, so they can tell you what food you must buy. Different kinds of cars have different safety features and crash ratings that statistically affect your healthcare costs in the event of an accident, so they can tell you what car to buy. Different areas of the country have healthier environments than others, so they can tell you where to live. Obesity causes all sorts of health problems and regular exercise makes you healthier, so they can make you buy a gym membership and command you to use it three times a week.

Just as in *Lopez* and *Morrison*, the federal government here argues a theory of government power that gives them unlimited power over every decision in your life, both for you and your family. It makes a complete mockery of the concept of limited government.

These are the stakes in the Obamacare cases working their way toward the Supreme Court. If the Court holds the individual mandate or any of the other challenged provisions unconstitutional, and holds that the unconstitutional provision cannot be severed from the rest of the statute, then we can strike down this whole thing once and for all. Then in 2013, with a new president and a new Congress, we can try to implement conservative healthcare cost reforms that improve the system for everyone.

Obamacare Is also Disastrous Policy

Although the unconstitutional individual mandate and employer mandate don't go into effect until 2014 (and hopefully will be struck down by the Supreme Court before then), various provisions of Obamacare have already started. Some of these cost a bundle. Such provisions that are already in effect include allowing younger adults to stay on their parents' policies until age twenty-six, banning copayments for preventive care, forbidding insurers from denying coverage to children with preexisting conditions, and prohibiting caps on total coverage.[46]

The Obama administration is predictably blaming the insurance companies. That in and of itself is disturbing, though, because the basic law of supply and demand—which is one of the most basic principles of both classical free-market economics and interventionist Keynesian economics—is that all mandates on products or service providers result in increased prices for consumers. In other words, whenever government makes businesses provide an additional benefit as part of their product, they pass the cost of that benefit along to the consumer. The administration's complaining about this fact reveals either a gross ignorance of basic economics, or a deception of the American people by demagoguing this issue. It's hard to know which is worse.

As anyone with a rudimentary understanding of economics could have predicted, health insurance companies are now confirming that they must increase healthcare premiums as a result of Obamacare's passage. Worse, these increases—of up to almost 10%—are for small businesses and individuals. Total premium increases could be as high as 20%.[47]

These companies are the job creators of our economy. Making healthcare more expensive means that fewer people will get it. Aside from the fact that this means sick people will go without treatment and get more sick (or even die), it means that those who can afford insurance will pay more for it, taking away money that they could use to buy a house or pay for a college education.

Once health insurers told the public the truth, President Obama's team responded with some of the ugliest thuggery you could imagine. Secretary Kathleen Sebelius of the Department of Health and Human Services—in the spirit of a Soviet commissar—fired off a warning letter to the insurance companies. This letter read, "There will be zero tolerance for this type of misinformation and unjustified rate increases." It continued, "We will also keep track of insurers with a record of unjustified rate increases: Those plans may be excluded from health insurance Exchanges in 2014."[48]

Such government coercion continues to increase the strain Obamacare imposes on the private sector. As increased mandates make healthcare too expensive for employers to provide without pushing themselves into insolvency, more and more companies will discontinue their plans. As that happens, more and more will go onto the public exchanges. When a critical mass of people end up on the public exchanges, the healthcare insurance industry will begin to lose structural integrity. As that happens, we'll finally get the government-run system called the "public option" that Nancy Pelosi and House Democrats initially pushed for, but that Middle America rejected. This resulted in the Senate version, which included these exchanges as a "moderate" alternative to the public option.

But the Left is merely biding its time in treating this as a temporary setback, confident that the chain of events we just explained will result in a public option. Then the public option will lead to a single-payer system—a national system where healthcare is exclusively provided and run by the government.

Fortunately, political will at the moment is keeping movement toward a public option on a knife's edge, as right now the Obama administration is issuing temporary waivers for yet another mandate, this one on businesses. This mandate has already gone into effect, and requires employers to devote at least 80% of healthcare premium payments to benefits, with less than 20% toward administration and overhead. It so happens that McDonald's very publicly announced that its healthcare plan for its employees—which, as you can imagine, is a scaled-down plan—would have to be dropped, since it couldn't keep costs below 20% for their simple plan.[49] McDonald's iconic status as an hourly wage employer grabbed headlines, whereupon the U.S. Department of Health and Human Services (HHS) quickly issued a waiver to avoid a PR black eye. Then other companies jumped on board, and now HHS has issued at least 733 waivers, and the number keeps going up.[50] (Of course, this also provides yet another way for the government to control businesses, as HHS can choose to reward the president's supporters with waivers while denying them to companies critical of the White House.)

Employers that can't afford to offer the kind of coverage required by Obamacare currently have political cover. But again, the Left is biding its time, believing that they can continue building political momentum for a public option.

The public option will take us down the same path as Canada. The Canadian healthcare problem started in 1946, when a socialist running one Canadian province, Tommy Douglas, enacted legislation providing government insurance for hospital treatment. By 1961 this became comprehensive medical coverage. Once healthcare was "free," medical visits doubled. As costs spiraled out of control, Canada responded by reducing payments—which is rationing.[51]

Thus a public option eventually drives insurance companies into bankruptcy, at which point the central government takes over with a "single payer" system. Once the government is in charge, everything changes—for the worse.

MEET DR. RATION—
HE'LL DECIDE WHAT'S BEST FOR YOU

President Obama's pick to run the Centers for Medicare & Medicaid Services, Dr. Donald Berwick, said, "Any healthcare funding plan that is just, equitable, civilized and humane must—must—redistribute wealth from the richer among us to the poorer and less fortunate."[52] In other words, Dr. Berwick believes government must allocate healthcare resources. That's what we call "rationing."

Berwick is a chilling choice to run our healthcare system, given his lengthy record of socialist statements. Berwick said, "I cannot believe that the individual health care consumer can enforce through choice the proper configurations of a system as massive and complex as health care. That's for [government] leaders to do."[53]

Consistent with what conservatives have always predicted, Berwick readily admits that the government would have to ration care. "You cap your health care budget, and you make the political and economic choices you need to make to keep affordability within reach."[54] You cannot create a national healthcare system without rationing. Berwick admits, "Indeed, the Holy Grail of universal coverage in the United States may remain out of reach unless, through rational collective action overriding some individual self-interest, we can reduce per capita cost."[55]

At another time, Berwick tipped his hand as to what this is really all about. He said it's "important also to make health a human right because the main health determinants are not health care but sanitation, nutrition, housing, social justice, employment, and the like."[56]

Look at that list: housing, employment, nutrition. Berwick says that government healthcare must have authority to allocate all those things. That's socialism, plain and simple. It would require an authoritarian government, and be the bane of the free market and individual decision making.

INEVITABLE RATIONING AND SHORTAGES

The reality is that the subsidies Obamacare promises cannot help but destroy the private insurance industry. For example, people making $31,521 a year are entitled to a $14,176 subsidy. Those making $35,500 are entitled to a $13,385 subsidy. And even those making $59,250 are entitled to a $7,530 subsidy.[57]

The private market cannot bear the cost of these subsidies. How will they be paid for? As consumers balk at the cost, government will push for power to cut insurance reimbursements to doctors. There is already a growing shortage of doctors,[58] and many doctors are now retiring because of Obamacare. Cutting how much a doctor can make, after countless years of sacrifice and training to be able to practice medicine, will result in many older doctors deciding to retire early. This will worsen the shortage, resulting in longer waits for vital care.

The situation will be no different than in other countries, where government steps in to supposedly fill the void. If you want to see the results of government-run healthcare, just look at the countries where it exists. For example, take a woman in Canada who had a miscarriage in the waiting room, because she was kept waiting while she bled through her jeans, sobbing at both the trauma and the humiliation of this happening in a room full of people.[59] Or a Swedish man who sewed up his own leg after being kept waiting for someone to treat his deep cut (and then was reported to police for using the medical supplies to treat himself).[60]

Government-run healthcare is a recipe for disaster. It will cause suffering, and even death. The American healthcare system is far from perfect, but it's infinitely better than what inept government bureaucrats can do.

Constitutional Conservative Healthcare

America does not have a healthcare crisis. Instead, we have a healthcare *cost* crisis. That's where conservatives must act to help contain costs.

It's also where the fight must begin, to get the terminology right. The Far Left succeeds—whether it's Barack Obama, Hillary Clinton, or whoever—whenever it wins the battle of the dictionary to define the terms. Conservatives must always emphasize that American doctors provide the best healthcare in the world. We just need to tackle spiraling costs.

America spends around $2.6 trillion a year on healthcare, which is about 17% of the U.S. gross domestic product. This is a phenomenal amount of money. We need to bring down costs, but not at the expense of care.

It takes much more space than we have in this chapter to go into all the details of what ideal healthcare cost reform looks like. But here follows a number of items that should be put before the American people, found in various reports and recommendations from over the past decade.

PUTTING PATIENTS IN CHARGE

First, insurance coverage should be focused on the individual, rather than on the employer. Right now companies get an unlimited tax break for what they offer employees, but individuals have no such credit or deduction. Redirecting that provision toward individuals or families would make insurance tremendously more affordable to the tens of millions of Americans who are self-employed or work for a small company that can't provide coverage.

A related second point is that the individual must be incentivized to avoid reckless costs. Right now millions pay only a fixed copay, regardless of cost or prudence. Governor Tim Pawlenty of Minnesota says it's like if someone told you, "Go buy a TV—any TV you want. Then just bring me the receipt, and you'll have a $50 co-pay, and I'll pay the rest, no matter how much it is." Pawlenty asks, "If I made you that offer, how many of you would go get a twenty-inch black-and-white? You'd get a sixty-inch plasma-screen instead."

That's a perfect illustration of what's wrong with the employer-centered system. Individual consumers have no sense or appreciation of costs, and so instead of acting as a rational consumer, they severely overconsume. This quickly uses up healthcare resources, which then drives up costs. (This is also why when government takes over healthcare, no one has any appreciation of costs, and supplies become completely exhausted—resulting in rationing.)

A good example of a consumer-based system is the one Governor Mitch Daniels instituted for Indiana state employees. The state deposits $2,750 each year into a Health Savings Account (HSA) for each employee, and also pays the premium for the plan. Anything left over each year the employee can keep as personal wealth. If the amount is entirely used, the employee then pays part, and the state-employer pays part, up to $8,000. After that, the employee is completely protected to insure against catastrophic illnesses.[61]

As such, employees carefully manage their healthcare dollars. They don't forgo necessary tests or medicines, but they make decisions as rational consumers. Only 4% of plan participants use up the entire $2,750. This consumer-based model has brought down costs significantly, while informing consumers and improving care. Many states are now examining this model for themselves.[62]

Third, small businesses should be able to contractually join with other small businesses to have the same bargaining leverage as large companies. That would enable small businesses and one-man businesses to extend healthcare coverage to millions of Americans by making it affordable. This would also make it easier for small businesses to grow, by offering better benefits for employees.

Fourth, Americans should be able to purchase health insurance across state lines. That way everyone in America could search across the entire country to find a package that best fits the needs and resources for their particular family, instead of being at the mercy of their particular state government. They should also be able to carry that insurance with them if they move to a different state.

Fifth, medical records should be made electronic. Many billions of dollars are spent every year on routine tests to obtain medical information that has already been found for that patient in a previous clinical setting. A portable system that a provider could access from any location would prevent the cost and possibly deadly delay that accompany running those tests again. Also, many people suffer injuries or death each year because of incomplete medical histories or inadvertent clerical or diagnostic errors. A comprehensive system that knows every health condition the patient has, any allergies he has, his complete family medical history, and any current medications he's on would instantly detect and flag all of those potentially deadly dangers. The time, redundancy, record keeping, and error rate in the current medical record system literally add up to hundreds of billions of dollars a year.

One caveat for such a system, however, is privacy. A way must be found to make this information accessible to the individual, but not to the government. Medical information can be some of the most embarrassing or personally damaging information out there. Government can never be trusted with such information on our citizens.

EMTALA REFORM

A sixth recommendation is to amend EMTALA, the Emergency Medical Treatment and Active Labor Act.[63] Under EMTALA, emergency rooms treat everyone who comes to an ER, regardless of their ability to pay. While it's a great humanitarian measure enacted in 1986 to help people, it's terribly abused and needs to be amended.

Many people go to an ER because they don't want to pay their copay for a regular physician! People of sufficient financial means to afford health insurance go for free treatment rather than get insurance. And people go for a nonemergency full workup at a price of many thousands of dollars that the healthcare system has to take as a loss, rather than spend a couple of hundred dollars at a family doctor's office. Some employers are also part of the problem, telling employees to get a medical slip if they're sick. Worse, a few family doctors contribute to the problem, sometimes advising their patients to go to the ER for an expensive test like a CT scan that the doctor knows insurance will not approve because the patient doesn't meet the criteria for the test. Many women go to the ER for a "free" pregnancy test, because they don't want to pay fifteen dollars at a drugstore for their own test!

Many thousands more go as drug seekers gaming the system. They complain of vague pain that the doctor doesn't believe the person is experiencing, and then (as one doctor told us jokingly) essentially say with no symptoms of pain, "I'm in pain, and I'm allergic to Motrin, Tylenol, Aleve, and anything that doesn't start with *P* and end in *ercocet.*" (Percocet is a narcotic frequently sought by drug abusers at hospitals.) They go from hospital to hospital, complaining of the same symptoms to obtain narcotics. (Again, a universal electronic system would instantly reveal that this person had visited a different hospital the previous day with exactly the same complaint, seeking drugs.)

Doctors are compassionate individuals who focus their careers on helping people. So ER doctors must be empowered to assess that a person does not belong in the emergency room and turn them away. They must document the event and the reason for turning the person away, but billions of dollars will be saved every year by doing so. When people go to an ER for treatment for a virus—for which antibiotics will not help—doctors need to be able to tell the patient to go home and take Motrin and Tylenol, but that prescription medication will not benefit them and thus should not be handed out.

MEDICAL MALPRACTICE REFORM

And seventh is medical malpractice liability reform, often called tort reform. Both of us know many doctors (and Klukowski's wife is a board-certified ER physician), and have heard plenty of horror stories of "defensive medicine," also called "legal medicine." Literally hundreds of billions of dollars a year are wasted in tests and procedures that the doctor doesn't believe are necessary under the circumstances.

Doctors do this because they are beset by countless lawsuits. Often terrible things can happen to a loved one if they're sick enough to go to the hospital. This is especially true where children are involved. When someone is injured or tragically dies, often a grieving parent or family member is desperately looking for someone to blame, understandably lashing out in their pain and loss. And rather than go to the trouble of litigation, too often the lawyers for the hospital or insurance company will immediately settle. Sadly, many predatory trial lawyers encourage a lawsuit that they think is weak on the merits in the expectation that the defendant healthcare provider will immediately make a settlement offer.

There are five things we can do to radically improve this system.

First, all providers must be legally able to have their patients sign a commitment that in the event of malpractice, the patient agrees to submit to binding arbitration, which is far quicker and less expensive than litigation. If patients don't want to consent to this, then they should be free to find another provider.

Second, any medical malpractice suit must immediately go to a state malpractice board composed of three doctors who specialize in whatever the relevant type of medicine is for a particular case (for example, neurology, obstetrics, or orthopedic surgery). Both the provider and the patient can be represented by a lawyer, and the doctors may ask either the lawyers or the parties themselves any question relevant to the case. On that basis, the doctors issue a report on the case and vote on whether malpractice occurred.

If the panel unanimously sides with the doctor, then the patient can appeal to a second panel. If that panel is also unanimous against the patient, then the suit cannot proceed to court. If the panel is anything other than unanimously for the doctor, then the case can go to court, but the loser pays all legal bills for *both* parties, and the panel's report will be accepted as evidence by the court.

This is the third improvement: The loser pays. In cases where a panel rules unanimously against a doctor, you can bet that the hospital or insurance company will settle the suit in a heartbeat to avoid additional cost. But where a panel is divided, the lawyers will seriously advise their clients on how strong or weak the case is, resulting in many frivolous cases being dropped to avoid the risk of having to pay all the costs for both parties.

And fourth, there must be liability caps through federal legislation. All injured parties must be able to sue for all economic damages without limit. If a doctor injures a patient economically as a result of a botched medical performance, then the patient must be made whole.

But there should be a national limit of $250,000 for noneconomic compensatory damages. That means "pain and suffering." Many lawsuits claim millions of dollars for "mental anguish." Again, the patient can sue for every dollar of economic damages, even if it's $10 million. Lost limbs, blindness, and so on can cost a lifetime of wages or salary. But for noneconomic compensation, the limit should be a quarter-million dollars.

There should also be a national limit of $500,000 for punitive damages, and they should be allowed only for fraud, intentional harm, or recklessness (not merely negligence). Those are damages where you admit that it doesn't compensate you for anything, you're just punishing the defendant. Sometimes punitive damages might be justified, but half a million dollars should be the limit.

And finally, federal law trumps state law through what's called preemption. Some states may want to impose more restrictive limits than those discussed here. For the reasons discussed in Chapter 4 on the national benefits of federalism, each state should have that option. Therefore the federal statute must specify that these are absolute limits, but that if any state imposes more restrictive limits, then the state law is not preempted by this federal law.

With all these changes, conservatives could start delivering the kind of improvements to healthcare that Americans deserve.

9

CULTURE WAR OF FAITH AND FAMILY

"Of all the dispositions and habits which lead to political prosperity, religion and morality are indispensible supports. In vain
would that man claim the tribute of patriotism, who should
labor to subvert these great pillars of human happiness, these
firmest props of the duties of men and citizens."

—George Washington, Farewell Address, 1796

America cannot succeed without rebuilding our culture. If we
become a people without faith, or if our families disintegrate,
or if we lose our American heritage, then it doesn't matter
if we fix our current economic woes or rebuild our national defenses.
Although we might be okay for a few years, in the coming decades we
will decline until we either collapse from within or are unable to defend
ourselves from threats abroad.

As Congressman Mike Pence of Indiana warned at the Values
Voters Summit in 2010, "Those who would have us ignore the battle
being fought over life, marriage and religious liberty have forgotten the
lessons of history." To this Pence—who declined to run for president
in 2012 and is instead the prohibitive front-runner for governor of Indiana (and could easily be a top-tier presidential contender a few years
from now)—added the sobering thought, "America's darkest moments
have come when economic arguments trumped moral principles."[1]

AMERICA'S FOUNDING FREEDOM:
RELIGIOUS LIBERTY

As we saw earlier in this book, when the Pilgrims came, they came seeking religious liberty. Many call religious liberty America's First Freedom.

The freedom to seek God, to understand him and learn his truth and his will, is a drive that spans the human consciousness. As Augustine prays to God at the beginning of his *Confessions,* "Our hearts are restless until they rest in you." This yearning of the human heart is seen in every culture since the beginning of our race, and is so compelling that when people don't know God, they'll even make one up.

The first permanent colonies in America were established so that Americans could worship God according to biblical teaching. Because so many have different beliefs regarding our Creator or different understandings of his Word, when we adopted the Constitution it became the cornerstone of American liberty that people must be free to worship and serve God, living according to their understanding of his precepts, according to the dictates of their own conscience. That is why the First Amendment begins with the Establishment Clause and the Free Exercise Clause.

Parts of American society have become so radically secular that it's easy to lose sight of this. It's now considered politically incorrect to identify anything as "Christian" unless it's being twisted to support some left-wing cause in the name of "compassion" or (President Obama's favorite) "being your brother's keeper." But this is a critical issue facing millions of Americans, with profound implications for the long-term prosperity and stability of American civilization.

The significance of the advance of militant secularism cannot be overstated, and it's seen all over the country. One example is the "War on Christmas," which many on the Left deride as a bogeyman; but in fact it continues to advance, to the point now that major U.S. cities are having a "holiday" parade or festival, rather than a Christmas event. Militant leftists sue over a benediction being given at a presidential inauguration. They sue to have the National Day of Prayer declared unconstitutional. They sue to stop a state government in Utah from allowing a highway patrol association to erect a cross to commemorate a trooper who fell in the line of duty (a cross approved by the trooper's family). They sue over a cross in the Mojave Desert or another in San Diego dedicated as war memorials. These cases are just a few from 2010, and are good examples of the Left's unending efforts to secularize America.

Anything resembling our historic faith is under assault in the United States.

Hijacking Christianity

Even though there have always been American politicians trying to play on religious sentiments to drum up public support for their policies, something has shifted in recent years. Many on the Left are secular (as referenced above), but in recent years more leftists have tried to claim a Christian mandate for liberalism.

It's gotten to the point today where some leftists are actually hijacking Christianity, twisting and distorting orthodox doctrines of the Christian faith to advance their political agenda.

Most disappointing, some of the best examples of this come from President Obama, his religious advisors, and his political allies.

We know that "hijacked" is a loaded term, but we use it advisedly because Barack Obama is the one who used it first. In June 2007, Senator Obama claimed that Christian Right leaders had "hijacked" Christianity.[2] Hijacked? How dare any politician currently holding public office claim that a group of clergymen upholding the traditional beliefs of the Christian faith is "hijacking."

Yet after winning the White House, President Obama had the audacity to claim a biblical mandate for his agenda. On August 19, 2009, the president held a conference call with Christian clergy, urging them to endorse his healthcare legislation as a moral issue, and claiming that their Christian duty to care for their brother obligated them to support him.[3] Now *that* is what hijacking Christianity looks like.

President Obama is not the first to do this, to be sure. In previous decades and centuries, some who called themselves conservatives mis-cited biblical text to justify segregation, Jim Crow laws, and even slavery. Time doesn't permit us to include a lengthy refutation here, but we'll just add that those who did such things were also hijacking Christianity.

But others on the Far Left are following the president's example.

For instance, we have the utterly bizarre case of (former) Speaker of the House Nancy Pelosi, who decided to follow President Obama's lead in claiming that God directs her lawmaking, invoking the Bible as her legislative road map. If a conservative Republican did this, it would be headline news.

On May 6, 2010, Pelosi engaged in a rambling, redundant, somewhat incoherent monologue in which she claimed that "the Word" directed her—meaning "the Word made flesh": Jesus Christ. She elaborated that she makes policy decisions, "in keeping with the values of Jesus."[4] (Watch the video on this at the link given in the endnote. It's disturbing.)

Pelosi said:

> My favorite word? That is really easy. My favorite word is the Word, is the Word. And that is everything. It says it all for us. . . . And that word is, we have to give voice to what that means in terms of public policy that would be in keeping with the values of the Word. The Word. Isn't it a beautiful word when you think of it? It just covers everything. The Word.[5]

Bizarre.

As two Christians who read the *whole* Bible (not just parts that support our natural preferences), we're not sure where in its pages Nancy Pelosi found the inspiration for her top legislative priorities. Since the Bible is the sacred text of the Christian faith, and the exclusive record of the teachings and values of Jesus, where else could she be enlightened to the values of Jesus?

We don't recall ever reading in the Bible "Thou shalt require every person to buy health insurance" or "Thou shalt oppose charter schools and homeschooling." We'd have to rename the Ten Commandments the "Twelve Commandments" instead. How do those Pelosi priorities embody the "values of Jesus"?

Nor do we remember being taught, "And Peter spoke unto them, saying, 'The Lord commands that you shall pass a cap-and-trade tax which shall tax all the people, that they may inherit a greener planet.'" We can't imagine what Bible Pelosi is reading. Perhaps she thinks God speaks to her directly. The Bible does not sanction same-sex marriage or abortion. It does not command heavy taxes on employers and professionals to pay for government handouts.

Instead, the Bible speaks of God and man, the relationship between the two and how that relationship can be restored forever. It reveals the moral character of God, the divine plan for the ages, and explains the purpose and duties of man, and how a holy God can satisfy the demands of justice while extending mercy to people by the forgiveness of their sins.

Yet we find time and again on the Left that, although they often push a secular (and sometimes militantly atheistic) agenda, many of them often try to wrap their redistributionist, government-control policies in Christian trappings to claim a moral justification—or worse, a divine mandate—for their actions.

Liberation Theology

Of all these twisted distortions of biblical truth, none of the perverted religions that leftists use to advance their radical agenda is more abhorrent than Liberation Theology.

Liberation Theology arose in Latin America and Africa in the 1960s, based on earlier writings from European theologians (especially German). It's a system that says Christianity is about helping the poor and liberating the oppressed through political and social action, and inserts Marxist principles into religion. It portrays Jesus Christ as a poor man who was killed by the political elite of his day for rousing the people to overthrow them, and says that Christianity is about improving the condition of those at the bottom of the economic and political ladder.[6]

Leftist religious leaders in this country have increasingly employed Liberation Theology to subvert the efforts of orthodox Christians to restore traditional Christian faith here. They demand "social justice," which despite the fact that some well-meaning people use that term loosely, commonly refers to the idea that government needs to reengineer society to be more "just." Nine times out of ten, it refers specifically to government redistribution of income, all in the name of "helping the poor."

One of the most visible promoters of this pernicious heresy is Jim Wallis, editor and leader of the far-left Sojourners (one of the groups that endorsed the communist "One Nation" rally in Washington, D.C., on October 2, 2010). Wallis, who now serves on President Obama's White House Advisory Council on Faith-Based and Neighborhood Partnerships, began as a leader of the violent, militant Students for a Democratic Society (SDS). *Sojourners* magazine has openly supported communist regimes, and Wallis himself wrote in one 1976 book that America is "the great seducer, the great captor and destroyer of human life."[7]

Wallis is also supported financially by none other than George Soros, the socialist, antigun, rabidly anti-Christian European billionaire. Our hats are off to the editor in chief of *World* magazine, Marvin Olasky, who after Wallis denied receiving such funding, examined financial statements for Soros's Open Society Institute, where he found hundreds of thousands of dollars given to *Sojourners*.[8]

Wallis was asked during a radio interview in 2006, "Are you then calling for the redistribution of wealth in society?" Wallis responded, "Absolutely. Without any hesitation. That's what the gospel is all about."[9]

Liberation Theology is revolutionary Marxism posing as Christianity. It's a counterfeit of biblical Christianity, and it's all the rage on the Far Left.

BLACK LIBERATION THEOLOGY

One derivative of Liberation Theology compounds the problem. When mixed with Black Nationalism here in the United States, the result is Black Liberation Theology. This hybrid is worse, because in addition to all of Liberation Theology's harmful elements, Black Liberation Theology also fosters bigotry.

President Obama's own former pastor did not hide the violent

Marxist roots of Black Liberation Theology. Sean Hannity first discovered in 2007 the hatemongering of Barack Obama's spiritual guide, Jeremiah Wright, and had Wright on his TV show to confront him. (Our hats are also off to Sean on this, as he broke this story on March 1, 2007, a full year before any of the other national shows paid attention to it.) In that interview, Wright freely admitted that James Cone was one of the originators of the Black Liberation Theology that Wright taught.

Cone effectively sets forth what Black Liberation Theology teaches, as he writes: "Black Theology refuses to accept a God who is not identified totally with the goals of the black community. . . . If God is not for us and against white people, then he is a murderer, and we had better kill him. The task of Black Theology is to kill gods who do not belong to the black community." [10] Beyond that, Cone has said on video:

> If the powerful in our society, the white people, if they want to become Christians, they have to give up that power and become identified with the powerless. If you're going to become a Christian, you can't be identified with the powerful and also a Christian at the same time. . . .
>
> The only way in which your repentance, your forgiveness can be authentic, your reception of it can be authentic, your repentance can be authentic, is that you give back what you took—and white people took a lot from black people. [11]

So in this last part, Cone indicates that a white person cannot have genuine repentance without supporting reparations for slavery (redistribution of wealth), to the tune of *trillions* of dollars.

James Cone is a bigot who evidently hates white people, and whose venomous hatred has infected his twisted theology. Such racism and hatred are widespread in Black Liberation circles.

One reason that Black Liberation Theology has gotten traction in parts of the black community is that it's a way of venting understandable anger and frustration over white racism. Countless blacks suffered many years of terrible discrimination, abuse, and insults that deny their human dignity and disrespect the fact that every black person, like every white person, is made in the image of Almighty God, and is due all the honor and respect accompanying that status.

One of the lessons from Martin Luther King, Jr., is that you cannot fight evil with evil. The solution to white racism is not black racism. A Christian response to racism must be filled with love, compassion, and forgiveness. It's a response that rejects sin, then seeks the restoration and reconciliation of the sinner.

Black Liberation Theology is a lie. It is a damnable perversion of the Word of God and the truth taught by Jesus Christ, and must be denounced.

Whatever god James Cone worships, it's not the God of the Bible.

Such a false religion is what leads Jeremiah Wright to shout on camera in a sermon, "God bless America? No, no, no! Not 'God bless America.' God damn America! It's in the Bible! For killing innocent people! God damn America!"[12]

Many would say to us, "How dare you judge another person's religion. That's un-American." For three reasons, we reject their assertion. First, James Cone—and his disciple Jeremiah Wright—sit in judgment of all of us. According to Cone, you aren't a Christian if you're white and do not give up whatever political authority you have, or if you do not support reparations for slavery. Where's the outcry against this outrageous claim that all those who professed the Christian faith for two thousand years were never Christians before Cone and Wright concocted their false religion?

Second, Americans have every right to do this. The First Amendment gives to every American the legal right to be theologically wrong. But all that means is that you cannot be discriminated against by the government for your religious beliefs. It does nothing to stand in the way of other Americans condemning your beliefs if they're based on hate and lies, such as calling upon Almighty God to damn this great country of ours.

And third, even though it's not politically correct, both of your authors have a Christian duty to denounce the false religion of both Liberation Theology and its subset, Black Liberation Theology. We're both Evangelical Christians, and as such we take seriously the biblical command to proclaim the gospel of Jesus Christ and oppose false religions that seek to destroy the gospel, such as the counterfeit Christianity of Liberation Theology.

The Bible teaches that every human being is a sinner, and that we are saved by grace, received through faith.[13] This faith is in the life and sacrificial death on the cross of Jesus Christ, a man who was also God himself in the flesh. Jesus's resurrection is the proof that God accepted Jesus's sacrifice as full payment for sin.[14] And this Jesus, who physically ascended into Heaven, will one day come again in glory to judge the living and the dead, and inaugurate the eternal kingdom of God. Jesus saves from their guilt and sin everyone who genuinely turns to him in faith, from every corner of the world, regardless of anything about them—including their skin color. That's the *real* gospel of Jesus Christ.

The Bible lays out special duties for dealing with those who twist the Christian faith into something that it's not. Titus 1:9 commands us to "hold firmly to the trustworthy message as it has been taught, so that [we] can encourage others by sound doctrine and refute those who oppose it."[15] Jude commands that we are to "contend for the faith that was once for all entrusted to the saints."[16] When it comes to denouncing those who corrupt the gospel of God's grace and the salvation of needy people, the Apostle Paul further says in Galatians, "Evidently some people are throwing you into confusion and are trying to pervert the gospel of Christ. But even if we or an angel from heaven should preach a gospel other than the one we preached to you, let him be eternally condemned!"[17] As Evangelicals, the two of us are duty-bound to publicly reject the perversion of Christianity spread by James Cone and Jeremiah Wright.

More recent events call for a fresh response, though. In response to Glenn Beck calling out the president on Liberation Theology, the White House responded by saying that President Obama is a "committed, mainstream Christian" and specifically rejected Beck's contention that Liberation Theology is about dividing people into two accounts: oppressors and victims.[18]

First of all, as two men who are affiliated with a Christian university (Liberty University) and work with one of America's premier religious liberty organizations (Family Research Council), we're deeply disturbed by the White House thinking that they have the power to designate the president's faith as "mainstream" Christianity. Are they saying that Jeremiah Wright is mainstream? The president has refused to join a church since leaving Wright's, so we have nothing else to which we can look. When President Obama looks at traditional Christian clergy (who really are mainstream), he says they've "hijacked" Christianity. And who are government officials in the White House to pronounce which Christian beliefs are "mainstream"?

This is exactly the kind of religious judgment the Establishment Clause was written to forbid. Although they can denounce religiously inspired calls for jihad or other violent movements, government officials cannot make proclamations to designate certain Christian beliefs "mainstream," while calling others "hijacking." A private citizen has every right to do that, but the spokesman for a U.S. president does *not*. Regardless of your personal faith or what you think of the role of religion in public life, when these things happen, we should all be concerned.

What the Constitution Says—and Does Not Say— About Religious Freedom

Of all the many ways in which the Left has twisted the Constitution in the past century, perhaps none exceeds how leftists have turned religious liberty on its head. Religious liberty and religious influence on society are now the exact opposite of what the Framers gave us.

The First Amendment contains provisions about religious liberty that are collectively referred to as the Religion Clauses. They read, "Congress shall make no law respecting an establishment of religion, or prohibiting the free exercise thereof. . . ."[19] The second of those two clauses is the Free Exercise Clause. This was one of the driving forces behind the settlement of the American colonies.

When government action stops a person from doing something required by their religious faith, the courts can determine whether this government act violates the Free Exercise Clause. That constitutional provision has suffered in recent years, in that it used to be that a law burdening religious practices would be struck down unless the law served a compelling public interest.[20] The Supreme Court then narrowed the protection of the Free Exercise Clause, holding that generally applicable laws (such as a law against using peyote, which was used in a Native American ceremony) don't violate the First Amendment, and courts will not rule that such a law is unconstitutional as applied to people acting for a sincere religious purpose.[21] Although the government can regulate hallucinogenic drugs, this recent narrowing of the clause's protection is incorrect and should be overruled.

Where the Court has really gone off the rails, however, is with the Establishment Clause, where the Court's decisions are a mess. The Establishment Clause was created to protect churches and people of faith from government attempts to influence our religious practices or limit our engagement on public issues. Instead it's often been turned into the exact opposite, as a hammer to pummel Christians and to drive us from the public square.

The most liberal year in U.S. Supreme Court history was 1968. That was the year where LBJ got all of his liberal justices on the Court—including Thurgood Marshall, who ties with William Brennan as the most liberal justice in history (at least to date)—but before Richard Nixon had the opportunity to appoint moderates and conservatives starting in 1969.

In 1968, the Supreme Court held that the Establishment Clause grants citizens or groups like the American Civil Liberties Union standing to bring lawsuits under the Establishment Clause that could not be brought under any other provision of the Constitution.[22] This created the only exception to the idea we saw in Chapter 6 that to have standing to sue, you must claim a personal injury that's different from that of the public at large. That year the Court also definitively held that the Establishment Clause not only requires government to be neutral between religions but also requires government never to favor religion over irreligion.[23]

Since that time religious liberty has been entirely hit-or-miss in the Supreme Court. In 1971 the Court instituted the infamous *Lemon* test, from *Lemon v. Kurtzman,* under which a law involving religion violates the Establishment Clause unless it has a secular purpose, neither advances nor inhibits religion, and doesn't excessively entangle government with religion.[24] This test only made things worse, since the Court can never agree on what it means. One variation it's led to is Justice Sandra Day O'Connor's endorsement test, under which a government action is unconstitutional if it gives the appearance of endorsing religion.[25] This test is energetically rejected by Justice Anthony Kennedy (who with O'Connor's retirement is the new swing vote on the Court), who instead argues for a coercion test, under which a law is unconstitutional if a citizen feels coerced to lend support (or to give the appearance of support) for a government action involving religion.[26] Conservatives continue to condemn the *Lemon* test as historically and legally wrong, and call for overruling it.[27] And because *Lemon* is such an infuriating mess, every few years the Supreme Court unceremoniously sets it aside completely when deciding an Establishment Clause case.[28]

We're in a crucial time for religious liberty. Even though America welcomes people of many divergent faiths, the reality is that as a nation we are increasingly dealing with adherents of religions that played little or no role in American life at the time of the Founding. The Founders did not deal with people who believed they were divinely commanded to kill innocent people—including children—and would be rewarded for doing so. The Founders did not consider honor killings or ritualistic violence. Instead they presumed religious practices that would either be consistent with Christian moral teachings, or at least with Judaism. Our religious liberty presumed that commandments such as "You shall not murder," "You shall not commit adultery," and "You shall not steal" would be universally accepted principles. The Founders formulated religious liberty presuming that "Do unto others as you would have them do unto you" and "Love your neighbor as yourself" would be the sorts of beliefs taught and practiced by the people. If there was ever a time when we need a constitutional conservative examination of religious liberty, this is it.

The frustrating fact is that we've not had five conservatives on the Supreme Court at the same time since 1936. That's why religious liberty keeps seesawing back and forth between liberal outcomes and moderate outcomes. With a fifth conservative on the Supreme Court—and only with five—we can finally work to restore the Establishment Clause to its correct meaning. Then we can all again live in the country where the First Amendment protects religious liberty, instead of muzzling it.

IT'S A FAMILY MATTER

It's simply amazing that we've reached a point where it's politically incorrect to defend family in America. The Framers would be astounded to be told that the Constitution they gave us included a woman's right to end the life of an unborn child, or the right of homosexuals to demand that the basic unit of human civilization be redefined. Yet that's where we are today.

It's become politically incorrect to fight for moral truth because it turns out that every person advocating for morality has their own moral failings. The Left—supported by the media—suggests that if you've ever done anything wrong, you can never speak out for what is right.

They also say that you can't legislate morality. That's completely absurd. Every criminal law legislates morality. We say it's wrong to murder. It's wrong to steal. It's wrong to assault someone. It's wrong to lie under oath. We declare those moral standards, make it a crime to violate those standards, and punish those who do.

The issue here is a matter of ideals, not of being unrealistic. "All have sinned, and fall short of the glory of God."[29] Our Christian faith teaches us that every human being is a sinner; no one's perfect, and everyone needs forgiveness for many things. America's rich and beautiful tradition as a compassionate, merciful, and forgiving nation stems from our long-held and widely held religious heritage emphasizing redemption and understanding.

The fallacy of the Left is to say that anyone who falls short on a moral standard forfeits the right to advocate those standards because they're hypocrites. That statement is ridiculous. The fact that all of us fall short of our moral ideals cannot be an excuse for not having moral standards at all. Who argues that because the police cannot ticket every single person who speeds, speeding laws are all illegitimate, and no police officer can rightfully issue such a ticket if that officer has ever exceeded the speed limit himself? Then we wouldn't be able to punish tax cheats, because the government doesn't catch them all. (Ask Treasury

Secretary Timothy Geithner about that, since he knows from personal experience.) We wouldn't be able to punish theft, because many thieves are never caught. We couldn't even punish murder, because unfortunately many homicides go unsolved.

There are multiple purposes for laws embodying values. (And all criminal laws embody values, because when we criminalize something, we deem it to be toxic to society—injurious to the social fabric—and task the government with going after those who commit crimes, even if the victim doesn't want to press charges.) One purpose is retribution; we exact justice on those who do wrong. That's a purely moral rationale. Another is deterrence. We want to make an example of those who do wrong. That's a form of moral coercion.

Marriage

Obviously one major issue in America right now is the definition of marriage.

First, however, we want to make a point that is too often lost. The Left tries to portray anyone who doesn't support same-sex marriage as a hatemonger and bigot. Unfortunately, some opponents of same-sex marriage, or homosexuality in general, have given grist to the Left's mill by making caustic or humiliating statements, heaping scorn on homosexuals or their supporters, sometimes with venomous invective.

We reject that entirely. The Bible some of these people cite also commands us to love our neighbor as ourselves, speak to others only in a manner that is wholesome and honorable, and to speak the truth in love. The Christian response to this, as in all such situations, is to be kind, gentle, humble, and peaceful. We don't pull punches from speaking the truth. But it's important to share the truth in the right way.

Your two authors have fought as hard as anyone to protect traditional marriage. Blackwell was the chairman and lead spokesman for the 2004 Ohio marriage amendment, and championed that issue in the campaign. Blackwell has also worked with other states to protect marriage in their state constitutions, and is an advocate for the Federal Marriage Amendment. Klukowski is one of the lawyers involved in the fight for marriage in the case *Perry v. Schwarzenegger.* This case from

California is currently before the U.S. Court of Appeals for the Ninth Circuit. Unless dismissed for a procedural reason referred by the Ninth Circuit to the California Supreme Court, this case could go to the U.S. Supreme Court sometime in 2012. So same-sex marriage may be an issue on Election Day 2012.

President Obama has done a number of things to mainstream gays into American culture. For example, he's now recognizing as "nurturing families" those in which children are raised by "two fathers."[30] Another is repealing Don't Ask, Don't Tell, discussed elsewhere in this book.

President Obama has also ordered the Justice Department to stop defending the Defense of Marriage Act (DOMA). The Constitution tasks the president with upholding the law, and DOJ declines to defend a law only when it infringes upon the president's executive power, or when no reasonable argument can be made supporting it. With DOMA, President Obama is saying that he supports marriage as between one man and one woman, but that any law saying exactly the same thing is irredeemably irrational and unconstitutional. That's ridiculous.

The biblical standard is that sex should be reserved to married couples. Neither of us is naïve, and the reality is that sex outside marriage is common in this culture and other cultures. Sexual drive is one of the strongest human passions. Even some people whose sincerely held faith leads them to believe that they should wait until marriage for sex find themselves falling short of that standard.

But such imperfections do nothing to diminish the sanctity or monumental importance of marriage. Supporters of marriage should unapologetically defend it, despite the fact that many urban elites and media pundits call them names for doing so.

In 2000, California voters passed Proposition 22, clarifying that marriage in California is between one man and one woman, as how it has always been in Western civilization for more than 2,000 years. The California legislature passed a civil unions law, allowing the same public benefits for same-sex couples as married couples. But some homosexuals demanded to be called "married" and filed a state lawsuit claiming that Proposition 22 violated the California Constitution.

In 2008, the California Supreme Court agreed, holding 4–3 that Proposition 22 was unconstitutional because it violates an implied right to marry in the California Constitution. In response, the voters of California amended their state constitution. They passed Proposition 8, providing that marriage is the union of one man and one woman. The amendment left intact California's civil unions law.

Unwilling to accept the will of the voters, several same-sex couples filed another lawsuit. This one was filed in federal district court in San Francisco, arguing that this part of the California Constitution violates the U.S. Constitution. The plaintiffs in *Perry v. Schwarzenegger* are being represented by former U.S. solicitor general Ted Olson, perhaps the most formidable Supreme Court lawyer alive today, a libertarian (and sometimes conservative) who takes a hard-line libertarian position on this issue. His cocounsel is liberal trial lawyer David Boies.

California's elected leaders refuse to defend their constitution in court. Arnold Schwarzenegger and Jerry Brown—the former governor and current governor, respectively—publicly announced that they would not defend marriage or the will of California's voters.

So the court allowed a group to intervene. Dennis Hollingsworth and other individuals affiliated with ProtectMarriage, which successfully fought to pass Proposition 8, joined the lawsuit to defend traditional marriage in *Perry.*

They are represented by Charles Cooper, the Reagan-Meese Justice Department legal advisor we discuss in Chapter 10. Cooper's firm is partnered with the Alliance Defense Fund (ADF), a national organization dedicated to protecting religious liberty and related SoCon issues, such as marriage and the sanctity of life.

This case is profoundly important. Should same-sex marriage become a constitutional right, every nonprofit group—including every church—that refuses to recognize it could lose its tax-exempt status and be denied public platforms. This would cripple countless thousands of churches, ministries, and Christian schools and businesses. Moreover, businesses refusing to provide services to same-sex couples due to religious beliefs (such as a photographer declining to work a same-sex wedding) could lose their business license. Speakers who support traditional marriage could be denied access to radio and TV airwaves. It's even possible that parents who teach their children biblical truth about sexuality could be accused of child abuse for "teaching hate."

Yet this case in the U.S. District Court for the Northern District of California was heard by Judge Vaughn Walker, an openly homosexual federal judge. Judge Walker made this a show trial, with elaborate proceedings, and even seeking to broadcast the trial on TV. It took an emergency order from the U.S. Supreme Court to prevent the broadcast, based on the clear showing that many supporters of traditional marriage were being threatened and harassed.

Predictably, Judge Walker held this provision of the California Constitution unconstitutional, violating the Due Process Clause and the Equal Protection Clause of the Fourteenth Amendment. He struck down Proposition 8 and ordered that state workers begin performing same-sex marriages even before an appeal could be considered.

Today this case is before the Ninth Circuit—which is the most liberal federal appeals court in America. Nonetheless, the Ninth Circuit immediately issued an emergency stay of Walker's decision, ordering that no same-sex marriages occur while *Perry* is on appeal. (Appellate courts do not appreciate it when inferior courts try to force their hand by implementing controversial decisions before an appeal can be heard. Walker's attempt to do so was outrageous.)

Regardless of the outcome in the Ninth Circuit, this case is likely going to the Supreme Court. Thus the issue of whether the Constitution requires same-sex marriage is about to be resolved.

Constitutional conservatism means being faithful to the original meaning of the Constitution, regardless of the outcome. The Constitution is silent on marriage. The courts have long held that the Constitution implicitly protects marriage. But as we explained in Chapter 4, implied rights are those found in the history and tradition of the American people, such that they are essential to an American scheme of liberty. Moreover, implied rights must be narrowly and carefully defined. Putting these rules together, it means that the only forms of marriage protected as an implied constitutional right are those that have been universally embraced by the American people since 1789. Only the marriage of one man and one woman meets those criteria.

Thus any other forms of marriage, such as same-sex marriage or polygamy (which is practiced in dozens of countries across the globe, such as Islamic nations), are not part of any constitutional right.

We've repeatedly made the point that the family is the basic unit of our civilization in every sense. It's not just the basic unit of social culture, it's also the basic unit of economic production and economic consumption, and is also the basic unit from which we derive security in society—including physical security.

Parents' Rights

Another social issue not getting the media attention it deserves is parents' rights.

Given the overarching interest in strong families, a father and a mother together must be respected as the leaders in the unit of government called the family. In the case of a single-parent home, he or she is the only leader in that unit of government. To preserve the primacy of the family, we must recognize and uphold the rights of parents—especially natural parents.

At least since 1923 the Supreme Court has recognized in the Constitution an implied right for parents to raise their children.[31] The Court holds this to be a fundamental right, such that laws burdening raising children are upheld only if they satisfy "strict scrutiny," meaning that they're narrowly tailored to achieve a compelling public interest. Any parent will attest that they would give up almost anything before they'd give up their children or the right to make the decisions that a parent ought to make.

This right is seen in the decisions made for children every day. The biggest influence on children aside from parents comes from the people who teach them in school five days a week for thirteen years, so an immediate decision is where children go to school. Another is what faith children are brought up in, such as what church the family attends and what that church teaches. There are decisions that must be made on how late children can stay out, whom they spend time with, who their influences are, and how they are disciplined for misbehaving.

These parental rights are under an ongoing threat from government expansion. As this book is being edited, the Supreme Court is considering whether a judge must issue a warrant before a public school can allow social workers to interrogate a child at school without the parents' knowledge regarding possible abuse, or if school officials have the power to act as parents to consent to the interrogation without a warrant. When government grows, it includes growing in the direction of controlling how children are raised. An expanding state inevitably invades the home.

PARENTAL RIGHTS AMENDMENT
MIGHT BE A BAD IDEA

An even bigger concern than the U.S. government invading the home is having a foreign authority dictate family decisions. That's the concern many have regarding the United Nations Convention on the Rights of the Child. This treaty declares civil, economic, and social rights of children.

President Bill Clinton signed this treaty on February 16, 1995, but under our Constitution a treaty must be ratified by two-thirds of the Senate to be effective, and the Senate has not done so. This opposition is driven by conservatives, who are extremely concerned about foreign standards for how children are raised—standards that would be administered by the United Nations.

In response to this, some conservatives support a Parental Rights Amendment (PRA) to the U.S. Constitution. But there's a real risk in the PRA. If there's one instance of governmental policy where the cure *might* be worse than the disease, the PRA might be it.

We emphasize "might." This amendment would declare that parents have a fundamental right in the upbringing of their children, and that foreign law cannot be used in assessing those rights. If in fact this treaty were ratified and the international community attempted to interfere with American families, then the PRA could be invaluable.

But if the UN never attempts such a move or is rebuffed, then the PRA could leave federal judges deciding how to raise our children. First, as the Supreme Court said in its landmark case on the constitutional status of treaties, *Reid v. Covert,* treaties and statutes are of equal authority in our country, and so any treaty that violates our Constitution (in this case, the right to raise our children) would be unconstitutional if it attempted to supersede parents.[32] Second, because statutes and treaties are of equal authority, under the last-in-time rule, if a statute and a treaty conflict, the most recently passed one trumps.[33] So if this treaty were ratified and became a problem, passing a federal law would override it. Third, the president has the unilateral power to terminate any treaty consistent with the treaty's terms,[34] so if this treaty became a problem, given that Article 52 of this treaty allows for withdrawal with one year's notice, a president (presumably not President Obama) could withdraw from it.

Contrast that with one enormous danger of enacting the PRA. Right now the Supreme Court is very careful about interfering with parents' rights, regarding it as an issue wherein federal judges should not become heavily involved. But if a *federal* constitutional amendment is passed, then this 100% becomes the Court's business, from that day on and forever. The Supreme Court would then have power to override the wishes of any president, Congress, state legislature, *or parent* in defining parents' rights.

Sobering warnings on this danger come from three noteworthy sources.

First, Justice William Rehnquist (before he became chief justice) wrote a dissenting opinion in a 5–4 Supreme Court case in 1982. Joined by Chief Justice Warren Burger and Justices Byron White and Sandra Day O'Connor, the conservative Justice Rehnquist wrote:

> I believe that few of us would care to live in a society where every aspect of life was regulated by a single source of law, whether that source be this Court or some other organ of our complex body politic ... By [issuing today's ruling], the [Court's] majority invites further federal court intrusion into every facet of state family law. If ever there were an area in which federal courts should heed the admonition of Justice Holmes that "a page of history is worth a volume of logic," it is in the area of domestic relations. This area has been left to the States from time immemorial, and not without good reason. .... State intervention in domestic relations has always been an unhappy but necessary feature of life in our organized society. .... We have found, however, that leaving the States free to

experiment with various remedies has produced novel approaches and promising progress. Throughout this experience, the Court has scrupulously refrained from interfering with state answers to domestic relations questions.[35]

Second is Justice Antonin Scalia's warning from a 2000 case. In arguing (and this point helps the PRA) that he doesn't believe he has power to enforce parental rights unless they're mentioned in the Constitution, Scalia then adds that on the other hand:

> If we [the Supreme Court] embrace this unenumerated right [of parents to raise children], I think it obvious . . . that we will be ushering in a new regime of judicially prescribed, and federal prescribed, family law. I have no reason to believe that federal judges will be better at this than state legislatures; and state legislatures have the great advantage of doing harm in a more circumscribed area, of being able to correct their mistakes in a flash, and of being removable by the people.[36]

Third, Justice Anthony Kennedy—who's an interesting voice here because he usually wants federal courts to decide all sorts of things—added:

> The protection the Constitution requires, then, must be elaborated with care, using the discipline and instruction of the case law system. We must keep in mind that family courts in the 50 states confront these factual variations each day, and are best situated to consider the unpredictable, yet inevitable, issues that arise.[37]

In other words, right now family disputes are handled by local judges in family court. Those judges reflect the values of the community, they come from that community, and they are usually easily reversed if their decision is bad or easily removed if they don't consistently make good decisions. By contrast, if federal judges decide parental rights, their decisions have the full force and authority of the U.S. Constitution and become protected precedent under stare decisis—and those judges are confirmed for life. All things being equal, it's better to deal with a family law judge in your local town.

Beyond that, one provision in the PRA gives agenda judges carte blanche to do whatever they want. Section 2 essentially says that federal or state laws burdening family rights are okay if they satisfy strict scrutiny by being narrowly tailored to promote public interests of the highest order. History shows that liberal judges simply declare any laws they like to satisfy strict scrutiny. That's how the Supreme Court upheld the unconstitutional parts of the McCain-Feingold campaign finance law (discussed in Chapter 14) in the 2003 case *McConnell v. FEC,* and that same year upheld racial preferences in school admissions in *Grutter v. Bollinger.* Thus judicial activists could simply declare new "compelling interests" as they did in *McConnell* and *Grutter,* and conveniently uphold whatever laws they want anyway. But liberal judges are the ones eroding family rights, so they're the ones PRA is designed to rein in. By itself, Section 2 might render PRA ineffective.

Finally, so much power radiates from a constitutional provision that they can create new doctrines. As mentioned in Chapter 4, the Commerce Clause gave birth to the "dormant commerce clause," which violates federalism by wrongly limiting states' being able to make all sorts of business laws. And although the Establishment Clause was designed to protect churches and people of faith from the government, it's been inverted to close the public square to churches and people of faith.

The same could happen with the PRA. By providing that parents have a fundamental right in the raising and educating of children, the PRA empowers life-tenured federal judges to declare parents' rights. But the power to declare what specifically is included within the category of parental rights carries with it the power to say what things are *not* parental rights. If an activist Supreme Court says that the right to make educational decisions doesn't include the right to send your child to a religious school, then it doesn't, regardless of the fact that such an outcome flatly contradicts the words of the amendment. (After all, it's the Supreme Court. It can say whatever it wants if it's interpreting a provision in the Constitution.) Also, parents' rights regarding children can be read as conversely including children's rights against parents. The Court could declare a right to a public-school education, or the right to not attend church, or the right to not be spanked. Once the Court has a constitutional provision to work with, you never know what will happen a century down the road.

Again, though, we said the PRA *might* be a bad idea. If this treaty is ratified, and if the UN tries to use it to supplant America's parents, and if our president refuses to withdraw from it, and if they could be trusted to be faithful to the limits of the PRA's textual mandate, then the PRA would be an invaluable help to America's parents.

But those are a lot of ifs. The Founders chose to not make family affairs a federal issue, and instead as part of federalism left it as an issue for state and local governments. Family law is a close cousin to the police power that we examined in Chapters 4 and 5, and is safer there. Unlike a constitutional amendment to protect marriage or the unborn, precisely worded to ensure those outcomes, the PRA uses broad language of a "fundamental right" but leaves it to the courts to define them. We're not willing to put such extraordinary power in the hands of federal judges, and neither were conservative judges such as Justices Rehnquist and Scalia, or even moderate judges such as Justices O'Connor and Kennedy. Families are too important to be entrusted to the federal judiciary.

Abortion

Another issue that keeps recurring in our national life is abortion. This is the ongoing national disgrace of *Roe v. Wade*.

On January 22, 1973, the U.S. Supreme Court declared that the U.S. Constitution includes a right for a woman to have an abortion to end the life of her unborn child. Although that right is nowhere referenced in the Constitution, this decision came about as an extension of the 1965 *Griswold v. Connecticut* decision, declaring an implied constitutional right to privacy. And from beginning to end, the most outrageous thing about the opinion in *Roe* is that it's a bizarre mix of philosophical meanderings, presumptive discussions of theology, and examinations of how ancient cultures thought of life. There's not a single paragraph of legal reasoning in the whole misbegotten thing. (And for good reason—there's no principle from the Constitution or American law that could support *Roe*'s outrageous holding.)

For years, millions of people have fought to see *Roe v. Wade* overturned, and it's become a central issue in U.S. Supreme Court confirmation battles. Pro-life activists were hopeful that *Roe* would be overturned after additional changes on the Court, when in 1989 Justice Kennedy joined a couple of known pro-life justices in *Webster v. Reproductive Health Services,* harshly criticizing parts of *Roe*'s holding and suggesting that *Roe* might need to be overruled.[38] Those hopes were dashed three years later when Kennedy became the fifth vote to uphold a right to abortion in *Planned Parenthood v. Casey* in 1992.[39]

Nonetheless, *Casey* undermined *Roe.* It replaced several key parts of *Roe* and downgraded abortion from a fundamental right to nonfundamental status. Liberal and moderate justices refused to allow this to make a difference, subsequently even striking down a ban on the hideous and gruesome practice of partial-birth abortion in 2000.[40] But the equation shifted when Justice Alito replaced Justice O'Connor in 2006, and Justice Kennedy was willing to become the fifth vote to uphold a new ban on partial-birth abortion in 2007.[41]

This isn't about a woman's being able to do whatever she wants with her own body. It's not her body. It's a smaller body inside hers. It has its own genetic makeup that is 50% different from hers, so the cells of that body are not the cells of her body. The baby has its own heart, brain, stomach, and other organs. They're not part of her. This is a separate person, breathing and moving and even feeling. It's the miracle of life.

Roe v. Wade must be overruled. It will go down in history as one of the worst cases of all time. The reality is that if *Roe* is overturned, it will not make abortion illegal. Instead it will restore to each state the power to make laws regarding abortion, pursuant to states' police power to make laws for public health and morality. At that point pro-life advocates will have to convince their fellow citizens that every baby is a precious human being made in the image of God, deserving of all the dignity and respect that attend such a sacred status.

DEFINING LIFE

When does life begin? You can't defend abortion unless you argue that what loses its life in the process is not a human being. (If you say it's a human being but that it's okay to kill it for convenience as a form of birth control, then that's a deeply disturbing thought.)

The problem with the Left is its unwillingness to take a stand as to when life begins. A perfect example of this is the statement from 2004 Democratic presidential candidate Wesley Clark, who said, "Life begins with the mother's decision."[42] In other words, life begins whenever the mother decides it does.

This is an amazingly absurd statement. It's ridiculous on a galactic scale, as it reflects something that is self-evidently untrue. We have scientific measurements to detect life. It's only in the absence of such indicators that a doctor will pronounce a patient dead. Within a few weeks, an unborn child has a heartbeat and brain-wave activity. To any doctor in America, a patient showing those two things is declared to be alive.

Then again, at least it was an answer. When he was still a candidate, Barack Obama said that determining when life begins is above his "pay grade." Of course, how can you support abortion if you're not ruling out that a human being might be losing its life? Being president is about leadership. You can't be a leader by refusing to take a stand on the tough issues, especially when lives are at stake.

And there are a great many human lives at stake. There have been almost 50 million abortions since *Roe v. Wade*. Fully 35% of American women have had an abortion by age 45. And the horrible tragedy is that 93% of these abortions are for convenience—no rape, incest, or health concerns, just an after-the-fact form of birth control. It's heartbreaking.[43]

Fortunately, technology has helped us here in amazing ways. It's been an unconscionable lie of the abortion industry that unborn children are unfeeling, senseless blobs of tissue. With 4-D ultrasound, a woman in her OB's office can look with eyes full of wonder at a real-time video showing her little baby moving his hands and his feet, and even sucking his thumb. Millions of women—and men too if they're sitting in the room as the father—find their wide eyes soon full of tears as they gaze at the unspeakable beauty of a new human being getting ready to enter our world. They stand amazed at witnessing human life.

It is a heinous indictment of our society that this precious life can be crushed before that baby draws her first breath. May God grant this generation to come to understand that whatever your hardships may be or how challenging your circumstances are, every baby boy and girl deserves to live.

Economic and Security Impact of Family Troubles

These issues are not only for social conservatives. The priorities of ECons and SafeCons are likewise impacted by the strength of our families.

A perfect example of this is from Klukowski's friend Jared, who owns and runs a day care in Phoenix, Arizona. Jared told him about one mother whose children are in his day care. This mother, Maria (not her real name), has seven children by five different men. She freely told Jared through various conversations how much she gets per child from the government. She gets welfare, food stamps, food assistance (free milk, butter, cheese, etc., for each child), day care (Jared's business), and healthcare. Jared was shocked to find that she receives about $6,500 per month. She works, making around $10 an hour. At full time, this amounts to $20,000 per year. But she receives about $78,000 a year from the taxpayers.

Likewise, our security is at stake. Men with a wife and children have something to live for, and also something to die for if duty calls. Children raised in stable households tend to be more law-abiding, and are taught to serve and to sacrifice as adults. All such people are far less susceptible to being drawn into murderous ideologies, or to betraying the neighbors or their country. Strong families keep America safe.[44]

For the reasons we discussed in Chapters 3 and 4, strong families and personal faith provide better workers, better consumers, and better investors, and help raise the next generation of honest, honorable, courageous citizens who make excellent soldiers, emergency workers, and police officers. Yet another example of how all three types of conservatives stand or fall together.

10

TO KEEP AND BEAR ARMS

"The Second Amendment is a doomsday provision, one designed for those exceptionally rare circumstances where all other rights have failed—where the government refuses to stand for reelection and silences those who protest; where courts have lost the courage to oppose, or can find no one to enforce their decrees. However improbable these contingencies seem today, facing them unprepared is a mistake a free people get to make only once."

—Judge Alex Kozinski, *Silveira v. Lockyer,* 328 F.3d 567, 570 (9th Cir. 2003)

(dissenting from denial of rehearing en banc)

There is one more social issue: guns. It's often not portrayed as a social issue, because those who oppose social conservatives don't want to square off against gun owners as well. The reason is that when the Left opposes the Second Amendment, they lose elections.

But gun rights are unquestionably a social issue. The Second Amendment right to keep and bear arms goes to the heart of American traditions and our American identity. If gun ownership is not a social issue, then we don't know what is.

Your authors speak with authority on this issue. Blackwell is a member of the board of directors of the National Rifle Association of America, the flagship gun rights organization in the United States. And Klukowski worked for the NRA as special assistant and later senior advisor to former NRA president Sandy Froman (who continues to serve on the NRA board and the NRA executive council), and Klukowski's scholarly works on the Second Amendment have been cited by federal courts in several major cases across the country.

"Call Me Gabby"

We approach the issue of gun rights shortly after the shooting tragedy in Tucson. Such times call for a serious discussion of both safety and liberty, and what these things mean in our national life.

"Call me Gabby." Those were the first words Democrat Gabrielle Giffords said to me (Klukowski) when we met in 2003. I was working at the Arizona State Senate where she was a state senator, three years before she was elected to Congress. She knew I was a Republican and that I served under a Republican senator. While I was on a first-name basis with all the Republican senators I met on the campaign trail and helped with their elections, none of the Republican senators I had met only within the Senate building as a staffer extended me such a privilege. I addressed each one by rank and title, which is of course reasonable and proper.

I made it a point to meet all thirty senators. I introduced myself to her by saying, "Good morning, Senator Giffords. I'm Ken Klukowski." All of them responded courteously, but in a way that maintained the expected distance between senators and staff. So I was floored when this state senator from the *other* party gave me an earnest handshake and a warm smile, and said, "Call me Gabby." And I did.

I lived twelve minutes from the Safeway grocery store where Gabby was shot in Tucson, Arizona, where several Americans—including an honorable federal judge and an innocent little girl—lost their lives to a depraved murderer. I used to work in the office of the NRA president just four minutes from there. My wife and I would often shop there after church.

The challenge with laws involving firearms is the balance they must find. For the reasons discussed in this chapter, the Second Amendment right to bear arms is central to American safety and liberty, both individually and as a people. But the Second Amendment does not secure gun rights for violent predators and convicted felons. Thus the task is formulating laws that fully protect and uphold the rights of law-abiding citizens, while protecting innocent people from degenerate thugs. It's difficult, but it must be done to protect our liberties.

Political and Policy Battles

There haven't been many gun control fights at the national level in recent years. Despite the fact that the national leaders of the Democratic Party in the past forty years—such as President Obama and President Clinton, Secretary Hillary Clinton, Senator John Kerry, Vice President Al Gore, and congressional leaders such as Nancy Pelosi and Tom Daschle—have been rabidly antigun, there's no one issue that has cost the Democrats more dearly than opposing the Second Amendment. And they know it, so now they try to keep quiet. Even though zealous antigunners like Eric Holder, Charles Schumer, and Dianne Feinstein just can't seem to restrain themselves from lashing out at gun owners whenever the topic comes up on camera, most national Democrats have learned from one painful whipping after another that on this issue they had better stay silent.

The Obama administration's antigun administrative actions thus far have been fairly subtle. For example, in mid-2010, President Obama's Bureau of Alcohol, Tobacco, Firearms and Explosives (BATFE, better known as ATF) reversed a decades-old policy on temporary gun transfers. Every retail gun sale requires the person buying the gun to fill out Form 4473, where the buyer gives his full name, home address, and information for a federal background check to confirm that he's not a felon, and that attests whether he's a U.S. citizen. But a temporary transfer of firearms, such as to journalists so that they can do a media story involving a gun, or to an engineer to evaluate some scientific issue involving that model of gun, has never required such forms because it's a temporary transfer for professional reasons, after which the gun is returned. This policy had been in place since 1969, the year after the most draconian and oppressive law in American history was passed, the Gun Control Act of 1968. But without any reason, the Obama BATFE has reversed this policy, requiring even temporary custodians of guns to fill out Form 4473. Proposed ATF rules would also require gun stores to report certain firearm sales to the government. And Hillary Clinton has decreed that certain rifles now cannot be imported into the United States.[1]

Another measure is that the Environmental Protection Agency

(EPA) tried to move forward on an item from the gun control wish list: banning lead ammunition. The idea is to say that lead is a pollutant, and therefore the EPA can claim jurisdiction to regulate it. In this case, "regulating" means banning. Lead ammo is half the price of most other ammunition—such as ammo made from copper—so if you ban it you make it much more expensive to shoot a gun.

This type of gun control is insidious. It sounds mundane and bureaucratic, nothing that would ever grab the headlines. The result of such tactics is that it raises an alarm only among those who are fully versed in Second Amendment and gun rights issues, and plugged in with organizations like the NRA.

The Unsung Heroes Who Really Saved the Second Amendment

Two of the past four years, 2008 and 2010, have seen historic victories for gun rights in the U.S. Supreme Court—the two greatest such victories in American history. A couple of the radical libertarian crusaders (see Chapter 4) who hopped on this issue in recent years are now being hailed by some for "saving" the Second Amendment.

There are indeed several people who saved the Second Amendment. If not for them, no one reading this book would have any enforceable constitutional right to buy or own a gun.

But they're not the people you've seen on the news or interviewed by those who aren't particularly involved with gun rights. These are the men who really saved the Second Amendment for us and future generations. They haven't received the media attention they deserve, and even in conservative circles certain radical libertarians have been given the spotlight to the exclusion of those whose years of faithful effort brought us to where we are today.

The Left came to dominate higher education in the 1960s and '70s. As part of this, law schools became increasingly more liberal. New Deal supporters who hailed the Supreme Court's leftward lurch in 1937 became law professors in the 1940s and '50s, and their students in turn became even more liberal law professors in the 1960s and '70s.

Along with this leftward shift in academia came a leftward view toward the Second Amendment right to keep and bear arms. When the big push started in 1968 to ban all handguns in America, the consensus view in legal academia was that complete bans wouldn't violate the Second Amendment because no one had any right to own a gun.

In this environment, it was considered laughable when Don Kates published a lengthy scholarly piece on gun rights in the elite *Michigan Law Review* in 1983.[2] This was followed by a book by Stephen Halbrook, and more law review articles by David Hardy and Nelson Lund.[3] The evidence started mounting, until in 1989 a major liberal constitutional law professor published "The Embarrassing Second Amendment" in *Yale Law Journal,* mainstreaming debate on the Second Amendment. This launched a flood of scholarly pieces, with the names of academic researchers such as Bob Cottrol, Joyce Lee Malcolm, and David Kopel joining the small but growing list of lawyers and professors examining this little-understood provision of the Constitution.[4]

THE PUBLIC VERSION OF *HELLER* AND *MCDONALD*

In 2008 the Supreme Court handed down its first significant opinion on the Second Amendment in American history. It was the landmark case *D.C. v. Heller.*

Under local law, residents of Washington, D.C., were not permitted to have a gun in their homes. In 2003, six D.C. residents who wanted to keep a gun in their home for self-defense filed a lawsuit, claiming the D.C. gun ban violated their rights under the Second Amendment to keep and bear arms. This lawsuit, *Parker v. District of Columbia,* lost in federal district court. But a three-judge panel of the U.S. Court of Appeals for the District of Columbia Circuit reversed the district judge, holding that the Second Amendment guarantees a right to private citizens to keep and bear arms. The opinion was written by Judge Laurence Silberman, who was appointed by President Reagan while Attorney General Ed Meese was advising on judicial nominations.

Since the D.C. Circuit also held that only one of those plaintiffs, Dick Heller, had standing to bring this lawsuit in federal court, the case was renamed *District of Columbia v. Heller,* and the Supreme Court took it. In *Heller,* the Supreme Court, in a long and detailed opinion, held that the Second Amendment is in fact an individual right, and struck down the D.C. ban.

But the Constitution's Bill of Rights gives American citizens rights only against the federal government. After the Civil War, the Fourteenth Amendment extended most—but not all—of the Bill of Rights to also apply against state and local governments. So everyone knew that the next big question was whether the Second Amendment applies (or is "incorporated," to use the legal term) to the states.

The Second Amendment applies directly to D.C. because the District is federal territory. After *Heller,* the next question was whether the Second Amendment is incorporated to the state through the Fourteenth Amendment. On June 26, 2008 (the day *Heller* was decided), both the NRA and the radical libertarians who argued *Heller* separately filed lawsuits challenging Chicago's handgun ban, which was almost as restrictive as D.C.'s. The cases went up the ladder, and on June 28, 2010, in *McDonald v. Chicago* the Supreme Court held that the Second Amendment applies to the states.

Three lawyers argued the case in *McDonald.* In addition to Chicago's lawyer, the libertarian who argued *Heller,* Alan Gura, presented a libertarian argument. Former solicitor general Paul Clement argued for the NRA.

For the reasons explained below, it's worth noting that the radical libertarians didn't win these cases on their legal theories. All rights that have been "incorporated" to the states have been so through the Fourteenth Amendment Due Process Clause. In *McDonald,* the libertarians' primary argument was that the Court should incorporate the Second Amendment through what's called the Fourteenth Amendment Privileges or Immunities Clause. To do this, they claimed (wrongly, as shown below) that the Court would have to overrule the *Slaughter-House Cases,* which we learned about in Chapter 4. Overturning *Slaughter-House* has been an article of faith for some libertarians for decades, but the Supreme Court would have none of it.

The conservative justices lit into Gura. Chief Justice Roberts cut him off only seconds into his argument, saying that "it's a heavy burden for you to carry to suggest that we ought to overrule that decision." As Gura continued undeterred, Justice Scalia came in with guns blazing, first asking if it was easier to win this case through overruling *Slaughter-House* or going through the conventional route with the Due Process Clause. When Gura admitted the latter was easier, Scalia pressed him. "Why are you asking us to overrule ... 140 years of prior law, when ... you can reach your result under [the conventional approach]." Scalia then finished with a caustic backhand that elicited laughter throughout the courtroom: "unless you're bucking for—a place in some law school faculty."[5]

After this pummeling was over, Clement rose and gave a quick, straightforward application of how the Court had incorporated rights for the past century through the Due Process Clause, and why that perfectly applied to the Second Amendment. He easily parried the questions from the liberal justices, and then took his seat. It was over. There was no way Chicago could win the case.

This is not to say that these libertarian crusaders didn't do something significant. They were the ones who designed these two big lawsuits, initiated them, and adroitly pursued them to a successful conclusion. The cases were well planned and shrewdly executed, and it took good lawyering.

But for those of us who have been involved in this issue for years, who know the lawyers and scholars who toiled for years to bring this day about, the same people who are the ones now doing much of the heavy lifting as the real work begins, it's profoundly disappointing to see those who laid all the groundwork for these cases, and who created the unique facts to get these cases going, not get the credit they're due.

This is especially true from my perspective (Klukowski). I personally know all of these players. I helped research one of the briefs in *Heller* and published a law review article on the Second Amendment shortly before the Supreme Court decided *Heller*. I also authored one of the larger briefs in *McDonald* (representing the American Civil Rights Union, Let Freedom Ring, the Committee for Justice, and the Family Research Council) and published another law review article on how the Second Amendment applies to the states.

But I'm not one of these pioneers. I have enough skill and background to fully evaluate each of these lawyers and scholars, but can't be accused of sour grapes because I admit these cases would have been won just as easily if I had never been involved.

THE TWO MEN WHO SAVED
THE SECOND AMENDMENT

More than any others, these victories were possible because of two men. They are Charles Cooper and Nelson Lund.

Chuck Cooper, whom we referenced in the previous chapter, is one of the top constitutional litigators in America. He graduated at the top of his law school class from Alabama, clerked for a judge on the Fifth Circuit, then clerked for Justice William Rehnquist on the Supreme Court (before Rehnquist became chief justice). When Attorney General Ed Meese took over the Justice Department in President Reagan's second term, Meese asked that Reagan appoint Cooper as the assistant attorney general in charge of the Justice Department's Office of Legal Counsel (OLC). This is one of the two elite legal teams for the U.S. government, with OLC writing legal memos to advise the president and attorney general on the most complicated and serious legal issues facing the country. (Cooper's deputy was a brilliant lawyer named Samuel Alito.)

After OLC, Cooper went on to a career litigating some of the most important constitutional cases in America. As noted, Chuck is the lead counsel for defenders of traditional marriage in the California same-sex marriage case. Cooper also now handles some major Second Amendment cases for the NRA, and is involved in First Amendment issues, campaign finance, and any number of other issues.

Nelson Lund is a law professor and the foremost Second Amendment legal scholar in the United States. He holds a Ph.D. from Harvard and received his J.D. from the University of Chicago, where he was the law review's executive editor. He clerked for a judge on the Fifth Circuit, then for Justice Sandra Day O'Connor on the Supreme Court. When Cooper was the head of OLC, Lund was one of the top lawyers serving under Cooper and Alito. Lund also served on the other elite legal team in the government, the Office of the Solicitor General. He then served as associate White House counsel under Bush 41, and in the early 1990s became a law professor. Lund is the Patrick Henry Professor of Constitutional Law and the Second Amendment at George Mason University, the only endowed professorship involving the Second Amendment in America. Lund's prolific scholarship on the Second Amendment has been published by prestigious law reviews and been cited by numerous federal courts.

Around 1990, Second Amendment strategists were concerned about the antigun sentiment in legal circles, and decided that the groundwork must be laid for an eventual Supreme Court case declaring the Second Amendment as an individual right. In the early 1990s, the NRA had some newer board members who were high-powered attorneys. One of these was the aforementioned Sandy Froman, first elected to the NRA board in 1992. Froman—a graduate of Stanford and Harvard Law School, who was a partner at the largest law firm in Arizona and a former law professor—helped put together the first law school academic symposium to organize research efforts building on the scholarly works we've already mentioned.

As this scholarship began to emerge in the 1990s, the next step was bringing it to the attention of federal judges. Every federal appeals court to weigh in on the Second Amendment in the previous decades had held that the Second Amendment was about either the power of states to have militias (meaning National Guard) or for individuals to have firearms only in connection with uniformed militia service. None had held that the Second Amendment was an individual right.[6]

In 1998, a Texas doctor going through a messy divorce, Timothy Joe Emerson, had a restraining order issued against him. Emerson was a gun owner. Under federal law, anyone under any sort of restraining order cannot own, possess, or touch a gun.[7] (This is an example of a law that might not survive now that the Second Amendment is being enforced in court, in that restraining orders can be issued in a routine fashion in situations like divorce, often without the other party even having a lawyer or opportunity to argue against the order. We don't allow constitutional rights to be taken away by a judge without due process. Lund has an excellent law review article analyzing this issue.[8]) A Clinton-appointed U.S. attorney discovered that Emerson still had a gun, and prosecuted him.

Emerson was convicted. As the case went on appeal to the Fifth Circuit, Chuck Cooper and Nelson Lund got involved. This was an appropriate case to argue why the Second Amendment is a right held by private citizens, like every other provision in the Bill of Rights. Emerson's public defender welcomed the help Cooper and Lund offered, and worked with them to bring all of their legal scholarship and evidence to the court's attention.

The result was spectacular. In a seventy-one-page opinion by Judge William Garwood, in the 2001 case *U.S. v. Emerson,* the Fifth Circuit became the first federal appeals court to hold that the Second Amendment is an individual right. The court went on page after page quoting and citing the mountain of legal evidence Cooper and Lund presented, proving that the original meaning of the Second Amendment was for individual law-abiding Americans to own and carry firearms without any connection to militia service.[9]

Emerson is what made the later Supreme Court victory in *Heller* possible, if not almost inevitable. As Lund described *Emerson* to Klukowski, "It was instantly clear that this was the most significant legal victory for Second Amendment rights in American history, and it was also clear that it was only a first small step toward securing the Second Amendment's proper place in American jurisprudence." As a result of *Emerson,* a liberal panel of the Ninth Circuit the following year took another case backed by the NRA, *Silveira v. Lockyer,* and wrote a lengthy opinion arguing that *Emerson* was wrong, holding that the Second Amendment was not an individual right.[10] With a well-developed split between the federal appeals courts, the Supreme Court was ready to consider the issue. The opportunity came several years later in the *Heller* case.

When the Supreme Court decided *Heller,* they did not adopt the radical libertarians' theory on the meaning of the Second Amendment. Instead, Justice Kennedy (who was the fifth vote in *Heller*) indicated that what he found persuasive was an argument that he said during oral argument was *not* found in Dick Heller's brief, instead coming from an amicus brief.[11] The argument Kennedy then described (about how to uncouple the two clauses in the amendment) was Lund's argument in the brief he filed, as recognized both by Second Amendment scholar David

Kopel and another law professor.[12] Taken with various scholarly works the Court cited, including some by Steve Halbrook and Joyce Malcolm (undoubtedly the two top historians on the Second Amendment—especially Halbrook, whose many works are widely cited), the Supreme Court issued a lengthy decision adopting an individual right.

Unlike *Heller*, in one sense no one can claim credit for the *McDonald* win. It was just a straightforward application of Supreme Court precedent, though Paul Clement deserves credit for a smooth and flawless performance before the Court. (Clement was smart to take this case. As solicitor general, he had filed a brief for the U.S. government in *Heller* that was surprisingly unfriendly to the Second Amendment. Since Clement is on the Republican short list for a Supreme Court nomination, representing the NRA helps rehabilitate his record on this issue.)

What is noteworthy is that some radical libertarians thought they could unanimously win on getting the Court to overrule the *Slaughter-House Cases*. They're half right. It was unanimous; they unanimously *lost* that argument, as all nine justices rejected the idea that *Slaughter-House* should be overruled. The four liberal justices voted not to incorporate the Second Amendment, just as the four liberals voted against an individual right in *Heller*. Four justices voted to incorporate the Second Amendment through the Due Process Clause (which is unfortunate, in that this approach is not at all conservative).

Justice Clarence Thomas was the only principled originalist in *McDonald*, voting to incorporate the Second Amendment through the Privileges or Immunities Clause, but without overruling *Slaughter-House*. (This is exactly the approach Klukowski argued for in his Supreme Court amicus brief in *McDonald*, as Professor Lund acknowledged in Lund's law review article examining *McDonald*, published by *Florida Law Review*.[13]) With Thomas's vote, there was a clear five-justice majority holding that the Second Amendment is a fundamental right, extending the right to bear arms to the states.

Justice Thomas's approach should have been the majority holding for the Court. It was radical to push for overruling *Slaughter-House*. Lawyers from over a dozen organizations gathered for a conference to coordinate support for *McDonald* when the Court announced it would take the case. Your author Klukowski was among them. With all of us seated around a large table at the Heritage Foundation, taking turns addressing the group, a lawyer representing Otis McDonald tried to discourage me from writing a brief explaining to the Court how it could incorporate the right to bear arms to the states through the Privileges or Immunities Clause without overruling *Slaughter-House*. As a lawyer, you usually welcome alternative arguments that can win your case. The coplaintiffs in the *McDonald* case included gun rights organizations, which presumably cared only about extending the Second Amendment to the states. McDonald's legal team then filed its consent with the Court allowing all outside groups to file amicus briefs. It was a blanket consent that didn't object to my brief, so they didn't formally try to block me. Nonetheless, it's hard to see how urging me to drop the brief would have helped their clients' case. This case was about gun rights but was hijacked by radical libertarians to advance their economic agenda in a way that could have endangered this case for the gun rights clients by seeking to exclude other arguments that could win the case. Evidently Justice Thomas agreed with the other conservative justices that the principled way to win this case was to keep it focused on the right to keep and bear arms, where it belongs.

The Future of the Second Amendment

Heller and *McDonald* were only the beginning of what will now be perhaps a thirty-year fight for gun rights. As Lund tells Klukowski, "The biggest misperception of *Heller* and *McDonald* is that they provide a robust and secure foundation for gun rights in the courts. Without further substantial victories, *Heller* and *McDonald* could turn out to be relatively insignificant as a practical matter."

What Nelson is talking about here is that *Heller* and *McDonald* were the low-hanging fruit. *Heller* held that the Second Amendment was an individual right, and *McDonald* held that this right extends to the states. All those cases require is that the government cannot completely ban you from having any common firearms in your house. It's unclear at this point whether the courts will uphold the Second Amendment as protecting anything more.

Now the real work begins. There are around 85 million gun owners in America. They possess 200 million firearms. And there are 20,000 gun laws in this country. Looking at that picture, there are infinite possibilities for lawsuits. What standard of review should courts apply in deciding Second Amendment cases? Who has standing to bring these lawsuits in the first place? What are your Second Amendment rights when you leave your house? What about public places? What about firearms other than handguns, shotguns, and rifles? Do you have a right to carry firearms that are concealed in public? These are only six of many questions the courts will have to face in the coming quarter century.

As a result of the Supreme Court's recent historic cases, Second Amendment cases are now flooding the federal courts. As Judge Diane Sykes of the U.S. Court of Appeals for the Seventh Circuit wrote in one important recent case, *U.S. v. Skoien,* "The Second Amendment is no more susceptible to a one-size-fits-all standard of review than any other constitutional right. Gun-control regulations impose varying degrees of burden on Second Amendment rights, and individual assertions of the right will come in many forms."[14] Thus courts have begun the long and complex process of developing a framework for considering how the 20,000 or so gun regulations on the books impact America's 85 million gun owners nationwide.

Any way you look at it, we are at the beginning of a new era of constitutional law. How these cases are decided will depend on who wins the White House in 2012, and the Supreme Court that president helps create. This is an economic issue, in that personal protection and home security protect property and contract rights, and guns are invaluable for self-protection against criminals. It is a national security issue, in that the police can't be everywhere, and so in an age of terrorism and when a lone malevolent killer might start shooting at a crowd around a congresswoman at a grocery store, everyone who wants to protect themselves and their families needs the right to do so. This is a perfect coalition builder for constitutional conservatives and will be a major issue for years to come.

11

A NATION SAFE AND SECURE

"A truly successful army is one that, because of its strength and ability and dedication, will not be called upon to fight, for no one will dare to provoke it."

—President Ronald Reagan,
Speech at the U.S. Military Academy at West Point, May 27, 1981

During times of financial anxiety, it's natural for the federal government to posture by saying that its number-one job is helping to create jobs. But as important as a growing economy is, the fact remains that the Constitution says the federal government's top priority is national security. And Republicans need to unapologetically push a constitutional conservative policy to secure the lives and interests of American citizens both at home and abroad.

It's a tremendous challenge to find the right balance when it comes to security. In a free society, it's easier for criminals or terrorists to threaten others. On one hand, government power must be constrained by the Constitution and uphold the rights of American citizens. On the other hand, the Constitution isn't to be construed in a fashion that gets us all killed. The constitutional conservative approach is to adhere to the proper balance of liberty and security.

The Obama administration has proven itself incompetent regarding this paramount purpose of the federal government. We see it in securing classified information, bringing terrorists to justice, detecting threats, and in using the military for social engineering. The president's worst national security failure, though, is something you might not have seen before, and we'll explore it at the end of this chapter.

Protecting the Homeland Against Terror

We must protect the American homeland against an ongoing threat of Islamic jihadist terrorism. We need to accept that militant Islam constitutes an existential threat to Western civilization in general, and to the American way of life in particular.

BRINGING TERRORISTS TO JUSTICE

We must deal with all the terrorists we capture on the battlefield. John Brennan, President Obama's White House terrorism czar (whose operational activities are unconstitutional, by the way), noted that of the terrorists we capture on the battlefield and take to Guantánamo Bay, Cuba (Gitmo), but later release, at least 20% return to the battlefield to kill Americans. Brennan said that percentage is rather good, and not something for which we should be overly concerned.[1] That number has since risen to 25%.[2]

Nor is this an isolated example. President Obama has now nominated James Cole to be America's deputy attorney general, the top post at the Justice Department aside from the attorney general himself. When even his Democratic Senate couldn't confirm Cole, Obama gave him a recess appointment. Cole has compared the 9/11 terrorists to drug dealers, and believes that acts of terrorism are crimes that can be handled through our domestic law enforcement system, rather than acts of war.[3]

The administration's tone on this issue helps explain Barack Obama's naïve and wrongheaded promise to close Gitmo within a year of taking office (a promise he's long since broken). President Bush sent detainees to Gitmo both because the marines there are an extremely disciplined military force, making Gitmo an impregnable fortress, and because Bush was advised that the writ of habeas corpus would not apply, so terrorists couldn't bring everything into civilian court.

The Supreme Court later held by a narrow 5–4 vote in 2008 that habeas corpus does apply to Gitmo.[4] This decision from *Boumediene v.*

Bush is the worst national security decision issued in American history, sparking a dissent by four conservative justices, in which Justice Scalia wrote:

> Today the Court warps our Constitution in a way that goes beyond [this] narrow issue.... It blatantly misdescribes important precedents.... It breaks a chain of precedent as old as the common law that prohibits judicial inquiry into detentions of aliens abroad absent statutory authorization. And, most tragically, it sets our military commanders the impossible task of proving to a civilian court, under whatever standards this Court devises in the future, that evidence supports the confinement of each and every enemy prisoner.
>
> The Nation will live to regret what the Court has done today.... [5]

This issue involves American sovereignty and American exceptionalism (discussed below) and shows how agenda judges are rewriting the constitutional order. The Constitution draws a bright line between national security and law enforcement. It's a line between military and police, between foreign policy and domestic policy, between foreigners and citizens. The Constitution exists to protect innocent citizens from their own government, with the presumption of innocence, proof beyond a reasonable doubt, the right to an attorney, and the right to a jury trial. The Constitution affords foreigners who are wartime enemies against the United States no such protections, especially when fighting our military on foreign battlefields. The Supreme Court got *Boumediene* wrong, and leftist politicians from Barack Obama to Hillary Clinton cheered this decision.

But you can't win a war this way. Proof of this is seen in the case of Ahmed Ghailani, one of the terrorists who bombed the U.S. embassies in Kenya and Tanzania in 1998, killing 280 people. In a knee-jerk fit of liberalism, President Obama decided to allow Attorney General Eric Holder to treat Ghailani as a common criminal in a U.S. civilian court, where the prosecution is severely restricted by the Federal Rules of Criminal Procedure, the Federal Rules of Evidence, and the Fourth, Fifth, Sixth, and Eighth Amendments in the Bill of Rights.

Predictably, the trial was a disaster. The Clinton-appointed federal judge in this civilian trial excluded a key witness because that witness had been subject to harsh interrogation. All sorts of other procedural issues were in play in Ghailani's favor. In the end he was acquitted (because of government's not being able to prove every element beyond a reasonable doubt) of 284 out of 285 charges of conspiracy and murder. He was convicted on only a single count of conspiracy to destroy a government building.[6]

The U.S. criminal justice system is premised on the idea that it's better for a hundred guilty people to go unpunished than for a single innocent person to be condemned. As a result, you can't get a conviction unless every single procedural obstacle is overcome, and everything proven beyond a reasonable doubt. Consequently, guilty people go free all the time.

However, war is about defeating the enemy by any means. Fighting a war involves limited information, scant evidence, and calculated risks. Those work on a battlefield, but they usually don't hold up in a courtroom.

That's why Ghailani isn't getting what he deserves. He's thirty-six years old. He'll get twenty years in prison, after which he'll be a free man when still middle-aged and with perhaps a long, happy life ahead of him. Instead he should be executed. But thanks to the abysmal failure of President Obama and Attorney General Holder, the former refusing to treat this war *as a war* and the latter for his boneheaded insistence on treating foreign enemy terrorists like American citizens, this mass-murdering foreign enemy will eventually go free.

Ghailani is the first Gitmo terrorist given a civilian trial. Other cases were pending, including that of 9/11 mastermind Khalid Sheikh Mohammed. President Obama and General Holder continued saying these terrorists should get civilian trials, though the president added that some terrorists may get military trials if they might be acquitted in civilian trials.

Of course, this sacrifices principle. If military trials are acceptable for anyone, then they're okay for everyone. Denying a civilian trial to someone who's entitled to it because they might be acquitted is manifest injustice. The constitutional conservative view is that all of the terrorists are entitled to military tribunals only. The entire Obama-Holder approach to the War on Terror is a spectacle.

Which is why on April 4, 2011, the White House reversed course.

Several post-*Boumediene* cases in the federal system had gone to the D.C. Circuit federal appeals court, where the court held against the terrorists. On April 4, the Supreme Court refused to review those D.C. Circuit decisions in two cases petitioning for certiorari, *Al-Odah v. U.S.* and *Awad v. Obama.* When the Supremes declined to delve back into terrorist rights in civilian court, the White House reversed course over Holder's public dissent, and announced that these terrorists will now go back to the military tribunal system that then-Senator Obama previously condemned.

There was a day when Democrats were not weak on national security. During World War II eight German saboteurs secretly came ashore in New Jersey. Federal agents captured them. Democrat FDR, acting as a wartime president, correctly decided that under international law these German soldiers were not entitled to prisoner-of-war status because they were not in uniform. Despite the fact that they had been captured on U.S. soil, FDR then ordered them tried in secret—we repeat, in *secret*—by a military commission. Less than three *weeks* after their capture, he ordered them summarily executed, even before the U.S. Supreme Court had issued a final opinion on what their rights were under these circumstances.[7]

President George W. Bush—a Republican—enacted a system that is far more careful and generous to these terrorists than was ever the case during World War II. All Gitmo detainees should be subject to military commissions in Gitmo. The system should be expedited, without many of the procedures used in civilian trials for Americans. And those found guilty should get the justice they deserve, without leftist antimilitary sympathies.

MISMANAGING OTHER TERRORIST PROSECUTIONS

It's not just Gitmo detainees, though. The failed approach was evident in trying other terrorists, such as those we capture here on U.S. soil. One example is Umar Farouk Abdulmutallab. He's the Christmas Day "underwear bomber" who sewed plastic explosives into his underwear and tried detonating them on an international flight on December 25, 2009, shortly before it landed in Detroit. Had he succeeded, 289 people would be dead.

The attack was foiled when a passenger realized what Abdulmutallab was doing and subdued him. Abdulmutallab was arrested in Detroit and taken into federal custody, and President Obama allowed Attorney General Holder to attempt a civilian prosecution of this terrorist. It took almost a full year just to get Abdulmutallab arraigned in court, which finally happened on December 16, 2010. Although we hope this case ends in a conviction on all counts, there would be little doubt that if this Nigerian-born terrorist (not an American) were to go before a military tribunal he would quickly and surely be found guilty.

"ISRAELIFICATION" OF AIRPORT SECURITY

This raises the separate issue of our insane airport security. Simply put, it's lousy.

In a free society there will always be ways that terrorists can try to kill innocent people, but this isn't about that undeniable fact. Ten years after 9/11, the United States has not secured our airlines, the point of vulnerability that cost three thousand American lives.

We still see this vulnerability. An Iranian-American businessman named Farid Seif forgot to remove his Glock handgun from his computer case when he went to the airport. It went through security, he boarded the plane and flew to his destination, and didn't realize he was carrying a gun until he was unpacking at his hotel. He alerted authorities.[8]

Think about this. This wasn't some sweet grandma who had a .22 pistol buried in a big purse as she shuffled along with her walker at the airport. Although Seif is evidently a good American, this man looks like a Middle Easterner, has a Middle Eastern name, hails from the world's leading state sponsor of terrorism, and managed to board a U.S. airplane *with a gun.* What if he had been a jihadist terrorist, instead of a law-abiding businessman?

The numbers bear out the infuriating reality that Seif's story is the *norm,* not the exception. Janet Napolitano's Department of Homeland Security has at least three classified reports showing that the *majority* of the time, you can sneak guns *and even bombs* onto an airplane. In New Jersey in 2006, undercover agents were able to sneak guns and bombs past security 20 out of 22 times. In Los Angeles, undercover agents succeeded getting past security 50 out of 70 times. And in Chicago, agents got past security 45 out of 75 times.[9]

From the sublime to the ridiculous: A fifty-year-old airline pilot was arrested by federal marshals after posting a series of six video clips he recorded at San Francisco International Airport on YouTube, which showed flight crews being forced to go through Transportation Security Administration (TSA) screening while ground crews—who have access to secure areas of an airplane—were seen simply swiping a card to get through security.[10]

This should be one of the biggest scandals in America. Not simply because DHS has failed to secure the airports, but for two other reasons. First, DHS is not being forthright with the American people as to how vulnerable we still are. Ignorance is *not* bliss. And second, because another nation shows us a completely different way to handle airport security effectively.

We should study how some version of the Israeli airline system could be implemented here. In Israel, you go through a couple of levels of security where you're not even stopped, but you're being watched and asked questions, as officials look for telltale signs of trouble. Then every passenger goes through a brief interview with a trained security agent. These agents have four years of training before they're deployed. They psychologically profile every person, asking specific questions, and evaluating not just the answers, but how they compare with other answers, the tone and mannerisms of the passenger, body language, and other indicators. One interesting thing is that they look intently at your face the entire time, which causes certain reactions in people who are trying to hide something. They're trained to detect all manner of signs that something might be amiss.

At the end of the interview, they put a number on the boarding pass, between one and six. A one means that you go straight onto the airplane without any delay at all—much faster at that point than a U.S. airport. The higher the number, the more scrutiny you then undergo. If you get a six, you'll be in the airport for hours. Trained agents will sequester you alone, unpack all of your bags, and examine all the contents. They do in-depth follow-up interviews, can run background checks, check your computer, pictures in your camera, find out what you were doing at each location and why.

This is profiling, but not racial profiling. It's psychological profiling, by trained experts looking for signs of anxiety, hostility, nervousness, or deceit. They consider everything about the passenger, and if the right warning signs are present they'll dig through everything to confirm you're not a threat. That's why for many years the only security breach in Israel was when one nonthreatening man accidently (like the businessman above) forgot to unpack his gun in 2002.

This contrasts with the self-evident ineffectiveness of the American model. Why does TSA mess up at the horrifying rate seen in the reports above? Because every agent knows that the odds are overwhelming that he'll go his whole day at the scanner without ever having someone try to sneak a weapon past him. Inevitably, you drop your mental guard as hundreds of bag images flash on the screen before you. Things make it past. That's a recipe for a terrorist attack succeeding.

America's airport security needs to be like Israel's, and our Constitution allows it. Security is not about political correctness; it's about making sure no one gets killed. The "Israelification" of U.S. airport security would literally be a lifesaver. The Fourth Amendment bars only unreasonable searches and seizures, and the Supreme Court would easily uphold a system designed to detect threats through profiling, along with full searches when danger signs are present (since the search would be reasonable in light of the warning signs that the agents detected). Constitutional conservatives must demand the Israelification of U.S. airport security.

MASS-CASUALTY ATTACKS

The United States also needs a constitutional conservative policy on protecting our homeland from a massive attack. The 9/11 attacks were the worst civilian attack we've experienced in our history. Yet the terrible death toll from that day—more than three thousand of our fellow Americans—was the result of four airliners crashing into buildings (or, in the case of Flight 93, from crashing in a Pennsylvania field after passengers rose up against the terrorists) and would be eclipsed by the loss of life that can result from other attacks.

We are under constant threat from nuclear, biological, and chemical weapons. Those threats will only increase as rogue nations continue to pursue weapons of mass destruction, given our ineffective strategies toward North Korea and Iran.

But there are other, less discussed dangers, such as that from an electromagnetic pulse (EMP). Fission bombs (atom bombs) on average explode with only roughly 1% of the force of the fusion bombs (hydrogen bombs) that America and Russia have in their nuclear arsenals, but are much easier to make and can still destroy part of a city. (The bombs America dropped on Hiroshima and Nagasaki were fission bombs.) If a terrorist group were to obtain a single fission bomb, they might not have to smuggle it into the United States and detonate it in a city. Instead they could load that bomb on a small missile carried by boat, stay perhaps two hundred miles off the Eastern Seaboard, and then launch the missile westward and upward to detonate perhaps fifty miles above the Mid-Atlantic region. Nuclear bombs generate an EMP that travels for hundreds of miles. Although an EMP would not be inherently dangerous to human beings or other living creatures, it would be devastating to electronics.

Even a relatively weak nuclear device, if it were high enough in the atmosphere, could project an EMP that would knock out most electronic devices from New York City to Atlanta, hitting Philadelphia, Baltimore, Richmond, Raleigh, Charlotte, and—of course—Washington, D.C. An EMP would shut down office buildings and hospitals. Thousands of cars driving on the highways and hundreds of airplanes flying in the air would literally have their onboard computers shut down while still moving at full speed. Almost everything with a circuit breaker would blow the breaker until restarted, and things without circuit breakers would be permanently ruined.[11]

Any electronics that were not "hardened" (insulated from electronic surges) would be affected, unless underground or otherwise shielded from an EMP. The damage would be massive in scope, and possibly catastrophic in overall impact. When we tested nuclear devices in the Pacific in the 1940s and '50s, a high-altitude nuclear detonation affected power systems in Hawaii hundreds of miles away.[12]

In the face of such a catastrophe, government is severely limited. Families must be able to protect themselves and provide for themselves. Families must be strong, and work with other families to ensure strong neighborhoods. Citizens would have to act much more through local and state governments, as the national government would be unable to act. Although it's easy for such scenarios to sound alarmist or apocalyptic, it is the role of government to prepare for every catastrophic scenario, from nuclear fallout to biological attacks, to financial meltdowns and market collapses, to this—the aftermath of an EMP attack.

The dangers America faces are manifold, and they are growing. The threat these dangers pose is enhanced by the weakness of liberal responses, given the Left's domination of the Democratic Party. But even many Republicans have not paid sufficient attention to these threats, which desperately call for a constitutional conservative response.

Constitutional conservatives need to have in place continuity-of-government systems to ensure this country is able to defend itself and get back on its feet in the event of such a nightmare.

KEEPING CLASSIFIED INFORMATION SECURE:
WIKILEAKS AND THE LEFT

One recent event highlights the need for protecting America's security, and the Obama administration's need to protect us: the recent scandal with WikiLeaks.

An Australian named Julian Assange is an antigovernment activist who runs a website dedicated to revealing classified material, under the woodenheaded delusion that revealing American government secrets will promote justice in the world. In July 2010, WikiLeaks released 92,000 U.S. military documents concerning the Afghanistan war. And in November 2010, the site released 250,000 documents from the State Department. While at the time of this writing authorities suspected that disgruntled army private first class Bradley Manning was the source of the documents, it's still being investigated, including the question of whether others were also involved.

The fallout continues. Assange is also accused of multiple sex crimes in Sweden, so it's unclear when—or if—he'll ever be held to account in the United States. There's also a question of what crime he may have committed. It's possible that Assange is to be charged with espionage,[13] and anyone with security clearance who gave that information to Assange could definitely be charged with espionage,[14] and possibly even with treason (which carries the death penalty, but which is also very hard to prove under the Constitution).[15]

The issue, though, is what to do about it. Robert Gibbs, the hapless former White House press secretary, mocked the idea that this release damaged national security, saying, "We're not scared" of a lone website operator.[16]

Yet classified information is information that—if disclosed—endangers national security. Although much of the disclosed documents were merely embarrassing, hundreds were classified. Some of these documents were marked "confidential," which means the disclosure of the information could reasonably cause *damage* to national security. Others were "secret," which federal law defines as meaning that disclosure is expected to cause *serious damage* to national security. (Fortunately, none of the documents on the system that was illegally accessed were "top secret," which is information where disclosure would cause *grave damage* to national security.)[17]

So the disclosure of these documents by definition means that U.S. national security was damaged, and we're still assessing the extent of that damage. It's clear for example that the Obama administration has agreed to share with Russia our knowledge of Britain's nuclear arsenal, which has obvious diplomatic implications.[18] Also when the *New York Times* contacted the White House regarding releasing these documents, the White House objected to some of the releases, but not others—despite the fact that they were all sensitive.[19]

Setting aside Gibbs's predictably silly comments, the lack of blanket condemnation reflects one of the most serious problems with the Far Left. There is an idiotic notion out there that governments shouldn't keep secrets. But even the constitutional lawyer who fought the Pentagon Papers case involving Daniel Ellsberg at the Supreme Court, Floyd Abrams, wrote how this situation was entirely unlike that Vietnam War scandal, and condemned what WikiLeaks and Assange have done.[20] The world is a dangerous place, and to protect ourselves and our children in such a world, we need to keep secret those things that could harm us.

Following the Constitution in a National Crisis

Sooner or later America will again face a national security crisis. That crisis might be a conventional foreign military threat, such as North

Korea launching a war against South Korea, or Russia invading Chechnya or one of the Eastern Bloc countries, or Iran attacking Israel. Or it could be domestic terrorism, an attack on a large number of people as in a sports stadium or a large building or a crowded area such as Times Square. It's a question of "when," not "if."

When that happens, the Constitution becomes more important than ever. The Constitution is always the Supreme Law of the Land. It can never be suspended or set aside. It's during times of crisis that government is most tempted to seize unfettered powers, taking advantage of the "whatever it takes" attitude that temporarily gains majority support in the wake of a shocking event. The Constitution allows massive exertions of power in response to emergencies, in keeping with Justice Robert Jackson's famous statement in 1949 that the Constitution is not a suicide pact. But where the law allows government to take an inch, it's often inclined to take a mile.

The Constitution is written as a charter of government, especially for times when the political will to restrain power might be flagging. During times of true emergency, the freedom of speech, the holding of full and free elections on the day set by law, and the Second Amendment right to keep and bear arms tend to be among the first rights targeted.

The way to best protect our constitutional rights during times of emergency is by electing and appointing men and women who truly revere our Constitution. In times of stress or of outright panic, when voters are not watching our political leaders as closely or carefully, we most need those who take seriously their oath to support and defend the Constitution of the United States.

EXECUTIVE SUBJECT TO CONGRESSIONAL OVERSIGHT AND UPHOLDING CIVIL RIGHTS

Another failure of leadership, mostly by the current administration but partly by previous Republicans as well, involves classified information and the Constitution. On one hand, the government must keep classified information secure while sharing that information between appropriate intelligence agencies and Congress. On the other hand, the Constitution must be upheld throughout this delicate process.

The Obama administration has not fulfilled its legal obligation to subject itself to congressional oversight on intelligence. Even Democratic senators are railing against the fact that the Obama White House is not sharing intel with Congress that federal law requires them to share.[21] Senator Feinstein wrote, "Having to fight over access to counterterrorism information is not productive and ultimately makes us less secure."[22]

While this shows one side of the problem, another story sounds a cautionary note from the Bush years regarding adhering to the Constitution.

Former deputy attorney general James Comey, when testifying before the Congress in hearings that were designed to go after the Bush administration, recounted one story that makes this point. Attorney General John Ashcroft—who is a solid conservative—was ill in the hospital in March 2004. However, a controversial program passed as an emergency measure immediately after 9/11 required frequent reauthorization by the attorney general to continue. We still don't know exactly what this program was, only that it granted the federal government broad powers in the name of security. That's a term that's often necessary, but that any true conservative looks at skeptically because it's a buzzword of statists and authoritarians that can be used expansively to trample the liberties of the citizens that those government officials are supposedly protecting. (National security conservatives are not at all minimalists when it comes to security; the government needs robust powers to protect citizens in a dangerous world. But such power must be watched very closely.) All we know is that this particular program was considered very intrusive into the lives of American civilians.

Deputy Attorney General Comey had properly assumed all of Attorney General Ashcroft's duties while Ashcroft was in the hospital. The program mentioned above was about to expire, and so Comey would be the one to decide on whether to continue it. Comey found out while in his official car that instead of coming to him, White House chief of staff Andrew Card and White House counsel Alberto Gonzales had gone to Ashcroft in the hospital to get him to sign off on continuing the program. Comey ordered his motorcade to turn on its lights and sirens and rush to the hospital.

Comey entered Ashcroft's room, only to find Card and Gonzales already there. He then recounts that Ashcroft lifted himself up in his bed and argued against what the White House was requesting. Attorney General Ashcroft went on about how the program went too far, and that he would not continue it.

Potential abuses are always possible, especially in wartime. That speaks to the importance of having constitutional conservatives in national security leadership posts. We don't need to know extremely sensitive national security secrets, just as we may never know what this particular program involved. Nor do we doubt that Andrew Card and Alberto Gonzales had very good reasons for wanting this program to continue, and were focused on protecting the nation. But we do need those making these top-secret decisions to rightly understand the Constitution and to faithfully fulfill their oaths of office to uphold it.

START IS A NONSTARTER

Another example of President Obama's poor leadership is the new START treaty between the United States and Russia. In reaching the new mandated number of warheads for both countries, that number being 1,550, America will have to dismantle more than 80 warheads more than the Russians. The United States will have to eliminate 150 delivery vehicles (which are either missiles or bombers—either of which "delivers" the warhead to its intended target), while the Russians can add 130. It will also impede America's ability to deploy a missile defense system.[23] In other words, it looks like we're giving up something for nothing.

This treaty had not been ratified by the U.S. Senate, out of serious concern regarding missile defense, but it was then rammed through in the last days of the 2010 lame-duck congressional session before the vanquished November candidates left office. International law is messy, in that treaties are binding upon signatories only according to their public understanding of those treaties. (If that sounds like a catchall that could be abused to get out of treaty obligations all the time, that's because it's exactly that.) The Russians have publicly stated that they understand the new START treaty to mean that the United States cannot deploy a missile shield of the nature we've planned for years. The treaty was held up because some Senate Republicans rightly insisted on knowing what assurances our State Department undersecretary in charge of this treaty (liberal former congresswoman Ellen Tauscher) gave to Russia in that regard. Conservative Republicans would not vote for such a treaty if in fact Tauscher gave up missile defense in the negotiations.

But President Obama put together the votes to ratify the treaty nonetheless. This is terribly reckless, because in a world where nuclear weapons are proliferating, America needs a comprehensive missile defense to protect ourselves. This serves as yet another reminder that our nation is safest when our commander in chief is a constitutional conservative.

THE MYTH OF MISUNDERSTANDING

Some on the far left say that much of the terrorist problem comes from a lack of understanding of their cultures, or perhaps their extreme poverty. This is ridiculous. The problem is that the cultural understanding of Islamic jihadists is that it's okay to kill those who refuse to join their religion, even children. The problem isn't that we fail to understand these extremists; the problem is that they're evil. All we need to understand about them is that they will never settle for anything less than our religious conversion or our death, and we need to respond accordingly.

Nor is the problem that they don't understand us. The new operations chief of Al Qaeda lived in the United States for fifteen years. This is someone who has seen the beauty of freedom and experienced the goodness and the richness of the American people. He's lived with us and enjoyed all the blessings of our country. Having that wealth of knowledge and experience, he still wants to kill us all.

Nonetheless, it's an ongoing delusion of the Left that the problem is that America's worldview is not as enlightened as the rest of the world's. We've seen that time and again from the current president, whenever he apologizes for the United States to foreign leaders and foreign audiences, or whenever he bows before them—both figuratively and literally.

At least President Obama managed to find his soul mate on American sovereignty with his VP. Evidently failing to grasp that America is the leader of the free world—or at least that he's supposed to root for his own country—Vice President Joe Biden told the Belgians in Brussels that their city may be the "capital of the free world."[24]

As Sarah Palin said during the 2008 VP debate, "Say it ain't so, Joe! Say it ain't so!"

The vice president acknowledged that as the second-highest elected official in the country (though thankfully one without any inherent power except for breaking tie votes in the Senate), he was probably out of line. He said, "As you probably know, some American politicians and American journalists refer to Washington, D.C., as the 'capital of the free world.'"[25]

Yes we do, Mr. Vice President, because it is. But instead, Biden went on talking (a shocker, we know) to make the case for why Brussels could lay claim to the title. What the heck is wrong with Joe Biden? Yet Barack Obama decided that Joe Biden is the man who should be a heartbeat away from the presidency.

Picking a VP is one of the first acts of leadership of a president. When it comes to national security, in picking Vice President Biden, President Obama once again failed to lead.

American Sovereignty and International Power

A belief in American exceptionalism leads to a commitment to American sovereignty. When you understand the American system of ordered liberty and government, the excellence of our free-market economy, and our devotion to transcendent truths and human dignity, you fiercely support the idea that we can never allow foreign powers to exert authority over us.

President Obama told our military that the world needs a new "international order" to maintain global peace. He stood before the graduating class of new army officers at West Point in May 2010, and told these American soldier leaders, "Our adversaries would like to see America sap its strength by overextending our power." The solution to this supposed problem is, according to our current commander in chief, that "we have to shape an international order that can meet the challenges of our generation."[26]

The president continued by explaining: "The international order we seek is one that can resolve the challenges of our times—countering violent extremism and insurgency; stopping the spread of nuclear weapons and securing nuclear materials; combating a changing climate and sustaining global growth; helping countries feed themselves and care for their sick; preventing conflict and healings its wounds."[27]

The depressing reality of having our commander in chief make those comments is that the Constitution makes him almost completely in charge of this decision. As the Supreme Court explained, "The President is the sole organ of the nation in its external relations, and its sole representative with foreign nations. . . . The President is the constitutional representative of the United States with regard to foreign nations."[28]

Yet we need to push for a constitutional foreign policy with the current president, even as we work toward electing a new one.

We must never join the Treaty of Rome, which created the International Criminal Court and could subject American troops to foreign prosecution. We cannot rely on the United Nations to contain sponsors of terrorism such as Iran from getting nuclear weapons, or to maintain effective inspection regimes of rogue nations such as North Korea. And we must never waver in our support for the nation of Israel, which often stands alone against the world.

AMERICA THE EXCEPTIONAL

A recurring criticism of President Obama is that he fails to protect America's national security interests. That stems from his rejection of American exceptionalism.

As we first discussed in *The Blueprint,* American exceptionalism is the understanding that there's something special about the United States. We're not like other countries around the world. We have a singular advantage of a distinctive set of values and priorities (largely derived from our religious heritage and our Judeo-Christian moral philosophy), abundant natural resources, and the most carefully planned and successfully executed governmental system ever devised. America truly is what Puritan Reverend John Winthrop and President Ronald Reagan called a Shining City on a Hill, adapting that phrase from Jesus Christ's Sermon on the Mount.[29]

In contrast to President Reagan, President Obama said (to a *foreign* audience), "I believe in American exceptionalism, just as I suspect that the Brits believe in British exceptionalism and the Greeks believe in Greek exceptionalism."[30] In other words, America isn't exceptional in any way that Britain and Greece aren't exceptional, and no doubt he believes that Haiti, Kenya, and Qatar are exceptional, and so on around the planet. Translation: Despite having the greatest economy in the world, having the greatest military in the world, being the world's sole superpower, and being a beacon of light for all humanity, there's nothing special about America.

It's appalling that any American president would be unwilling to proclaim to any audience that we are the greatest nation on earth. As Governor Tim Pawlenty remarked, "This is somebody who I think is embarrassed by America and our success, and at times I think the feeling is mutual."[31]

Perhaps it's this embarrassment that has led to President Obama's failure of leadership on national security issues.

Ask and Tell About "Don't Ask, Don't Tell"

A fantastic example of a failure of leadership is President Obama calling on Congress to repeal the "Don't Ask, Don't Tell" law (DADT). Ever since the founding of the Republic, homosexuals have not been able to serve openly in the military. Setting aside religious beliefs, moral convictions, and natural law, this still makes sense, given that in the military you are often forced into quarters so close that they're sometimes nothing short of intimate, with no privacy or personal space whatsoever in an extremely stressful, emotional, and adrenaline-filled environment. As a sop to the gay rights community, when Democrats had control of both Congress and the White House, President Bill Clinton softened this policy to say that it was still illegal for gays to serve in the military, but that no one could ask you about it so you were okay as long as you didn't tell anyone or get caught doing anything.

It was an article of faith on the Left to repeal DADT. This is amazing, in that there is an unprecedented split here with the military Joint Chiefs of Staff. Some of the chiefs—the army chief of staff, the air force chief of staff, and the commandant of the U.S. Marine Corps—openly say that repealing DADT would jeopardize U.S. national security by impairing military performance, and therefore oppose changing the policy. Even in the Pentagon's study, which was rigged because it asked military members about *how* they would implement the change, rather than *whether* the change was a good idea, a majority of marines and combat troops said they oppose the change.[32]

The military is no place for social engineering. No doubt many homosexuals can be trusted not to make sexual advances, just as many heterosexuals can likewise be trusted in close quarters. But we don't allow men and women to bunk together, or deploy them alone together in a forward position with no privacy, even though we trust them to remain professional and adhere to standards of conduct. Homosexuals should not get any special treatment denied to heterosexuals.

But the purpose of America's military is to fight and win wars. Congress has the power to make whatever policy it chooses regarding our military. But voters need to demand that Congress base those decisions only on what makes our military the best fighting force it can be after careful consideration of the judgment of our top military officers, without regard to any political consideration. Otherwise our security is not what it should be, and members of Congress who allow anything other than national security to impact their vote should be kicked to the curb.

A SHOCKING CASE OF JUDICIAL ACTIVISM

Late 2010 saw a shocking and outrageous federal court decision striking down DADT. It's far worse from a judicial standpoint even than the California same-sex marriage decision (it's difficult to believe, because that decision was terrible by so many legal standards).

This is not to say that this military decision in *Log Cabin Republicans v. U.S.* necessarily has more of an impact on society than redefining the institution of marriage. After all, marriage is the fundamental institution of human civilization.

What makes *Log Cabin* worse is the judicial interference in the military. This decision came from the U.S. District Court for the Central District for California. As Judge Virginia Phillips acknowledges in her opinion, courts must give special deference to the president and to Congress when it comes to national policies concerning military readiness. But then she completely ignores the fact that DADT is the policy judgment of the president acting as commander in chief, enacted by Congress pursuant to its constitutional power to raise military units.

There's no constitutional right to serve in the military. Someone who is blind cannot serve in combat, no matter how patriotic they are and how willing they are to risk their lives for their fellow countrymen. You can't even serve if you're *color-blind*. Same thing for someone who is hearing impaired. Or even someone with allergies or foot problems.

So it is utterly outrageous—a level of judicial activism almost never seen in America—for a federal judge to invoke a supposed civilian right to homosexual conduct, declare it a fundamental right (which the Supreme Court never did when it legalized sodomy in the 2003 case *Lawrence v. Texas*, which we mentioned in Chapter 6), and use it to strike down a military law.

The Supreme Court has made clear that the federal courts are the least qualified branch of government to determine national security policy, and that the Constitution does not permit them to override military judgments of the president, especially when Congress concurs.

This decision paints a perfect picture of an agenda judge, and a reminder of how the courts are implicated in the national security aspect of constitutional conservatism.

Yet in the closing days of the 2010 lame-duck session of Congress, President Obama managed to get through a law that will repeal DADT once the defense secretary and the chairman of the Joint Chiefs of Staff certify that the repeal won't impact military readiness. This is convenient. Since Obama made sure that he picked a defense secretary and a chairman who support repeal, and since several of the other chiefs oppose repeal, he made sure the other chiefs' approval was not necessary. So the Left scored a big victory on DADT, a reminder that elections have consequences.

Greatest National Security Threat Is Our National Debt

However, the greatest threat to national security is our national debt. No one's talking about it this way, but our debt has now reached the point where it is endangering our country's ability to defend itself.

As noted in Chapter 7, Admiral Mike Mullen, chairman of the Joint Chiefs of Staff, somberly declared that our national debt is the most dire threat to our national security.[33] By the time of the next presidential election, our national debt will be more than $15 trillion, making the annual interest alone on that debt $600 billion, which is more than our entire military budget.

To put a finer point on it, though, in the first fiscal year of the Obama presidency (October 2009 through September 2010), of our heart-stopping $1.69 trillion deficit for that year, we borrowed $734 billion from foreign countries. As a result, as of September 2010, China held over $900 billion of U.S. debt.[34]

If you jump off the Empire State Building, it's not the fall that kills you. It's the sudden stop when you hit the ground that ends your life.

The same is true with national debt. What happens if China decides it won't buy more U.S. debt? We'd immediately have to issue debt that other countries pick up at loan-shark interest rates that would crash our financial system, or the U.S. government would shut down until we passed emergency legislation to balance our budget in a process that would wreck the entire governmental infrastructure in this country. Either way, the result would be catastrophic.

These numbers are real, and this situation is dire. This isn't about having to cancel long-term research projects on next-generation weapons systems. It's about every paycheck to every military family instantly stopping until we passed emergency legislation of a nature never before seen in this country. And it would be several hours or days of paralysis during which one of our enemies might try things that they wouldn't dream about now, knowing that while America would surely act to repel an attack on our homeland, we would suddenly be crippled enough that we couldn't protect any of our allies or interests abroad.

Once again, the three legs of the conservative movement rely upon each other. We need a balanced budget for the sake of protecting our very lives, and must preserve our culture to protect our way of life. Losing any of these things would mean losing everything.

12

A COUNTRY OF IMMIGRANTS

"The simple truth is that we've lost control of our own borders, and no nation can do that and survive."

—President Ronald Reagan

One issue America must address is immigration. It was a back-burner issue for many years, but since 2006 it's become a major flashpoint. Immigration has implications for the economy, our culture, and our security. It's an issue we need to get right with a constitutional conservative approach.

At the outset, we want to emphasize one very important point. Although there are some on the Right who are "soft" on immigration, meaning they favor some avenue to allow illegals currently here to remain here—a concept usually referred to as "amnesty"—they do so for very different reasons than those on the Left.

Specifically, there are many social conservatives who favor some form of amnesty (fully defined below, so everyone can understand what we mean). Many of these SoCons are Christian conservatives, driven by compassion for foreigners desperately looking to make enough money to support their families, and especially by compassion for those who have been working in the United States for some time, developing relationships here in America. These SoCons' policy recommendations are driven by charity, mercy, and compassion, and we respect our good friends who support some form of amnesty for these reasons.

Many social conservatives support various forms of amnesty for many laudable reasons. We appreciate the sincerity of their beliefs. For the reasons that follow, we don't believe that any form of amnesty is the right approach, especially a form that confers American citizenship. But we welcome an honest and open conversation on the options available to the country, respecting that many who disagree with us do so for all the right reasons.

As Senator Marco Rubio—the son of Latino immigrants from Cuba—has rightly said, America cannot be the only nation on earth that refuses to enforce its immigration laws.[1] It's not fair to those who have followed the law. It's toxic to the concept of the rule of law. It makes a cheap mockery of the magnificence of American citizenship, and in fact it is the ultimate entitlement mentality to think that any foreigner affirmatively deserves citizenship. American citizenship is a precious privilege, and as a sovereign nation we have not only the right, but the *duty*, to have an orderly immigration system that promotes American culture and political philosophy, and to demand that those who would receive United States citizenship submit to an American system of laws, and face consequences for lawbreaking.

DECADES OF FAILURE

One reason immigration deserves a chapter in this book is that it's a textbook example of how both parties have completely failed to adhere to a constitutionally conservative approach. This problem predates both George W. Bush and Barack Obama, although it's been especially bad in recent years. Thirty years ago, when the problem was a fraction of what it is today, Justice Lewis Powell wrote in a Supreme Court opinion, "This is a problem of serious national proportions, as the Attorney General recently has recognized. Perhaps because of the intractability of the problem, Congress—vested by the Constitution with the responsibility of protecting our borders and legislating with respect to aliens—has not provided effective leadership in dealing with this problem."[2]

Democratic Failure

Even though both parties have failed, for the reasons that follow it's clear that Democrats have done far worse.

Just look at the statistics. In the last two Bush years, the number of U.S. Immigration and Customs Enforcement (ICE) arrests of illegals at workplaces was 4,077 and 5,184 in Fiscal Years 2007 and 2008, respectively. Under Obama, the numbers for Fiscal Years 2009 and 2010 are a paltry 1,644 and 927, respectively.[3]

Senator Jon Kyl, the Senate Republican whip, on camera in a town hall discussion, described a White House meeting with President Obama to discuss immigration, in which Senator Kyl and others pushed for border enforcement: " 'The problem is,' [the president] said, 'if we secure the border, then you all won't have any reason to support comprehensive immigration reform.' In other words, they're holding it hostage. They don't want to secure the border unless and until it is combined with comprehensive immigration reform."[4]

While the White House denied it, saying in a press briefing that Kyl's statement was false, their denial was ridiculous. Anyone who knows Jon Kyl—as both of us do—will tell you that he's never been known to exaggerate. Senator Kyl is an honest and straight shooter. If White House deputy press secretary Bill Burton denies it, then Burton is not telling the truth. Whether he's speaking of things he does know, or intentionally deceiving the press, doesn't really matter, in that the American public should never tolerate any White House spokesman telling falsehoods.

Due to these shenanigans, career immigration officers have no confidence in the Obama administration. (We hear reports that many of them didn't have confidence in the previous administration, either.) In August 2010, it became public that 259 career ICE officers in the union (affiliated with the Democrat-friendly AFL-CIO) were surveyed on whether they had confidence in ICE director John Morton and assistant director Phyllis Coven, and signed a letter directed to the secretary of DHS.[5] In a *unanimous* 259–0 vote, nonpolitical ICE officers said, "No!"

It's no wonder that career ICE officers have no confidence in the president's political hacks. Morton and his political subordinates refuse to do the job the law requires of them, and they deceive the American public. For example, when Fox News reported that ICE was dropping deportation proceedings against many illegals as a form of de facto amnesty (because if ICE refuses to deport you, then you could stay in the United States forever), ICE denied it. But then Fox obtained a confidential internal ICE memo from Morton in which he announced the "new policy" that if there are not "adverse factors" such as "criminal convictions, fraud and national security," then he wanted deportation proceedings dropped, even against illegals already in ICE custody.[6]

Democrats support amnesty—and by that we mean a process to convert millions of foreigners into permanent, voting citizens. For the reasons we discuss below, this is not about making America a welcoming country for immigrants. It's instead about creating permanent class warfare, with millions of voters who support unsustainable social programs, paid for by taxes on the middle class and job creators.

Such an insidious plan isn't about welcoming new citizens or enriching our country; it's instead about control.

Arizona's Immigration Law

Most people are familiar with Arizona's S.B. 1070, a law that, among other provisions, penalizes employers who hire illegal aliens. This law was designed by GOP rising star Kris Kobach, now Kansas secretary of state. Listening to the media on this law, you'd think this law was a fascist monstrosity somehow rammed through despite overwhelming public opposition.

Yet polls show that Arizona's law is popular. For example, a CBS poll (hardly conservative) showed 57% think the Arizona law is "just right," 23% think it "goes too far," and 17% think it "doesn't go far enough."[7] In other words, 74% of Americans—three-fourths of those asked—think that Arizona's law is a step in the right direction.

Despite these numbers, the Left (and a few honestly mistaken people on the Right—some of them friends and colleagues of ours) says, "That law's unconstitutional! Only Congress can make immigration

laws!" They say that the Arizona law violates the Constitution by invading a region where only the national government can tread, trespassing
on federal territory by camping out in Congress's backyard.

While immigration is a federal issue, that's irrelevant, because the
Arizona law is *not* an immigration law.

The Supreme Court explained in *De Canas v. Bica,* "Power to regulate immigration is unquestionably exclusively a federal power. But the
Court has never held that every state enactment which in any way deals
with aliens is a regulation of immigration and thus per se pre-empted
by this constitutional power, whether latent or exercised."[8] The Court
then cites a number of cases from over the decades, and reaffirms their
holding that "the fact that aliens are the subject of a state statute does
not render it a regulation of immigration."[9] The Supremes explain that
this is because as far as the Constitution is concerned, immigration "is
essentially a determination of who should or should not be admitted
into the country, and the conditions under which a legal entrant may
remain."[10]

The Court then added that the only other component of Congress's
immigration power is to decide who can become an American citizen,
and what requirements they must meet to gain citizenship. Quoting
two older cases from the early and mid-1900s (showing that this was a
long-held rule of constitutional law, not something they were just making up), the Supreme Court said:

> The Federal Government has broad constitutional powers in determin-
> ing what aliens shall be admitted to the United States, the period they
> may remain, regulation of their conduct before naturalization, and the
> terms and conditions of their naturalization. Under the Constitution the
> states are granted no such powers. . . . State laws which impose discrimi-
> natory burdens upon the entrance or residence of aliens lawfully within
> the United States conflict with this constitutionally derived federal
> power to regulate immigration, and have accordingly been held invalid.[11]

The *De Canas* decision was a *unanimous* decision of the U.S. Supreme
Court. Not only did it enjoy the support of conservative justice William Rehnquist, it was also joined in full by the two most liberal justices

in Supreme Court history (unless recent appointees are further to the left): Justices William Brennan and Thurgood Marshall (more liberal than John Paul Stevens or Ruth Bader Ginsburg). For that matter, the opinion was *written* by Justice Brennan.

It's extremely unfortunate that even many supporters of Arizona's law don't understand this. Many have argued that states can enforce immigration law so long as it does not conflict with federal law. That's the route to disaster, because all it takes is a federal court latching on to the Supreme Court's holding that immigration is *exclusively* a federal issue, and then striking down a state law that does the same thing as federal law.

Instead, the critical point to remember is that rather than an immigration law, the Arizona law is a state police power law. You'll recall from Chapter 5 that the police power—which states possess, but which the federal government does not under the Tenth Amendment—is the power to make laws for public health, safety, morality, social order, and general welfare.

Arizona's law arises entirely from the basis of the police power. Illegal aliens who lack the vaccinations Americans obtain destroy our "herd immunity" for many diseases such as whooping cough and meningitis. ("Herd immunity" is a medical term for diseases against which almost everyone is inoculated. As a result, the "herd" is immune, and even if some isolated member of the herd without immunity gets the disease, it doesn't spread to others because everyone else he comes into contact with is immune.) It's also a public safety law, given the number of aliens involved in drugs and violent crime. It's a morality law, in that states have the power to tell businesses to reflect certain ethical standards in employing someone, and since federal law requires certain documents to get employment, an illegal alien is engaged in fraud by presenting fake documents. It's also a general public welfare law, because the millions of illegals who are not gainfully employed are instead drawing billions of dollars (that's *billions* with a *b*) of welfare benefits.

This law was demagogued by our nation's leaders in Washington. Attorney General Eric Holder blasted it, then admitted he hadn't read the law (which is only a few pages long). The same is true for Secretary Janet Napolitano. President Obama—not to be outdone—shamed his office by an episode involving a foreign ruler, President Felipe Calderón of Mexico. Calderón's nation continues to function only by countless billions of dollars flowing from illegal workers in this country, coupled with many billions more of American tourist dollars. He stood as a guest on our soil, next to our head of state, and condemned the sovereign state of Arizona for trying to enforce the rule of law within its own state borders. And President Obama approved.

The bottom line is that even without this being immigration per se, the federal government still has the power under Article VI to preempt state sovereignty on a law like this. But preemption generally requires Congress to express its intent to do so. The issues covered by S.B. 1070 aren't covered by a federal law expressing an intent to preempt.

The public outrage motivating Arizona is found in other states as well, for example, leading Governor Susana Martinez of New Mexico to tell her police that they should check immigration status.[12] Arizona's law is in the courts as we write this, and could likely end up before the Supreme Court.

A Generous Guest Worker Program Without Citizenship

Anger and frustration over cynical politics and tales of criminal actions by some illegal aliens have impeded a productive conversation about worthwhile policy. America could use cost-effective labor that would improve the lives of millions of foreign families.

Millions of foreigners come here desperately seeking an opportunity to provide for themselves, and in many instances working to provide for families back in their home countries. If employers here are seeking to fill jobs that pay a legal wage, and workers from other countries are willing to work at that wage because it beats wages back home, we can make that happen.

We should have a complete overhaul of the part of our immigration system dealing with work visas and temporary resident aliens. There should be a federal database, with tens of thousands of companies searching for labor, and millions of aliens who would like to work here temporarily. If a foreigner passes a background check and public health check and has no criminal record, they should be able to be added to this database.

Such a worker can be matched to a job involving appropriate skills as a temporary worker. This guest worker must have an ID card with biometric data. Payroll taxes must be deducted, and there should be a serious debate about whether they're entitled to Social Security and Medicare, or instead if these taxes would be an ongoing fee that guest workers pay for working here. (This could be part of saving those entitlement programs by backfilling its missing revenues. Remember that these are temporary workers, so they're going to be here only a few years and will not be allowed to live in this country permanently once they're no longer in the workforce. These entitlement programs are retirement programs, and foreign workers would not be retiring here.)

The foreign worker would not be eligible for any public assistance. They're here to add to our economy and enrich themselves in the process. They're not here to get government handouts that America simply cannot afford. (Remember, we're already going bankrupt. Entitlement programs are for citizens; they're not global humanitarian aid that leaves us unable to provide for American children.) No food stamps, housing subsidies, welfare payments, or Medicaid. You pay your own way off what you earn. If your job isn't economically worthwhile, then you should return to your own country. No subsidized college tuition or similar benefits. And all workers will include a payroll deduction for medical insurance, so that we don't get millions of foreign workers showing up uninsured in hospital emergency rooms for extremely expensive healthcare that the American taxpayer must provide.

To be enrolled into the guest worker program an alien must consent to expedited removal proceedings. First, a criminal conviction of any sort must result in immediate deportation (after any applicable prison sentence), with a lifetime ban on returning to the United States.[13] Second, if any foreign worker is even charged with a crime, immigration authorities have the discretion to deport him if they think it's warranted. (Authorities often arrest someone and are ready to bring charges, but realize that the case is of a nature where it would take weeks or months to prosecute, at substantial taxpayer cost. Many cases are dropped as a result. This fact should not complicate matters if the person involved is a foreigner with no vested right to be here.) If the worker is fired from his job or if that job ceases to exist, then if the government does not immediately reassign the worker to a new job, he must be immediately deported, although he's eligible to return in the future if a new job opens up. Remember—they're here to work. If they're not working, then they're a drain on the American economy and must leave. Such proceedings must be quick and efficient, with no right of appeal.

For anyone deported, the rule is simple. Anyone caught having illegally entered the United States can be immediately deported with a single limited proceeding before an immigration judge, and is then barred for life from ever returning to this country. One way to reduce the number of people who repeatedly break into this country is to ensure that doing so means you can never return.

EMPLOYERS HAVE NO EXCUSE

With these elements, there's no reason a guest worker program cannot be designed that every employer can use. And once there's a system to match every willing employer with workers, there's no reason any company should ever be found knowingly employing an illegal alien or failing to go through the federal system with the biometric tracking card. Once the system is in place, employers who violate it should be subject to severe civil penalties, the funds from which can help pay for the system. For repeat offenses, in addition to increased civil penalties, the persons responsible at the company should be subject to criminal charges if their actions are found to be willful and deliberate. States should also have the authority to revoke the business licenses of repeat offenders if the state feels that move is justified, as in an Arizona law currently pending before the Supreme Court.[14]

That's the key to dealing with roughly 12 million illegal aliens already here. Once this system is in place, there should be a 180-day grace period wherein employers cannot be sanctioned. During this time employers will be able to check the status of everyone on their payrolls, letting go those here illegally. Not being able to get a job, those people will end up leaving the United States by the millions. (After all, you can't get a paycheck and you can't get public welfare programs. How are you going to live, aside from becoming a criminal?) As companies bring in legal workers to replace illegal ones, this turnover will gradually fix the problem on a company-by-company basis.

ANY PATH TO CITIZENSHIP SEPARATE FROM A GUEST WORKER PROGRAM

If someone in another country wants a job, why can't we have a system that provides a good-paying job for that worker, so that he can provide for his family and eventually return home? Why must such a program include a path to citizenship?

The key here is the doublespeak within the amnesty crowd. They say, "We want to build a middle class in Mexico." First, that's narrow-minded. Why only Mexico? There are illegal aliens here from many countries, and not just from other Central and South American countries like Guatemala and Ecuador, but also from Africa, Southeast Asia, and Europe. Don't we want to see middle classes arise and thrive in those countries as well, creating strong markets for American exports?

Second, this proves that the motivation of the amnesty crowd is completely inconsistent with what's necessary for true citizenship. *True* citizenship is about assimilating a person into *American* culture and political philosophy, to the diversifying enrichment of this nation. It's not about balkanizing the United States into clashing cultures with different languages. America is a melting pot, and a melting pot is where everyone melts into a *common* culture and allegiance.

Guest workers can become citizens, but on precisely the same terms as everyone else. Completely apart from the guest worker program, they can apply to become citizens through the same process that any foreigner abroad uses to try to become a U.S. citizen. If they're willing to go through *all* those steps just like *everyone* else, then as a country we welcome them with open arms.

Assimilation Is the Foundation for Immigration

The key to effective immigration is *assimilation*. To become an American, you must become one in your heart. You must leave allegiances to your old country behind and commit yourself fully and *exclusively* to the American nation, the American people, and the American Constitution.

President Teddy Roosevelt spoke to the issue of immigration, serving as chief executive during a time when America had lots of immigrants coming to make America their home (legally). Roosevelt said:

> In the first place, we should insist that if the immigrant who comes here in good faith becomes an American and assimilates himself to us, he shall be treated on an exact equality with everyone else, for it is an outrage to discriminate against any such man because of his creed, or birthplace, or origin. But this is predicated upon the person's becoming in every facet an American, and nothing but an American. . . . There can be no divided allegiance here. Any man who says he is an American, but something else also, isn't an American at all. We have room for but one flag, the American flag. . . . We have room for but one language here, and that is the English language . . . and we have room for but one sole loyalty and that is a loyalty to the American people.[15]

It's a good thing for all Americans to speak more than one language, and so if people from other countries choose to speak a different language at home, that's fine. And children should be taught a second language in school, whether that language is among the traditional choices of Spanish, German, French, or Latin or one of the newer options (in light of global developments), Arabic or Mandarin Chinese. Yet the necessity of everyone in our society's being able to speak one common language is part of the impetus driving various bills across the country calling for English to be the official language.[16]

American citizenship should be difficult to obtain. It must involve a clear mastery of the English language in both written and spoken form. It must involve passing a test showing a clear understanding of the Declaration of Independence and the U.S. Constitution, as well as the important aspects of our political philosophy, ideology, and history. It should also take a hard look at why the person wants to become an American. Such a process will result in our country continuing to grow in the right direction, with immigrants who are passionate about freedom and excited about their new home.

THE CHALLENGE OF DEALING WITH
THOSE WHO BREAK THE LAW

Roughly 40% of illegals in this country originally entered legally.[17] That shows our current visa and passport system is completely broken, in that millions of foreigners come here, then overstay, and we don't know who they are, where they are, or what they're doing. All we know is that whatever they're doing, they're breaking the law and straining our social services.

That statistic also means that the majority of illegals in this country—60%—entered illegally, committing crimes in the process. That number is absolutely unacceptable, especially since they commit illegal acts not only to get here, but on a daily basis to work and stay here. This shows a disregard for the rule of law that cannot be allowed to become part of the American body politic. Our country will decline if we cease to be a nation of laws.

RULE OF LAW ESSENTIAL TO EFFECTIVE
IMMIGRATION IN AMERICA

There are many reasons that those entering this country illegally and committing crimes as part of their activities here (identity theft, forging government documents, fraud, etc.) cannot simply be given a path to citizenship.

This is not just about aliens who commit criminal actions, though all by itself that's a huge problem.

An example is the case of Jose Lopez Madrigal, who in May 2010 was accused of raping a woman in Edmonds, Washington. Although ICE won't comment, it's since come to light that Madrigal had been deported nine times since 1989 and had a long rap sheet, where he had committed a whole range of crimes from drug dealing to a previous sexual assault. Yet he kept coming back into this country, brutalizing American women in terrible ways.[18]

To be sure, Madrigal is the exception, not the rule. Again, most illegals in this country are hardworking people who see themselves as not really harming anyone by being here illegally to do tough jobs to make enough money to support their family abroad. (Crimes such as identity theft, which are essential to working in this country as an illegal unless the worker is being paid cash—which means that the employer is breaking the law—do in fact hurt people, but illegals engaged in this theft don't mean to hurt anyone.)

Don't let anyone fool you by saying, "This shows the need for comprehensive immigration reform." No, if we had amnesty, or if we had a generous guest worker program, it would not prevent thugs like Madrigal from selling drugs and raping American women. The only thing that would stop that man—a man who would never qualify for a guest worker program—is to secure the borders.

We must also secure our borders for the sake of national security. One Muslim cleric linked to jihadist beliefs was caught being smuggled over the Mexican border, trying to enter the United States illegally.[19] There have also been unprovoked shootings, such as a Mexican gunman firing at people working on a highway in America.[20] Such shootings are becoming more common, and are a threat to the safety of Americans.

The problem is that lawlessness will destroy that which makes America a country that people want to break into. Recall our discussion from Chapters 5 and 11 on American exceptionalism. The reason we succeed as a rich and vibrant country is that we are a country under the rule of law. In other countries, people don't adhere to the standards of rigorous competition coupled with uncompromising adherence to the law on issues of property, contracts, torts, and crimes. Without those things, we're no better than the rest of the world, where poverty and scarcity are common features for most people.

If someone enters this country illegally and lives every day committing a variety of lawless acts—some of them criminal—it indicates a disregard of the rule of law. If that person is willing to become a guest worker and registers into a system, then so be it. But to become a citizen of the United States—the most important and valuable citizenship in the world—that person must apply like anyone else. But having committed a variety of crimes in our country, they would bear the burden of proving they respect the rule of law before they could successfully complete the naturalization process.

If we allow people to enter this country illegally it undermines the rule of law and embeds the same disregard for law that characterizes their native lands, and will degrade our business environment until our economy declines to the level of the countries they seek to escape. Rigid and unapologetic adherence to the rule of law—a hallmark of American exceptionalism—is essential to economic prosperity.

The Question of Birthright Citizenship

It's often said that the Fourteenth Amendment guarantees citizenship to anyone born on American soil. It's called birthright citizenship.

This statement is repeated all the time, but it's wrong. Some say it out of a lack of understanding of constitutional law or immigration law. Others say it to misinform the public, trying to help the case for various forms of amnesty by implying the Constitution is on their side.

There are several types of people who are not U.S. citizens even if they are born on U.S. soil. If a foreign diplomat, such as the wife of the British ambassador, here in America gives birth, that child does not become a U.S. citizen under current federal law. The same holds true if a visiting head of state were to have a baby, such as the wife of the French president. Or if an enemy soldier were held prisoner on U.S. soil, any child born to that soldier would not become a U.S. citizen. Federal law expressly provides for these exceptions.[21]

Yet federal law could not do this if birthright citizenship were guaranteed by the U.S. Constitution. The statutory provisions denying birthright citizenship to the three categories just mentioned would be unconstitutional; all those children would be Americans.

The reason for these exceptions is the Jurisdiction Clause. The relevant part of the Fourteenth Amendment reads, "All persons born or naturalized in the United States, and subject to the jurisdiction thereof, are citizens of the United States and of the state wherein they reside."[22] Foreign diplomats enjoy diplomatic immunity,[23] so they are not subject to the jurisdiction of the federal government. The same goes for a foreign head of state. Same for foreign soldiers; they serve a foreign sovereign power.[24] This understanding of the Jurisdiction Clause is that you are not "subject to the jurisdiction" of the United States if you are not required to obey U.S. law.

Some say it's possible to end birthright citizenship just by changing the current citizenship law, found at 8 U.S.C. § 1401(a). The idea is that although birthright citizenship is currently provided by federal law, that citizenship is not commanded by the Constitution.

Those arguing that the Constitution secures birthright citizenship often point out that in 1898 the Supreme Court appeared to side with birthright citizenship in *U.S. v. Wong Kim Ark,* where the Court rejected the government's effort to keep an American-born Chinese person from returning to America.[25] That might be a flimsy argument, though, because Wong was born to parents who were here legally, and in its opinion the Court expressly stated that it was declaring citizenship for "all children here born of resident aliens."[26] Thus the Court was considering only children born of legal aliens, not illegal.

Instead, the only Supreme Court support for birthright citizenship comes from a fairly recent (1982) activist decision, *Plyler v. Doe,* where the Court held 5–4 that a state could not refuse to pay for the public school education of children of illegal aliens. Writing for the narrow majority, Justice William Brennan—who was one of the most liberal justices to ever sit on the High Court—stated that "no plausible distinction with respect to Fourteenth Amendment 'jurisdiction' can be drawn between resident aliens whose entry into the United States was lawful, and resident aliens whose entry was unlawful."[27]

However, both history and law make a plausible argument that there is a difference.

After the Civil War, Congress passed the Civil Rights Act to secure all sorts of rights for black Americans now that slavery was abolished.[28] (They actually had to pass it twice, because President Andrew Johnson vetoed the first one, and the second time Congress overrode the veto.[29]) Many who voted against it supported its goals, but considered the bill unconstitutional.[30] One of these was Congressman John Bingham of Ohio, who went on to become the lead author of the Fourteenth Amendment, which was then proposed in Congress.

That's important because the Fourteenth Amendment was patterned after the Civil Rights Act, to extend to all Americans—including blacks who used to be slaves—all the rights of American citizens. It was the only way to extend those rights in such a way that they could not be taken away (as might have happened if the Supreme Court held the Civil Rights Act unconstitutional). More to the point here, the Civil Rights Act states, "All persons born in the United States, and not subject to any foreign power, excluding Indians not taxed, are hereby declared to be citizens of the United States."[31]

The Supreme Court laid hold of this meaning in 1884, making it part of constitutional law in *Elk v. Wilkins*. The case was about an American Indian born on a reservation, John Elk, who later in life moved off the reservation, renounced his Indian citizenship, and claimed U.S. citizenship under the Citizenship Clause, since the reservation was on American soil. The Supreme Court rejected Elk's claim of citizenship, finding that Indian tribes were "alien nations, distinct political communities."[32] This wasn't enough for the Citizenship Clause, because the Court held that "subject to the jurisdiction thereof" meant "not merely subject in some respect or degree to the jurisdiction of the United States, but completely subject to their political jurisdiction, and owing them direct and immediate allegiance."[33]

Saying that the Indian nations were essentially separate nations within U.S. borders, the Court went on to hold that an American Indian born on a reservation is "no more 'born in the United States and subject to the jurisdiction thereof,' within the meaning of the first section of the fourteenth amendment, than the children of subjects of any foreign government born within the domain of that government, or the children born within the United States, of ambassadors or other public ministers of foreign nations."[34]

At least Native Americans are born on American soil. The United States claims the land of an Indian reservation as land where U.S. law can extend, and no foreign power is permitted. So Native Americans have only a limited form of quasi-sovereignty. If that's insufficient to trigger the Citizenship Clause, then it's not hard to make a case that foreigners who owe their allegiance to a completely foreign nation are not fully subject to U.S. jurisdiction, and thus their children might receive citizenship under current federal law, but not because the Constitution requires it.

A number of conservatives find this material persuasive and argue that the Constitution does not promise birthright citizenship for the children of illegal aliens.

First is Judge Richard Posner of the U.S. Court of Appeals for the

Seventh Circuit. Every lawyer under age fifty likely recognizes Posner, as he's one of the two federal judges (aside from Supreme Court justices) most cited in law school textbooks. Far from a doctrinaire conservative (for example, he does not support the Second Amendment right to bear arms), Judge Posner has argued against birthright citizenship for illegals. Posner writes:

> We should not be encouraging foreigners to come to the United States solely to enable them to confer U.S. citizenship on their future children. But the way to stop that abuse of hospitality is to remove the incentive by changing the rule on citizenship.... A constitutional amendment may be required to change the rule whereby birth in this country automatically confers U.S. citizenship, but I doubt it.... The purpose of the rule was to grant citizenship to the recently freed slaves, and the exception for children of foreign diplomats and heads of state shows that Congress did not read the citizenship clause of the Fourteenth Amendment literally. Congress would not be flouting the Constitution if it amended the Immigration and Nationality Act to put an end to the nonsense.[35]

A second is Dean John Eastman of Chapman University School of Law. Eastman is a former law clerk to Justice Clarence Thomas, and an outstanding constitutional scholar. Eastman notes that the language of the Fourteenth Amendment deliberately tracks the Civil Rights Act of 1866.[36] He then notes what Senator Lyman Trumbull, one of the other authors of the Fourteenth Amendment, meant by "jurisdiction," such as excluding Indians. Trumbull said that he meant "complete" jurisdiction, meaning, "Not owing allegiance to anybody else."[37] Another major player, Senator Jacob Howard, mirrored this by saying it meant "full and complete jurisdiction," of the sort mentioned in the Civil Rights Act (which, as we just saw, excluded those who were citizens of another nation).[38] To this Eastman added material from Thomas Jefferson and other sources to argue that birthright citizenship for children of illegals violates the political theory embodied in America's founding documents, instead arising from European feudalism.[39]

Another top conservative who opposes the idea of birthright

citizenship is none other than the godfather of modern constitutional conservatism, Attorney General Ed Meese. With luminaries of that caliber supporting this theory, it's likely to spread in conservative circles.

This is not entirely a liberal-conservative split, though, because there are conservatives who say that birthright citizenship is found in the Constitution. Solicitor General James Ho of Texas, a former law clerk to Justice Clarence Thomas and chief counsel to the Immigration Subcommittee of the Senate Judiciary Committee, published a law review article making this argument.[40] This theory asserts that the general concept of birthright citizenship is based on the old English common-law doctrine of *jus soli,* recognized by the Supreme Court.[41] Ho argues that the Supreme Court's most infamous case, *Dred Scott,* is what jettisoned *jus soli* by denying that blacks were citizens by birth. Accordingly, the argument goes, the Citizenship Clause of the Fourteenth Amendment was intended to overrule *Dred Scott* by making birthright citizenship a constitutional rule. Of course, if birthright citizenship is commanded by the Constitution, then no statute can deny it to those born on American soil.

Most legal experts believe that birthright citizenship (except for people representing a foreign sovereign power—again, the Jurisdiction Clause) is a constitutional guarantee. If so, the only way to do something about it would be to pass a constitutional amendment. Senator Lindsey Graham—a moderate Republican—has even said he supports the idea.

Economic Fallout

While legal immigration has been a great blessing and will continue to be so, illegal entry into this country by those with no respect for the law will degrade and run down our economy. With such lawlessness comes an entitlement mentality.

Take as an example the 5–4 agenda decision (see Chapter 6) of *Plyler v. Doe,* mentioned above, in which the Supreme Court held that the children of illegal aliens could demand American taxpayers pay to educate their children. Writing for the four dissenters, Chief Justice

Burger—joined by Justice Rehnquist, Democrat-appointed Justice Byron White, and moderate Justice O'Connor—wrote in dissent that

> the Constitution does not constitute us as "Platonic Guardians" nor does it vest in this Court the authority to strike down laws because they do not meet our standards of desirable social policy, "wisdom," or "common sense."...We trespass on the assigned function of the political branches under our own limited and separated powers when we assume a policy-making role as the Court does today.[42]

We're facing an economic disaster in this country already. We cannot add to it the costs of entitlements if we make citizens of people with limited earnings potential, having little or no education and a skill set that can result only in limited economic productivity. In fact, if 12 million illegals were granted amnesty, the cost of long-term entitlements for them would amount to a crushing $2.6 *trillion*. Already, the cost of illegals in this country is a staggering $113 billion *every year*.[43]

Hardworking immigrants who live by the law and raise their children to be productive members of American society are part of the solution, not part of the problem. We should not only welcome such immigrants—we should celebrate them. But to make sure we have those kinds of immigrants, we need a system with demanding standards that advances our national interest.

ANCHOR BABIES

This problem continues to worsen: Some illegals come to America for the specific purpose of having an "anchor baby"—a baby who becomes a U.S. citizen upon birth, to give the parents a reason to argue they should be allowed to stay in this country for the rest of their lives. As of 2003, the official estimates were that 165,000 anchor babies are born *every year* in the United States.[44]

There is also a little-known reason that some are pushing for changing birthright citizenship. Evidently some people are running something of a scam, in which they take people—largely from China—who are several months pregnant and arrange for them to pay a lot of money in order to secure a three-month visa for them. These people then come to the United States on those visas, have the baby here, receive their postnatal care and recover, and then move back to China with their baby, who is now an American citizen for the rest of the child's life.[45]

This is just the latest aspect of an intolerable situation.

There is so much for conservatives to gain by fixing our immigration system, especially with regard to Hispanics. Our friend Reverend Sammy Rodriguez, speaking on Mike Huckabee's television show, said that Hispanics understand that marriage is the key to economic prosperity. Sammy went on to explain that married Hispanic families provide strong homes to ensure good educations for their children, keeping them off welfare and out of gangs, and enabling them to go on to successful professional careers and raise the next Hispanic-American generation with prosperity and security. These are core conservative concepts, and so fixing our immigration system in a way that fully upholds the rule of law will lay a firm foundation for reaching the growing Hispanic community with a conservative agenda.

We need to fix a broken immigration system. But to have a calm, deliberate discussion to develop such a policy, we need to secure the borders and enforce the law, so that we can make decisions that focus on economic improvement and advancing the rule of law, instead of holding this issue hostage in a cynical attempt to create Democratic voters. American citizenship is a precious privilege, one that should be carefully guarded and reserved for those who through honesty, hard work, and abiding by the rule of law pledge their allegiance exclusively to this country, intent on becoming an American in every sense of the word.

13

SAVE THE CHILDREN

"But with respect to future debt; would it not be wise and just for that nation to declare in the constitution they are forming that neither the legislature, nor the nation itself can validly contract more debt, than they may pay within their own age. . . ."

—Thomas Jefferson, September 6, 1789

Throughout this book, we've made the case repeatedly that our focus is on future generations. A future-oriented focus is the essential hallmark of responsible and virtuous government.

The Founders understood this, and explicitly wrote this into the Supreme Law of the Land. We see this in the Preamble of the Constitution, which begins:

We the People of the United States, in order to form a more perfect union, establish justice, insure domestic tranquility, provide for the common defense, promote the general welfare, and secure the blessings of liberty for ourselves *and our posterity,* do ordain and establish this Constitution for the United States of America.[1]

This principle cannot be overstated, and perhaps nothing in the partisan divide is more infuriating to responsible public officials than how the Left has twisted and corrupted it. When deficit spending, liberals—and shockingly, even sometimes moderates—most often say, "It's for the children," when they are in fact harming our children by saddling them with horrific debt. It's on the two issues discussed in this chapter that public officials most often prove themselves manifestly unfit for high office and public trust, where they pander to the politics of the moment at the cost of the safety and happiness of future generations.

These two issues are entirely about the next generation. They are the two *E*s: Education and Entitlements.

THE ENTITLEMENT TSUNAMI

When earthquakes occur underwater, they release incredible amounts of energy. Most waves on the ocean are caused by wind, and go only a few feet deep. An earthquake's pulse of energy may appear to be only an ordinary wave out in the deep water, and feel like it to any boats going over it. But the energy pulse reaches all the way down to the ocean floor, often miles deep.

When it gets close to the shore and the ocean floor rises toward the surface of the water, that massive surge of energy becomes compressed, building in intensity. It draws surrounding water into it and rises above the water's surface, becoming a massive wave. This wave can tower above the surface to heights of fifty or even a hundred feet (and theoretically even higher), becoming an enormous wall of water with terrible, deadly force. It hits the shore as a massive destroyer that can kill thousands and demolish whole buildings.

This agent of death and destruction is called a tsunami.

There is a wave coming. It is a tsunami, a massive economic wave that if not dispelled will cause widespread economic devastation unlike anything this country has ever known. It is roughly an $88 trillion wave of obligations that our children and grandchildren must pay in entitlement spending. If that wave is not dispelled, it will crash into our children and everything they've ever built or saved, laying waste to our economy.

This tsunami is composed of our entitlement programs—Social Security, Medicare, and Medicaid. Governor Mitch Daniels of Indiana is not exaggerating when he calls these entitlements a tsunami of "Republic-ending magnitude." Nations can fall apart over financial disasters of such titanic size.

What follows looks mainly at Social Security, which was created in

1935. Although the numbers differ somewhat, the same problems and solutions apply to Medicare, created in 1965. Both are massive, unsustainable programs that must be completely overhauled.

The Long Creation of the Tsunami

Starting with the Sugar Act of 1764, Great Britain looked upon the American colonies as a revenue source. The English citizens in America came to be seen—and treated—as existing for the purpose of feeding governmental power through economic production and taxation.

From casting off the British for independence, one of the fiercest driving forces in the American psyche became that we each must be free to generate our own wealth and make our own way. We take responsibility for our own financial choices, and we neither look to anyone else to carry us nor consent to carrying others.

This is not to say that we're a heartless country. We're the most generous nation on earth by far. Programs that assist the disabled or those in unanticipated need are compassionate. But where disability insurance or other responsible measures are available, the onus is on the individual to think about how to provide for himself and his family, rather than assume someone else will do it.

ORIGINS OF A TIME BOMB

As America sank into the Great Depression an increasing number of people were in need. People burned through their investments, then their savings, then started selling possessions. More and more, people ran out of all those options. Many of the hardest hit were the elderly, who could show up at the daily lines looking for one day's work, but who would almost always be passed over in favor of young, healthy-looking men. Especially hard-hit were elderly women, usually widows, who had been stay-at-home housewives and thus didn't have as marketable a skill set as an older man who may have had forty years' experience in a craft or trade.

Thus, the Social Security Act became law in 1935. It was designed to provide a *minimal* level of income for older, retired Americans.

Unfortunately, some people started looking increasingly to government to provide a basic standard of living. Worse, this gave rise to a whole class of politicians who fed this mentality by campaigning on ever-larger government programs. As the idea of living off the government lost its stigma, millions more openly embraced it, and supported politicians who touted these handouts. Thus was born the New Deal Coalition and the modern Democratic Party.

But the numbers show the unsustainability of this policy approach. In 1950, social programs accounted for 33.4% of federal spending. Today they consume 61.3%.[2] That's almost double just as a matter of percentages. When you consider that the 1960s, the 1990s, and the past few years have seen enormous explosions in the size of government, the picture of a looming giant emerges.

Now these entitlements have reached a tipping point. For the first time since Ronald Reagan overhauled the program in 1983, extending its solvency, Social Security sank into the red in 2010, paying out more money than it took in.[3] In 2011, Social Security is running a deficit of $45 billion. This can be expected to grow every year, as the tsunami comes crashing onto our shore.[4] So now Social Security has begun draining its reserve funds.

SUPPLEMENTAL INCOME, NOT SUBSIDIZED LIFE

Under federal law, once the Social Security trust fund doesn't have enough money for full payments, then everyone's Social Security check will be *automatically* reduced by whatever percentage is necessary to match the amount of revenue flowing into the program. Everyone will take a big haircut, which is estimated to start at a drastic 30%.

As of 2008, fully one-third of Social Security recipients relied on the program for at least 90% of their income.[5] That means they just couldn't live without it. To cut those checks by 30% will leave millions of elderly Americans in desperate need.

The challenge we face is a demographical problem. When Social Security was created, average life expectancy in America was age 64. You didn't start claiming Social Security until you were 65. So less than half of seniors were ever eligible to receive Social Security payments, and most who lived long enough to receive benefits did so for only a few years.

Today life expectancy is age 78. When Social Security began, the understanding was that many millions of people would pay into it but never take anything out of it. However, as life expectancy has increased with people continuing to claim benefits at the same eligibility age, millions more every year are able to claim more years of benefits.

As a consequence, more people are looking to Social Security to provide a subsidized lifestyle for decades. This violates two key assumptions of the whole Social Security system. The first is that it would provide supplemental income for most seniors, who were expected to have their own retirement savings, or would at least provide enough money for the bare essentials of life for those few who have no retirement plan. The second is that it's something that would carry people for three or four years, not thirty or forty years as life expectancies continue to rise.

FUZZY MATH AND THE PIG IN THE PYTHON

The math is inescapable. In 1935, there were sixteen workers for every Social Security beneficiary. Today there are only four workers. Within less than two decades, the ratio will be two to one. It's a disaster.

The faulty Social Security model assumed manageable ratios of workers to beneficiaries. We've already looked at the issue of longer life expectancies. Another factor is that people today are having fewer children, reducing the number in the workforce relative to the population. Also in modern America higher education is often necessary, so people are not working full-time at a career-type job until several years later. Each of these facts makes the strains on the system worse, forcing the reality that we need structural reform.

Then comes what's called the "pig in the python." It's a phrase intended to convey the visual image of an enormous constrictor snake— a python—that has swallowed a massive pig, like you might see on a *National Geographic* show. Think of the huge bulge in the snake's belly as it moves down the serpentine body.

There's a pig in the demographic python in this country—baby boomers. It's a bulge of population moving up the age brackets. The massive number of children born from 1945 through 1964 created a huge surge of additional workers funding the Social Security system in the 1970s, '80s, and '90s. But starting in 2010, those baby boomers went from being contributors to becoming beneficiaries.[6] There are more than 70 million baby boomers, and every year now millions are retiring. The strains on the system are building to a level never before seen.

This is the tsunami bearing down on us.

SOCIAL SECURITY IS WELFARE, NOT PERSONAL PROPERTY

One important reason to discuss Social Security is that many conservative Americans—including many Tea Party voters—don't understand how Social Security works. Many people think that they're paying into an account with their name on it through the deductions to their paychecks every week.

They're not. Every Social Security deduction from your paycheck flows into one common account, from which all Social Security checks are paid. Millions don't understand that the moment the deduction happens, you lose that money forever. It goes to a current beneficiary, and the assumption (which is mathematically false) is that when your time comes, other people will be paying for you.

As a result, Social Security is a mandatory welfare program, the only requirement for which is having reached a certain age. It's not something you own and thus could pass on to your children.

This should be especially unacceptable to black men in America. Statistically, black men today don't live as long as other racial groups. (There are various causes for this, from nutrition to medical care to other factors, all of which we must work to overcome.) Also statistically, older black men overall have less in savings and investments than other racial groups. (Again, all for various factors that thankfully are now being overcome.) Consequently, the unfair reality that Social Security is not personal property that can be passed on hits black America harder than it does the rest of the country. That alone should motivate minorities to push for a complete overhaul of the system.

Fixing Social Security and Medicare

So we must completely overhaul Social Security and Medicare. To do that, the first step is a national consensus that massive change is needed.

That's a problem, in that one of our major parties refuses to admit the problem exists. The Democrats' position is perfectly represented by socialist independent U.S. senator Bernie Sanders. Senator Sanders says:

> The White House deficit commission is reportedly considering deep benefit cuts for Social Security, including a steep rise in the retirement age. We cannot let that happen.
>
> The deficit and our $13 trillion national debt are serious problems that must be addressed. But we can—and we must—address them without punishing America's workers, senior citizens, the disabled, widows and orphans.
>
> First, let's be clear: Despite all the right-wing rhetoric, Social Security is not going bankrupt. That's a lie![7]

That's the Democratic line. Social Security is fine. And unfortunately, many moderate Republicans essentially say the same thing through their failure to support any major changes.

Space doesn't permit a detailed plan on changing the system, but several elements are clear and they arise from two absolutes. First, we must reduce payouts. And second, we must reduce dependency on those payouts.

It's a political reality that the system as it exists today must be retained for all current beneficiaries, and preserved for those about to start receiving benefits, whether that means age 60, or even age 55. Our proposed changes are for workers who have not yet attained that age.

There are several concrete steps that can be taken to reduce payouts. First, the retirement age needs to be adjusted upward to account for longer lives. This upward adjustment can also be justified on the grounds that modern medical advances allow more people to be economically productive for more years. Many suggest age 70 as doable.

A second change is means-testing. Right now, the more you pay into the system by way of income (up to a maximum at about $90,000), the more you get in benefits down the road. The reverse is actually true, in that the more you make, the less you need from Social Security. It should be openly acknowledged as a welfare system. As people earn

$150,000 or $200,000, the amount received in Social Security can progressively decrease as people earn more.

Then the issue becomes reducing dependency. That can be accomplished only through personal retirement accounts. There is plenty of debate over what percentage of paychecks would go into such a system, or where such deductions could be invested.

But the reality remains that Social Security currently provides less than a 2% return on investment. Even the lowest-risk personal investment portfolio more than doubles that 2% rate over any significant time horizon. So something akin to a mandatory individual retirement account (IRA), with the mandatory deductions going to rock-solid conservative investment allocations, would allow for compound interest to grow workers' wealth over a working lifetime of fifty years or so.

This benefit should multiply, in that investing is a mentality. The key is being aware of compound interest and making decisions whereby that interest works for you, instead of against you. If a person has 2% deducted from their paycheck, and they learn enough to decide how to allocate those funds, then they're more likely to deduct another 2% or 3% out of each paycheck to direct into an investment account that is unrestricted, where they can decide to go with more aggressive investment options such as small-cap or small-growth stocks, or emerging markets such as Africa or Eastern Europe, and possibly even a small amount in futures or commodities. Even if part of an investment portfolio loses money, such supplemental funds will continue to be a net contribution to retirement accounts. And if someone at age 30 or 35 loses 10% in aggressive investments, they're more likely to become more cautious while still young enough to amass quite a bit of money by the time they're ready to retire.

Again, all of these same principles apply to Medicare as well. Mandatory Health Savings Accounts (HSAs) would direct funds on a bi-weekly or monthly basis into conservative investment-type vehicles to fund medical expenses. This will also make consumers more focused on cost-effective healthcare decisions, conserving resources and getting the most out of their dollars.

Overhauling Social Security and Medicare gets back to the keys of constitutional conservatism for a Sovereign Society that we enumerated in Chapter 4. By educating Americans on how to be self-sufficient and giving them the means to act on this knowledge, we can move back toward a culture of individualism and family, instead of one in which the government is the center of our universe, on which we rely for our daily bread.

EDUCATION

This leads to the other issue that dominates the future of our children and grandchildren: education.

The American people understand just how broken the educational system is in America. In a recent NBC/*Wall Street Journal* poll, only 5% of Americans think our public schools "work well," 36% think "some changes needed," and a staggering 58% say "major changes or *complete overhaul needed.*"[8]

They're right. It's a national embarrassment that the wealthiest, most powerful nation on earth has educational scores well below the average industrialized nation. In 2010, out of 30 such nations the United States ranked 25th in math and 21st in science. Our high school graduation rate is 20th on that list of 30.[9]

We're in a period of unprecedented need. In the wake of globalization, work can increasingly be done by workers in other countries. And with developing technology, good-paying jobs cannot be performed without an educated skill set. If our children continue falling behind children in other countries, then a generation from now our kids will be working for them.

Failure of Unions, the Department of Education— and Families

Why is it that having every advantage, our students don't succeed on the level of their less resourced counterparts? There are at least two reasons.

The first is the power of the teachers' unions. Education should be about children, not bureaucrats or systems. Why do public school teachers need tenure? They're not professors, where tenure serves to protect professors from retaliation for unpopular ideas or provocative research. Teachers should not have any job protection that private-sector workers do not enjoy. Pay should be based on merit. Principals and schools should be able to enforce discipline in the classroom, and then should be held responsible for doing so.

Teachers' unions, however, are all about money and power. They fight for more pay for teachers and more benefits, while increasingly protecting teachers from discipline or accountability. It's virtually impossible to fire a lousy teacher at a public school.

Beyond that, teachers' unions are generically left-wing political organizations embracing causes that have nothing to do with education. Teachers' unions in California are supporting the same-sex marriage fight in federal court there. Other teachers' unions have taken actions supporting abortion, affirmative action, and gun control. Others support a government takeover of healthcare. These unions exist to serve themselves and advance liberal ideology, not to give our children the most challenging education they can handle.

The second reason is the U.S. Department of Education. There's nothing unconstitutional about the federal government choosing to spend federal tax money on education, and to make decisions on allocating that funding. But the Constitution does not empower the federal government to set education policy or priorities. And just because federal funding is constitutional doesn't mean that it's good policy. Since the Department of Education was created in 1978, educational test scores have continued to decline. Educational policy should instead be fully returned to state and local communities.

This is pursuant to one of the eight constitutional conservative keys in Chapter 4: federalism. States must be sovereign to make laws embodying their priorities, answerable to their voters. If they succeed, other states are free to follow. If they fail, then people can move to a state that shows it can make education work.

EMPOWERING FAMILIES

Too often, educational results are determined by family more than anything else. Within the same school, the top students tend to be children from families that are stable, involved, and focused on their children's performance, enforcing discipline and priorities in the home and working with teachers. Students from chaotic homes tend to have poor grades. While there are plenty of exceptions in both directions, no one can deny that the home environment has a major impact on student performance.

In that vein, education policy should empower families. That's why private schools, charter schools, and homeschooling are essential features for improving education. Your education tax dollars don't exist to feed a bureaucracy and left-wing politics. They should support your children instead. What matters most is what our children are learning in the academic fields covered in primary and secondary education. So long as children can meet or exceed required scores, parents should be free to have their children educated in whatever form and setting they think best.

This gets back to another constitutional conservative key from Chapter 4. It's family autonomy, enabling parents to make decisions for their children.

The College Tuition Problem

Although most of those issues don't apply to colleges, there is one issue that has to be addressed regarding higher education: tuition.

Modern education aid programs have opened tremendous opportunities for millions of students who come from families that cannot afford college tuition to obtain financial aid. But this has unbalanced the market forces at work in tuition and needs to be corrected.

Prices should be set by supply and demand. But when you tell an eighteen-year-old that all he has to do is sign on the dotted line, he can party for four years (and maybe learn something in his spare time), and he won't need to pay it off until he's in his thirties, he'll sign for a whole lot of money because the money doesn't seem real to him at that moment.

Universities are like sponges in a bucket of water. If you pour more water in the bucket, the sponge will soak it up. The more easy money (which feels like "free" money at the moment of decision) you pump into the higher education market, the higher tuition will rise.

That's why tuition is rising at more than twice the rate of inflation, despite the fact that family incomes are not increasing.[10] Professors' salaries are rising, campus beautification projects are proliferating, and shiny new student gyms are being built. Because there are suddenly so many kids with access to so much money, universities are going for a country club look to attract new students, knowing that they can hike tuition to pay for it and the kids will pay.

There's a solution that doesn't invite more federal power. First, the federal government can condition federal grant funding on certain restrictions on tuition increases. Second, the feds could really put the squeeze on this runaway tuition problem by making those tuition increases a condition for being eligible for student loan money, which no university could do without.

What would be much better, however, would be if the states would do this with their own state schools as well. As public universities become increasingly affordable relative to private schools, those private schools will have to voluntarily follow the same approach, or soon be left with kids from wealthy families, but losing the best and the brightest to state schools.

Education is the future. We need tremendous improvements in education if America is to continue to be the world's superpower in the next century, and to face the challenges that we will surely face. Education has been far too liberal for far too long. It's time for a constitutional conservative approach to teaching the next generation.

The nation recently saw these two issues of entitlements and education collide with the union protests in Wisconsin, Ohio, Indiana, and other states. It showcased the power of the teachers' unions, as well as other government unions. Despite the fact that many of these people make more than their private-sector counterparts (some more than $100,000 a year) and the states are bankrupt, they protested having to take the same cuts as private workers. Government union pensions and benefits—including those for government teachers—are enormous contributors to our unsustainable debt. That system must change.

This is not an indictment of all unions or collective bargaining, only *militant* tactics by *government* unions. Even FDR—a Democratic president who relied on union support—strongly objected to government workers' striking. Every government worker consumes taxpayer money. Many of these workers are vital to public safety, but many are not. Those who are not cannot be allowed to demand *your* money. Our answer must be "No more."

Constitutional conservatism demands these changes. There is no fundamental right to collective bargaining; it's not in the Constitution. There is no right to taxpayer money. There is no right to a job, only the freedom to compete for a job. We need to get back to constitutional government.

The biggest downside risk inherent to democracy is that politicians get so focused on the short term that they neglect the long term. That's how our entitlement system has reached a crisis state: Too many politicians were too scared of losing their next elections to talk about reforming such popular programs. The same goes for education, in that too many politicians have focused on increasing government power and appeasing unions rather than on laying a solid foundation for future prosperity.

Constitutional conservatism is about restoring our Framers' vision for America. That includes the Constitution's preamble, of securing liberty and prosperity for our children and grandchildren. It's time we demanded policies that our children will thank us for a generation from now.

14

THE TRUTH SHALL SET YOU FREE

"Speech is an essential mechanism of democracy, for it is the means to hold officials accountable to the people. . . . The right of citizens to inquire, to hear, to speak, and to use information to reach consensus is a precondition to enlightened self-government and a necessary means to protect it. . . . For these reasons, political speech must prevail against laws that would suppress it. . . . Premised on the mistrust of governmental power, the First Amendment stands against attempts to disfavor certain subjects or viewpoints. . . . By taking the right to speak from some and giving it to others, the Government deprives the disadvantaged person or class of the right to use speech to strive to establish worth, standing, and respect for the speaker's voice. The Government may not by these means deprive the public of the right and privilege to determine for itself what speech and speakers are worthy of consideration. The First Amendment protects speech and speaker, and the ideas that flow from each."

—Justice Anthony Kennedy, *Citizens United v. Federal Election Commission*, 130 S. Ct. 876, 898–899 (2010).

Reviving and reorienting the Republican Party through a resurgence of constitutional conservatism as we've discussed in this book can happen only if you make it happen by what you do on Election Day. Americans must be *informed voters*. They must regularly vote each time Election Day comes around, and that vote must be responsibly informed by due diligence into the candidates' views and an understanding of the important issues facing the country.

That will turn on how you and your fellow Americans act with two of our fundamental rights found in the Constitution. They are our right of free speech and our right to vote.

SPEAKING THE TRUTH

Late 2009 gave us one particular episode of how President Obama and his allies regard your right to speak against them and hold them accountable.

This example of an attempt to censor and punish speech was seen during the Obamacare debate. Humana (a major health insurance provider) sent a letter informing its customers that if the Obamacare bill became law, it would reduce or eliminate various Medicare benefits. In response, the Obama administration (through far-left Secretary Kathleen Sebelius of the Department of Health and Human Services) responded with a dire threat and a gag order: If Humana didn't shut up, the government would cut Humana out of all Medicare programs, a move that could drive Humana into bankruptcy.[1]

This violates the doctrine of unconstitutional conditions. Under that doctrine, "the government may not deny a benefit ... on a basis that infringes [a person's (including corporations)] constitutionally protected ... freedom of speech even if [that person] has no entitlement to that benefit."[2] Free speech is a fundamental right.[3] Here the government said that you must forfeit your right to inform your customers of your honest assessment of the government's proposed law. The Constitution does not allow such authoritarianism.

This incident is important, because the free communicating of facts, opinions, and ideas is essential to having a free society. (If President Obama and Sebelius had not backed off, they would have lost an embarrassing court fight.)

This is of a piece with how President Obama and his staff regard media outlets that disagree with them, as seen in how they speak of Fox News Channel. The White House communications director said that Fox is "opinion journalism masquerading as news,"[4] and "what is fair to say about Fox and certainly the way we view it is that it is really more a wing of the Republican Party."[5] The White House senior advisor said Fox is "not really a news station."[6] The White House chief of staff said, "the way . . . the president looks at it [and] we look at it is it's not a news organization. . . ."[7]

The pattern here is disturbing. If you do any business with the government and we don't have your full support for our agenda, we'll cut off your livelihood. If you're a news outlet reporting to the public, we'll say you're our political opponents, not real media. In the world of the Left—whether Barack Obama or Hillary Clinton—free speech is never free.

This becomes all the clearer when the media has at times schemed to protect President Obama from public scrutiny. We congratulate Tucker Carlson and his team at the *Daily Caller*, who broke the story that prominent journalists for mainstream (that means liberal) publications conspired to prevent the Jeremiah Wright story from catching on, even saying in emails that they should brand as racist any commentator who raised concerns about Barack Obama choosing to raise his children under Wright's savage, bigoted venom.

Why We Have a First Amendment— Free Speech Restored in *Citizens United*

In *Citizens United v. FEC,* the Supreme Court struck down the most intolerable part of the Bipartisan Campaign Reform Act (BCRA), also known as McCain-Feingold.[8] This provision made it a felony for ordinary people to give their money to a public interest organization to speak out within thirty days of a primary or sixty days of a general election.[9]

This is an issue of simple fairness. Billionaire George Soros is free to spend $1 million on any election activities he wants. (For example, he could run $1 million worth of TV ads.) But if 10,000 ordinary people who don't have millions of dollars lying around wanted to each give $100 to an organization to buy that same $1 million worth of ads, those people responsible for buying the ads would be guilty of a federal felony and could be sent to prison for five years. BCRA allowed ultrarich leftists to do almost anything they want, but muzzled everyday Americans to shut them out of the democratic process of trying to persuade their fellow citizens.

The Court in *Citizens United* declared that "political speech [is] speech that is central to the meaning and purpose of the First Amendment."[10] Beyond that, "If the First Amendment has any force, it prohibits Congress from fining or jailing citizens, or associations of citizens, for simply engaging in political speech."[11] As the Court explained, under BCRA the following would be felonies:

> The Sierra Club runs an ad, within the crucial phase of 60 days before the general election, that exhorts the public to disapprove of a Congressman who favors logging in national forests; the National Rifle Association publishes a book urging the public to vote for the challenger because the incumbent U.S. Senator supports a handgun ban; and the American Civil Liberties Union creates a Web site telling the public to vote for a Presidential candidate in light of that candidate's defense of free speech. These prohibitions are classic examples of censorship.[12]

Justice Anthony Kennedy then made one of the best formulations of the Framers' rationale for the Free Speech Clause of the First Amendment ever penned by the Supreme Court, when he wrote for the Court majority:

> Speech is an essential mechanism of democracy, for it is the means to hold officials accountable to the people.... The right of citizens to inquire, to hear, to speak, and to use information to reach consensus is a precondition to enlightened self-government and a necessary means to protect it.... For these reasons, political speech must prevail against laws that would suppress it.... Premised on the mistrust of governmental power, the First Amendment stands against attempts to disfavor certain subjects or viewpoints.... By taking the right to speak from some and giving it to others, the Government deprives the disadvantaged person or class of the right to use speech to strive to establish worth, standing, and respect for the speaker's voice. The Government may not by these means deprive the public of the right and privilege to determine for itself what speech and speakers are worthy of consideration. The First Amendment protects speech and speaker, and the ideas that flow from each.[13]

OBAMA'S AUTHORITARIAN CRUSADE
AGAINST FREE SPEECH

When *Citizens United* was decided, the Left screamed with a shrill, statist wail. Such screeds came from the likes of Senator Chuck Schumer of New York, who called the Court's decision un-American.

But the coup de grâce came from President Obama, who as we saw in Chapter 1 tried to shame the U.S. Supreme Court on national television during the 2010 State of the Union address. In doing so, the president said that "the Supreme Court reversed a century of law to open floodgates for special interests—including foreign corporations—to spend without limit in our elections. Well, I don't think American elections should be bankrolled by . . . foreign entities."[14]

That statement is irrefutably false. Either he made an inexcusably ignorant statement, or President Obama deliberately deceived the American people. The audacity of Obama's false statement is what caused Justice Samuel Alito, sitting in front of the president, to be caught on camera shaking his head in disbelief, saying under his breath, "That's not true."

Three reasons President Obama's statement is false: First, the Supreme Court expressly stated in *Citizens United*, "We need not reach the question whether the Government has a compelling interest in preventing foreign individuals or associations from influencing our Nation's political process."[15] The plaintiff in this case was a public interest organization named Citizens United, led by D.C. veteran David Bossie. It's a domestic corporation, so the Court didn't need to address a separate statutory bar to foreign financing of American elections.

Second, *Citizens United* didn't reverse a hundred years of law. President Obama had to be referring to the Tillman Act, which in 1907 was enacted to forbid corporate contributions to political campaigns.[16] *Citizens United* didn't change this law at all; it simply restored the ability of corporations to make *independent* expenditures to support a candidate, *not* to give any money to any campaigns.

Third, as Judge A. Raymond Randolph of the U.S. Court of Appeals for the D.C. Circuit noted, in *Citizens United* the Supreme Court cited *twenty-three* previous cases in which the Supreme Court had held that corporations have First Amendment rights.[17] (Full disclosure: Judge

Randolph was Klukowski's professor for First Amendment in law school.) The Supreme Court could hardly have been clearer over the years, stating as it had in the 1978 case *First National Bank v. Bellotti:*

> [Free speech is] indispensible to decisionmaking in a democracy, and this is no less true because the speech comes from a corporation rather than an individual. . . . We thus find no support in the First Amendment, or in the decisions of this Court, for the proposition that speech that otherwise would be within the protection of the First Amendment loses that protection simply because its source is a corporation. . . . [Such a rule] amounts to an impermissible legislative prohibition on speech based on the identity of the interests that spokesman may represent in public debate. . . .[18]

That long line of cases was changed for the first time in 1990 in *Austin v. Michigan Chamber of Commerce.*[19] The Court compounded that mistake when it upheld BCRA in *McConnell v. FEC* in 2003.[20] In *Citizens United* the Court overruled those two bizarre anomalies, restoring the First Amendment as it had existed since the Framing. In explaining the need to do so, it held: "When Government seeks to use its full power, including the criminal law, to command where a person may get his or her information or what distrusted source he or she may not hear, it uses censorship to control thought. This is unlawful. The First Amendment confirms the freedom to think for ourselves."[21]

OBAMA AND THE DEMOCRATS DECEIVING VOTERS

Democrats tried again to misinform the public as the Left was panicking over imminent losses in 2010. In the closing days of the 2010 midterms, President Obama engaged in a deceitful and Orwellian campaign against supporters of business and free enterprise. He said on the campaign trail in October 2010, "the American people deserve to know who is trying to sway their elections."[22] Just in case you missed the insinuation, Obama went on to say of those who support Republicans, "It could even be foreign-owned corporations."[23]

This is appalling and reprehensible. There's no evidence of any foreign involvement, of course, but that seems to be irrelevant to this president when he's accusing Republicans and their supporters of criminal behavior.

The Democratic National Committee produced an election ad with this theme. In it, the Democrats name two top Bush White House political operatives (Karl Rove and Ed Gillespie). They then accuse two groups of "stealing our democracy" funded by "secret foreign money." [24] This ad, worthy of *Pravda,* was part of a concerted White House effort to demonize the political opposition with no evidence whatsoever.

And when leftist pundits started yammering that this was all *Citizens United* again, they were again dead wrong. As Judge Randolph pointed out, in *Citizens United* the Court upheld the disclosure requirements by an 8–1 vote. [25] So even if there was foreign money, it wouldn't be secret.

Even the *New York Times*—which often bends over backward to defend this president—called him out on this one. The *Times* editorialized, "there is little evidence that what the chamber does . . . is improper or even unusual. . . ." [26] The *Times* quoted others using terms such as "smear tactics" in describing Democrats' actions, and ended by quoting a Republican campaign finance lawyer saying, "It's really just unfortunate and irresponsible rhetoric from the White House." [27]

Rather than changing course after the *New York Times*'s chastisement that the president's tactics were shameful, the White House doubled down with Vice President Joe Biden's renewing the attack the following day. While anyone familiar with our loquacious VP could reasonably conclude that the White House decided to change course but Biden just didn't get the memo (again), the fact that they continued on this attack for the next couple of weeks makes it clear that Barack Obama decided the *Times* was just too weak-stomached when it came to crushing enemies of the state.

Obama Administration Seizes Control of the Internet

Given this authoritarian attitude toward silencing dissent, it's no surprise that the Obama administration has taken the first step to seizing control of the Internet. Once again, the Constitution stands in the way of President Obama and his lieutenants.

Ever since Barack Obama took office, the Federal Communications Commission (FCC) has been threatening to take control of parts of the Internet. On December 21, 2010, FCC chairman Julius Genachowski called for an immediate vote on proposed rules to give the FCC power to regulate broadband access to the Internet under the name of "net neutrality." The FCC adopted these rules by a 3–2 vote, with three Democrats voting for them and two Republicans against.[28]

Net neutrality is the first step to controlling access to the Internet. If you can control who has access, then you can control what information is shared. You can use it to silence political enemies, or keep citizens from getting access to truthful information. All this censorship is in the name of serving and protecting the public.

What makes Genachowski's move on behalf of President Obama particularly outrageous is that it slaps a federal appellate court in the face. Just eight months earlier, the D.C. Circuit held in *Comcast v. FCC* that the FCC has no statutory authority to regulate the Internet.[29] It was a unanimous decision of three well-respected judges, two conservative (David Sentelle and the aforementioned Randolph), and one liberal (David Tatel), showing that even many liberal judges don't read the law as allowing government to simply declare control of something the size of the Internet.

Now Verizon has filed an appeal with the D.C. Circuit, challenging the FCC's action. The case is pending before the court as this book goes to print.

Add to this the proposed legislation to create an Internet "kill switch" that would allow a president to control Internet traffic in the event of a cyber-attack. While there are real security concerns about a widespread Internet-based attack that could devastate our economy or national security, only measures safeguarding free speech can be allowed. Sharing information is vital to a free society.

SOLUTION IS THE NONDELEGATION DOCTRINE, NOT CONGRESSIONAL REVIEW ACT

Many Republicans are promising to roll back this FCC power grab. The Congressional Review Act (CRA) provides that when an agency promulgates regulations carrying the force of law, Congress can pass a joint resolution of disapproval.[30] This would nullify the regulations. The only problem is, CRA does nothing beyond the normal lawmaking process. A CRA disapproval resolution must be signed by the president, or requires two-thirds of Congress to override a presidential veto, just like any statute. Otherwise it would violate the Constitution's Presentment Clause, which requires any congressional action to be presented to the president.[31]

Needless to say, President Obama will veto anything that undoes his regulations. Although Republicans made major gains in the 2010 midterms, the odds are slim that Republicans can pick off enough Democrats to reach a two-thirds supermajority in both the House and Senate to override a veto. That's what it takes under CRA to trump regulations.

If that seems weak, it's because the Supreme Court correctly struck down the idea of a legislative veto in *INS v. Chadha*.[32] Congress cannot negate executive action by anything resembling a veto, and so in 1983 the Court invalidated provisions in various laws allowing Congress to trump the executive branch.

Regulations That Make Laws Are Unconstitutional

But there is a solution. It's the nondelegation doctrine.

Only Congress can make laws.[33] The executive branch administers the laws Congress makes, but cannot make law.[34] In carrying out laws, Congress can authorize agencies to make regulations. The courts have allowed such regulations to make public policy, so long as they're not "major" policies.[35] (This rule is problematic, but it's the one on the books.)

Congress cannot delegate its legislative power. While Congress can authorize agencies to make regulations, those regulations cannot be of such scope that they make major public policy. Regulations that sweeping would become de facto statutes, usurping the constitutional role of Congress.[36] Since 1928, the Supreme Court has held that Congress must set forth an "intelligible principle" in a statute, and agencies are authorized to make only regulations that follow Congress's intelligible principle.[37] The Court struck down two major parts of FDR's New Deal for violating this principle.[38]

It's time to revive the nondelegation doctrine. The Court hasn't struck down anything for violating this doctrine since 1935, but it's still good law. Not since the 1930s have we had an administration so far to the left of the Supreme Court. The FCC's "net neutrality" rules would be a perfect test case, since Congress clearly has not authorized the FCC to take over the Internet.

This is even worse than nondelegation, however. In those previous cases, the Court struck down a law where Congress gave too much power to an agency, saying that Congress had delegated its power to the executive branch. In the Obama administration, Congress refused to give such power, and President Obama's agencies seized that power anyway.

In all of American history, no administration has tried such a sweeping power grab. Now more than ever, we need the Supreme Court to fulfill its role as the guardian of constitutional government.

VOTE FOR FREEDOM

It's not just enough to have information. Millions who live in authoritarian countries have access to the Internet, through which they learn about what their government is doing, but those people can do nothing about it. In our country, we can vote.

Free Elections Are Both a Right and a Duty

Your author Blackwell knows something about elections. For eight years Blackwell served as Ohio secretary of state, the top elections official in a large state that's also one of the critical swing states in presidential elections. (No Republican has ever won the White House without carrying Ohio.)

Secretaries of state are the guardians of democracy in America, working to ensure that every eligible voter has a reasonable opportunity to cast a vote. Each "SOS" must then ensure that every legal vote is accurately tabulated. And they must ensure that no illegal or tainted votes are counted, votes that would corrupt the vote totals. As both of your authors wrote in a piece for *Yale Law & Policy Review,*

> How do citizens know which candidate actually won in any given elec-
> tion? Election results are legitimate only to the extent that the returns
> include every legal vote—and only those votes—undiluted by fraudu-
> lent or otherwise unacceptable votes.... Thus the secretary of state is
> involved in the unique act of balancing the duty to ensure access to the
> ballot box with protecting the integrity of the voting process.[39]

As we explain in detail in that law review, there are two voting rights. You have a right to have your legal vote counted, and a related right that your vote not be diluted or canceled out by someone else's illegal vote or by tampering.

PROTECTING THE BALLOT BOX

That's why Americans should be very concerned by those from the Far Left seeking to get involved in voting. One major concern that we discussed in *The Blueprint* was ACORN, formerly a formidable group (which Blackwell fought for years) but now fallen apart, since their support for criminal actions became a national story—undercover videos surfaced of ACORN willing to aid and abet underage prostitution and federal housing fraud.

But many concerns still remain. For example, the New Black Panther Party was caught on video intimidating voters in Philadelphia, where the Bush Justice Department nailed them in court. But then the Obama-Holder Justice Department let them go in a major scandal that Republicans should now investigate.

The corrupting specter of fanatical-left billionaire George Soros also looms large over the electoral process. Soros is funding millions of dollars into the Secretary of State Project through the Democracy Alliance, which Soros and other far-left authoritarians like fellow billionaire Peter Lewis have set up to channel hundreds of millions of dollars to advance leftist causes and candidates.[40] This SOS project has already elected several far-left chief elections officers, such as Jennifer Brunner, who succeeded your author Blackwell as Ohio secretary of state. (Brunner didn't run for reelection.)

These SOSs can make all the difference when elections are close. For example, one of the most liberal secretaries of state in America is

Minnesota's Mark Ritchie, whose wrong decisions are widely believed to have allowed liberal embarrassment Al Franken to barely win a U.S. Senate seat in Minnesota by only 312 votes out of millions cast.[41] If not for such a stridently liberal SOS who made every possible call to help Franken, Norm Coleman would still be in the U.S. Senate, and the Democrats would never have had their sixtieth vote to pass Obamacare. Ritchie was a prime recipient of support from Soros's SOS project.[42]

VOTING IS YOUR PATRIOTIC DUTY

Voting is unique. First, voting is a fundamental right.[43] But it is one of the only—if not *the* only—right that is also a duty. As we explained in *Yale Law & Policy Review*, when casting a vote each citizen is acting as the sovereign, the ultimate authority in our republic.[44] When you vote, you are deciding which persons should be given the power to rule our nation, as well as your state, city, and county.

This is why the Framers debated long and vigorously about terms of office. For example, some argued that the president should serve one seven-year term. In the end, the Framers decided that House members should have a two-year term, so that they'd be most accountable to the people because they'd always be worrying about getting reelected. Senators should serve a six-year term, so that they could make unpopular decisions that the voters don't like, and be given up to six years to prove the wisdom of their decision. But then they still had to stand for reelection eventually. (However, as was discussed in Chapter 5, until 1916 senators were chosen by state legislatures rather than the people, to maintain even more distance from popular angst and to ensure that senators would vote for the states' interests, not necessarily those of the people.) And the president is given a four-year term to give him some time to prove his unpopular actions to be in the national interest, with the right to seek an additional term if he proves himself worthy.

Because voting is a duty, we can place certain requirements on it that we can't place on other rights. Voting isn't all about convenience, though the Left has been pushing that incessantly for decades. Ideas such as 100% voting by mail, absentee voting for any reason or no reason, early voting, and even wrongheaded suggestions for Internet voting are all designed to make voting as easy as possible.

The Left also opposes every effort to safeguard the ballot box. Laws requiring government-issued photo identification to vote and proof of residency are vital to ensure that people vote only where they live, and vote only once.

Aside from the fact that all of these issues entail terrible potential for abuse, voting is a duty. There's nothing unreasonable about requiring a person to go to the county seat of government to register to vote. Political campaigns are designed to fully inform a vote by Election Day, not a month before Election Day, so laws requiring that a person can vote early by absentee ballot only for certain reasons are beneficial, not burdensome.

Voting should not be something done flippantly or casually. It is as serious an issue as we face, and requiring voters to undertake reasonable actions to impress upon them the seriousness of their vote and the solemnity of the voting process will encourage them to understand the issues and vet the candidates. Only then can their vote be informed and responsible.

Be Careful About Impeachment

It's also for these reasons that Americans should always be very careful about impeachment and removal of government officers. The Constitution gives the U.S. House the exclusive power to impeach.[45] If an officer is impeached, he's still in office, but must then undergo a trial in the U.S. Senate. By a two-thirds vote, the Senate can remove any officer impeached by the House.[46] This power extends to any executive officer, including the president and vice president, as well as to any federal judge, including Supreme Court justices.

It is critically important to use the impeachment process only under the very narrow circumstances set forth in the Constitution. Article II says that executive branch officers shall be removed only for "treason, bribery, or other high crimes and misdemeanors."[47] Article III states that all federal judges serve for life, contingent only upon the requirement that they "hold their offices during good behavior."[48]

These terms are left to the House and Senate to define. In theory, a president could be removed from office for wearing an ugly tie. But the records of the Constitution's drafting and ratification show that the Framers intended for impeachment to be used only for serious felonies. When Article II references treason and bribery, the Framers meant that only crimes of such magnitude should be used to remove a president. The same goes for the "good behavior" language for judges in Article III.

We are not a parliamentary system, where all branches of government are subordinate to the legislature and can be removed at will by a vote of no confidence. The Constitution creates three coequal branches of government, so while officers of other branches can be removed by Congress, it should be only for extraordinary circumstances. We do not and should not impeach a president just because we don't like his policies, or a Supreme Court justice because we don't like how they vote on a case.

The reason we must be careful is that we are a democratic republic, and as such the people's choice must be accorded tremendous respect. Through the Electoral College, the American people choose a president for four years, and give him that length of time to prove his actions right. That's why we have elections, to change officeholders at that point, not before. Federal judges are appointed (by the people through the president and the Senate) for life, specifically to shield them from public reactions.

Impeachment is also usually not necessary for a lower executive branch officer. All of them are appointed by the president or by someone who answers to the president. Most serve at the pleasure of the president, and those who don't are still removable for good cause. If a person is engaged in criminal behavior, or in most circumstances even just outrageous (but still legal) behavior, the president removes that person himself.

Democracy is about accountability. Impeachment is about stopping an egregious violation of the Constitution or laws. But impeachment is not about redoing an election. If Congress abuses its impeachment and removal power, then the voters will remove those members of Congress.

Protecting and Restoring the Vote

So we must protect voting as among our most sacred rights. On it rests our destiny as a nation.

First, we must protect the sovereignty of states to make voting laws, subject only to certain restraints. Some of these restraints are constitutional, such as not disenfranchising people on the basis of race or gender, as guaranteed by the Fifteenth and Nineteenth Amendments, respectively. Others are federal statutes, such as Congress using the Constitution's Article I authorization to set a nationwide day for congressional and presidential elections.[49]

Other laws might have to be changed from time to time. For example, the Voting Rights Act (VRA) was passed to deal with racial discrimination, pursuant to the Constitution's express mandate in the Fifteenth Amendment.[50] Section Five of VRA was enacted to address egregious and systemic racism in various states in the South.[51] Section Five imposes severe restrictions on these states, such as not allowing them to change the slightest aspect of their voting procedures (or to engage in redistricting) without approval beforehand either from the U.S. attorney general or a three-judge panel of the U.S. District Court for the District of Columbia. The Supreme Court originally upheld these major restrictions because voting rights violations in those areas were sometimes so severe that "exceptional circumstances justify legislative measures not otherwise appropriate."[52]

Those conditions have now improved to the point where America can elect a black man as president of the United States. So now the Supreme Court has suggested that provisions like Section Five may no longer be constitutionally acceptable and that it would welcome a case to consider the question.[53] Justice Clarence Thomas has gone further and also called for the Court to strike down Section Five as being beyond what the Fifteenth Amendment authorizes in our present reality.[54]

Redistricting and Reapportionment

Finally, when you vote you have an opportunity to vote for all sorts of officers. Aside from the president, you vote for U.S. Senate and U.S. House, for governor, state senator and state house, and depending on the laws of your state you may also be voting for secretary of state, attorney general, treasurer, and any number of other state officials, as well as city and county officials.

The president and vice president are offices that appear on every ballot every four years, while your options for governor, U.S. senator, and other statewide officials vary by state. Many of the offices on your ballot depend on your exact address. Your candidates for U.S. House and various other offices such as state senate and state house are determined every ten years through the redistricting process.

Every ten years the Constitution requires that a national census be taken. Those results are certified and made official. From the census, 435 House seats are distributed among the fifty states as evenly as statistically possible. That's called reapportionment. Within each state, the census numbers are designed to draw district lines for U.S. House, state senate, and state house with all districts having the same number of people. That's called redistricting.

This is something your author Blackwell has experience with. He served as cochairman of the 2000 U.S. Census Monitoring Board, and currently serves as vice chairman of the Redistricting Committee of the Republican National Committee. This process is vitally important to make sure that every U.S. citizen enjoys full and equal political representation.

Reapportionment also has implications for presidential races. The president is elected by the Electoral College. Every state has adopted a law by which the Electoral College members from that state are chosen according to which presidential candidate they support, where a slate of electors pledged to the candidate who won the popular vote in that state are the ones who vote in the Electoral College. The Constitution gives each state a number of Electoral College votes equal to its total number of U.S. House and Senate members, which changes when the House seats are reapportioned every decade.

The trends in this country tend to favor Republicans. People tend to move to states with stronger families and lower taxes, growing the populations of more conservative states and giving them more Electoral College votes. Also people become more conservative as they get married, have children, and get older (each of these factors has a significant impact) and are more likely to vote Republican. (Again, another reason why the Republican Party must be the conservative party in America.)

The 2010 census bears this out. Texas—a conservative state—picked up four congressional seats, with additional gains for states such as Arizona, Georgia, South Carolina, and Utah. States that lost seats include liberal bastions such as New York, New Jersey, and Illinois. Although this pattern wasn't completely consistent nationwide, it shows overall that people gravitate to states with more freedom, which lays the foundation for a stronger economy, rather than the automatic handouts of large government funded by higher taxes.

It is critical to keep voting as a civic duty, one in which the voter takes it upon himself to study the issues and vet the candidates. If Republicans make a conservative case for the GOP, then a fair voting process on Election Day should yield good results.

The First Amendment secures two types of rights. The first is to be able to believe and worship according to the dictates of conscience, and freely live out that faith. The second is to be able to speak and persuade. Every American may speak out on issues and candidates, as individuals or as groups. The press has the freedom to publish and circulate such speech. And people have the right to gather together to let their voices be heard, and to call our leaders to account. We must be able to pool our resources, share with others, and freely speak through television, radio, newspapers, magazines, emails, and the Internet so that the democratic process keeps our republic free.

This freedom lasts only if the right people are elected to public office. Conservatives must work hard to ensure that the Republican nominee for each race is the most conservative nominee who can win the general election. These conservatives should work to earn the vote of every voter, informing them of how constitutional conservatism provides the brightest future for them and their children.

CONCLUSION

"WHAT A GLORIOUS DAY!"

"If we lose freedom here, there is no place to escape to. This is the last stand on Earth. And this idea that government is beholden to the people, that it has no other source of power except to sovereign people, is still the newest and most unique idea in all the long history of man's relation to man. This is the issue in this election. Whether we believe in our capacity for self-government or whether we abandon the American Revolution and confess that a little intellectual elite in a far-distant capital can plan our lives for us better than we can plan them ourselves."

—Ronald Reagan, "A Time for Choosing," October 27, 1964

Whether the Republican Party becomes the vehicle through which America regains a path toward prosperity depends on whether the Constitution becomes truly resurgent in American life. As this book shows, constitutional conservatism is the governing philosophy through which all three major aspects of public policy—economic, social, and national security—can take a sharp turn in the right direction. This would do more than pull us back from the brink of the precipice. It would begin the long, difficult journey back to our Founding Fathers' house, as we discussed in the Introduction.

Citizen Activists

A constitutional conservative agenda cannot happen without you. This book is about making you a *citizen activist*.

That's what the Founders intended in laying the foundation of this country in our Declaration and Constitution. When the Founders first wrote, "We hold these truths to be self-evident," which we discussed in

Chapter 5, they were not just speaking for those in the room. They had been elected by the colonies to meet together as the Continental Congress. When they wrote "We" they meant all the people of the United States.

They understood that in a republic, the role of an elected leader is to be both a delegate and a trustee. As a delegate, they represent the views and wishes of their constituents. As a trustee, they make decisions in accordance with what they believe to be in the best interests of their constituents and the nation as a whole, leaving it to the voters to keep them in office if time proves their actions wise and beneficial. They were each to be citizen-legislators, who came from the people, represented the people, stood accountable to the people, and would one day return to the people as a private citizen.

This became perfectly clear in the Constitution, which they began, "We the People of the United States." Referencing those who had lost their lives in the Battle of Gettysburg to save the Constitution and the Union, our greatest president, Abraham Lincoln, said in the Gettysburg Address:

> Four score and seven years ago our fathers brought forth on this continent a new nation, conceived in liberty, and dedicated to the proposition that all men are created equal.... It is rather for us to be here dedicated to the great task remaining before us—that from these honored dead we take increased devotion to that cause for which they gave the last full measure of devotion—that we here highly resolve that these dead shall not have died in vain—that this nation, under God, shall have a new birth of freedom—and that government of the people, by the people, for the people, shall not perish from the earth.

What they struggled to save—and by God's providence succeeded in saving—is what you have today. You must make good use of what you have. Each of us has a role to play.

In the Parable of the Talents, the Lord Jesus Christ speaks of three men, given talents of silver by their lord as he left on a long journey. (A talent was a metal bar.) One had five talents. A second man had three, and the third had one. Upon returning, the lord called each of them to account. The one with five earned five more, and the one with three earned three more. Both men were praised for their work.

But the third man had hidden his talent. He never put it to use to earn interest or a return on investment, so all he had to show was that single talent of silver, no more. He was scolded by his master for failing to make use of his talent, and cast out from his lord's house.

The lesson here is that we're expected to make use of each talent—each resource—God gives us. It wouldn't be enough for the man with five talents to have earned three. This is consistent with how Jesus ended another parable, the Parable of the Faithful Servant, by saying, "To whom much has been given, much will be expected."

In this country, we're blessed with many talents of self-government. We are intended to be a self-governing people. Although it's our patriotic duty as citizens to vote on Election Day, our duty does not end there. As we saw in Chapter 14, our vote must be an informed vote, requiring us to study the issues and the candidates. And it is to cast a vote not in our narrow and petty self-interests, but instead in the best interest of our families and children, our neighbors, and our country as a whole.

But as important as it is to cast an informed vote, we're given resources to do so much more than vote. We have the First Amendment right (a "talent") to speak out, to inform our fellow citizens and hold accountable our elected leaders and candidates for public office.

We have the right to pursue and advance the eight keys of constitutional conservatism explored in Chapter 4. We have the right to work to ensure the blessings of liberty for ourselves and our posterity, just as the Framers proclaimed they were doing in the Preamble of the Constitution. We have the right to marry and raise our children, to worship God and learn that which is true and right. We have the right to protect ourselves, our families, and our liberties against any who would endanger them.

America can succeed only with active citizenship. You don't have any rights that you don't understand and value. When Ben Franklin said that he and his fellow Framers had given us "a Republic—if [we] can keep it," he was speaking of the hard work that is required of every generation to preserve a democratic republic. The price of liberty truly is eternal vigilance.

Pressing Forward to the Year 2021

We are two years into a twelve-year cycle to enact a constitutional conservative vision for America. Not long ago people were talking about 2010, and now they're talking about 2012. While such benchmarks are important, true leaders must look further. As discussed in Chapter 1, one of the greatest causes of the failure of our current political leaders to make the right decisions, to do what's truly in the best interests of the nation, is their excessive focus on the next election. To paraphrase one (liberal) movie, *The American President*, they're so busy trying to keep their jobs that they forget to *do* their jobs.

This isn't about one congressional cycle or one presidential election cycle. It might be, if this were merely about the Republican Party retaking the majority in both houses of Congress and winning the White House.

While that's what many Republicans are focused on, it's not enough to save the United States. As we've argued from the outset, although your authors are committed Republicans, we're Americans first. As Americans, we need constitutional conservatives in control of the House, the Senate, the White House, and the Supreme Court. Then—and *only* then—can America move back in the direction we need to save our country for our children and their children after them.

It will take until the year 2021 to get us on that track.

The first step is already behind us. The 2010 election was about taking back the House, and doing so by a sufficient margin to guarantee that no additional legislative monsters will make it through Congress. As an additional check, we also needed several Senate seats to be able to filibuster legislation that's dangerous to the United States.

The second step is to establish a unified constitutional conservative government. A conservative Republican must take the White House, and we must build on our House majority by twenty-five or more seats and take back the Senate by a sixty-vote filibuster-proof margin, or at least come close to it. (This means targeting thirteen Senate seats.) The

Left will be in crisis mode, and will more likely be defiant than despondent over their rout when the new president lays out an extremely ambitious legislative agenda. The only constitutional conservative we've elected since 1924 was Ronald Reagan, and given that lesson of history, we need wide enough margins to pass legislation over the defections of moderate and business-as-usual Republicans.

The third step is 2014. There's a natural pushback in the first midterm election of a new president. (Thankfully, America was saved in 2010 by a pushback of such magnitude that it amounted to a repudiation, even more so than the elections of 1994.) Some of the changes a constitutional conservative Republican president must make will be opposed by many, as they'll involve deep cuts to popular programs. But we have no choice. We're facing a financial tsunami that will otherwise cause an economic meltdown and inflict more economic pain than any of us has ever experienced. So we must engage in a two-year education campaign to keep the public's eye on why we must make these drastic changes. In doing so, we must not only prevent losing House seats—we should work to target what could be up to nine vulnerable Senate seats. The goal, by 2014, is to have the votes for constitutional amendments, even if no Democrats possess an instinct for self-preservation to vote for a Balanced Budget Amendment and other needed constitutional provisions.

The fourth step is in 2016. One presidential term will not be enough to complete changes of the magnitude we discuss in this book. It took eight decades to get into this mess, and it will take eight years—not just four—to fully reset our course out of it. The Left will understand that a half century of trying to turn America into a socialist country is unraveling before their eyes, and by this time moderate voters will have a solid understanding of why liberal policies are to blame for the years of cutbacks and sacrifices we will be in the midst of making. So the goal in 2016 is to finish the job by maintaining a conservative—not just Republican—government. A single-term presidency can't get the job done.

The fifth step is handing off the presidency to a second constitutional conservative president in 2020. That will be something the country has not seen for more than a century. Major changes in public policy have a wet-cement quality; it takes years to dry, and once it does it's very hard to change. (That's why Social Security and Medicare have continued unchanged for decades. It's also why the Department of Education still exists at all.) If America has a total of at least twelve years of a constitutional conservative president, then we can be firmly set on a constitutional conservative course for the next quarter century to restore America's greatness. If the president sworn in on January 20, 2021, is a constitutional conservative, then we just might make it.

There are two specific issues that will take until 2021 to fix.

The first is that profound changes to the entitlement systems will take years to show their value. These changes will involve people getting acclimated to the reality of not relying upon government. They'll also involve personalized accounts for retirement and healthcare that will need years of growth to give voters the sense that an individual-based system will serve them better than a socialized retirement system.

The second is the U.S. Supreme Court. There should be three or four Supreme Court vacancies between now and 2021. (We're referring to Justices Ginsburg, Scalia, and Kennedy, and if there's a fourth it would likely be Justice Breyer.) Right now the Court has two committed constitutional conservatives, a third who's a constitutional conservative half the time, a fourth who is a moderate-conservative chief justice, a fifth who is a moderate, and four who are liberals. If we have no vacancies before the next presidential election, and then elect a two-term constitutional conservative Republican president, America could have a conservative Supreme Court for the first time since 1936.

For the reasons discussed throughout this book, we must perish any thought that this country can return to constitutional government without a major change on the U.S. Supreme Court. It's not possible with just two branches of our three-branch government. It takes all three. And when you're talking about upholding the Constitution, no branch is more important than the only branch with the power to authoritatively declare what the Constitution means. We're just one or two votes away from a Supreme Court that can restore the Constitution.

An Eighty-Year Revolution

In 1928, America elected a moderate Republican president who moved America on a disastrous moderate course, an approach openly embraced by some Republicans today. When our markets crashed as a result, Democrats seized power in 1932 with a president and Congress that pushed through a radical expansion of government power and enacted programs designed to make millions of Americans dependent on the government for their literal survival.

Thus began eighty years of forsaking the Constitution. In all that time, we had a president for eight years willing to work to return us to the Constitution, but never a conservative Congress to allow that to happen. Aside from that time, we've had a couple of presidential terms that were somewhat conservative and years where one or both houses of Congress were Republican, but never conservative Republican. Even the 1994 midterms didn't give us a conservative majority.

The 2010 elections were historic in this regard. Constitutional conservative candidates won elections outright, and millions of Americans finally seemed engaged in the seriousness of our situation. We might finally have a chance, the first chance we've had in four generations.

But as just discussed, it will take a twelve-year strategy to reach this result. We're two years into it, but we have ten to go.

When the Founders spoke of revolution, they meant it in the literal sense of "revolving"—that is, coming around in a circle. The idea of a revolution, from the Greeks and the Romans, was that of an apathetic or corrupt government coming back to first principles to restore effective government. They believed that any new form of government would likewise eventually fail, and that the people would again throw off that government to return to first principles. This picture of moving in an ongoing circle is what the ancients conceived of as a revolution, and it's what the Founders believed as well.

"What a Glorious Day!"

It's impossible to know here at this writing in early 2011 whether we'll succeed. Although our faith tells us that God is ultimately in control of America's destiny, we do not presume to know what that future is.

This book is about your *legacy*. It's not just about the next twenty or thirty years. It's about the fact that most of you reading this book will be *ancestors* of many future generations. It's about the next fifty, hundred, even two hundred years. This book is about doing what the Framers did, in fundamentally bringing America back to our founding principles, to renew America's promise for future generations. How do you want your great-grandchildren to speak of you a century from now?

It reminds us of a story. We wrote earlier in this book that on April 19, 1775, a British soldier fired the Shot Heard Round the World, which launched the American Revolution and inaugurated eight years of terrible war. It commenced trying times of terrible loss and sacrifice, times in which those fighting for freedom did not know what the ultimate result would be.

Yet people hoped. When the Continental Congress heard of the fateful shot and realized we were at war, Samuel Adams turned to John Hancock and said, "What a glorious day!" Adams was mindful of the gravity of the situation. The shooting was on Lexington Green in Adams's own state of Massachusetts, the colony that had suffered the most under the British.

But Adams understood that revolution was the only way to establish a truly principled government, or create a truly free nation on the American continent. He knew the coming years would be terrible, and that he and his fellow patriots—including Washington, Jefferson, Madison, and his own cousin John Adams—were risking their lives in this endeavor. That's why when they signed the Declaration of Independence, they meant it when they wrote, "And for the support of this Declaration, with a firm reliance on the protection of Divine Providence, we mutually pledge to each other our lives, our fortunes, and our sacred honour."

We do not face such times now. There will be no bloodshed in this peaceful revolution. And we cannot declare independence, because the whole world is now explored, and there is no rich, abundant landmass waiting to be colonized.

But it will indeed be a revolution if it brings us back to our Declaration and Constitution. It will throw off decades of abuse and restore a nation under a written Constitution faithfully upheld as our Supreme Law under God, and put us again on a path of faith and family, freedom and opportunity, strength and security.

Such a revolution would reorient us to a follow a new course where each of us can honestly believe that our children will enjoy a better life than we have today. Should we be in the beginning stage of such a revolution, then we can say with hope and thankfulness:

"What a glorious day!"

NOTES

INTRODUCTION: THE PRODIGAL NATION

1. Terence P. Jeffrey, "111th Congress Added More Debt Than First 100 Congresses Combined: $10,429 Per Person in U.S.," CNSNews, Dec. 27, 2010, http://www.cnsnews.com/news/article/111th-congress-added-more-debt -first-100.

2. Gallup Poll, June 25, 2010, http://www.gallup.com/poll/141032/2010-Con servatives-Outnumber-Moderates-Liberals.aspx.

3. Ibid.

4. Gallup Poll, July 22, 2010, http://www.gallup.com/poll/141512/Congress -Ranks-Last-Confidence-Institutions.aspx.

5. Jeffrey M. Jones, "Congress' Job Approval Rating Worst in Gallup History," Gallup, Dec. 15, 2010, http://www.gallup.com/poll/145238/Congress-Job-Ap proval-Rating-Worst-Gallup-History.aspx. For comparison, even during the two years in recent decades that proved to be wipeouts for the majority—1994 when Republicans took over and 2006 when Democrats took over—Congress's approval rating was higher at 21% both times. *USA Today*/Gallup Poll, in "Poll Shows Approval Rating for Congress at Historically Low Levels," *RTT News,* Sept. 20, 2010, http://rttnews.com/Content/PoliticalNews .aspx?Node=B1&Id=1423440.

6. It is one consistent with Greek and Roman philosophy as well as Judeo-Christian theology. It formed the basis of political and social theory during the patristic, medieval, Renaissance, Baroque, and colonial eras. It was even consistent with the thinking of the Enlightenment, even as Enlightenment

philosophers tried to distance themselves from faith to understand the world in which we live in entirely materialistic terms.

7. James Madison, *The Federalist* No. 51.

8. Ibid.

9. The only exception to having both representatives and senators at the state level is Nebraska. Every other state has a bicameral legislature like Congress, with two chambers—a house and senate. Nebraska, however, has a unicameral legislature, meaning it only has one chamber.

10. The communist is former green jobs czar Van Jones, the former chief of staff is Rahm Emanuel, and the socialist is energy czar Carol Browner.

CHAPTER 1: DEMOCRATS AND REPUBLICANS HAVE BOTH FAILED AMERICA

1. Barack Obama, Transcript of Democratic Primary Presidential Debate, CNN, Jan. 31, 2008, http://www.cnn.com/2008/POLITICS/01/31/dem.debate .transcript/.

2. Clementi Lisi, "Obama promised 8 times during campaign to televise health care debate," *New York Post,* Jan. 6, 2010, http://www.nypost.com/p/news/ national/obama_falls_short_on_campaign_promise_5gFAG1TwuLUSW6M n7h6hWN.

3. Julie Mason, "C-SPAN pledge comes back to haunt Obama," *Washington Examiner,* Jan. 7, 2010, http://www.washingtonexaminer.com/politics/C-SPAN -pledge-comes-back-to-haunt-Obama-8727172-80812497.html.

4. Letter from Brian P. Lamb, Dec. 30, 2009, http://www.c-span.org/pdf/ C-SPAN%20Health%20Care%20Letter.pdf.

5. Barack Obama Campaign Promise No. 234, *PolitiFact,* http://www.politifact .com/truth-o-meter/promises/promise/234/allow-five-days-of-public -comment-before-signing-b/.

6. Ibid.

7. Klukowski has a law review article (a scholarly publication) coming out early in 2011 that discusses this issue. See Kenneth A. Klukowski, "Making Executive Privilege Work: Formulating a Multi-Factor Test in an Age of Czars and Congressional Oversight," 59 *Cleveland State Law Review* (publication forthcoming 2011).

8. As we explain in *The Blueprint,* Browner was on the board of the Commission for a Sustainable Society, the political action arm for Socialist International.

9. The situation with Elizabeth Warren is especially bad. Democrats created a statist agency to exert authority over the entire financial lending industry, called the Consumer Financial Protection Bureau. The director of that new agency is a Senate-confirmed position. President Obama nominated Warren, but despite an overwhelming fifty-nine Democrats in the Senate, she couldn't get

confirmed. In response, Obama created a new White House advisory position with the power to—this is unbelievable—set up the new agency. This is exactly the same job Warren would have received if she had been confirmed, so this move is a gross subversion of the Senate confirmation process. Any private entity receiving any orders from Warren should immediately file a lawsuit, because any such order would be unconstitutional.

10. "Hapless SEC Can Now Hide Its Secrets," *Washington Examiner,* July 31, 2010, reprinted in *RealClearPolitics,* http://www.realclearpolitics.com/2010/07/31/hapless_sec_can_now_hide_its_secrets_238733.html.

11. Seton Motley, "A Minimum Wage Trap," The Arena, *Politico,* Oct. 5, 2010, http://www.politico.com/arena/perm/Seton_Motley_41A04D1E-FDF5-45A2-A46C-D1CE35715CEA.html.

12. 18 U.S.C. §§ 210, 595 (2006).

13. Barack Obama, Speech at a Rally in Philadelphia, Oct. 10, 2010, http://www.realclearpolitics.com/articles/2010/10/10/obamas_speech_at_a_rally_in_philadelphia_107514.html.

14. Barack Obama, in Toby Harnden, "Barack Obama: Arrogant US has been dismissive of allies," *Daily Telegraph,* April 3, 2009, http://www.telegraph.co.uk/news/worldnews/northamerica/usa/barackobama/5100338/Barack-Obama-arrogant-US-has-been-dismissive-to-allies.html.

15. Allahpundit, "Obama's turnout pitch to Latinos: Get out there and punish your enemies," *Hot Air,* Oct. 25, 2010, http://hotair.com/archives/2010/10/25/obamas-turnout-pitch-to-latinos-get-out-there-and-punish-your-enemies/.

16. *Citizens United v. FEC,* 130 S. Ct. 876 (2010).

17. Barack Obama, State of the Union address, Jan. 27, 2010, http://www.whitehouse.gov/the-press-office/remarks-president-state-union-address.

18. John Roberts, in Linda Feldmann, "Chief Justice John Roberts and Obama White House: A tit for tat," *Christian Science Monitor,* March 10, 2010, http://www.csmonitor.com/USA/Politics/2010/0310/Chief-Justice-John-Roberts-and-Obama-White-House-a-tit-for-tat.

19. For example, another issue is reconciliation. In a halfhearted, you-can't-seriously-think-this-will-work measure (which regrettably is quite common in Washington, D.C.), in the 1970s the Senate adopted a process called "reconciliation." As federal deficits spun out of control (they were only a fraction of what they are today), senators adopted a rule under which any law designed to reduce the federal deficit could not be filibustered. That is to say, any measure that the Congressional Budget Office (CBO) said would reduce the annual deficit could be passed with just 51 votes, not being subject to a filibuster that takes 60 votes to end.

It's always been accepted by both parties that reconciliation can be used only for measures that honestly would reduce the deficit. But CBO must base its projection on assumptions given to it. For example, if Harry Reid tells the

CBO to calculate the budget impact of Obamacare, and the CBO includes in the assumptions that Congress will cut Medicare by $500 billion, then the CBO must deduct that $500 billion from the price tag, even when it's clear that Democrats will never pass any measure that bends the cost curve in Medicare by cutting funding.

Senators Harry Reid, Dick Durbin, and Chuck Schumer all said that they were willing to use reconciliation for bills that they can't get sixty votes to advance. The Democratic leader can simply declare it to be a reconciliation measure, regardless of whether their cooked books say that it reduces the deficit or not. Because once the leader calls something a reconciliation measure, the president of the Senate—who is Vice President Biden—rules on whether such a designation is proper. If Republicans object, they can appeal the ruling of the chair. But it takes only fifty votes (plus the VP's tiebreaking vote) to uphold the ruling of the chair. So if you keep almost all of the Democrats together, you can declare anything you want to be a reconciliation measure. Whether it's Obamacare, cap-and-trade, card-check, or whatever you want, it can be passed with just fifty Democratic votes.

This becomes much more important now than it was two years ago. This of course is designed to ram through items that couldn't even keep all the Democrats together. While we can hope that a GOP House will be able to reject such wrongheaded legislation, anything that does pass could then be slipped through the Senate with reconciliation.

20. *United States v. Comstock,* 130 S. Ct. 1949, 1956 (2010) (quoting *McCulloch v. Maryland,* 17 U.S. (4 Wheat.) 316, 405 (1819)) (internal brackets and quotation marks omitted).

21. Mosheh Oinounou, contr., "McCain Strategist Warns GOP Risks Becoming 'Religious Party,'" Fox News, April 17, 2009, http://www.foxnews.com/politics/2009/04/17/mccain-strategist-warns-gop-risks-religious-party/.

22. Ibid.

23. Former congressman John Shadegg proposed the Enumerated Powers Act several times during his tenure in Congress. One of the new constitutionalist members of Congress should take up this proposal and force every member of Congress to go on record on it.

CHAPTER 2: PARTY SPLIT IN 2012? A REPEAT OF 1912 IS OBAMA'S BEST CHANCE

1. Rush Limbaugh, *Rush Limbaugh Show,* video on *On the Record with Greta Van Susteren,* Fox News Channel, Oct. 19, 2010.

2. Ken Blackwell and Ken Klukowski, "Obama Wins if GOP Flinches on Marriage," *Huffington Post,* Aug. 28, 2010, http://www.huffingtonpost.com/ken-blackwell/obama-wins-if-gop-flinche_b_697249.html.

3. *McCulloch v. Maryland*, 17 U.S. (4 Wheat.) 316 (1819). *McCulloch* is one of the most important cases in U.S. history because it clarified the doctrine of enumerated powers—that the Constitution only gives the government the powers found in the document, or those that are implicit in being able to carry out those enumerated powers.

4. Teddy Roosevelt was the first to significantly expand the ranks of White House personnel. George Washington had only a single staffer in 1789—a secretary. Seven decades later, when Abraham Lincoln became president, the White House had only two staffers. When Teddy Roosevelt became president, he decided to make the White House much more energetic, with an internal staff that did not have to rely entirely upon personnel in the various agencies. As a consequence, he increased the size of the White House staff to twenty. To accommodate this staff, Roosevelt built the West Wing of the White House, including the most famous office in the world—the Oval Office.

5. No candidate gained the necessary majority in the Electoral College in 1800, so the choice went to the U.S. House of Representatives, as required by the Constitution. Article II of the Constitution provides that if no presidential candidate receives a majority of the Electoral College, then the issue goes to the House of Representatives. But in the U.S. House for this purpose only, each state gets only one vote. Whoever gets the most states supporting him or her in the House becomes the new president. But as would come to characterize realignments, Democratic-Republicans gained large majorities in the House and the Senate. The deadlock in the House broke in Jefferson's favor, creating a unified government under President Jefferson, and also holding the dominant positions among governorships and statehouses across the early Republic.

6. Some will argue that the Democrats were not a new party. While their position is reasonable, it's more useful to see 1828 as having created a new political order. The Democratic Party that emerged from that campaign and endured to this day is so fundamentally different from the Democratic-Republicans of the previous three decades that we think it's more accurate to refer to the 1828 campaign as the birth of the Democrats. Democrats may celebrate Jefferson-Jackson dinners for party fund-raisers (Republicans have Lincoln Day dinners), but Democratic Party principles are so at odds with the strictly limited and decentralized government envisioned by Jeffersonian democracy that modern Democrats cannot trace their lineage to Thomas Jefferson.

7. This election was a rematch of 1824, wherein Jackson won the popular vote but not the Electoral College. The 1824 election thus went to the House for the reasons explained in note 5.

   The Federalist Party essentially dissolved in 1814, leaving America under one-party rule by the Democratic-Republicans. Ten years later, the election of 1824 marked the first time where one person, Senator Andrew Jackson of

Tennessee, clearly won the popular vote (by a significant margin) but failed to take a majority in the Electoral College. There were four candidates running for office, each taking a portion of the Electoral College. As in 1800, the House of Representatives did not immediately elect a president.

Eventually, one of the four candidates, Speaker of the House Henry Clay, made a deal to support Secretary of State John Quincy Adams. In exchange for securing Electoral College votes for Adams to become president, Clay became Adams's secretary of state (the stepping-stone to the presidency). Outraged at having lost the White House to what he saw as a corrupt bargain, Jackson organized the first grassroots campaign. Taking the White House in 1828, Jackson also brought in a governing majority of the new party, the Democrats.

Clay made this deal because during this time, the secretary of state was seen as the best office to hold to be the next successful candidate for the presidency, in the same manner that the vice presidency is perceived today. For three consecutive presidencies, the current secretary of state went on to become president. Jefferson was our third president, and his secretary of state, James Madison, became the fourth president. Madison's secretary of state, James Monroe, became our fifth president. And Monroe's secretary of state, John Quincy Adams, became our sixth president. Even before that, during the tenure of the first president, George Washington, John Adams was vice president, and Thomas Jefferson was secretary of state. There were no tickets before the Twelfth Amendment where one person ran for president and another ran for vice president. Instead, per Article II of the Constitution, the person with a majority in the Electoral College became president, and the runner-up became vice president. Vice President Adams edged out Secretary of State Jefferson in 1796, with the odd result that President Adams had a former opponent in Vice President Jefferson. Adams had just appointed his own secretary of state to the Supreme Court, and Jefferson had been secretary of state immediately before vice president. Thus the general expectation in 1824 was that being secretary of state would lead to the presidency.

8. Far more Americans voted Democrat than Republican in the 1860 presidential election. However, the Democratic Party split along geographical lines. (There was also a fourth candidate, John Bell, who was the candidate for the brief existence of the Constitutional Union Party.) Democrats in the North nominated the man who had defeated Lincoln for the U.S. Senate in Illinois, Stephen A. Douglas, while in the South, Democrats nominated John C. Breckinridge. This split, and the very serious policy disagreements underlying it, allowed Lincoln to carry enough states to gain a majority in the Electoral College with just under 40% of the popular vote, becoming America's sixteenth president.

9. This election was not the worst defeat in terms of the Electoral College or the popular vote. Instead, it was the essential splintering of the Democratic Party,

which they didn't recover from politically until thirty-six years later, in 1932 with FDR. (Democrats' only White House victory in those years, Woodrow Wilson, occurred when Republicans split into two parties for the 1912 election.)

10. Although there are disagreements as to why this happens, some suggest that both parties ossify around certain issues, and those battle lines continue until a generation has passed, but the parties haven't updated their positions. As such, one party finally becomes outdated and loses the voters, forcing a complete reorientation of the parties.

11. Although Dwight Eisenhower was elected in 1952 and reelected in 1956, Ike was clearly and stridently moderate, not conservative, so his election was not at all a sign of realignment as he did nothing to repudiate the overall governing philosophy of his Democratic predecessor (Harry Truman), and his enormous public respect as America's victorious Supreme Commander in Europe and Africa during World War II was a broad-based, bipartisan appeal. Likewise, although Herbert Hoover was elected in 1928, he ran as a moderate. (Hoover was not strident in his moderate politics, however, because before 1932 the American people were not calling for major entitlements or a large regulatory state.) Thus the last time that someone ran as an unapologetic conservative was Calvin Coolidge in 1924.

12. See, e.g., Burton Folsom, *New Deal or Raw Deal? How FDR's Economic Legacy Has Damaged America* (New York: Threshold Editions, 2009).

CHAPTER 3: WE'LL HANG TOGETHER, OR WE'LL SURELY HANG SEPARATELY

1. See Chapter 2, note 5.

2. Heritage Expert, "Edwin Meese, III," The Heritage Foundation, http://www .heritage.org/About/Staff/M/Edwin-Meese.

3. Bernard Bailyn, *The Ideological Origins of the American Revolution* (Cambridge, Mass.: Belknap, 1967), 1–9.

4. *Zorach v. Clauson*, 343 U.S. 306, 313–14 (1952).

5. Speech of Oliver North to the National Rifle Association of America, http:// www.youtube.com/watch?v=XXViw9MGLdk.

6. Mike Pence, "Value Voters Summit 2010," in Jonathan Martin and James Hohmann, " 'Values voters' tell Republicans: You still need us," *Politico*, Sept. 18, 2010, http://www.politico.com/news/stories/0910/42370.html.

7. Associated Press, "Study: Divorce, Out-of-Wedlock Childbearing Cost U.S. Taxpayers More Than $112 Billion a Year," Fox News, April 15, 2008, http:// www.foxnews.com/story/0,2933,351300,00.html.

8. Pranay Gupte, "It's Personal for a Top NYC Divorce Lawyer," *New York Sun*, May 17, 2005, http://www.nysun.com/business/its-personal-for-a-top-nyc -divorce-lawyer/13956/.

9. "The Mount Vernon Statement: Constitutional Conservatism: A Statement for the 21st Century," Conservative Action Project, Feb. 17, 2010, http://www.themountvernonstatement.com/.

10. "The Manhattan Declaration: A Call of Christian Conscience," Nov. 20, 2009, http://www.manhattandeclaration.org/the-declaration/read.aspx.

11. Plato also wrote of a timocracy, which was a military-based social system. When Aristotle wrote on this, he simplified it to the three mentioned in this chapter.

CHAPTER 4: THE EIGHT KEYS OF CONSTITUTIONAL CONSERVATISM TO CREATE A SOVEREIGN SOCIETY

1. 1 Thessalonians 4:11 (NIV).

2. Ephesians 4:28 (NIV).

3. 2 Thessalonians 3:10 (NIV).

4. Proverbs 22:7 (NIV).

5. Ken Blackwell, "Reversing America's Culture of Debt," *RealClearPolitics*, April 8, 2009, http://www.realclearpolitics.com/articles/2009/04/reversing_americas_cultu.html.

6. Gretchen Morgenson, "Debt's Deadly Grip," *New York Times*, Aug. 21, 2010, http://www.nytimes.com/2010/08/22/business/22gret.html?ref=todayspaper.

7. Ibid.

8. Ronald Reagan, "Remarks at the Ecumenical Prayer Breakfast, Dallas, Texas, Aug. 23, 1984," http://www.reaganfoundation.org/pdf/SQP082384.pdf.

9. James Madison, *The Federalist* No. 46.

10. U.S. Constitution, Amendment II.

11. Congress later proposed the Fifteenth Amendment to end voter discrimination based on race, which the states ratified in 1870. The Thirteenth, Fourteenth, and Fifteenth Amendments are collectively known as the Reconstruction Amendments, passed in the aftermath of the Civil War.

12. U.S. Constitution, Amendment XIV, § 5.

13. *Barron ex rel. Tiernan v. Mayor of Baltimore*, 32 U.S. (7 Pet.) 243, 247 (1833).

14. *McDonald v. City of Chicago*, 130 S. Ct. 3020, 3031 (2010).

15. *Washington v. Glucksberg*, 521 U.S. 702, 720–21 (1997).

16. *Duncan v. Louisiana*, 391 U.S. 145, 149 n.14 (1968).

17. For example, the Fifth Amendment right to be indicted by a grand jury before having to stand trial for a felony is not a fundamental right, and so does not apply to the states. *Alexander v. Louisiana*, 405 U.S. 625, 633 (1972). And the Seventh Amendment right for a jury trial in all civil matters involving more than twenty dollars is not fundamental. *Minneapolis & St. Louis R. Co. v. Bombolis*, 241 U.S. 211, 217 (1916).

18. *Loving v. Virginia*, 388 U.S. 1, 12 (1967) (holding that people have a funda-

mental right to marry); *Meyer v. Nebraska,* 262 U.S. 390, 399 (1923) (holding that parents have a fundamental right to raise their own children).

19. *City of Boerne v. Flores,* 521 U.S. 507, 524–35 (1997). A law is congruent if the federal legislation matches Congress's factual findings as to the nature of the problem it addresses. And it is proportional if it doesn't go too far by infringing upon the states more than necessary.

20. *Glucksberg,* 521 U.S. at 720–21.

21. "Overcriminalization, Solutions for America," Heritage Foundation, Aug. 17, 2010, http://www.heritage.org/Research/Reports/2010/08/Overcriminalization. We would also like to note the fantastic work that Brian Walsh at the Heritage Foundation has done on this issue, under the guidance of former attorney general Meese.

22. Ibid.

23. Paul Rosenzwieg and Brian W. Walsh, *One Nation Under Arrest: How Crazy Laws, Rogue Prosecutors, and Activist Judges Threaten Your Liberty* (Washington, D.C.: Heritage Foundation, 2010).

24. John D. Podesta and Robert A. Levy, "Marriage equality for all couples," *Washington Post,* June 8, 2010, http://www.washingtonpost.com/wp-dyn/content/article/2010/06/07/AR2010060703593.html.

25. David Boaz, "Phony solutions for real social ills," *Los Angeles Times,* Feb. 7, 2011, http://www.latimes.com/news/opinion/commentary/la-oe-boaz-social-conservatives-20110207,0,4157527.story.

26. *Slaughter-House Cases,* 83 U.S. (16 Wall.) 36, 60 (1873).

27. Id. at 66.

28. Id. at 82.

29. Id. at 74.

30. Id. at 81.

31. Executive Order 12612, Oct. 26, 1987, 52 Fed. Reg. 41,685, http://www.archives.gov/federal-register/codification/executive-order/12612.html.

32. Executive Order 13083, May 14, 1998, available at *Patriot Post,* http://patriotpost.us/document/executive-order-12612/.

33. *New State Ice Co. v. Liebmann,* 285 U.S. 262, 311 (1932) (Brandeis, J., dissenting) ("There must be power in the States and the nation to remould, through experimentation, our economic practices and institutions to meet changing social and economic needs.").

34. Rick Perry, *Fed Up: Our Fight to Save America from Washington* (New York: Little, Brown, 2010), 4.

35. *Whalen v. Roe,* 429 U.S. 589, 597 (1977).

36. *United States v. Sprague,* 282 U.S. 716, 731 (1931) (citing various Supreme Court cases).

CHAPTER 5: THE TENFOLD PROMISE OF AMERICA

1. "America as a Religious Refuge: The Seventeenth Century, Religion and the Founding of the American Republic," Library of Congress, http://www.loc.gov/exhibits/religion/rel01-2.html.

2. First was the Sugar Act in 1764. Then came the Stamp Act and Quartering Act in 1765. Then the Townshend Act in 1767. Then in response to the 1773 Boston Tea Party (which has served as the inspiration for the modern Tea Party movement) came the aptly named Intolerable Acts in 1774.

3. People sometimes notice the different words of *inalienable* and *unalienable*. In modern English we say "inalienable," but in 1776 the proper form of the word was *unalienable*. Both words mean the same thing, but the first form is the right way to say it today.

4. Each of the new American states was a sovereign republic. But the Founders understood that each state standing alone—and with nothing more than treaty-type agreements with other states—would likely not endure. In fact, once we dealt with the common danger of British oppression, we could end up like Europe, squabbling and jockeying, until eventually some states might even be at war with others.

5. U.S. Constitution, Amendment X.

6. *Marbury v. Madison,* 5 U.S. (1 Cranch) 37, 176 (1803).

7. *McCulloch v. Maryland,* 17 U.S. (4 Wheat.) 316, 405 (1819).

8. U.S. Constitution, Article I, § 10, cl. 3.

9. *Gonzales v. Oregon,* 546 U.S. 243, 270 (2006).

10. *District of Columbia v. Heller,* 554 U.S. 570, 600 (2008).

11. *Kasler v. Lockyer,* 2 P.3d 581, 602 (Cal. 2000) (Brown, J., concurring).

12. *Silveira v. Lockyer,* 328 F.3d 567, 570 (9th Cir. 2003) (Kozinski, J., dissenting from denial of rehearing en banc).

13. *Congressional Quarterly's Guide to U.S. Elections* (Washington, D.C.: Congressional Quarterly, 1985).

14. Transcript of interview with André Bauer, *On the Record with Greta Van Susteren,* Fox News Channel, March 30, 2010, http://www.foxnews.com/story/0,2933,590083,00.html.

CHAPTER 6: GOD SAVE THIS HONORABLE COURT

1. Tom Harkin, in Jeffrey Rosen, "Now Playing for Center Court," *Time,* May 24, 2010, 28.

2. The Supreme Court is identified by the name of the chief justice, so the Roberts Court began with John Roberts's confirmation as chief justice in 2005. Before that, it had been the Rehnquist Court. All nine justices have the same voting power on cases, however, so the eight associate justices are independent in terms of their actions and opinions.

3. *Christian Legal Society v. Martinez,* 130 S. Ct. 2971 (2010).

4. *Graham v. Florida,* 130 S. Ct. 2011 (2010).

5. *Boumediene v. Bush,* 553 U.S. 723, 792–95 (2008).

6. *Massachusetts v. EPA,* 549 U.S. 497, 526 (2007). Article III of the Constitution requires plaintiffs to have standing, which requires among other things a concrete, definite injury, not a theoretical and debatable injury, such as arguing that global warming is man-made. Also, for one to have standing, a court must be able to fix the injury. That wouldn't be possible even if global warming was real, since 80% of greenhouse emissions come from foreign sources outside the jurisdiction of U.S. courts.

7. Barack Obama, in Michael Powell, "Strong Words in Ohio as Obama and Clinton Press On," *New York Times,* March 3, 2008, http://www.nytimes.com/2008/03/03/us/politics/03campaign.html?_r=1.

8. We say likely, because we still don't have too much of a record on Justices Sotomayor and Kagan. While both are clearly very liberal, it remains to be seen if they are as far to the left as Ginsburg.

9. *McDonald v. City of Chicago,* 130 S. Ct. 3020, 3120, 3122 (2010).

10. Id. at 3136.

11. Editorial, "The case against Kagan," *Washington Times,* June 24, 2010, http://www.washingtontimes.com/news/2010/jun/24/the-case-against-kagan/; Ken Blackwell and Ken Klukowski, "Kagan Opposes Second Amendment Gun Rights," *Big Government,* May 14, 2010, http://biggovernment.com/kenandken/2010/05/14/kagan-opposes-second-amendment-gun-rights/.

12. Roll Call on Vote 245, Nomination of John G. Roberts, Jr., 109th Congress, 1st Sess., Sept. 29, 2005, http://www.senate.gov/legislative/LIS/roll_call_lists/roll_call_vote_cfm.cfm?congress=109&session=1&vote=00245.

13. Roll Call on Vote 1, On the Cloture Motion of the Nomination of Samuel A. Alito, Jr., 109th Congress, 2nd Sess., Jan. 30, 2006, http://www.senate.gov/legislative/LIS/roll_call_lists/roll_call_vote_cfm.cfm?congress=109&session=2&vote=00001.

14. Remarks of Senator Barack Obama, Confirmation of Judge John Roberts, September 2005, http://obamaspeeches.com/031-Confirmation-of-Judge-John-Roberts-Obama-Speech.htm.

15. Ibid. (emphasis added).

16. Tom Daschle, in Thomas L. Jipping, "Democrats Will Try to Filibuster Judicial Nominees," *Human Events,* Nov. 18, 2002, reprinted by Committee for Justice, http://www.committeeforjustice.org/articles/articles/old/news111802_he.aspx.

17. These nominees included Judge Terrence Boyle and William Haynes to the Fourth Circuit, Henry Saad to the Sixth Circuit, and Carolyn Kuhl and William Myers to the Ninth Circuit.

18. Prominent nominees who were ultimately confirmed, including Priscilla Owen to the Fifth Circuit and William Pryor to the Eleventh Circuit.

19. "Pickering, Charles Willis Sr.," *Biographical Directory of Federal Judges,* Federal Judicial Center, http://www.fjc.gov/servlet/nGetInfo?jid=1883&cid=999& ctype=na&instate=na.

20. Orrin G. Hatch, Floor Statement, "Nomination of Charles Pickering, Sr., for Fifth Circuit," Oct. 30, 2003, http://hatch.senate.gov/newsite/index.cfm? FuseAction=PressReleases.Detail&PressRelease_id=214302&Month=10& Year=2003.

21. Dianne Feinstein, in Thomas Jipping, "Judging personal beliefs," *WorldNetDaily,* Feb. 28, 2002, http://www.wnd.com/index.php?fa=PAGE.printable&pageId= 12945 (emphasis added).

22. U.S. Constitution, Article VI, § 1, cl. 3.

23. Letter from Elena Kagan to Lindsey Graham, July 12, 2010, found at http:// legaltimes.typepad.com/blt/2010/07/in-letter-elena-kagan-praises-miguel -estrada.html.

24. Goodwin Liu, in news release from Jeff Sessions, "President Obama Pushes Five Fringe Court Picks," Sept. 28, 2010.

25. Ibid.

26. Federal Judgeship Act of 2008, 110th Cong., 2nd Sess., S. Rep. No. 110– 427, Mar. 13, 2008, http://thomas.loc.gov/cgi-bin/query/D?c110:2:./temp/ ~c1103pcD58.

27. Federal Judgeship Act of 2009, 111th Cong., 2nd Sess., S. 1653, Sept. 8, 2009, http://thomas.loc.gov/cgi-bin/query/z?c111:S.1653.

28. Some of these were names like Judges J. Michael Luttig on the Fourth Circuit and Edith Clement on the Fifth Circuit, which were no surprise because they'd been talked up for years as possible Supreme Court picks.

29. Stuart Taylor, Jr., "The Bork Hearings; Burger and a Former Carter Aide Praise Bork's Civil Rights Record," *New York Times,* Sept. 24, 1987, http://query.nytimes .com/gst/fullpage.html?res=9B0DE6DD173AF937A1575AC0A961948260& sec=&spon=&pagewanted=all.

30. *Scott v. Sandford* (*Dred Scott*), 60 U.S. (19 How.) 393, 587 (1857).

31. *Steel Co. v. Citizens for a Better Env't,* 523 U.S. 83, 94 (1998) (quoting *Ex parte McCardle,* 74 U.S. (7 Wall.) 506, 514 (1869)).

32. *Barron ex rel. Tiernan v. Mayor of Baltimore,* 32 U.S. (7 Pet.) 243, 247 (1833).

33. The Court held that the Bill of Rights applied to the states in this case on the theory that these new states used to be territories, and so continued to treat them as territories where the Bill of Rights did apply since territories were under federal control.

34. *Plessy v. Ferguson,* 163 U.S. 537 (1896).

35. *Roe v. Wade,* 410 U.S. 113, 129 (1973).

36. *Griswold v. Connecticut,* 381 U.S. 479 (1965).

37. *Roe,* 410 U.S. 163–165.

38. *Lawrence v. Texas,* 539 U.S. 558, 578 (2003).

39. *Bowers v. Hardwick,* 478 U.S. 186 (1986). Recall our discussion of the police power in Chapter 5.

40. *Graham v. Florida,* 130 S. Ct. 2011 (2010).

41. Id. at 2030.

42. Id. at 2033–34.

43. *Roper v. Simmons,* 543 U.S. 551 (2005).

44. *Atkins v. Virginia,* 536 U.S. 304 (2002).

45. *Kennedy v. Louisiana,* 554 U.S. 407 (2008).

46. *United States v. Comstock,* 130 U.S. 1949, 1954 (2010).

47. Jess Bravin, "Chief Justice Decries Brawling Over Judicial Nominees," *Wall Street Journal,* Jan. 1, 2011, http://online.wsj.com/article/SB100014240527487 0385920457605433301180044 2.html?mod=WSJ_hp_LEFTTopStories.

48. Some readers might consider thirty days too short of a time to both answer all these questions and compile all these documents. But one needs to understand that many of these documents and questions have already been assembled before a nomination is made. Candidates for a possible judicial nomination are rigorously vetted before a president decides whom to nominate for any given judicial seat. The Office of Legal Policy at the Justice Department examines potential candidates, and then the White House Counsel's Office must also sign off. Many of these documents are the ones looked at during this stage, and the nominee typically knows days in advance that the president has decided to nominate that person. So much of this work has already been done, and it's not quite as much of a chore for the nominee to just make another copy of all the same documents.

49. There is a Senate tradition of allowing a senator to move for a nomination to be held over for a week. This is part of the tradition of senatorial courtesy, and is often done as a respectful courtesy by the chairman to minority senators. This tradition of one week's delay does not upset the timeline we've given. Let's say a committee hearing is held in the first week of the third thirty-day period, and then the nominee returns answers to follow-up questions in the second week. A committee hearing should then be held during the third week. If there's no cause for delay, the members can vote the nomination out of committee on that day. If a senator requests a one-week delay, then the nomination can be voted out in the fourth week. Either way, then, the nomination should be out of committee before day 90.

50. The U.S. Department of Justice is led by the attorney general. Second in charge is the deputy attorney general. Third is the associate attorney general and fourth is the solicitor general. Then comes the various assistant attorneys general, of which the one in charge of the Civil Division is the most senior.

51. It's usually about being an associate and then a partner at a high-powered firm, where you get years of experience handling complex trials dealing with all sorts of questions of procedure, evidence, and weaving those things into legal arguments.

52. Confirmation Hearing on the Nomination of John G. Roberts, Jr., to be Chief Justice of the United States: Hearing Before the Senate Committee on the Judiciary, 109th Cong. 55 (2005) (statement of John G. Roberts, Jr.).

53. Id. at 56.

54. It's worth noting that Sam Alito made a similar comment during his confirmation. When pressed (by a Democrat) as to whether he would use the courts to look out for the "little guy" (obviously framed in such a way that the senator considered that a good thing), Alito responded that no, he was for the law. If the law was on the side of the little guy, the little guy would win. But if the law was on the side of the big guy—the corporation, or whoever—then the big guy would win. Conservative Judge Diarmuid O'Scannlain on the Ninth Circuit makes a convincing case that an even better analogy is that a judge is like a football referee. See Diarmuid F. O'Scannlain, "The Role of the Federal Judge under the Constitution: Some Perspectives from the Ninth Circuit," 33 *Harvard Journal of Law & Public Policy* 963, 963–966 (2010).

55. Alexander Hamilton, *The Federalist* No. 78.

56. Ibid.

57. Brian Bix, *Jurisprudence: Theory and Context* (5th ed., 2009), in O'Scannlain, *supra* note 54, at 966.

58. O'Scannlain, *supra* note 54, at 967.

59. Id. at 967–68.

60. Id. at 968 (quoting Judge Stephen Reinhardt).

61. Mia Reini and John Shu, "ABA's biased judicial ratings: Same old dog, same old tricks," *Daily Caller,* Aug. 20, 2010, http://dailycaller.com/2010/06/30/abas-biased-judicial-ratings-same-old-dog-same-old-tricks/.

62. These are in chronological order, not order of importance. The first four were the first four U.S. presidents, for their lasting impact on the first years of the Republic, which shaped the basic institutions of the new constitutional order. Although several other presidents—William Howard Taft, Warren Harding, and Richard Nixon—had as many appointments to the Court, those appointments did not result in the ascendancy of a new governing framework for interpreting the Constitution.

63. First was George Washington, who appointed the entire original Supreme Court, and with it determined the course of the Court's first decisions. This included the first chief justice of the United States, John Jay (one of the three authors of *The Federalist Papers*), as well as Jay's successor.

64. The second was John Adams, despite the fact that Adams served only one term

as president. In the final days of his presidency, before Thomas Jefferson was sworn in, Adams appointed a number of judges to the federal courts, including nominating his secretary of state, John Marshall, as chief justice of the United States. Chief Justice John Marshall is the most influential judge in all of American history, leading the Court from 1801 to 1835, and writing for it in a number of its most consequential decisions that still direct the course of America today, including the Court's most important decision, *Marbury v. Madison.*

65. The third was Thomas Jefferson, who appointed the first Democratic-Republicans to the Court, and in so doing moved the Court in a profoundly new direction of recognizing the primacy of voters' decision in a democratic republic.

66. The fourth was Jefferson's protégé James Madison, because of the combined impact of his appointees, including Justice Joseph Story, and his role in drafting the original Constitution and cowriting the Bill of Rights.

67. The fifth was Abraham Lincoln, who had five Court appointments that then determined the scope of the post–Civil War Constitution after the adoption of the Thirteenth, Fourteenth, and Fifteenth Amendments, which fundamentally changed the nature of the federal-state balance of power in this country.

68. The sixth was Franklin Roosevelt, who through his five appointments to the Court created a pro–New Deal majority that, starting in 1937, introduced vast expansions of federal power than had ever been previously allowed, forever changing the reach of the federal government into people's lives.

69. The seventh was Ronald Reagan. First, in his two terms he appointed four Supreme Court justices. Elevating William Rehnquist to chief justice put an intellectual conservative powerhouse at the head of the Court. Another, Antonin Scalia, is one of the most brilliant and memorable staunchly conservative justices to ever be appointed to the Court. Reagan also attempted to put Judge Robert Bork on the Court; Bork is if anything even more intelligent than Scalia, and also more conservative. (Bork matches Clarence Thomas in his originalist conservatism.) But beyond these, relying upon the recommendations of his trusted right hand, Ed Meese, Reagan filled the circuit courts and district courts of the nation (which are the appeals courts and the trial courts, respectively) with literally hundreds of judges, a great many of which were conservatives. It filled the pipeline for the next generation. Dozens of top judges today were lower-ranking judges in the early Reagan years, or were brilliant young members of the Reagan White House or Reagan Justice Department.

70. Edwin Meese III, Speech Before the American Bar Association, July 9, 1985, in *Originalism: A Quarter-Century of Debate,* edited by Steven G. Calabresi (Washington, D.C.: Regnery, 2007), 53.

71. Edwin Meese III, Speech Before the D.C. Chapter of the Federalist Society Lawyers Division, Nov. 15, 1985, in ibid., 73–75.

72. There is a thirteenth court, called the Federal Circuit in D.C., but it hears cases only on certain issues such as patent or intellectual property cases.

73. Fifth Circuit Court of Appeals Reorganization Act of 1980, Pub. L. 96–452, 94 Stat. 1994 (1980), codified in relevant part at 28 U.S.C. §§ 41, 44, 48 (2006).

74. *Lochner v. New York,* 198 U.S. 45, 52, 64 (1905).

75. *Massachusetts v. EPA,* 549 U.S. 497, 526 (2007).

76. U.S. Constitution, Article III, § 2, cl. 1.

77. *Lujan v. Defenders of Wildlife,* 504 U.S. 555, 560–61 (1992).

78. *Hein v. Freedom From Religion Foundation,* 551 U.S. 587, 611 (2007). (Kennedy, J., concurring) (quoting *Richardson v. Ramirez,* 418 U.S. 166, 188 (1974). (Powell, J., concurring)).

79. *Valley Forge Christian College v. Americans United for the Separation of Church and State, Inc.,* 454 U.S. 464, 473–474 (1982) (citations omitted).

80. Id. at 475–476.

81. *Boumediene v. Bush,* 128 S. Ct. 2229, 2262, 2275 (2008).

82. Id. at 2294–96.

83. *Log Cabin Republicans v. United States,* 716 F. Supp. 2d 884 (C.D. Cal. 2010).

CHAPTER 7: A BALANCED BUDGET AND FAMILY FLAT TAX

1. AP-GfK/CNBC Poll, in Alan Fram and Jennifer Agiesta, "AP-CNBC Poll: Cut services to balance budget," Associated Press, Nov. 30, 2010, http://apnews.myway.com/article/20101130/D9JQCLT80.html.

2. Policy analysis by some suggests that the marginal economic impact of increased government spending starts to be negative once spending becomes 23% of GDP. Much of the relevant material supporting this theory is done by the National Tax Limitation Committee, http://www.limittaxes.org.

3. *Frothingham v. Mellon,* 262 U.S. 447, 487–88 (1923).

4. Jonathan Weisman, "Voters Back Tough Steps to Reduce Budget Deficit," *Wall Street Journal,* Aug. 16, 2010, http://online.wsj.com/article/SB1000142405274 8703723504575425851623589976.html?mod=WSJ_WSJ_US_News_5.

5. Jennifer Ciminelli, quoted in ibid.

6. Tax Policy Center Joint Committee on Taxation, shown in interview with Austan Goolsbee, *Fox News Sunday,* Sept. 12, 2010.

7. Scott A. Hodge, "Why more Americans pay no income tax," CNN, April 15, 2010, http://articles.cnn.com/2010-04-15/opinion/hodge.non.taxpayers_1_in come-tax-tax-policy-center-credits-and-deductions?_s=PM:OPINION.

8. Hank Adler and Hugh Hewitt, *The FairTax Fantasy: An Honest Look at a Very, Very Bad Idea* (n.p.: Townhall, 2010).

9. Steve Forbes, *Flat Tax Revolution: Using a Postcard to Abolish the IRS* (Washington, D.C.: Regnery, 2004).

10. Tom Blumer, "It's the Spending, Stupid," *Pajamas Media*, Sept. 1, 2010, http://pajamasmedia.com/blog/its-the-spending-stupid/.

11. Thomas Sowell, "Political Fables," *Townhall*, Sept. 7, 2010, http://townhall.com/columnists/ThomasSowell/2010/09/07/political_fables.

12. Andrea Neal, "What's not to like about money-back guarantee?" *Indianapolis Star*, Dec. 22, 2010, http://www.indystar.com/apps/pbcs.dll/article?AID=2010 12220307.

13. IBD Editorials, "Jobbed in America," *Investor's Business Daily*, Aug. 13, 2010, http://www.investors.com/NewsAndAnalysis/Article/543800/201008131907/Jobbed-In-America.aspx.

14. Hibah Yousuf, "Economists: The stimulus didn't help," *CNNMoney.com*, April 26, 2010, http://money.cnn.com/2010/04/26/news/economy/NABE_survey/.

15. Steve Forbes, "Railroading the Taxpayer," *Forbes*, Aug. 11, 2010, http://www.forbes.com/2010/08/11/fact-and-comment-opinions-steve-forbes.html?boxes=opinionschanneleditors.

16. Ibid.

17. Ibid.

18. E.g., Timothy F. Geithner, "Welcome to the Recovery," *New York Times*, Aug. 2, 2010, http://www.nytimes.com/2010/08/03/opinion/03geithner.html?_r=1.

19. Ibid. (citing report by economic advisers Alan Blinder and Mark Zandi).

20. Barry Ritholtz, "2008 Bailout Counter-Factual," *The Big Picture*, Aug. 17, 2010, http://www.ritholtz.com/blog/2010/08/bailout-counter-factual/.

21. Jackie Calmes, "Obama Is Against a Compromise on Bush Tax Cuts," *New York Times*, Sept. 7, 2010, http://www.nytimes.com/2010/09/08/us/politics/08 obama.html?_r=1.

22. Eileen Norcross and Todd Zywicki, "How public worker pensions are too rich for New York's—and America's—blood," *New York Daily News*, Aug. 8, 2010, http://www.nydailynews.com/opinions/2010/08/08/2010-08-08_how_public _worker_pensions_are.html.

23. Ibid.

24. J. Richard, "Oops! Calif. Budget Deficit Actually Double What Legislators Thought," *AOL News*, Nov. 11, 2010, http://www.aolnews.com/surge-desk/article/oops-california-budget-deficit-actually-double-what-legislators/19713421.

25. Kaitlyn Ross, "Budget woes wait for governor-elect," *Your News Now*, Nov. 23, 2010, http://capitalregion.ynn.com/content/top_stories/524775/budget-woes -wait-for-governor-elect/.

26. J. P. Freire, "Let California drown, voters say," *Washington Examiner*, Jan. 6, 2010, http://washingtonexaminer.com/blogs/beltway-confidential/let -california-drown-voters-say.

27. Paul Krugman, "1938 in 2010," *New York Times*, Sept. 5, 2010, http://www
    .nytimes.com/2010/09/06/opinion/06krugman.html?_r=1.

28. Christina Romer, in "Romer Calls for Washington to 'Spend More and Tax
    Less' in Farewell Address," Fox News, Sept. 1, 2010, http://www.foxnews
    .com/politics/2010/09/01/romer-calls-washington-spend-tax-farewell
    -speech/.

29. Marco Rubio, "An Idea-Based Conservative Future," *Townhall*, June 1, 2010,
    http://townhall.com/columnists/MarcoRubio/2010/06/01/an_idea-based_
    conservative_future.

30. Thomas F. Cooley, "Why framing the wrong problem killed the summer of
    recovery," *Forbes*, Sept. 8, 2010, http://www.forbes.com/2010/09/07/economy
    -recovery-deficit-opinions-columnists-thomas-cooley.html.

31. Diana Furchgott-Roth, "Deficits Up, Unemployment Up," *RealClearMarkets*,
    July 29, 2010, http://www.realclearmarkets.com/articles/2010/07/29/deficits_
    up_unemployment_up_98595.html.

32. Alan Greenspan, *Meet the Press*, NBC, Aug. 1, 2010.

33. Mitch Daniels, interview with Chris Wallace, *Fox News Sunday*, Aug. 8,
    2010, http://www.foxnews.com/on-air/fox-news-sunday/transcript/gov-mitch
    -daniels-possible-gop-presidential-contenders?page=2.

34. Mike Mullen, "Mullen: National Debt is a Security Risk," *ExecutiveGov*, Aug.
    27, 2010, http://www.executivegov.com/2010/08/mullen-national-debt-is-a
    -security-threat/.

CHAPTER 8: OBAMACARE

1. Ken Klukowski, "Individual mandate insurance is unconstitutional," *Politico*,
   Oct. 20, 2009, http://www.politico.com/news/stories/1009/28463.html.

2. See *Florida v. U.S. Dept. of HHS*, 3:10-cv-00091-RV (N.D. Fla. Jan. 31, 2011),
   op. at 32, 64 n.27.

3. Id. at 64 n.27.

4. Erwin Chemerinsky, "Health care reform is constitutional," *Politico*, Oct. 23,
   2009, http://www.politico.com/news/stories/1009/28620.html.

5. Akhil Reed Amar, "Constitutional objections to Obamacare don't hold up," *Los
   Angeles Times*, Jan. 20, 2010, http://articles.latimes.com/2010/jan/20/opinion/
   la-oe-amar20-2010jan20.

6. Walter Dellinger, in Ruth Marcus (*Washington Post*), "The health care mandate
   is constitutional," *Oregon Live*, Nov. 25, 2009, http://www.oregonlive.com/
   opinion/index.ssf/2009/11/the_health_care_mandate_is_con.html.

7. Ibid.

8. David B. Rivkin, Jr., and Lee A. Casey, "Illegal Health Reform," *Washington
   Post*, Aug. 22, 2009, http://www.washingtonpost.com/wp-dyn/content/article/
   2009/08/21/AR2009082103033.html.

9. Ken Klukowski, "An Open Letter to Nancy Pelosi and Robert Gibbs," Fox News, Oct. 30, 2009, http://www.foxnews.com/opinion/2009/10/30/ken-klukowski-open-letter-pelosi-gibbs-constitution-individual-mandate/.

10. U.S. Constitution, Article I, § 8, cl. 3.

11. See, e.g., *Carter v. Carter Coal Co.*, 298 U.S. 238, 299 (1936); *Railroad Retirement Board v. Alton Railroad Co.*, 295 U.S. 330, 368 (1935); *A.L.A. Schechter Poultry Corp. v. United States*, 295 U.S. 495, 548 (1935).

12. *National Labor Relations Board v. Jones & Laughlin Steel Corp.*, 301 U.S. 1, 31 (1937).

13. *United States v. Darby*, 312 U.S. 100, 118 (1941) (upholding the Fair Labor Standards Act).

14. *Wickard v. Filburn*, 317 U.S. 111, 114 (1942).

15. Id. at 125.

16. These cases were *Heart of Atlanta Motel v. United States*, 379 U.S. 241, 252–53, 255–58 (1964), and *Katzenbach v. McClung*, 379 U.S. 294, 299–301 (1964).

17. *United States v. Lopez*, 514 U.S. 549, 567–68 (1995).

18. *United States v. Morrison*, 529 U.S. 598, 602 (2000).

19. Id. at 617–618.

20. *Gonzales v. Raich*, 545 U.S. 1, 12–20 (2005). Justice Scalia also voted to uphold the federal law, but wrote that this law is authorized by the Necessary and Proper Clause (which it's not, but Scalia wasn't about to join a decision that gave Congress such broad power under the Commerce Clause).

21. *Virginia ex rel. Cuccinelli v. Sebelius*, 728 F. Supp. 2d 768, 786 (E.D. Va. 2010).

22. *Florida v. U.S. HHS*, 716 F. Supp. 2d 1120, 1130–41 (N.D. Fla. 2010) (order denying motion to dismiss in part and granting in part).

23. *Rosenberger v. Rector & Visitors of the Univ. of Va.*, 515 U.S. 819, 841 (1995) (quoting *United States v. Butler*, 297 U.S. 1, 61 (1936)) (internal quotation marks omitted) (emphasis added).

24. *United States v. La Franca*, 282 U.S. 568, 572 (1931).

25. *United States v. Reorganized CF&I Fabricators of Utah, Inc.*, 518 U.S. 213, 224 (1996); *Dept. of Revenue of Mont. v. Kurth Ranch*, 511 U.S. 767, 799 (1994).

26. *Sunshine Anthracite Coal Co. v. Adkins*, 310 U.S. 381, 393 (1940); *Butler*, 297 U.S. at 61.

27. The Constitution says "duties and imposts," but imposts are just a particular type of duty tax, so it falls with the "duty" category and thus is only one type of tax.

28. U.S. Constitution, Article I, § 8, cl. 1.

29. *Helvering v. Davis*, 301 U.S. 619, 640 (1937); *Butler*, 297 U.S. at 64–68.

30. *Butler*, 297 U.S. at 64 (quoting Joseph Story, *Commentaries on the Constitution of the United States*, 5th ed., vol. 1, § 907 (1833)).

31. U.S. Constitution, Article I, § 8, cl. 18.

32. *United States v. Comstock*, 130 S. Ct. 1949, 1956 (2010) (citations omitted).

33. *National League of Cities v. Usery*, 426 U.S. 833, 845 (1976).

34. *Garcia v. San Antonio Metro. Transit Authority*, 469 U.S. 528, 531 (1985).

35. *New York v. United States*, 505 U.S. 144, 161–66 (1992).

36. *Printz v. United States*, 521 U.S. 898, 925–26 (1997).

37. *South Dakota v. Dole*, 483 U.S. 203, 211 (1987) (quoting *Steward Machine Co. v. Davis*, 301 U.S. 548, 590 (1937)).

38. See *Liberty University v. Geithner*, No. 10-2347 (4th Cir. argued May 2011).

39. *Planned Parenthood Affiliates of Michigan v. Engler*, 73 F.3d 634, 636 (6th Cir. 1996).

40. *Free Enterprise Fund v. Public Company Accounting Oversight Board*, 130 S. Ct. 3138, 3161 (2010).

41. *Alaska Airlines, Inc. v. Brock*, 480 U.S. 678, 685 (1987).

42. *Ayotte v. Planned Parenthood*, 546 U.S. 320, 330 (2006).

43. Patient Protection and Affordable Care Act, Pub. L. No. 111–48 § 1501 (a)(2) (G), 124 Stat. 119, 243 (2010).

44. E.g., *HHS*, 716 F. Supp. 2d at 1129, 1149 (order denying motion to dismiss in part and granting in part).

45. *Lopez*, 514 U.S. at 564.

46. Janet Adamy, "Health Insurers Plan Hikes," *Wall Street Journal*, Sept. 7, 2010, http://online.wsj.com/article/SB1000142405274870372000457547820094890 8976.html.

47. Ibid.

48. Letter from Kathleen Sebelius, in Michael Barone, "Gangster government stifles criticism of Obamacare," *Washington Examiner*, Sept. 10, 2010, http://www .washingtonexaminer.com/politics/Gangster-government-stifles-criticism-of -Obamacare-811664-102642044.html.

49. Janet Adamy, "McDonald's May Drop Health Plan," *Wall Street Journal*, Sept. 30, 2010, http://online.wsj.com/article/SB10001424052748703431604575522413101063070.html.

50. Milton R. Wolf, "Tawdry details of Obamacare," *Washington Times*, Jan. 28, 2011, http://www.washingtontimes.com/news/2011/jan/28/tawdry-details-of -obamacare-420960137/.

51. Sally Pipes, "Why ObamaCare Must Be Repealed," *RealClearPolitics*, Aug. 17, 2010, http://www.realclearpolitics.com/articles/2010/08/17/why_obamacare_ must_be_repealed_106780.html.

52. Donald Berwick, video, RedState.com, 2008, shown on *Hannity*, Fox News Channel, May 3, 2010.

53. Donald Berwick, in Dennis Henninger, "Berwick: Bigger Than Kagan," *Wall Street Journal*, July 15, 2010, http://online.wsj.com/article/SB10001424052748 703792704575367020548324914.html.

54. Ibid.

55. Ibid.

56. Ibid.

57. Study, American Action Forum, in *Special Report with Brett Baier*, Fox News Channel, May 28, 2010.

58. Suzanne Sataline, "Medical Schools Can't Keep Up," *Wall Street Journal*, April 12, 2010, http://online.wsj.com/article/SB10001424052702304506904575180331528424238.html?mod=WSJ_hpp_MIDDLENexttoWhatsNews Second.

59. Wayne Thibodeau, "Christine Handrahan describes hours of tension in emergency room," *Guardian*, July 29, 2010, http://www.theguardian.pe.ca/News/Local/2010–07–29/article-1632292/Peakes-woman-loses-her-baby%2C -dignity-while-awaiting-hospital-treatment-/1.

60. Peter Vinthagen Simpson, "Jonas, 32, sewed up his own leg after ER wait," *Local*, Aug. 3, 2010, http://www.thelocal.se/28150/20100803/.

61. Mitch Daniels, "Hoosiers and Health Savings Accounts," *Wall Street Journal*, March 1, 2010, http://online.wsj.com/article/SB1000142405274870423130457509160047029306.html.

62. Ibid.

63. Emergency Medical Treatment and Active Labor Act, Pub. L. No. 99–272, codified at 42 U.S.C. § 1395dd (2006).

CHAPTER 9: CULTURE WAR OF FAITH AND FAMILY

1. Mike Pence, Value Voters Summit 2010, in Jonathan Martin and James Hohmann, " 'Values voters' tell Republicans: You still need us," *Politico*, Sept. 18, 2010, http://www.politico.com/news/stories/0910/42370.html.

2. "Video: Obama says Christianity has been 'hijacked' by the 'Christian Right,' " *Hot Air*, June 25, 2007, http://hotair.com/archives/2007/06/25/video-obama-says -christianity-has-been-hijacked-by-the-christian-right/comment-page-1/.

3. See Bernie Becker, "Obama Casts Health Effort in Moral Terms," *New York Times*, Aug. 19, 2009, http://prescriptions.blogs.nytimes.com/2009/08/19/ obama-casts-health-effort-in-moral-terms/.

4. Nicholas Ballasy, "Pelosi Says She Has a Duty to Pursue Policies in Keeping With The Values of Jesus, 'The Word Made Flesh,' " *CNSNews*, June 1, 2010, http://cnsnews.com/news/article/66208.

5. Ibid.

6. Sinclair B. Ferguson, David F. Wright, and J. I. Packer, *New Dictionary of Theology* (1988), 387–91, s.v. "Liberation Theology."

7. Aaron Klein, "Not again! Meet Obama's new controversial pastor," *WorldNet-Daily*, March 15, 2010, http://www.wnd.com/index.php?fa=PAGE.view&pageId=128053. See also Ted Baehr, "Socialism has suffocated the people of God,"

WorldNetDaily, April 2, 2010, http://www.wnd.com/index.php?fa=PAGE.view &pageId=135109.

8. Marvin Olasky, "Sojourners and Soros: The Sequel," *Townhall,* Sept. 11, 2010, http://townhall.com/columnists/MarvinOlasky/2010/09/11/sojourners_and_ soros_the_sequel/page/full/.

9. Interview of Jim Wallis, Interfaith Voices, Jan. 13, 2006, replayed on *Glenn Beck,* Fox News Channel, Aug. 24, 2010, transcript at http://www.foxnews .com/story/0,2933,589904,00.html.

10. James H. Cone, *Black Theology and Black Power* (Maryknoll, NY: Orbis, 1997).

11. Video of James Cone, Transcript in "Glenn Beck: Liberation Theology and Social Justice," *Glenn Beck,* July 13, 2010, http://www.glennbeck.com/content/ articles/article/198/42891/.

12. "Video: Jeremiah Wright and God damn America," *Hot Air,* March 13, 2008, http://hotair.com/archives/2008/03/13/video-jeremiah-wright-and-god -damn-america/.

13. Ephesians 2:8–9.

14. Romans 3:21–28.

15. Titus 1:9 (NIV).

16. Jude 3 (NIV).

17. Galatians 1:7b–8 (NIV).

18. Associated Press, "White House defends Obama's 'mainstream' religion," *Daily Caller,* Sept. 2, 2010, http://dailycaller.com/2010/09/02/white-house-defends -obamas-mainstream-religion/.

19. U.S. Constitution, Amendment I, cls. 1 and 2.

20. *Wisconsin v. Yoder,* 406 U.S. 205 (1972); *Sherbert v. Verner,* 374 U.S. 398 (1963).

21. *Employment Division, Dept. of Human Resources of Ore. v. Smith,* 494 U.S. 872, 885 (1990).

22. *Flast v. Cohen,* 392 U.S. 83, 105–06 (1968).

23. *Epperson v. Arkansas,* 393 U.S. 97, 103–04 (1968).

24. *Lemon v. Kurtzman,* 403 U.S. 612–13 (1971).

25. *County of Allegheny v. ACLU,* 492 U.S. 573, 630–31 (1989) (O'Connor, J., concurring).

26. *Lee v. Weisman,* 505 U.S. 577, 588 (1992).

27. See, e.g., id. at 644 (Scalia, J., dissenting).

28. See, e.g., *Marsh v. Chambers,* 463 U.S. 783, 786–92 (1983); see also generally Kenneth A. Klukowski, "In Whose Name We Pray: Fixing the Establishment Clause Train Wreck Involving Legislative Prayer," 6 *Georgetown Journal of Law & Public Policy* 219 (2008).

29. Romans 3:23 (NIV).

30. Presidential Proclamation—Father's Day, White House, June 20, 2010, http:// www.whitehouse.gov/the-press-office/presidential-proclamation-fathers-day.

31. *Pierce v. Society of Sisters*, 268 U.S. 510 (1925); *Meyer v. Nebraska*, 262 U.S. 390 (1923).

32. See *Reid v. Covert*, 354 U.S. 1, 17, 18 (1957) (plurality opinion) (discussing *Missouri v. Holland*, 252 U.S. 416 (1920); id. at 18 n.34 (citing *Whitney v. Robertson*, 124 U.S. 190, 194 (1888)).

33. Id. at 18.

34. See *Goldwater v. Carter*, 444 U.S. 996 (1979).

35. *Santosky v. Kramer*, 455 U.S. 745, 770–71 (1982) (Rehnquist, J., dissenting).

36. *Troxel v. Granville*, 530 U.S. 57, 93 (2000) (Scalia, J., dissenting).

37. Id. at 101 (Kennedy, J., dissenting).

38. *Webster v. Reproductive Health Services*, 492 U.S. 490, 517–20 (1989) (plurality opinion of Rehnquist, C.J.).

39. *Planned Parenthood v. Casey*, 505 U.S. 833 (1992).

40. *Stenberg v. Carhart*, 530 U.S. 914, 930 (2000).

41. *Gonzales v. Carhart*, 550 U.S. 124, 132 (2007).

42. Wesley Clark, quoted in Steven Ertelt, "Wesley Clark Backs Abortion Until Birth, Won't Pick Pro-Life Judges," *Life News*, Jan. 8, 2004, http://www.lifenews.com/nat268.html.

43. See Dan Joseph, "Nearly 50 Million Abortions Have Been Performed in U.S. Since Roe v. Wade Decision Legalized Abortion," *CNS News*, Jan. 25, 2011, http://cnsnews.com/news/article/nearly-50-million-abortions-have-been-pe.

44. Our colleague Pat Fagan at the Family Research Council has published outstanding research on how children raised in a married household of one man and one woman, and also children raised in households of faith, tend to be better adjusted, attain higher educational levels, and become more economically productive members of society. See generally Patrick F. Fagan, et al., *The Annual Report of Family Trends: 2011*, Marriage and Religion Research Institute (Washington, D.C.: Family Research Council 2011), http://downloads.frc.org/EF/EF11B27.pdf.

CHAPTER 10: TO KEEP AND BEAR ARMS

1. Press Release, "BATFE Revises Policies on Firearms 'Transfers,'" *NRA Institute for Legislative Action*, June 3, 2010, http://www.nraila.org/Legislation/Federal/Read.aspx?id=5866; "BATFE Request to Track Semi-Automatic Rifle Sales Delayed," Jan. 7, 2011, http://www.nraila.org/Legislation/Federal/Read.aspx?id=6110; "Members of Congress to Clinton: Revisit Decision on M1 Rifles and M1 Carbines," Oct. 8, 2010, http://www.nraila.org/Legislation/Federal/Read.aspx?id=6051&issue=.

2. Don B. Kates, Jr., "Handgun Prohibition and the Original Meaning of the Second Amendment," 82 *Michigan Law Review* 204 (1983).

3. Stephen P. Halbrook, *That Every Man Be Armed: The Evolution of a Constitutional Right* (Albuquerque: University of New Mexico Press, 1984); David T. Hardy, "Armed Citizens, Citizen Armies: Toward a Jurisprudence of the Second Amendment," 9 *Harvard Journal of Law & Public Policy* 559 (1986); Nelson Lund, "The Second Amendment, Political Liberty, and the Right of Self-Preservation," 39 *Alabama Law Review* 103 (1987).

4. E.g., Robert J. Cottrol and Raymond T. Diamond, "The Fifth Auxiliary Right," 104 *Yale Law Journal* 995 (1995); Joyce Lee Malcolm, *To Keep and Bear Arms: The Origins of an Anglo-American Right* (Cambridge, Mass.: Harvard University Press, 1994).

5. Transcript of Oral Argument, pp. 4, 6–7, *McDonald v. City of Chicago*, 130 S. Ct. 2010 (2010) (No. 08–1521), Supreme Court of the United States, March 2, 2010, http://www.supremecourt.gov/oral_arguments/argument_transcripts/08-1521.pdf.

6. Kenneth A. Klukowski, "Citizen Gun Rights: Incorporating the Second Amendment through the Privileges or Immunities Clause," 39 *New Mexico Law Review* 195, 200 & nn. 39, 40 (2009) (listing various federal cases).

7. 18 U.S.C. § 922(g)(8)(A) (2006).

8. Nelson Lund, "The Ends of Second Amendment Jurisprudence: Firearms Disabilities and Domestic Violence Restraining Orders," 4 *Texas Review of Law & Politics* 157 (1999).

9. *United States v. Emerson*, 270 F.3d 203, 218–60 (5th Cir. 2001).

10. *Silveira v. Lockyer*, 312 F.3d 1052, 1092 (9th Cir. 2002).

11. Transcript of Oral Argument, pp. 5–6 (comments of Kennedy, J.), *District of Columbia v. Heller*, 554 U.S. 570 (2008) (No. 07–290), http://www.supremecourt.gov/oral_arguments/argument_transcripts/07-290.pdf.

12. David Kopel, "Oral Argument in D.C. v. Heller: The view from the Counsel Table," *Volokh Conspiracy*, March 31, 2008, http://volokh.com/2008/03/31/oral-argument-in-dc-v-heller-the-view-from-the-counsel-table/; Michael P. O'Shea, "The Right to Defensive Arms After *District of Columbia v. Heller*," 111 *West Virginia Law Review* 349, 363–66 (2009).

13. Nelson Lund, "Two Faces of Judicial Restraint (Or Are There More?) in *McDonald v. Chicago*," 63 *Florida Law Review* at n.97 (2011), http://papers.ssrn.com/sol3/papers.cfm?abstract_id=1658198.

14. *United States v. Skoien*, 587 F.3d 803, 813 (7th Cir. 2009), *vacated* 614 F.3d 638 (7th Cir. 2010) (en banc).

CHAPTER 11: A NATION SAFE AND SECURE

1. Lindsay Graham, interview with Chris Wallace, *Fox News Sunday*, Feb. 14, 2010.

2. Catherine Herridge and Mike Levine, "Gitmo Repeat Offender Rate Con-

tinues to Rise," Fox News, Dec. 8, 2010, http://www.foxnews.com/politics/2010/12/08/gitmo-recidivism-rate-continues-rise/.

3. AP contr., "GOP Fuming Over Recess Appointment of Lawyer Who Compared 9/11 to Drug Trade," Fox News, Dec. 30, 2010, http://www.foxnews.com/politics/2010/12/30/ gop-fuming-recess-appointment-lawyer-compared-drug-trade/.

4. *Boumediene v. Bush*, 553 U.S. 723, 755–56, 771 (2008).

5. Id. at 849–50 (Scalia, J., dissenting).

6. Guy Benson, "Debacle: Terrorist Ahmed Ghailani Acquitted on 284 of 285 Counts in Civilian Court," *Townhall*, Nov. 18, 2010, http://townhall.com/tipsheet/GuyBenson/2010/11/18/debacle_terrorist_ahmed_ghailani_acquitted_on_284_of_285_counts_in_civilian_court.

7. See generally *Ex parte Quirin*, 317 U.S. 1 (1942).

8. Matthew Mosk, Angela Hill, and Timothy Fleming, "Gaping Holes in Airline Security: Loaded Gun Slips Past TSA Screeners," ABC News, Dec. 16, 2010, http://abcnews.go.com/Blotter/loaded-gun-slips-past-tsa-screeners/story?id=12412458.

9. Ibid.

10. George Warren, "Sacramento-Area Pilot Punished for YouTube Video," News10 ABC, Dec. 22, 2010, http://www.news10.net/news/article.aspx?storyid=113529&provider=top&catid=188.

11. Jena Baker McNeil and Richard Weitz, "Electromagnetic Pulse (EMP) Attack: A Preventable Homeland Security Catastrophe," Heritage Foundation, Oct. 20, 2008, http://www.heritage.org/research/reports/2008/10/electromagnetic-pulse-emp-attack-a-preventable-homeland-security-catastrophe; Frank J. Gaffney, Jr., "EMP: America's Achilles' Heel," *Imprimus*, June 2005, http://www.hillsdale.edu/news/imprimis/archive/issue.asp?year=2005&month=06.

12. "Nuclear Weapon EMP Effects, Special Weapons Primer," Federation of American Scientists, Oct. 21, 1998, http://www.fas.org/nuke/intro/nuke/emp.htm.

13. 18 U.S.C. §§ 793, 798. It's unclear from the facts that have been reported thus far whether all the elements of espionage have been fulfilled.

14. 18 U.S.C. § 793(f) (making it a crime for anyone entrusted with access to classified documents to give those documents to an unauthorized person).

15. 18 U.S.C. § 2381 (including as treason anyone who owes allegiance to the United States giving aid and comfort to the enemies of this country). Treason is extremely hard to prove, being the only crime defined by the U.S. Constitution, and requiring at least two witnesses to an overt act. If a soldier were to provide information to Al Qaeda it would be treason, but it would be difficult to establish that WikiLeaks was deemed a wartime enemy at the time the leak occurred.

16. Trish LaMonte, "Press Secretary Robert Gibbs: 'We're not scared' of WikiLeaks founder Julian Assange," Syracuse.com, Dec. 1, 2010, http://www.syracuse.com/news/index.ssf/2010/12/press_secretary_robert_gibbs_w.html.

17. "Classification Levels," Federation of American Scientists, http://www.fas.org/sgp/library/quist2/chap_7.html.

18. Matthew Moore, Gordon Rayner and Christopher Hope, "WikiLeaks cables: US agrees to tell Russia Britain's nuclear secrets," *The Telegraph,* Feb. 7, 2011, http://www.telegraph.co.uk/news/worldnews/wikileaks/8304654/WikiLeaks-cables-US-agrees-to-tell-Russia-Britains-nuclear-secrets.html#.

19. See Michael Goodwin, "The worst of Times," *New York Post,* Jan. 30, 2011, http://www.nypost.com/p/news/local/the_worst_of_times_qq3CxZl5hIkiLq2t27jq0O/0.

20. Floyd Abrams, "Why WikiLeaks is Unlike the Pentagon Papers," *Wall Street Journal,* Dec. 29, 2010, http://online.wsj.com/article/SB10001424052970204527804576044020396601528.html.

21. Kara Rowland, "Senators: Administration keeps Congress in dark on intel," *Washington Times,* May 22, 2010, http://www.washingtontimes.com/news/2010/may/22/senators-obama-admin-keeps-congress-dark-intel/.

22. Dianne Feinstein, Letter to Barack Obama, in ibid.

23. Peter Brookes, "Not a New START, but a bad START," *Hill,* Sept. 13, 2010, http://thehill.com/opinion/op-ed/118523-not-a-new-start-but-a-bad-start.

24. "Biden Says Brussels Could Be 'Capital of the Free World,'" Fox News, May 25, 2010, http://www.foxnews.com/politics/2010/05/25/biden-says-brussels-capital-free-world/.

25. Ibid.

26. Barack Obama, in "Obama Call for 'International Order' Raises Questions About U.S. Sovereignty," Fox News, May 24, 2010, http://www.foxnews.com/politics/2010/05/24/obama-international-order-raises-questions-sovereignty/.

27. Ibid.

28. *United States v. Curtiss-Wright,* 299 U.S. 304, 319 (1936) (quoting Annals of Cong., 6th Cong., col. 613, March 7, 1800 (remarks of John Marshall)).

29. Ronald W. Reagan, Farewell Address to the Nation, Oval Office, Jan. 11, 1989; John Winthrop, "A Model of [Christian] Charity," from *Winthrop Papers, 1623–1630* (Boston: Massachusetts Historical Society, 1931), 2:295.

30. James Kirchick, "Squanderer in Chief," *Los Angeles Times,* April 28, 2009, http://articles.latimes.com/2009/apr/28/opinion/oe-kirchick28.

31. Tim Pawlenty, on *Hannity,* Fox News Channel, Nov. 3, 2010.

32. "U.S. Combat Troops Resist 'Don't Ask' Repeal," Fox News, Dec. 1, 2010, http://www.foxnews.com/politics/2010/12/01/pentagon-plays-combat-fighters-resistance-gays/.

33. Mike Mullen, "Mullen: National Debt is a Security Risk," *ExecutiveGov,* Aug. 27, 2010, http://www.executivegov.com/2010/08/mullen-national-debt-is-a -security-threat/.

34. Ken Blackwell, "America's Financial Future: Our Choice . . . But Not For Long," *Townhall,* Dec. 23, 2010, http://townhall.com/columnists/KenBlackwell/2010/ 12/23/americas_financial_future_our_choice_but_not_for_long.

CHAPTER 12: A COUNTRY OF IMMIGRANTS

1. Marco Rubio, in debate for U.S. Senate, CNN, Oct. 24, 2010.

2. *Plyler v. Doe,* 457 U.S. 202, 237 (1982) (Powell, J., concurring) (internal citations omitted).

3. Graph presented on *Special Report with Brett Baier,* Fox News Channel, Aug. 23, 2010.

4. Jon Kyl, video shown on *On the Record with Greta Van Susteren,* Fox News Channel, June 21, 2010.

5. Joel S. Gehrke, Jr., "Immigration enforcement union took a no-confidence vote in its leadership," *Washington Examiner,* Aug. 4, 2010, http://www.washington examiner.com/opinion/blogs/beltway-confidential/immigration-enforcement -union-took-a-no-confidence-vote-in-its-leadership-99976699.html.

6. Memorandum from John Morton, Aug. 20, 2010, shown onscreen and read on *America Live with Megyn Kelly,* Fox News Channel, Aug. 27, 2010; "New Immigration Policy to Halt Some Illegal Immigrant Deportations," Fox News, http://www.foxnews.com/politics/2010/08/27/new-immigration-policy-halt -illegal-immigrant-deportations/.

7. CBS Poll, July 13, 2010, on *Face the Nation with Bob Scheiffer,* CBS, July 18, 2010.

8. *De Canas v. Bica,* 424 U.S. 351, 354–55 (1976) (internal citations omitted).

9. Id. at 355.

10. Id.

11. Id. at 358 n.6 (quoting *Takahashi v. Fish & Game Commission,* 334 U.S. 410, 419 (1948)) (internal citation and quotation marks and emphasis omitted).

12. Fox News Latino, "Susana Martinez Tells Police to Check Immigration Status in New Mexico," Fox News, Feb. 1, 2011, http://latino.foxnews.com/latino/ politics/2011/02/01/new-mexico-governor-susana-martinez-tells-police-check -immigration-status/.

13. As part of this, any foreign worker who commits a capital offense and is sentenced to death by a jury will be executed, regardless of what their home country thinks of capital punishment.

14. *Chicanos Por La Causa v. Napolitano,* 558 F.3d 856 (2009), *cert. granted sub nom. Chamber of Commerce of the U.S. v. Whiting,* 130 S. Ct. 3498 (2010), *under advisement* (U.S. argued Dec. 8, 2010) (No. 09–115).

15. Theodore Roosevelt, 1907, http://www.snopes.com/politics/quotes/troosevelt.asp.

16. See Elizabeth Llorente, "English-Only and English as Official Language Bills Gain Momentum," Fox News Latino, Feb. 1, 2011, http://latino.foxnews.com/latino/politics/2011/02/01/states-considering-official-english-bills-sense-new-momentum/.

17. Debate between J. D. Hayworth and Luis Gutierrez, *Meet the Press*, NBC, May 30, 2010.

18. Chris Ingalls, "Investigators: Edmonds rape suspect deported nine times," King 5 News, May 21, 2010, http://www.king5.com/news/local/Investigators-Edmonds-rape-suspect-deported-nine-times-94637479.html.

19. Daily Mail Reporter, "Controversial Muslim cleric caught being smuggled into U.S. over Mexico Border," *Daily Mail*, Jan. 28, 2011, http://www.dailymail.co.uk/news/article-1351385/Controversial-Muslim-cleric-caught-smuggled-US-Mexico-border.html.

20. Adriana Gomez Licon, "Mexican gunman fires across border toward U.S. highway workers," *El Paso Times*, Jan. 14, 2011, http://www.elpasotimes.com/ci_17087113?source=most_viewed.

21. 8 U.S.C. § 1401(a).

22. U.S. Constitution, Amendment XIV, § 1, cl. 1.

23. Diplomatic Relations Act of 1978. See, e.g., *Abdulaziz v. Metropolitan Dade County*, 741 F.2d 1328, 1330–31 (11th Cir. 1984).

24. Geneva Convention Relative to the Treatment of Prisoners of War, Aug. 12, 1949, 6 U.S.T. 3316; Accord *United States v. Lindh*, 212 F. Supp. 2d 541, 553 (E.D. Va. 2002).

25. *United States v. Wong Kim Ark*, 169 U.S. 652–53 (1898).

26. Id. at 693.

27. *Plyler v. Doe*, 457 U.S. 202, 211 n.10 (1982).

28. Act of April 9, 1866, ch. 31, 14 Stat. 27 (1866) (codified as amended at 42 U.S.C. §§ 1981–82 (2006)).

29. Kenneth A. Klukowski, "Citizen Gun Rights: Incorporating the Second Amendment Through the Privileges or Immunities Clause," 39 *New Mexico Law Review* 195, 216 (2009) (citing *Congressional Globe*, 39th Cong., 1st Sess., 915–17 (1866)).

30. Andrew C. McLaughlin, *A Constitutional History of the United States* (New York: Appleton-Century, 1935), 2:654.

31. Act of April 9, 1866, *supra* note 28.

32. *Elk v. Wilkins*, 112 U.S. 94, 99 (1884).

33. Id. at 102.

34. Id.

35. *Oforji v. Ashcroft*, 354 F.3d 609, 621 (7th Cir. 2003) (Posner, J., concurring) (citing Peter H. Schuck and Rogers M. Smith, *Citizenship Without Consent:*

Illegal Aliens in the American Polity (New Haven, Conn.: Yale University Press, 1985), 116–17; Dan Stein and John Bauer, "Interpreting the Fourteenth Amendment: Automatic Citizenship for the Children of Illegal Immigrants," 7 *Stanford Law & Policy Review* 127, 130 (1996).

36. John Eastman, "From Feudalism to Consent: Rethinking Birthright Citizenship," Heritage Foundation, March 30, 2006, http://www.heritage.org/Research/ Reports/2006/03/From-Feudalism-to-Consent-Rethinking-Birthright-Citizen ship#_ftn3. Eastman also shows how in the *Slaughter-House Cases* (which we looked at in Chapter 10), the Court noted that the Citizenship Clause was to confer American citizenship on black Americans, and the purpose of the Jurisdiction Clause was to deny citizenship to the children of citizens of foreign countries even if those children were born within the United States. 83 U.S. (16 Wall.) 36, 73 (1873).

37. *Congressional Globe,* 39th Cong., 1st Sess., 2893 (1866) (statement of Sen. Trumbull).

38. Id. at 2890 (statement of Sen. Howard).

39. Eastman, *supra* note 36.

40. James C. Ho, "Defining 'American': Birthright Citizenship and the Original Understanding of the Fourteenth Amendment," 9 *Green Bag* 2d 367 (2006).

41. *Inglis v. Trustees of the Sailor's Snug Harbor,* 28 U.S. (3 Pet.) 99, 164 (1830).

42. *Plyler,* 457 U.S. at 242 (Burger, C.J., dissenting).

43. Ed Barnes, "Illegal Immigration Costs U.S. $113 Billion a Year, Study Finds," Fox News, July 6, 2010, http://www.foxnews.com/us/2010/07/02/immigration -costs-fair-amnesty-educations-costs-reform/.

44. *Oforji,* 354 F.3d at 621.

45. Interview with Lindsey Graham, *On the Record with Greta Van Susteren,* Fox News Channel, Aug. 3, 2010.

CHAPTER 13: SAVE THE CHILDREN

1. U.S. Constitution, Preamble (emphasis added).

2. Bureau of Economic Administration, cited on *Glenn Beck,* April 13, 2010.

3. Stephen Dinan, "Social Security in the red this year," *Washington Times,* Aug. 5, 2010, http://www.washingtontimes.com/news/2010/aug/5/social-security-red -first-time-ever/.

4. Matt Cover, "CBO: Social Security to Run $45 Billion Deficit in 2011," CNS News, Jan. 27, 2011, http://cnsnews.com/news/article/cbo-social-security-run -45-billion-defic.

5 Matt Sedensky, Associated Press, "No Inflation Means No Cost-of-Living Increase for Social Security Recipients," *CNSNews,* Oct. 12, 2010, http://www .cnsnews.com/news/article/no-inflation-means-no-cost-living-increa.

6. People can starting taking Social Security at reduced payments at age sixty-two, so really this problem began in 2007, but the primary wave began to hit in 2010 with people claiming full benefits.

7. Bernie Sanders, "Hands off Social Security," *Politico*, Sept. 1, 2010, http://www.politico.com/news/stories/0810/41628.html.

8. NBC/*Wall Street Journal* Poll, "State of Public Schools," taken Sept. 22–24, 2010, cited on *Meet the Press*, NBC, Sept. 26, 2010.

9. Jim Axelrod, "Other Nations Outclass U.S. on Education," CBS News, Sept. 14, 2010, http://www.cbsnews.com/stories/2010/09/14/eveningnews/main68666 63.shtml.

10. Alison Damast, "College Tuition: Going for Broke," *BusinessWeek*, Oct. 20, 2009, http://www.businessweek.com/bschools/content/oct2009/bs20091020_667493.htm.

CHAPTER 14: THE TRUTH SHALL SET YOU FREE

1. Chad Pergram and Associated Press, "McConnell Blasts Government Over 'Gag Order' on Private Health Provider," Fox News, Sept. 23, 2009, http://www.foxnews.com/politics/2009/09/23/mcconnell-blasts-government-gag-order-private-health-care-provider/. This column reports everything except the bankruptcy comment, which is our addition.

2. *Board of Commissioners, Wabaunsee County v. Umbehr,* 518 U.S. 668, 674 (1996) (citations and internal quotation marks omitted).

3. *Morse v. Frederick,* 551 U.S. 393, 443 n.6 (2007); *Burson v. Freeman,* 504 U.S. 191, 196 (1991) (quoting *Thornhill v. Alabama,* 310 U.S. 88, 95 (1940)); *Thornburgh v. Abbott,* 490 U.S. 401, 407 (1989).

4. Anita Dunn, in Michael Scherer, "Calling 'Em Out: The White House Takes on the Press," *Time,* Oct. 8, 2009, http://www.time.com/time/politics/article/0,8599,1929058,00.html.

5. Anita Dunn in interview, *CNN Reliable Sources,* CNN, Oct. 11, 2009.

6. David Axelrod, interview in *This Week,* ABC, in Mike Allen, "Fox 'not really news,' says Axelrod," *Politico,* Oct. 18, 2009, http://www.politico.com/news/stories/1009/28417.html.

7. Rahm Emanuel, interview in *State of the Union,* CNN, in Noel Sheppard, "Rahm Emanuel: Fox Isn't a News Organization Because it Has a Perspective," *NewsBusters,* Oct. 18, 2009, http://newsbusters.org/blogs/noel-sheppard/2009/10/18/rahm-emanuel-fox-isnt-news-organization-because-it-has-per spective.

8. *Citizens United v. FEC,* 130 S. Ct. 876, 917 (2010).

9. Id. at 887.

10. Id. at 892.

11. Id. at 904.

12. Id. at 897.

13. Id. at 898–99.

14. Barack Obama, Transcript of State of the Union, Jan. 27, 2010, http://www
.realclearpolitics.com/articles/2010/01/27/obama_transcript_first_state_of_
the_union_2009_100077.html.

15. *Citizens United,* 130 S. Ct. at 911.

16. Tillman Act, 34 Stat. 864 (1907).

17. A. Raymond Randolph, "Free Speech: Anonymity and the First Amendment,"
Federalist Society National Lawyers Convention, Mayflower hotel, Washington, D.C., Nov. 19, 2010.

18. *First National Bank of Boston v. Bellotti,* 435 U.S. 765, 777, 784 (1978).

19. *Austin v. Michigan Chamber of Commerce,* 494 U.S. 652 (1989).

20. *McConnell v. FEC,* 540 U.S. 93 (2003).

21. *Citizens United,* 130 S. Ct. at 908.

22. Barack Obama, in Dan Eggen and Scott Wilson, "Obama continues attack on
Chamber of Commerce," *Washington Post,* Oct. 11, 2010, http://www.washington
post.com/wp-dyn/content/article/2010/10/10/AR2010101004009.html.

23. Ibid.

24. Ryan Witt, "New DNC ad claims Karl Rove and Chamber of Commerce are
stealing democracy," *Political Buzz Examiner,* Oct. 10, 2010, http://www.examiner
.com/political-buzz-in-national/new-dnc-claims-karl-rove-and-chamber-of
-commerce-are-stealing-democracy-video.

25. *Citizens United,* 130 S. Ct. at 914–16.

26. Eric Lichtblau, "Topic of Foreign Money in U.S. Races Hits Hustings,"
New York Times, Oct. 8, 2010, http://www.nytimes.com/2010/10/09/us/politics/
09donate.html.

27. Ibid.

28. Joelle Tessler, Associated Press, "Divided FCC pushes through new Web controls," *Washington Examiner,* Dec. 21, 2010, http://washingtonexaminer.com/
news/business/2010/12/divided-fcc-adopts-rules-protect-web-traffic.

29. *Comcast v. FCC,* 600 F.3d 642, 661 (D.C. Cir. 2010).

30. Congressional Review Act, Pub. L. No. 104–21, 110 Stat. 857 (1996) (codified
at 5 U.S.C. §§ 801–08 (2006); 15 U.S.C. § 657 (2006)).

31. U.S. Constitution, Article I, § 7, cls. 2 & 3.

32. *INS v. Chadha,* 462 U.S. 919, 951 (1983).

33. U.S. Constitution, Article I, § 1, cl. 1.

34. U.S. Constitution, Article II, § 1, cl. 1.

35. *National Petroleum Refiners Association v. FTC,* 482 F.2d 672 (D.C. Cir. 1973),
cert. denied, 415 U.S. 951 (1974).

36. *Field v. Clark,* 143 U.S. 649, 692 (1892).

37. *Hampton & Co. v. United States,* 276 U.S. 394, 409 (1928).

38. *A.L.A. Schechter Poultry Corp. v. United States,* 295 U.S. 495 (1935); *Panama Refining Co. v. Ryan,* 293 U.S. 388, 430 (1935).

39. J. Kenneth Blackwell and Kenneth A. Klukowski, "The Other Voting Right: Protecting Every Citizen's Vote by Safeguarding the Integrity of the Ballot Box," 28 *Yale Law & Policy Review* 107, 107 (2009).

40. Matthew Vadum, "Soros-supported 'Secretary of State Project' dealt blow in midterm elections," *Daily Caller,* Nov. 9, 2010, http://dailycaller.com/2010/11/09/soros-supported-secretary-of-state-project-dealt-blow-in-midterm-elections/.

41. Byron York, "Republicans deserve blame for Democratic excesses," *Washington Examiner,* Dec. 9, 2009, http://washingtonexaminer.com/politics/republicans-deserve-blame-democratic-excesses.

42. Vadum, *supra* n. 40; Matthew Vadum, "Soros Eyes Secretaries," *American Spectator,* Dec. 4, 2009, http://spectator.org/archives/2009/12/04/soros-eyes-secretaries.

43. *Northwest Austin Municipal Utility District Number One (NAMUDNO), v. Holder,* 129 S. Ct. 2504, 2511 (2009) (citation omitted); *Reynolds v. Sims,* 377 U.S. 533, 555 (1964); *Wesberry v. Sanders,* 376 U.S. 1, 17 (1964).

44. Blackwell and Klukowski, *supra* note 39 at 112–13.

45. U.S. Constitution, Article I, § 2, cl. 5.

46. U.S. Constitution, Article I, § 3, cl. 6.

47. U.S. Constitution, Article II, § 4.

48. U.S. Constitution, Article III, § 1.

49. U.S. Constitution, Article I, § 4, cl. 1.

50. U.S. Constitution, Amendment XV, § 2.

51. Voting Rights Act of 1965, Pub. L. No. 89–110, Title I, § 5, 79 Stat. 439, codified as reauthorized in Pub. L. No. 111–290 at 42 U.S.C. § 1973c.

52. *South Carolina v. Katzenbach,* 383 U.S. 301, 334–35 (1966).

53. *NAMUDNO,* 129 S. Ct. at 2513, 2516.

54. Id. at 2519, 2525–527 (Thomas, J., concurring in part and dissenting in part).

ACKNOWLEDGMENTS

We begin by thanking our wives, Rosa and Amanda, for their love, patience, and support, and dedicate this book to them and to our children's future. We also thank:

At Liberty University School of Law, where we are faculty members, Mat Staver, Shawn Akers, Jonathan Falwell, Jerry Falwell, and our friends at Liberty.

At the Family Research Council, where we are senior fellows, Tony Perkins, Rob Schwarzwalder, and our friends at FRC.

At the American Civil Rights Union, where we are fellows, Susan Carleson and our friends at ACRU.

At the National Rifle Association, where Blackwell serves on the board, Wayne LaPierre, Sandy Froman, and our friends at NRA.

At the Club for Growth, where Blackwell serves on the board, Chris Chocola and our friends at the Club.

At the National Taxpayers Union, where Blackwell serves on the board, David Stanley and our friends at NTU.

At the Conservative Action Project, Ed Meese, Pat Pizzella, and our friends at CAP.

Alan Sears, Austin Nimocks and our friends at the Alliance Defense Fund; Colin Hanna and our friends at Let Freedom Ring; Bob Reccord and our friends at the Council for National Policy; our friends at the Freedom Federation; Drew Griffis; Ian Ivey Jim Lord; Nelson Lund; David McIntosh.

Our agent Jason Allen Ashlock; Mary Matalin, Anthony Ziccardi, and our team at Simon & Schuster.

INDEX